JERUSALEM IN THE TWENTIETH CENTURY

MARTIN GILBERT

PIMLICO

PIMLICO
An imprint of Random House
20 Vauxhall Bridge Road,
London SW1V 2SA

Random House Australia (Pty) Limited
20 Alfred Street, Milsons Point, Sydney
New South Wales 2061, Australia

Random House New Zealand Limited
18 Poland Road, Glenfield, Auckland 10, New Zealand

Random House South Africa (Pty) Limited
Endulini, 5A Jubilee Road, Parktown 2193, South Africa

Random House UK Ltd Reg. No. 954009

First published in the United Kingdom by Chatto & Windus 1996
Pimlico edition 1997

1 3 5 7 9 10 8 6 4 2

Papers used by Random House UK Limited are natural,
recyclable products made from wood grown in sustainable forests.
The manufacturing processes conform to the environmental
regulations of the country of origin

Printed and bound in Great Britain
by Mackays of Chatham PLC

ISBN 0-7126-7378-4

Contents

List of Photographs

List of Maps

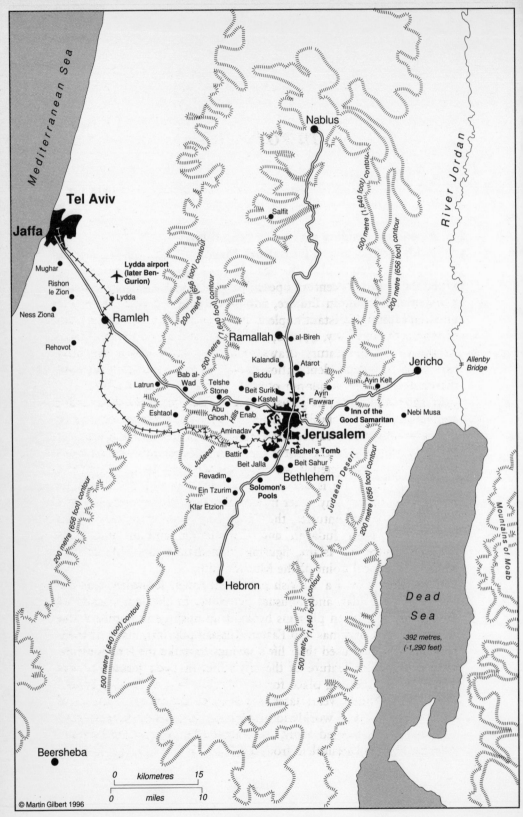

Jerusalem and environs

Introduction

When the twentieth century opened Jerusalem was a small provincial town of the Ottoman Empire, one of the towns furthest from the imperial capital, Constantinople. It had a population of only 70,000, of whom the majority, 45,000, were Jews, and 25,000 were Arabs. As the twentieth century draws to a close Jerusalem is the busy capital of an independent nation, Israel, with a population of more than half a million, a quarter of whom are Palestinian Arabs.

In 1995 and 1996, as Jerusalem celebrated the three-thousandth anniversary of the establishment of King David's capital on one of its many hills, its status as the capital of the Jewish State was not recognised by any of the world's leading powers. Although its Arab minority was disaffected it was also, for the most part, prosperous. The city's urban life is as varied, and for most of its citizens as fulfilling, as that of any other metropolis. It is, in addition, as it has been for so many centuries, the 'Holy City', the centre of religious worship for both Judaism and Christianity, and an important religious centre for Islam, figuring immediately after Mecca and Medina as a focal point of the Muslim faith.

Even when it was a Turkish provincial town, Jerusalem was the centre of particular and unusual activities. In the first decade of the century, Christian pilgrims brought an upsurge in numbers and activity every Christmas and Easter. Russian pilgrims, many of them peasants who had used their life's savings to make the long journey, were a particular feature of the city's life. In 1904 Jerusalem was chosen as the meeting place for the World's Fourth Sunday School Convention. Ninety years later it was to be the chosen location of more than a hundred worldwide groups and organisations every year.

In 1917 a British-led army, commanded by General Sir Edmund Allenby, liberated Jerusalem from the Turks. It was a British Government that then encouraged Jewish immigration to Jerusalem in the decade after the First World War. In Jerusalem today there is distress among Jewish Jerusalemites that the British Government does not recognise the city as Israel's capital. More than ten years ago the Anglo-Catholic writer Terence Prittie gave a book the title *Whose Jerusalem?*, as did two other authors after him. It was more than a rhetorical question: it was a cry of pain at the disputes that have bedevilled the city's ownership and status throughout this century – a century that has seen the city savaged by terrorism, bitterly divided by war and by violent strife, and cursed, even amid its great social, religious and cultural renaissance, by recurring conflict.

The Zionist movement, committed since 1897 to a Jewish home-land in Palestine, was encouraged after 1917 by the Balfour Declaration and the establishment of the British Mandate in Palestine to set up its self-governing institutions in Jerusalem from the first days of British rule. These included health and education. But the harbingers of conflict were quick to show themselves. Although there was a Jewish majority in the city in the 1920s, as there had been since the middle of the nineteenth century, the British chose an Arab as the first Mayor, and after that appointed only Arabs as his successors.

The growing number of Jewish institutions included the Hebrew University, on whose site Winston Churchill planted a palm tree in 1921, the Jewish National Library, and the Hadassah Hospital and Medical Centre. Three Jewish garden cities were set up, pioneers of modern suburban planning. But three Arab uprisings within two decades led to what was, in effect, the separation of Arab and Jewish neighbourhoods, including the creation of separate bus routes. Among the Jews murdered by Arabs in 1936 was Lewis Billig, an advocate of Arab-Jewish reconciliation. He was in his study working on an early Islamic text when he was killed.

British rule brought the amenities of modern life to Jerusalem, leading to an influx of Arab as well as Jewish immigrants. British census reports show that the increase in Jerusalem's population between 1921 and 1933 by immigration amounted to 20,000 Jews and more than 21,000 Arabs. These Arab immigrants came, like the Jews, from distant lands, including Morocco, Algeria, Libya and Yemen.

At the time of the battle for Jerusalem in 1948 there were 100,000 Jews and 65,000 Arabs in the city. The Jewish Agency for Palestine, established by the League of Nations at the start of the British Mandate to be the conduit for Jewish needs, accepted the United Nations' plan for a UN-administered Jerusalem, calling it a 'heavy sacrifice' which would nevertheless serve as 'the Jewish contribution to the solution of a painful problem'. The proposal was rejected by the Arabs. The plan contained a proviso that after ten years a referendum would be held to explore the desire of the inhabitants about the future regime of the city. Demographically, this would almost certainly have given the Jews the controlling voice.

During the battle for Jerusalem, Syrian soldiers were among those who cut the road to the coast. Iraqi soldiers took up positions in the centre of the city's western suburbs. At the same time, Egyptian soldiers entered the city's most southerly Jewish suburb, Ramat Rahel. By the end of the war, a divided Jerusalem had emerged, delineated by the cease-fire line, separated by large areas of No-man's Land, and demarcated by barbed wire and concrete barriers. The Arabs lost all their flourishing suburbs west of the cease-fire line. The Jews lost all their suburbs to the east and north. Israeli and Jordanian soldiers faced each other along the border that ran through the city.

The population growth between 1949 and 1966 accentuated the divisions. The Arab population increased by 28,000, reaching 70,000. The Jewish population increased by 111,000, reaching 195,000. This included many Jewish immigrants from Morocco, Iraq and other Arab lands in which they had long been harassed and persecuted.

In 1953 King Hussein of Jordan declared East Jerusalem to be 'the alternative capital of the Hashemite kingdom'. The real centre of Jordanian rule remained, however, in Amman. When, in June 1967, Jordanian troops, in support of Egypt, bombarded Mount Scopus to the north of the city and Ramat Rahel to the south, the die was cast for Jerusalem to become a battleground for the second time in less than two decades.

The Israeli Government had urged King Hussein not to enter the war. His decision to do so was decisive for the future of Jerusalem. Within two days of his troops opening fire, the former Jordanian sector of the city was under Israeli control. The physical barriers were thrown down. 'We earnestly stretch out our hands to our Arab brethren in peace,' declared Moshe Dayan, Israel's Minister of Defence, 'but we have returned to Jerusalem never to part from her again.' East Jerusalem, which constituted one-fifth of the built-up area of the city, was then incorporated by Israel and given new city boundaries.

Following the reunification of the city in 1967, new Jewish suburbs were built across the former Jordanian border, the cease-fire line of

1949. An influx of immigrants from the Soviet Union helped populate these new neighbourhoods. By the end of 1994 the Jewish population of Jerusalem had risen to more than 420,000, the Arab population to 155,000.

As a result of the policies of Teddy Kollek, Mayor of Jerusalem from 1965 to 1993, facilities were provided for the Arab population of East Jerusalem beyond anything introduced under Jordanian rule, including sewage, a piped water system, clinics, parks and gardens. Access to Israeli hospitals was unrestricted. The Arab neighbourhoods also grew both in size and prosperity. But the Christian Arab communities declined, many of their leading families emigrating as a result of Muslim hostility.

The Christian communities inside Jerusalem are the custodians of a precious heritage of worship and pilgrimage. Christian pilgrims come to the city in their hundreds of thousands every year. Christians of every denomination worship at the Christian Holy Places, which are often divided between several denominations. Those in search of the Garden of Gethsemane can choose three different sites. Two separate sites, one inside and one outside the present Old City walls, are both claimed as the true Calvary. Within the Holy Sepulchre, where the most-visited of these Calvaries is located, six separate Christian denominations have their custodians; each has its own altar and place of worship.

Orthodox Christians, Roman Catholics, Greek Catholics, Armenians, Protestants and Copts are the main Christian groups in the city. Each has its own needs, aspirations, properties, leaders and worshippers. The dedication of the Christian custodians and residents of the Holy Places, shrines, monasteries, nunneries, hospices and gardens is remarkable. In recent years a Mormon University has been built on Mount Scopus, its graceful arcaded façade overlooking the Old City.

Distant Christian interests are continually being asserted in Jerusalem. In the summer of 1994 the first Vatican emissary to Israel since 1948 asked for special consideration of Roman Catholic needs. Within a month, an emissary from President Yeltsin of Russia pressed the concerns of the new Russia for a voice in the city's Christian heritage. Israel responded by agreeing to uphold the needs of all Christian religious denominations, while insisting, as the Russian emissary was informed in no uncertain terms, that, whereas the spiritual rights of all religious groups would be scrupulously upheld, political rights, of which the Russians had also spoken, must be retained by Israel.

Since 1967 the American and British Governments have been among those which refused to move their Israel embassies to the capital city that they do not recognise as a capital. One senior American diplomat was recently refused permission by the State Department to participate in a meeting at the Jerusalem Hyatt Hotel, on the grounds that the hotel was located in East Jerusalem: it was in fact a few yards inside the Jordanian side of the 1949–67 line. As far as both Britain and the United States are concerned, Israel has neither de-jure authority in West Jerusalem nor de-facto authority in East Jerusalem, where, since 1967, she has been considered the occupying power, despite the Israeli Government's declared annexation of East Jerusalem, and its incorporation into Israel's capital.

In the summer of 1994 the agreement between the Israeli Prime Minister, Yitzhak Rabin, and King Hussein of Jordan, signed in Washington, confirmed another element in the complex matter of 'Whose Jerusalem?': the special position of the Hashemite Kingdom of Jordan with regard to the Muslim Holy Places in the city. At the same time, the Palestinian-Arab desire to see East Jerusalem as their capital intensified. This desire had first been articulated after the reunification of the city under Israeli rule. Since then it has become an established Muslim aspiration, constantly asserted. Thus the August 1994 Palestinian Pharmaceutical Conference, convened outside Jerusalem, held its final session in a hotel in the city, as a gesture of solidarity towards those Palestinian Arabs for whom the claim of Jerusalem as their capital is a central one, frequently asserted by their leading political and religious figures.

Also in summer 1994 King Hussein, flying over Jerusalem from west to east as a gesture of Jordanian-Israeli friendship, circled the Haram al-Sharif – the Noble Sanctuary on which are located the Dome of the Rock and the al-Aksa Mosque – and spoke by radio telephone with Prime Minister Rabin, who was on the ground. Fifteen years earlier the Egyptian President Anwar Sadat had gone to East Jerusalem and prayed on the Haram before addressing the Israeli Parliament in West Jerusalem. Both these events were electric moments in the history of the city, made all the more dramatic by the hope of reconciliation between Israel and its Arab neighbours which each of them presaged.

Meeting in Vienna early in 1994, Israeli and Palestinian officials exchanged views on what they described as 'the future status' of Jerusalem. On 16 August 1994 these talks were resumed in Casablanca and a week later moved to Marrakech. As part of the Oslo Agreements of that year between Israel and Yassir Arafat's Palestine

Liberation Organisation, Israel publicly recognised that the future status of Jerusalem was something that must eventually be brought to the negotiating table, and in the not too distant future.

Today, as throughout the almost thirty years that have passed since the city was reunited, the Jewish and Arab communities of Jerusalem live virtually separate lives. Some points of physical contact exist: hospitals, museums, the lobbies of hotels, and an increasing number of social-welfare and charitable institutions. The summer of 1994 saw a joint Arab-Jewish performance of *Romeo and Juliet* in the city. The summer of 1995 saw a meeting of Jewish and Arab youth groups in the calm rural surroundings of a Jewish suburban retreat, under the Israeli and Palestinian flags. But West Jerusalemites rarely visit the Arab residential neighbourhoods on a social basis, and vice versa. Shopping, eating out and recreation are seldom across the divide. Neither side has much idea, if any, of the daily life of the other, of the urban developments across the invisible border, or of the needs and desires beyond the undemarcated divide.

As the twentieth century enters its final half-decade, the divisions of Jerusalem still seem unbridgeable, but life there is as vibrant and stimulating as in any city in the world.

Merton College
Oxford
8 January 1996

Acknowledgements

My interest in Jerusalem was first stimulated a quarter of a century ago, when I was fortunate, on one of my first visits to the city, to meet Dr Helena Kagan, who had come to Jerusalem as a young medical doctor in the last years of the Ottoman Empire, determined to work for the children of the city; Edwin Samuel and Max Nurock, British officials from the earliest days of the Mandate; and Dr Bernard Joseph, who had been the Israeli Military Governor during the siege of the city in 1948. During those early visits I met many other men and women who had participated in Jerusalem's life and struggles. While I was writing the precursor to this volume, *Jerusalem: Rebirth of a City*, which spanned the nineteenth century, I was also fortunate to have had the chance to gain an important Palestinian-Arab perspective from Anwar Nusseibeh, a distinguished scion of one of Jerusalem's most distinguished Muslim families, and much help on photographic aspects of the city's history from Hanna Safieh, for many years the official photographer of the Arab Higher Committee.

Several hundred Jerusalemites have made their contributions to this volume, as experts, guides and friends. Considerable help was given me with regard to newspaper accounts by Enid Wurtman. David Harman gave the typescript the benefit of his scrutiny. On specific points of detail, and for recollections, I am grateful to Mikhail Beizer, Robert Craig, Helen Davis, Art D'Lugoff, Beth Elon, Tony Felce, Benjamin B. Ferencz, Ben Helfgott, Etan Kohlberg, Moshe Kohn, Herb Krosney, Nathaniel and Dalia Lichfield, Yehuda Litani, Menahem Milson, Martin Peirson, Jeremy and Anne Powell, Atara Rozik, Aumie Shapiro and Dr Jacob Raeder Marcus, who first visited Jerusalem in 1926. Kay Thomson let me use extracts from her 1990 diary, and also helped with the typing and correspondence.

During my work in collecting the photographs, I obtained access

Acknowledgements

to, and use of photographic material from, the Central Zionist Archives, the Elia Photographic Service, Isaac Harari, the Imperial War Museum, the State of Israel Government Press Office, the Jerusalem Municipality Photographic Archive, the Jerusalem Post Picture Collection, Keren Hayesod (United Israel Appeal), Efraim Kilshtok, David Rubinger, and Hanna Safieh. Three other Jerusalemite photographers have also influenced my approach to the city: Tim Gidal, G. Eric Matson and Josef Zweig.

In the final stages of the work I benefited considerably from the editorial help of Alison Samuel of Chatto & Windus, from the map-making skills of Tim Aspden, and from the textual scrutiny of Bob Davenport and Toby Buchan.

As with all my writing, my wife, Susie, gave me and the book the benefit of her wide experience, her fine judgement and her love of Jerusalem.

CHAPTER ONE

Awakenings,
1900–1909

A young Christian Arab, Mousa Kaleel, who lived in the town of Ramallah, fifteen miles north of Jerusalem, made his first visit there, by horse-drawn carriage, at the turn of the century. 'We saw no smoke coming out of tall chimneys, as we do on approaching cities in Western countries,' he later recalled. 'We saw spires of churches, bell-towers, minarets and square houses; we saw the wall girdling the city proper. We saw everything which reminded us of chivalry, religion and age, awakening the poetic in our natures.'

Yet the streets of Jerusalem were, Kaleel wrote, 'mean and narrow, and the private buildings are not imposing, but their humble appearance is effectively offset by the grandeur of the numerous churches, mosques, minarets, and public buildings'. From the minarets came the muezzins' call to the Muslim faithful: 'God is greatest; there is no God but Allah, and Mohammed is His messenger. Come to prayer. Come to salvation.'

On this first visit Kaleel also saw, to the north of the Old City, 'the "new Jerusalem", about twice as large as the city proper, and decidedly more modern looking. Here dwell the Jews who are assisted to return to the city by the Zionist Society. As a result of this immigration, the population has tripled in the last twenty years.'

Jerusalem, which had mouldered for so many centuries, had become a thriving city by 1900. No month passed without a new public building being started. On 7 October 1900 the first stone was laid for one of the most striking of all the city's buildings, the Church of the Dormition, on Mount Zion. This was a project of the Lazarist Fathers, favoured and supported by the German Kaiser, Wilhelm II, who had visited Jerusalem two years earlier, and wanted the Imperial German style and presence to be an important feature of the city.

Within a year a second substantial German building was under construction, the St Paul's Hospice, outside the Damascus Gate. Another builder in Jerusalem in the first decade of the century was the Ethiopian Empress Taitu, who commissioned a substantial church just off the Street of the Consuls, and built nearby an elegant two-storey residential building for Ethiopian residents and visitors.

The narrow-gauge, single-track railway from the coast, opened eight years before the turn of the century, brought a steady stream of visitors, most numerous being Russian and Greek Orthodox pilgrims, and Jewish settlers. The train travelled at the slowest of paces. In 1901 a Western missionary in the city, E. A. Reynolds-Ball, wrote: 'It requires only an ordinary amount of activity to jump out and pick the flowers along the line, and rejoin the train as it laboriously pants up the steep ascent – a feat I myself have occasionally performed.'

Even less reliable than the railway was Jerusalem's water supply. At the turn of the century the city's population depended on rainwater collected in cisterns. Although most houses had cisterns, these were almost always extremely old, and often unsanitary. Water was also carried into the city in large goatskin bladders by itinerant water-sellers, who drew it from the biblical Gihon Spring in the Kidron Valley. In 1901 the Turkish authorities laid an iron pipe from Solomon's Pools south of Bethlehem more than twelve miles across the hills to Jerusalem, converting an ancient tunnel under the Hill of Evil Counsel into a reservoir. But this water supply was dependent upon gravity flow over a terrain that, despite the Turks' best efforts, had upward as well as downward sections, and the quantity of water reaching the city through this pipe, never much more than about 20,000 gallons a day, decreased after a few years and was not improved.

*

The Jews of Jerusalem were subjected to Turkish laws, but many looked, as they had done for half a century, to the British for protection. On 3 February 1901 the most splendid of all the places of worship in the Jewish Quarter of the Old City, the Hurva Synagogue, was the scene of what the London *Jewish Chronicle* described as 'an impressive Memorial Service' for Queen Victoria. The service was presided over by the Ashkenazi Chief Rabbi, Samuel Salant. The large synagogue was 'filled to its utmost capacity, and policemen had to keep off the crowds, who vainly sought admission, by force'.

Among the Jews who visited Jerusalem that year was a newly ordained rabbi, the twenty-two-year-old Martin Meyer. Born in San

Francisco, he arrived in Jerusalem in September 1901 to spend a year at the American School of Oriental Studies. Reaching the city by train, he later recalled his first sight of the walls. 'How my heart beat. I wanted to do or say something. I wanted to sing. I wanted to shout. I hummed "The Holy City" and contented myself with some long deep-drawn sighs. This was once our home, where we bloomed and where we got the strength to be what we are now.'

Martin Meyer was taken from the station by horse and carriage to the Kamenitz Hotel, just off the Jaffa Road in the north-west of the city, where he was to stay. He was surprised to find 'no tramcars of any kind here, no gas or electric lights either'. On visiting the Old City he was even more shocked. 'Our New York and London ghettoes are paradise compared with our Jewish Quarter here,' he wrote. 'The streets are narrow, dirty, winding. Dirt is a mild term. Dung litters every corner, the offal of the shops is heaped in the midst of the streets. Filth of every description is accumulated here for years.' His American spirit was roused: 'We ought to have charge of the city for two months. A good sanitary engineer with a corps of workers could do wonders here.'

The life of the young religious Jews in their Talmudic academies also shocked Meyer: 'Within these dingy, musty walls, these boys wear away the best years of their lives, stooping so continually that they become narrow-chested and consumptive.' But at the Laemel School, not far from his hotel, Meyer was impressed. 'They learn the most important elements of modern education,' he wrote. 'You ought to hear the children speak Hebrew – this school being the first where Hebrew was introduced as a working, living tongue. I was amazed.'

In October 1901 Prince Adalbert of Prussia visited Jerusalem. 'The occasion gave me a good chance to see a Jerusalem crowd,' Martin Meyer wrote, 'and it must be confessed that it is as picturesque as can be imagined. Arabs of all ages, sexes and kinds, the men wrapped in their abbayes, the women enveloped in their various coloured izzars, Jews from Yemen, with their distinctive love locks, but distinctively Arabic otherwise in their appearance, the omnipresent Russian Jew with his caftan and cap, contingents from Morocco, Georgia and other innumerable sections of the east, monks in their distinctive garb, Franciscans, Jesuits, Armenians and Greeks. A few Europeans scattered here and there lend a certain staid and sombre colouring to the kaleidoscopic throng, and the stolid Turks in fez and frock coats suggested that curious intermingling of the east and west that we are now witnessing in the process.' Then, as the Prince drew near, came another contrast, the Turkish soldiers in their faded uniforms, and the German naval cadets in their well-starched white and blue.

*

One of those who had visited Jerusalem before the turn of the century was the Zionist leader Theodor Herzl. He went to the city at the time of the Kaiser's visit in 1898, hoping to persuade the Kaiser to support a Jewish land company in Palestine. The mission was a failure. Nor was Herzl impressed by what he saw of Jerusalem. 'Shouts, smells, tawdry colours,' he wrote in his diary, 'people in rags crowding the narrow, airless streets, beggars, cripples, starveling children, screaming women, bellowing shopkeepers. The once royal city had indeed sunk to the lowest depths.' But on 30 April 1902, while in Vienna, Herzl completed a novel based upon his vision of what might be, and what he felt ought to be, in the Holy Land. He called the book *Altneuland*, the 'Old-New Land', and in it he wrote eloquently about what he saw as the future of the city which had so displeased him four years earlier. It was, he wrote, to be 'a city of rejuvenated splendour, of activity and industry'.

Looking out over the new Jerusalem, the two heroes of Herzl's novel 'saw the Church of the Holy Sepulchre, the Mosque of Omar, and many other cupolas and roofs. But new and splendid buildings had been added. Over there, for instance – that large gleaming new building was the Peace Palace. The Old City seemed to sleep. But all around it the picture was entirely different. Modern suburbs had arisen, with a network of tramlines. The streets were broad and tree-lined. There were homes and office buildings, many parks, great educational institutes, emporia, some splendid public buildings and places of amusement. It was a cosmopolitan city of the twentieth century.'

Herzl's vision of a Jewish State, expounded in 1897, took fifty-one years to come to pass. His vision of a modern Jerusalem, expounded in 1902, was a reality ninety years later. Herzl also had a vision for Jerusalem in the international sphere, a vision in which today's municipal, educational, scientific and medical institutions are much involved, the participation of Jerusalem in the affairs of the wider world. In 1902 Herzl described the Peace Palace in the following words: 'This fine building has become a unique centre for all kinds of charitable and social ventures. Here work is done not only for the Jewish land and the Jewish people, but for other lands and other peoples too. Wherever in the world a catastrophe occurs – earthquake, flood, famine, drought, epidemic – the stricken country wires to this centre for help. Here there is always a stock of supplies, because both the gifts of such supplies and the requests for them are centralised here. A permanent Committee chosen from among all the nations sees to it that the distributions are justly made. But this is also a centre for inventors, artists, who need aid and are attracted by the Latin motto carved above its portals – *Humani nihil a me alienum puto* ('I regard nothing human as alien to me'). And indeed, these men obtain help here, if they are worthy of it.'

This was a remarkable vision for a man whose journey to Jerusalem in 1898 had led him to such disappointment when he saw the city itself. Barely a month after Herzl's novel was completed in Vienna, however, its vision was being doubted in Jerusalem by Martin Meyer, who, on leaving the city to return to the United States that June, took one last look at Jerusalem by moonlight. 'Such a beautiful sight,' he wrote. 'The houses are all of white stone or white washed and as they lay there under the silver light of the moon, quiet as a city of the dead, you could forget its dirt and its squalor and think only of its bygone splendours, when it was a city of kings and princes. It is only a trick of the imagination. The old Jerusalem is dead, passed away for all time.'

The old Jerusalem might be dead, but there were those who were determined to see a new Jerusalem come into being. Three months after Martin Meyer had gone, a group of Jerusalem Jews, among them the Jerusalem-born educator David Yellin, expressed their hopes for the city. In a leaflet published on 17 September 1902 Yellin and his friends wrote that their aim was to establish 'a Hebrew city, whose language will be the Hebrew language, and to achieve this goal we shall begin with a Hebrew neighbourhood, and all members of the community shall reside in one neighbourhood, if possible'.

Within two years Yellin had founded a Teachers' Association for all the Jewish teachers in Palestine. The factor that united all its members was the Hebrew language, which they were determined would be the language of teaching, of learning and of daily life throughout the land.

*

The most frequent visitors to Jerusalem in the first decade and a half of the twentieth century were Christian pilgrims. There seemed few limits to the exertions they were prepared to make for their faith. A group of Spanish pilgrims, setting off for a four-day spiritual journey on 19 April 1902, to pray at Roman Catholic sites, reached Jericho on the first day, the river Jordan and the Dead Sea on the second, and Bethlehem on the third, walking across a rough and wild terrain. Christians also came to Jerusalem for their conventions, setting a trend that reached a climax nine decades later. In the spring of 1902, as every spring, the ground was green with lush grass and bright with wild flowers, the sky was blue but no' harsh, the air fresh and invigorating before the dust storms and heat haze of summer.

The largest group of pilgrims in the first decade of the century were the Russian Orthodox Christians; in the 1990s the largest immigrant group to Jerusalem was of Russian secular Jews. The Russian Christian pilgrims came by boat from the Russian Black Sea ports to Jaffa, and then took the train up to Jerusalem. Their numbers were estimated at close on 10,000 in 1904. The city to which these pilgrims came, mainly at Easter but also at Christmas and for the New Year, was sizeable by the standards of the region. Four years before the turn of the century, the Ottoman authorities, conscious of their tax-gathering duties on behalf of distant Constantinople, had made a serious attempt to count the numbers of its citizens. The total population had been estimated, with somewhat dubious, or perhaps one should say hopeful, precision, as 45,472. Of these the Jews, a small minority in Palestine as a whole, were a substantial majority, their numbers estimated at 28,112. The Christian and Muslim Arabs of Jerusalem, totalling just over 17,000, were divided equally.

Christian Orders abounded, each one active in good works. Ten years before the turn of the century, the German Lazarists had established a hospice and a school in the city, and the Benedictine Sisters of Calvary an orphanage. In 1903 the Passionists established a dispensary. In 1904 the Salesian Fathers and the Salesian Sisters each established a school. In 1905 the Sisters of Charity of St Charles Borromeo built a convent and hospice in the German Colony, just south of the railway station. Not far to the east of them, at the top of an escarpment from which could be seen the Old City, the Mount of Olives, and, in the far distance, the Mountains of Moab, the French Poor Clares had built a convent: when war came in 1914 they were expelled to Alexandria, but they returned when the war ended, and have been there since.

The Greek Orthodox Church, the wealthiest of the Churches in Jerusalem, bought considerable amounts of land both inside and outside the Old City. Inside the Jaffa Gate it built hotels, and shops with residential quarters above them, as well as two modern markets,

6

one near the Jaffa Gate and one near the Church of the Holy Sepulchre. These new buildings, wrote the blind Jewish lexicographer, A. M. Luncz, in 1904, 'impart beauty and splendour to the Old City'. Outside the city walls, the fields and hillsides bought by the Greek Orthodox Church rapidly became residential neighbourhoods: among them the Greek Colony, Katamon and Abu Tor. The Old City, which most travellers saw and wrote about, was being overtaken in area and population by the New City, suburban and modern.

The quality of life in the Old City did not impress those who wrote the guidebooks. In 1901 Reynolds-Ball's *Jerusalem* was blunt in its portrayal of the Ottoman regime. 'It does not require more than a few hours' stay,' the author wrote, 'to realise that we are in a city of an effete and decadent power.' Strong words, and they were backed up with examples. 'The streets are not drained – few are wide enough for wheeled traffic. Attempts at sanitation are of the most primitive order. There is no water supply – no gas – no European shops – no postal delivery (except through the hotels) – and an inefficient and corrupt police.' Worst of all was the stench. 'It is highly advisable to walk very discreetly through the narrow malodorous alleys and lanes filled with garbage,' Reynolds-Ball warned. The garbage was only removed 'at long intervals in baskets slung on donkeys'.

Reynolds-Ball, like Theodor Herzl three years earlier, had little sense of the actual life of the city, whose inhabitants and buildings so often emerged in travellers' accounts as a collection of exotic, crumbling curiosities. But in 1901 a literary development took place, unnoticed by Reynolds-Ball or his contemporaries. This was the Turkish decision to allow the Russian-born Eliezer Ben Yehuda, who had insisted on modern Hebrew being the language of the Jews of Palestine, and was creating new Hebrew words where the Bible gave no guidance, to publish his own Hebrew-language newspaper, *Hashkafah*. The name chosen by Ben Yehuda, the Hebrew word for 'outlook', was intended deliberately to mirror two European newspapers of the time, the London *Observer* and the Paris *Observateur*. It appeared twice a week, with financial support from Baron Edmond de Rothschild, the man who made so many Jewish enterprises possible in Jerusalem, and throughout Palestine.

Each visitor to Jerusalem was surprised to find that the Jews were in a majority there. This had been so since the middle of the nineteenth century, when not only devoutly religious Jews but many secular ones as well had made the city their home. A considerable number of Jewish suburbs had been built outside the walls, their red-tiled roofs welcoming the travellers as they came along the Jaffa Road towards the Jaffa Gate, the main route from the coast. Travellers who arrived by rail, and walked or went by carriage to the Jaffa Gate, passed on their way two small suburbs, the Jewish suburb of Yemin Moshe, founded in 1892, and the much poorer Shaama quarter, founded in 1900. The Shaama houses were home to both Jews and Arabs. Only after three decades of living side by side did the Jews leave, made uneasy when the Jewish dead and wounded of the Hebron massacre of 1929 were brought past their houses on the way into the city.

It was a British traveller, Mrs A. Goodrich-Freer, who noted of her own first journey to the city at the turn of the century: 'We are so accustomed to think of the modern Jew as a recent immigrant to Palestine that it is somewhat surprising to find that Jerusalem is virtually a Jewish city. Out of about 60,000 inhabitants some 40,000 are Jews; a large part of the trade of the town is in their hands; not only have they overflowed in all directions their own quarter within the walls, but they have established themselves in various colonies, amounting to some half-dozen villages all within a mile or so from the city gates.'

Mrs Freer reached Jerusalem two years after the Kaiser's visit. 'The visit of the German Emperor', she wrote, 'is still marked with a white stone in the history of Jerusalem. Roads were made, gates were opened, the town was even cleaned in his honour, and he showed his warm appreciation of the welcome, general, and well deserved, by the truly cosmopolitan and Catholic spirit in which he presented to his subjects, in the Holy City, two sites, one for the erection of a Lutheran, the other of a Latin Church. Trade, agriculture and commerce in Jerusalem are never more flourishing than in the hands of Germans. The suburb known as the German Colony is an admirable example of cleanliness and order. It is, to all practical purposes, a picturesque German village, having its own church, public hall, band, drill-hall, schools, farm, gardens, and of course Bier Halle. Three immense orphanages, a large general hospital and a children's hospital, maintained by the Germans, are the only Protestant institutions of the kind upon any scale of magnitude.'

It was the rate of Jewish building that increased most in the first decade of the century, as more and more Jews arrived from Europe, many driven by idealism to live in the city which is mentioned more than 600 times in the Bible, others desperate to escape the poverty of so much of Eastern Europe, and the pogroms of Tsarist Russia. Seven new Jewish quarters were established between 1903 and 1908. Behind their somewhat formidable and almost faceless stone façades were lively courtyards and synagogues reflecting the different regional origins of newcomers.

Among the Jewish immigrants in that first decade of the century was a Lithuanian-born Jew, and Paris-trained sculptor, Boris Schatz. Moving to Sofia in 1895, Schatz had become the court sculptor of King Ferdinand of Bulgaria, and a founder of the Royal Academy of Art in Sofia. In 1903 he had met Theodor Herzl and been inspired by him to travel once again, this time as a Zionist. In 1905, at the Zionist Congress in Basle, he had proposed the setting-up of an art school in Jerusalem whose aim would be to teach and to promote a 'Jewish style' of art. This was accepted, and within a year, in 1906, he founded the Bezalel School of Art. The name was that of the biblical craftsman who constructed and decorated the Ark of the Covenant.

Schatz brought with him from Bulgaria to Jerusalem the first six students for his school. It was set up in a recently built crenellated stone building, originally designed as an orphanage. Schatz was determined to create Jewish craft industries for the Jews of Jerusalem and of Palestine. Each of his fine-arts students was expected both to learn a craft and to play a musical instrument. The crafts were carpet-weaving, filigree, copper-ware, carpentry, lace, metalwork, ivory-carving and lithography. Modern Hebrew was also taught at the school. This was an important counterweight to those Jews – and there were many in the city – who felt that the German language, which many of them spoke, and which was the language of one of the great European powers, ought to be the daily language of the Jews, with Hebrew reserved, as in the Diaspora, for prayer.

Ironically, the initial financial support for Schatz's Bezalel school came from a German philanthropist, Otto Warburg, and a group of German Zionists, who also helped market the finished products of the craft workshop. Today, some of the fine pieces in the Israel Museum in Jerusalem are items made at Bezalel. Schatz had been emphatic that the style of the work done in the school should be both 'Jewish' and commercially viable. In this he was successful. Within five years there were 460 students and craftsmen at the Bezalel school and its workshops.

The European powers were not to be outdone by Jewish enterprise. Each of them wished to have its authority recognised in Jerusalem. In 1900 both the French and the German authorities in the city opened a special post office. Here, letters could be posted and received, stamped with special French and German stamps, and dispatched to Europe and beyond in the safety of European efficiency.

The Russian Empire was quick to follow, in 1901, with its own post office and special stamps of the Russian Post Offices in the Levant. In 1908 the Italians did likewise. The most magnificent of all the buildings just inside the Jaffa Gate was the Austrian Post Office.

Stimulated by this European activity, the Turkish Post Office, slow and cumbersome though it was, set up a branch office at the railway station in 1901, so that pilgrims could send their thoughts homeward before returning home. Two further Turkish branch post offices were opened specifically for the Jews, in 1904 in the Jewish suburb of Mea Shearim, and five years later in Mahane Yehuda. The volume of postal communication with Europe constantly grew. As more Russian Jews reached the city, their letters urging relatives to follow them competed with other letters seeking alms. The arrival of postal bank money orders from Europe was a daily occurrence.

The fact that the Jews were a majority in the city impressed itself on many visitors not only as a demographic fact but as a spiritual one. The Christian missionaries were particularly conscious of the Jewish attachment to the city, and the messianic tradition whereby the Messiah would one day appear, or in Christian perspective reappear, in Jerusalem. As well as missionaries, Christian archaeologists were looking for evidence of many aspects of biblical history, both Old Testament and New, under the streets and courtyards of the Old City. In 1900 the American School of Oriental Studies had been set up in the Grand New Hotel, just inside the Jaffa Gate. It owed its creation to the vision of Joseph Henry Thayer, a professor at Harvard. Its main focus was on biblical studies, through the geography and history of the Holy Land. Two years later the German Evangelical Institute for the Study of Antiquities in the Holy Land was established. Fifty German theologians worked there, under the leadership of Dr D. Dalman, and public lectures were given, in German, to recount the links between the Bible and the city.

*

The Muslim and Christian Arabs of the city – a minority, but a substantial one – felt aggrieved at the new-found Zionism of so many Jews. Most Jerusalem Jews at the beginning of the century were content to live under Ottoman rule, and had no aspirations to being anything more than citizens and subjects. But, since 1897, the Zionist movement had pressed for some form of Jewish entity in Palestine – sometimes described as a Jewish Commonwealth, sometimes envisaged as a future Jewish State – and this was at the centre of Zionism's appeal for Jewish immigration.

Nowhere was the fear of eventual Jewish statehood felt more strongly than among the Arabs of Jerusalem. When, at the end of 1900, the Ottoman authorities promulgated regulations making Jewish entry to Palestine, and also Jewish land purchase, easier, a number of Jerusalem Arabs holding official positions in the local government collected signatures to protest to Constantinople.

Nothing came of this protest, but the unease which it revealed was not to go away.

*

By the end of the first decade of the century there were nearly twice as many people living outside the city walls as inside them. The city's main thoroughfare was no longer the crowded, stench-filled, dusty bazaar, which in winter could be a swirling current of mud and water. Outside the Old City, along the Jaffa Road and the Street of the Consuls, as well as in the continually expanding Jewish suburbs, could be found hotels, shops, the European post offices and the consulates, including the American and the Italian. It was the duty of the consuls to protect those living in the city with citizenships other than Turkish, including the many Russian Jews who were determined to retain the protection of a Great Power to safeguard their rights, and if necessary to seek reparation for any alleged indignity or injustice.

Fine private houses were being built outside the walls in the first decade of the century. In 1908 a Jewish merchant from the Russian Central Asian province of Bukhara, Mashiach Borochoff, built a splendid house on the Jaffa Road whose archways, Corinthian columns and gates with sculpted lions were visible to all who passed by. Hotels also flourished as the new century advanced. In his *New Guide to the Holy Land* of 1908, Father Barnabas Meistermann noted that just inside the Jaffa Gate was the Grand New Hotel, 'kept by Morcos, a Catholic' and the Central Hotel 'kept by Amdurski, a Jew'. Once outside the walls, he wrote, on the Jaffa Road 'we come successively to the Park Hotel, kept by Hall; then farther on, to the left, the Hotel Hughes, kept by Hughes, an Englishman; and on the right, near the French Consulate, the little Hôtel de France, kept by Dominique Bourrel'.

Mrs Goodrich-Freer had published her full account of life in Jerusalem four years before Father Meistermann's guidebook. Mrs Freer had spent more than two years in the city, and from her vantage point in the Hotel Fast, built by the Armenian Patriarchate just outside the Jaffa Gate, had explored every nook and cranny, and got to know members of the different communities. One of her observations concerned the provision of water in the city. 'There is an element of humour', she wrote, 'in the accounts published, in various directions, of the new Jerusalem waterworks. "In the way of public works", continues our Blue Book, "the most noteworthy undertaking during the year 1901 was that for supplying Jerusalem with water, which was brought in iron pipes from a spring situated about seven miles distant south of the city and known as the Sealed Fountain of Solomon's times." It is very picturesque to see the citizens of Jerusalem, men with goatskins carried on their backs, or with donkeys carrying empty kerosene cans, pannier fashion; women with jars on their heads, crowding round the fountain on the Bethlehem road to fetch water, in the rainy season without price, in summer to buy; but as the modern aqueduct, in contrast with that attributed to Solomon, is a wrought-iron pipe a few inches in diameter, laid, for a considerable part of its way, overground, any little London boy armed with a straw and a tin tack would quench his thirst at a lower rate than five piastres a cubic metre, the price quoted to us today. Indeed, there are many directions, which it might not be judicious to indicate, in which the Street Arab could "give points" to his Oriental cousin.'

Mrs Freer compared the 'Street Arab' of Jerusalem with a London urchin. The London boy, she wrote, was certainly 'a better sportsman, and would scorn the Jerusalem method of fighting, juvenile or adult; knives are drawn on very small provocation, and we have personally seen a man disabled for taking too low a fare for a carriage, which, however, is only trades-unionism; or for trying to draw water out of his turn, or when a stronger than he had a mind to precede him; but these again are only the methods of Nature herself. Even Whitechapel would cry shame on combatants who, after fighting at arms' length for some minutes, their long sleeves flying in the air, finally close, biting each other's shoulders, pulling each other's hair, scratching each other's faces and finally rolling together in the dust, when the uppermost will seize a stone – the Holy Land formation lends itself to such weapons – and belabour his adversary on head, face, hands or breast as most easily accessible.'

One of the newest buildings in Jerusalem at the turn of the century was a hospital just outside the Jaffa Gate, 'an admirable Moslem hospital,' Mrs Freer wrote, 'supported by Government, and – in itself a fact of interesting significance – under the management of the sisters of St Vincent de Paul, commonly known as Sisters of Charity. The order and completeness of all arrangements are abundant testimony that it could not be in better hands. The building is admirably planned; there is well organised accommodation for out-patients, the dispensary, and operating room, wards on a separate floor for women, a Mosque, accessible at all hours; supervision of doctors, native and European, carefully trained Arab-speaking nurses, the frequent attendance of a Moslem committee of management and a separate building, under the charge of police for criminals needing medical attention.

'There is a carefully tended garden for the use of convalescents, and it is pleasant to notice everywhere, even in the dispensary, the presence of flowers. The rules of the Order forbid the attendance of the sisters upon obstetric and syphilitic cases and at certain operations; but in the cause of humanity even these are set aside if the case is urgent or the auxiliary nurses inadequate. The Sisters are a magnificent illustration of the grand rule "laborare est orare." Even the ritual requirements of their faith have to be arranged with a view to the exigencies of service, and their daily Mass is heard at four o'clock in the morning, in order that their patients may not lack their work, even when gaining by their prayer.'

Observing Jews and Arabs in the street, Mrs Freer came to a somewhat startling conclusion. "When one compares the physique of the Arab and the Jewish races, as represented in Jerusalem,' she wrote, 'one cannot but reflect that Ishmail must have been much better-looking than Isaac; or, perhaps, as it is chiefly among the women that the fact strikes us, it might be fairer to say that one can hardly wonder, considering their respective ages, that the daughters of Hagar should be so much more pleasing in appearance than those of Sarah.'

Mrs Freer spent some time inside Muslim homes, and came to certain conclusions about the Muslim woman, who, she wrote, 'has few amusements beyond that of receiving and visiting her friends. Social festivities take place largely out of doors, and there are some half-dozen spots around Jerusalem, more or less shady, where, in the afternoon, you are sure to find groups of women drinking coffee and eating sweets and nuts. You may track them by nut-shells.' As for the Muslim men whom she was able to observe, Mrs Freer wrote that they 'have their cafes, where they smoke water-pipes, drink coffee and play cards or tric-trac at intervals all day.'

Mrs Freer also wrote about the roads of Jerusalem, noting that shoes, 'made to measure at ten francs a pair, are difficult to wear out, even on the Jerusalem roads, many of which look as if a wall had been casually spilt upon them. You can get a good riding-horse for five shillings, and a very good victoria and pair for about sixteen shillings a day, and for sixpence you can call in style upon any one within a mile of Jerusalem. There are no omnibuses.'

Jerusalem entered the twentieth century slowly. The first bicycle seen in the city had appeared on the Jaffa Road in 1898. 'Motor cars have been seen in Beirut,' wrote Mrs Freer, 'but have not yet reached the Holy City.' Many other scenes caught her attention. 'You may see one man carry a cottage piano, or an iron girder, or a twenty-foot section of railway line,' she wrote. As to laundry, 'it comes home snow-white, and the price includes dresses and all the "white wear" essential to the climate'. Furniture 'used to be costly and scarce, but you can now get any design in wood and metal-work copies at a very reasonable price in the workshops of the Alliance Israelite'.

The Alliance Israelite which Mrs Freer had mentioned, its full name being the Alliance Israelite Universelle, was an example of Jewish self-help in Jerusalem. Founded in Paris in 1860, it was set up as a world organisation of 'fortunate Jews' to help their fellow Jews in lands of oppression and poverty. Russia and Roumania were the main focus of its early activities. By 1912 'the Alliance', as it was known, had fifty-two schools in European Turkey and sixty-three in Turkey-in-Asia, including two schools in Jerusalem: one for boys, established in 1882, and one for girls, established in 1906.

Also in Jerusalem was the Evelina de Rothschild School for Girls, founded in 1880, and since 1898 the responsibility of the Anglo-Jewish Association. It had more than 500 pupils. Hebrew was the normal language of the pupils there, and half the formal instruction was in Hebrew. Other Jewish educational establishments in the city included a teachers' seminary with seventy student teachers, three kindergartens, and the long-established Laemel School, with more than 300 boys. Founded in the Old City in 1856, the Laemel School moved to the New City in 1903.

The Turkish authorities allowed these various Jewish educational institutions in Jerusalem, including the Alliance schools, to teach unimpeded. It was the Muslims who had greater grievances about their Ottoman masters. 'It is in many respects upon the Moslem population that the Turkish yoke presses most heavily,' Mrs Freer noted. 'Their position is somewhat anomalous.' On the one hand the Supreme Head of the State, the Ottoman Sultan, was 'the successor of the Prophet and the Caliph – vice-regent of God – and to obey him is a religious duty'. On the other hand, 'to the Syrians, the Turk is, equally with the Arab or the Hebrew, an alien, a perpetual reminder that they are a conquered race; while to the Arab he is the descendant of the Tartar conquerors of Arabistan, the representative of the modern reform which is a perplexity to their faith – a departure from the pure Moslemism of the Koran.'

The Jerusalem Jew, however, 'like the European under consular protection, has his special privileges. The Chief Rabbi ranks next to the Pasha, and is always presented with a key of the city gates when a new Sultan comes to the throne. The key is associated with a religious ceremonial, and is blessed and anointed with oil and spices. Accounts differ as to whether its possession is permanent, but it would seem unlikely, otherwise why should the presentation be renewed? As large baksheesh is paid for what seems, if temporary only, a useless privilege, one must conclude that there is for the Jews some esoteric signification, some allusion to the repossession of the city of their forefathers; some prophetic gratification, in the process of its return, of, as it were, bestowing it upon the Turkish authorities; some symbolic satisfaction in being, if only for the moment, in virtual command of the situation.'

The beginning of the century was a time of comparative prosperity for the Jews, Mrs Freer wrote. Jerusalem as a city had 'in many respects so much benefited by their presence'. Yet the Jews were subjected to 'many inevitable humiliations'. She then listed the disabilities facing the Jews of Jerusalem. 'Jewish children, girls especially, have to be protected mainly from the other children, Christian and Moslem. On the way to and from school; one frequently wonders at the patience – the heritage of centuries – with which Jews ignore the insults shouted after them in the streets; and, considering how much they contribute as citizens to the welfare of Jerusalem, it is sad that large sums of money should be paid for permission to pray beside the western wall of the Temple enclosure, to the villagers of Siloam for not disturbing the graves east of the village, and to the Arabs for letting alone the Jewish share of the Tomb of Rachel on the road to Bethlehem.'

The ability of Jews to pray without impediment at the Tomb of Rachel is as much an issue at the end of the twentieth century as it was at the beginning. During 1995, more than nine decades after Mrs Freer's visit, many hours of complex negotiations took place between Israel and the newly-established Palestinian Authority, representing the Palestinian Arabs of Gaza and the West Bank, as to what rights of access Israeli Jews would have to that same shrine. Under the plans then being discussed for Palestinian autonomy on the West Bank, Rachel's tomb would lie 400 yards inside the areas to be patrolled by Palestinian police once the autonomy agreement was concluded. Would Israeli Jews be guarded on the short journey by Israeli police? Would there be joint police patrols? Into whose custody would an Arab stone-thrower, or a Jew retaliating against an attack, be brought? Under whose jurisdiction would they be tried? The structure of the Tomb, unchanged since Mrs Freer's time, had, since the outbreak of a Palestinian Arab uprising in 1987, been protected from stone-throwers and bomb-throwers by two large, concrete slabs.

'To the casual observer,' Mrs Freer wrote of the Jerusalem Jew, 'his position is essentially modern: he is an immigrant, a foreigner, more distinctly so perhaps than even in London or New York. He is rigorously excluded from even the courtyard of the Holy Sepulchre, even when, as recently happened, he is represented by a distinguished English novelist with, as far as one knows, no anti-Christian prejudices. From the Temple area, now entirely in the hands of Moslems, he voluntarily excludes himself, lest, it is said, he should accidentally profane the Holy of Holies, though it would seem that without the Divine Presence and the presence of the Tables of the Law the Holy of Holies could not virtually exist.

'It is in the well known Wailing Place that one realises that the Jew is a homeless exile, heir to all the sufferings of what Zangwill has called "the long cruel night in Jewry which coincides with the Christian era". There, not only at the conventional hour on Friday afternoon, when the Jews assemble in large numbers, but all day, and every day, and even, at certain seasons, all night, one may witness scenes of obviously real personal sorrow. On the ninth day of the month of Ab, a time when for nine days the Jews fast from meat and wine, when there are no marriages and no rejoicings, then above all it is, in the words of their own litany, that "for the palaces laid waste, for the Temple destroyed, for the walls laid low, for the glory which has gone, for the great ones perished", they "sit solitary and weep".'

And yet, wrote Mrs Freer, 'when one sees the work effected by the Jewish Colonisation Association, by the Anglo-Jewish Association, and by the Alliance Israelite, one realises that even unscrupulous charity cannot wholly degrade, nor Rabbinical obstructionism entirely depress, a people whom repeated dispersions have failed to disunite, and two thousand years of persecution have not sufficed to destroy.' Reflecting on the Jewish aspirations with regard to Jerusalem, Mrs Freer continued: 'If numerical superiority be a criterion of possession, and achievement a measure of power; if the higher civilisation be that of the more effective philanthropy, and true part and lot in the soil be that of him who restores it to cultivation; then, mysterious as may seem to us the workings of God's providence, the deep tragedy of their existence, the dark problem of their destiny is approaching solution and Jerusalem is for the Jews.'

*

In the summer of 1908 a magnificent ceremony took place outside the Damascus Gate, when the playing of Turkish military bands and the firing of triumphal guns celebrated the revival of the Ottoman constitution. Turkey, the long-standing 'sick man of Europe', was being renewed by the exertions of the Young Turks, and there were great hopes of a more liberal regime for the outlying areas of the empire. Two Jerusalem Muslims, Ruhi Bey al-Khalidi and Said Bey al-Husseini, became members of the Ottoman Parliament in Constantinople. This did not necessarily bode well for the Jews of Jerusalem. One of the two new Muslim members, Said Bey al-Husseini, when President of the Municipal Council in Jerusalem in 1905, had done his utmost to prevent the sale of land to Jews at Motza, the small Jewish village just below Jerusalem on the road up from the coast. It was in this village that Theodor Herzl had planted a tree on his way to the city in 1898.

One effect of the new constitution caused distress in Jerusalem. For the first time, Christian Arabs as well as Muslims were liable for military service. 'They loathed it,' recalled Estelle Blyth, daughter of the Anglican Bishop of Jerusalem, 'and indeed, the rough and wretched life into which they were thrust as soldiers pressed more hardly upon the Christians, who, however poor they may be, have a higher standard of life than their Moslem confreres. Nominally, a man was exempt if he could prove he had a wife with no other supporter than himself; actually, this excuse was not always accepted. I remember that one of the stone-masons at St George's, finding himself about to be called up for that year's "askari" (conscripts), married a beggar-woman, and having thus clearly proved his wife's complete dependence upon himself, obtained relief. Being free, he promptly divorced her, with no ill will on either side. Another man we knew, a young fellow of eighteen, the only supporter of his mother and several little brothers and sisters, managed somehow to save and borrow fifty Turkish pounds to buy his release. His officer took the money and sent him home; but before he was gone two days' journey he was seized again, and sent on active service east of the Jordan.'

The life of the recruits, Estelle Blyth wrote, 'torn from plough and field without regard to the work of the country, was hard in the extreme. The old barracks at Jerusalem were very small, but numbers of recruits were dragged in from all parts of the country and penned up there like sheep, until the authorities were ready to move them to other stations. One very hot summer a number of recruits were brought in to Jerusalem, and shut up in the Tower of David, the citadel, and then in the old barracks. No one troubled to feed them very regularly or very often, and which was far worse, no one remembered to give them water. They were just forgotten. A Church of England missionary happened to be walking home past the barracks, and he heard agonised voices crying from above him, "For the love of God, give us water!" Looking up he saw hands thrust out through the bars above his head. He went at once to the Turkish commandant and reported this, and, as the matter seemed to be of little moment at headquarters, he asked and obtained leave to supply these wretched men with water from his own cistern, which he and his servant carried to the barracks in pails.'

Estelle Blyth also left a picture of the life of the Bishop's domestic helpers, from the kawass, or principal servant, downward. 'At one point,' she wrote, 'the kawass and the stable-boy were Moslems, the cook and the kitchenmaid Bethlehem women (Greek Orthodox Christians, that is), the housemaid an Armenian, the gate-keeper a Moor, and the gardener as great a rogue as ever came out of the Greek Levant. They all got on excellently together, and the breezes, chiefly on religious topics, though lively at the time, were short and infrequent. I should explain that a kawass is an official manservant, a Moslem, whose presence in the households of patriarchs, bishops and consuls was obligatory under Turkish law. In the early days he was answerable for the life and safety of his foreign Christian master; latterly, of course, the post was purely formal. The kawass wore a picturesque uniform, full baggy trousers of scarlet or blue cloth, a bright-coloured silken sash round the waist, and a short jacket and close waistcoat, all embroidered in gold braid. When out with his master or with any members of the household, he wore a long curved scimitar with solid silver handle and a sheath embossed in silver. Our kawasses spent a good deal of time rubbing up these silver embellishments, but the scimitars were old, and though the blades were beautifully patterned I do not think they could have wounded even a finger very severely. The kawass always walked in front (other servants behind, unless carrying a lantern at night); his business was to clear the way for you, which was a great convenience, for any such thing as a rule of the road for man, beast, or vehicle, never entered into the heads of the Turkish officials nor anyone else.'

*

On 13 February 1909 the Young Turk revolution gathered added momentum when the Grand Vizier was overthrown in Constantinople. In Jerusalem, Muslims, Christians and Jews joined together to form not only a local branch of the Young Turk Committee of Union and Progress but also a literary and political club, the Jerusalem Patriotic Society. David Yellin, who was teaching in Jerusalem, wrote to a friend in Berlin that 'we see for the first time in these societies Muslims (and of the upper class) associating with Jews and Christians'. At the end of that year, as a Jewish initiative, a joint-stock company was formed to help improve the local Arab agriculture: 5,000 of the 6,000 shares were held by non-Jews.

*

Each guidebook to Jerusalem captured some elements of the city's character in a particular decade. The 1907 edition of Thomas Cook's *Handbook for Palestine and Syria* was no exception. There was in Cook's opinion only one hotel worth mentioning, the Grand New Hotel, 'near Cook's office'. There were six physicians recommended for travellers: 'English, Drs Wheeler, Masterman, and Cant; German, Drs Grüssendorf and Einsler; French, Dr Roux'. Dr Masterman was co-editor of the handbook.

As to first impressions, the guide commented: 'Most travellers have a feeling of disappointment on first seeing Jerusalem, its magnitude is so much less than the imagination had pictured. Associated as it is with the grandest and most sacred events of history, it is difficult to feel that this little town, around whose walls you may walk in an hour, is the Holy City. And, indeed, it is not; for the city whose streets Jesus trod was about a third larger. Then Zion, a large part of which is now a ploughed field, was covered with palaces; and on every side, where now the husbandman pursues his toil, or desolation reigns, were magnificent structures befitting a great capital.' It was 'only gradually', the guide conceded, 'that the explorer finds out how much that is ancient – Jewish, Christian, and Arab remains – can still be seen in and around the city'.

*

For Mrs Freer, in her survey of Jerusalem in 1904, the behaviour of the Christians in the city was as disappointing as the small size of the city and its lack of physical grandeur. 'The heart of Jerusalem,' she wrote, 'its Holy of Holies, and alas! its battlefield, is the Church of the Holy Sepulchre. Here, as in the Holy Stable of Bethlehem, while the Christians pray, the Turkish soldiery must sit by to see that they do not steal, nor even murder. This is no figure of speech. Under the altar which marks the birthplace of our Lord there is a silver star which belongs to the Latins. In 1847 it was stolen, it is believed, by the Greeks. Replaced in 1852, another attempt to carry it off was made in 1873. Close by the same spot in 1893 the Latin sacristan was killed, and three of his companions injured by the Kawass of the Russian pilgrims, who fired his revolver on being requested to make way for the passage of the procession; and, so lately as in November 1901, seventeen Franciscans were severely wounded by the Greeks in the courtyard of the Holy Sepulchre.'

As a Christian, Mrs Freer wrote that she was 'thankful that there should be some 12,000 Christians in Jerusalem, of whom some 1,400 are Protestants, mostly German', and she earnestly wished 'new life to the mission-fields'. There were also some remarkable eccentrics, of the sort that Jerusalem has attracted in every decade. 'We have a lot of cranks come to Jerusalem every year,' the veteran American tour guide Rolla Floyd wrote home on 7 January 1907. 'There are about sixty Americans called the Sanphardites, twelve of whom came two years ago, the others quite lately. Sanphard says he is Alijah and the Agent of the All Mighty. They pretend to send the Holy Ghost out to their friends in all parts of the world. They have hired a large house here and one at Jaffa. Some come saying they will never die. I have met several of these people. Three of them have died since they claimed they would never die. And others I think will soon follow. There are quite a number of different sects, all differ as to the true meaning of the Scriptures. Each declare that they are the only ones that are right. So it is quite a babble. At the same time it is interesting (to me) to hear them all.'

*

The year 1902 was cursed by a lack of the winter rains. It was a year, Mrs Freer wrote, which 'threatened to end disastrously with a drought, and the anxiety felt upon the subject of rain can scarcely be comprehended except by those who have lived where there are no rivers, lakes, nor even the springs, and where the water supply is almost dependent upon the rain caught in the domestic cistern.'

To bring about rain, 'the Moslems inaugurated a procession of penitence; the chief men of the city, with the Pasha, walking barefoot around the sacred Haram enclosure, which occupies one-sixth of the entire city. The Jews, too, fasted and prayed – let us hope the Christians followed suit. Finally, in despair, the Moslem authorities, who seem to preserve a certain intermittent regard for the Hebrew faith, appealed to their fellow-sufferers and offered to the Jews free entrance into the Sacred Courts if they would assemble there and beseech the mercy of Heaven.'

The Jews declined the Muslim offer to enter the Haram al-Sharif, the Noble Sanctuary on which stood the Dome of the Rock and the al-Aksa Mosque. For many Orthodox Jews it is forbidden to go on to what, for them, is the traditional site of the twice-destroyed Temple. They did, however, ask permission, wrote Mrs Freer, 'to pray at the Tomb of David, a jealously guarded sanctuary of Moslem fanaticism, and receiving permission, assembled there on December 17. Before evening the rain fell in torrents, and a glorious rainbow spanned the Holy City.'

*

Mrs Freer was scathing about the architecture of Jerusalem. 'Beyond the colouring of the mosque and the façade of the Holy Sepulchre,' she wrote, 'there is nothing of artistic beauty in Jerusalem. The charm is in colour, not in form, in association, in the persistence of historic custom, in the psychology of the Oriental. The large new suburbs of the Jews are ugly and purely utilitarian, those of the Germans have the irrelevant prettiness of a model village. The English have spent incredible sums upon a hospital for the bodies and a church for the souls of the Jews, with results which are gratifying neither to the artist nor to the utilitarian. The Collegiate Church of St George, a fraction of a building intended to be of the proportions of Oxford Cathedral, goes far to atone for failure elsewhere.

'The modern French buildings of the Dominicans (S. Etienne), in spite of French taste in stained glass, are pleasing of their kind; the restored church of St Anne follows early Crusading lines, and has considerable archaeological interest; the tiled chapel of Notre Dame de France is effective in colouring; the large church built for the accommodation of the Reparatrices is coldly handsome.'

The decorations of the Greek Orthodox churches, Mrs Freer wrote with the superior attitude which Protestant observers readily adopted, 'are beneath criticism – crotchet, patchwork, Christmas-tree balls and artificial flowers; in the Russian alone one finds art, sometimes of really high quality. There are beautiful and costly objects, amid much that is crude, in the Armenian Church of St James; and the new Lutheran Church of the Redeemer has much purity and dignity of outline. The new Moslem suburb is pleasing so far, though getting perilously near to the type mysteriously called "Queen Anne", from which, however, it may be ultimately preserved by Oriental love of space and sense of dignity.'

*

European visitors to Jerusalem came to stare, to pray, and to give alms. In 1902 the Austro-Hungarian Prince zu Windischgrätz came on his honeymoon: his bride was the daughter of the Archduke Rudolf, the heir to the Habsburgs who had died in mysterious circumstances in his hunting-lodge at Mayerling. A chapel in the deepest section of the Church of the Holy Sepulchre, at the place where the Byzantine Empress Helena discovered what she believed to be pieces of the True Cross in the fourth century, was (and is) a monument to Habsburg devotions. It had been dedicated forty years earlier by the young Archduke Maximilian, later Emperor of Mexico, executed by the Mexicans in 1867 at the age of thirty-five.

Muslim, Christian and Jewish pilgrims added to the babble of tongues which struck all European visitors, more accustomed on their travels to the more muted tones of English, German, French or Italian. Even the languages of India were to be heard in the streets of Jerusalem, not only among Muslim pilgrims from the Indian subcontinent who were visiting the Haram, but among those Christian followers of the Apostle Thomas who lived on the Malabar Coast of India. There were also, Mrs Freer noted, Jerusalem Jews and Armenians who were 'in constant relation with India and receive large numbers of pilgrims and merchants, so that one often hears various languages of India in walking through the streets of Jerusalem'.

During the first decade of the twentieth century, Jerusalem was certainly as varied, colourful and exotic a city as Constantinople,

Cairo or Baghdad. It also contained the potential for rapid growth, as well as for distressing conflict.

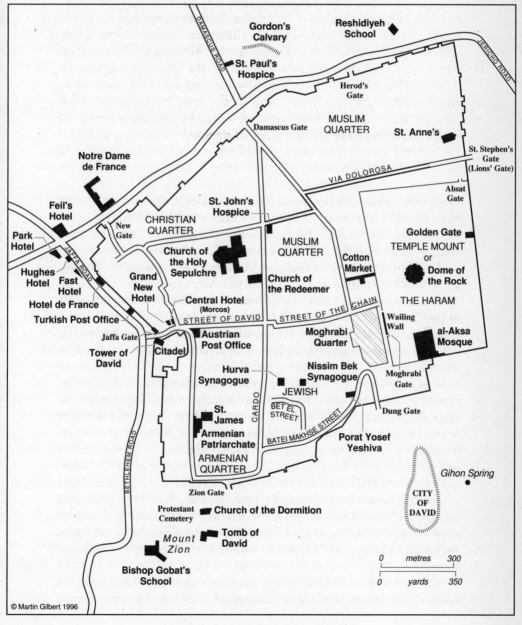

Old City and Jaffa Road before 1914

CHAPTER TWO

Conflicts,
1910–1914

Among the visitors to Jerusalem in 1910 was the Kaiser's son, Prince Eitel Fritz. Twelve years had passed since his imperial father had entered the city on horseback, through a special breach made for him in a low-lying section of the Ottoman wall, just south of the Jaffa Gate. Two monuments to the imperial visit were visible outside the city walls in 1910, the Church of the Dormition, dominating the skyline of Mount Zion, and the Augusta Victoria Hospice, dominating the ridge between Mount Scopus and the Mount of Olives. The architecture of both buildings was massively Germanic, and designed by German architects.

The Dormition church was designed by Heinrich Renard, best known for his buildings in the Rhineland, who modelled the new church on the ancient Worms Cathedral, overlooking the Rhine. For the interior he designed a replica of Charlemagne's palace chapel at Aix-la-Chapelle. The exterior of the church dominates the southern part of Jerusalem, and can be seen from almost every vantage point, north, south, east and west. Father Hoade wrote in his guidebook after the Second World War: 'Its massive towers, more suited to the Rhine Valley, give it the appearance of a medieval fortress'. Yet Renard had appreciated, and used to the full in the buttresses and bell-tower, the sandy-pink Jerusalem stone, which with every sunset glows with a golden light.

The Augusta Victoria was designed by Robert Leibnitz. Scorning local traditions, and even importing cement, in the centre of a twenty-acre compound given to the Kaiser by the Sultan he built a massive medieval German fortress, complete with a high tower which, on clear days, is visible from the banks of the river Jordan, twenty miles to the east and 3,700 feet below it. The interior fittings made the building the most modern in Jerusalem: lighting from an electric generator, and sanitary plumbing including European-standard baths and lavatories, the first of their kind in Jerusalem.

All this the Kaiser's son could look on with national, and indeed imperial, pride. Ronald Storrs, a British visitor to Jerusalem in 1910, later recalled how he and a friend, searching in vain for a Bible printed in Jerusalem, 'twice drove into and sundered Prince Eitel Fritz's State Procession'. Looking back on that visit a quarter of a century later, Storrs wrote: 'Russian establishments held pride of place outside the walls, with a Quarter covering many acres, and a Cathedral and public squares for the accommodation of their great Easter pilgrimages.' But Germany seemed to be fast overtaking. Not only were there the Augusta Victoria Hospice and Dormition Church outside the walls, but also 'the towering Lutheran Church of the Redeemer within the City; and covering the Damascus Gate and the intersection of the roads to Syria and Trans-Jordan, the crenellated Roman Catholic Hospice of St Paul'. The longer-established French and Italian monasteries and hospitals, Storrs wrote, 'though for the most part equally large and even more hideous, seemed to be less conspicuous'.

There was also Zionist activity in Jerusalem in 1910, when a twenty-four-year-old recent immigrant from Russia, David Gruen, who took the writing name Ben-Gurion, joined the small editorial board of the Labour Zionist journal *Ahdut* ('Unity'). He was poor and unknown, but in endless discussions with his colleagues he planned for, and dreamed of, a Jewish State. Some of this dreaming was done, as the future Prime Minister's biographer Michael Bar-Zohar writes, in an Arab café in the Old City 'that boasted the latest in modern technology: a gramophone that poured forth a stream of oriental melodies'.

In February 1912 another Russian Jew reached Jerusalem. He was Mendel Beilis. After two years in prison in Russia without trial, accused of carrying out a ritual murder on a twelve-year-old Christian boy, he had been found not guilty. His trial had aroused violent anti-Semitic feeling in Russia, and had made him a famous figure at the time, both for Jews and non-Jews. When he reached Jerusalem the Muslim Arabs not only allowed him to visit the al-Aksa Mosque but welcomed him there as one of the 'great Jewish heroes'. Like many Russian Jews, however, Beilis chose the new town of Tel Aviv for his home.

A month after Beilis had reached Jerusalem, J. E. Wright, a British Protestant clergyman, arrived in the city. He was distressed when an expected letter never came. 'The reason is,' he wrote in his diary, 'that some postmen who drive the mail cart up from Jaffa were shot at by some Indian Moslem fanatics, who killed three of them and the four horses, ransacking the mail with the hope of getting money.' Travelling eastward to Jericho, Wright visited the Inn of the Good Samaritan. 'It has been the scene of quite a few murders recently,' he wrote. Such were the hazards of the roads around Jerusalem.

Yet the building of amenities was continuous. In 1912 the blind Jerusalemite Abraham Moshe Luncz, whose annual published calendar was the main source of knowledge in Jerusalem of daily activities there, set up a Jewish Institute for the Blind at the entrance to the city on the Jaffa Road, thirty years after the opening of the British-built Ophthalmic Hospital to the south. The Ophthalmic Hospital had been established by the Order of St John, just below the Sultan's Pool, at the beginning of the road to Bethlehem and Hebron.

Jewish aspirations were also expressed in the search for new suburbs that could have an entirely Jewish aspect. On 7 November 1912 a Tel Aviv-based Hebrew-language magazine reported that a 'Talpiot Association' had been founded 'in order to establish a new and attractive neighbourhood in Jerusalem, just as large as Tel Aviv in Jaffa, and even more beautiful'. The building of Talpiot would begin the following spring. 'As is known, the association has purchased the plot near the German Colony, next to the railroad track, and this will also be just as nice as Tel Aviv.' In his calendar of Jewish events in the city for 1913, A. M. Luncz announced: 'The rebuilding of Jerusalem is drawing near.'

A British observer was less optimistic. On 23 November 1912 the British Consul in Jerusalem, P. J. C. McGregor, informed the British Ambassador in Constantinople of problems he was having with regard to the characteristics of twenty of the British-born Jews who were entitled to his protection. 'Like the great majority of the Jews who have flocked into Palestine during the last few years,' he wrote, 'most of the twenty persons on the annexed list are paupers without occupation. Meyer Goral, Gabriel Goral, Harris Shirwinter, Suma Epstein, Aaron Friedman and Sarah Swift possess property whereas nine live on alms (Khaluka) supplied by different Jewish Societies here, and three have recently made an unsuccessful application through this Consulate to be placed on the lists of the Jewish Central Benevolent Committee (Vaad Kola Kolalim).

'All of these people, with two exceptions, are of a low physical type and live in a condition of squalor aggravated by inability to adapt themselves to the conditions of existence in a semi-tropical climate. In fact, the opinion of medical authorities here is that, if Jerusalem is becoming increasingly unhealthy, it is mainly on account of the influx of a degenerate and unwholesome Jewish population, in itself a potent instrument for the spread of disease, especially malaria in all its forms.

'Only two of the persons named in the list can be said to have given this Consulate much trouble in regard to litigation during recent years, and I am far from wishing to stigmatise the British naturalised Jews here as being the most unfavourable specimens of the Hebrew community at Jerusalem. On the other hand, it cannot be maintained that they are other than foreign in every essential respect, as the briefest possible interview would suffice to prove. Only three of them have a working knowledge of the English language; perhaps six possess a smattering and the remainder speak only Yiddish: while in dress and customs they are undistinguishable from their congeners who throng the slums of modern Jerusalem.

'The numbers of Jewish heads of families registered at this Consulate as British subjects, and exclusive of those belonging to the category dealt with above, is sixty and, as the great majority of them are Orientals whose tendency is to become more and more assimilated to the native population among which they dwell, I venture to express the opinion that any gratuitous increase of such a colony in a land where the status of the individual so greatly affects the prestige of the flag protecting him, is greatly to be deprecated.'

McGregor added that the United States Government, 'with the express object – as I am informed by my American Colleague – of checking the influx of naturalised Jews into Palestine, has passed a law providing that prolonged residence in a foreign country shall render naturalisation in the United States null and void'.

In his discussions with Zionist Jews, McGregor was less scathing. In a dispatch of 29 January 1913 he reported on his conversation with 'one of the most cultivated and zealous leaders of the Zionist movement here', who denied current accusations that had appeared in various British newspapers that the Jews of Palestine were pro-German and pro-Ottoman. This leader had 'declared with emphasis' that those who argued that the Zionists were pro-German and pro-Turk 'did not voice the opinions either of the responsible leaders or of the mass. He said that the Jews had at one period hoped for much from the Turks, and even after this hope had been abandoned, considerations of policy had naturally compelled them to continue wearing the mask of Ottoman patriotism. In the same way they had been obliged to work the Zionist movement through German Jews, these being the natural leaders of the Yiddish-speaking race; but they had always striven to secure the protection of the British flag for their institutions, being convinced that under no other auspices could they hope to attain their object, viz., the settlement of a Hebrew-speaking Jewish population in the land of their fathers.'

*

In 1912 one of the most philanthropic Jews of America, Nathan Straus, established a Health Bureau in Jerusalem, equipped with the most modern hospital equipment which he could ship from the United States. That same year a leading American Zionist, Rabbi Judah L. Magnes, during his second visit to Jerusalem, proposed merging Straus's hospital with a scientific research institute. Magnes hoped that such an institute could be the first step in creating a Jewish academic institution, a fully fledged university, in Jerusalem. Straus decided, however, to concentrate his efforts on the practical side, and when he sailed from New York on 12 January 1913 he had with him two American Jewish nurses, Rose Kaplan and Rachel Landy, who were to set up a Nurses' Settlement, financed and supported by the Hadassah Women's Zionist Organisation of America. The 'settlement', which soon became known as the 'Hadassah' nursing clinic, began its work in Jerusalem that spring. It was assisted from the outset by a remarkable Russian-born Jewish woman, Dr Helena Kagan, who at the age of twenty-four had qualified as a doctor in Geneva. Not allowed, because she was a woman, to practise medicine by the Turkish authorities in Jerusalem, she joined forces with the two Hadassah nurses.

Magnes, meanwhile, was looking in another direction for the furtherance of his university idea. 'A beginning should be made with a School of Archaeology, which should develop into a School of the Humanities,' he wrote during 1913 to the Russian-born Zionist leader Dr Chaim Weizmann. Later that year Magnes changed his ideas again, extending his vision. 'The University in Jerusalem should begin with a School of Art,' he wrote. 'Jewish teachers and ministers from all over the world would endeavour to spend some time at it. For me the chief importance and attraction of such a School, as of the university in general, would be that humanities would be taught by Jews, primarily on the basis of Jewish documents and of Jewish life.'

The idea of a Jewish university in Jerusalem had been put forward at successive Zionist Congresses since 1902. It had been a central theme of another Russian-born Zionist leader, Menachem Ussishkin, at Jewish public meetings throughout Russia. It was supported with vigour by Dr Weizmann, who since 1906 had been a professor at Manchester University in England. In 1913 Weizmann had electrified the Zionist Congress in Vienna by his call for a Jewish university in Jerusalem. One of his listeners, Israel Cohen, wrote that Weizmann made the case for such a university 'partly in furtherance of the Jewish cultural renaissance, and partly in the interests of the Jewish students of Central and Eastern Europe who had already become victims of harsh discrimination at various universities'.

One of those who was considered a possible teacher at the future university was Paul Ehrlich, a German Jew and an active member of the Society for Combating Malaria in Palestine. He had been offered a research post at Frankfurt. 'If Ehrlich works in Frankfurt he is no use to us; he will be eaten up by Germans,' Weizmann wrote. 'If he were to work in Jerusalem it would be one of the greatest things for Jerusalem.' But first the money had to be found to establish a university. To this task Weizmann began to devote much time. In Manchester he found an ally in Harry Sacher, a journalist who felt strongly that a Jewish university in Jerusalem would be of benefit to Jews worldwide, both educationally and as an intellectual and moral focus.

*

Archaeological explorations in Jerusalem – a growing feature of the European presence in the second half of the nineteenth century – intensified in the early years of the twentieth century. In 1910, on the Mount of Olives, the remains were uncovered of an ancient Byzantine church, built in the fourth century, later destroyed by the Persians, rebuilt by the Crusaders, and then destroyed again. Also in 1910 the commercially driven excavations of Captain Montague Parker – he was in search of the treasures of the Second Temple – penetrated under the Haram al-Sharif. This caused deep distress not only in Muslim Jerusalem but throughout the Ottoman Empire.

Estelle Blyth, the Anglican Bishop's daughter, later recalled how, at the time of Captain Parker's digging, which took place when the Muslim festival of Nebi Musa, commemorating the death of Moses, coincided with Easter, 'Jerusalem was filled to the brim with excitable pilgrims and strangers belonging to various creeds, whose physical resistance in many cases had been undermined by the long and rigid fasts which preceded the festivals, and who were therefore as dry tinder and ready to blaze up at the slightest suggestion. Into this inflammable mass of humanity fell as a bombshell the report that the English excavators had broken into an old underworld passage, leading from under the Rock in the Mosque to the Golden Gate.

'The right of guardianship over the sacred area belonged to a Moslem family, who had jealously preserved it for several generations; it was held to be impossible that any one could have carried on digging operations, and finally have emerged within the Mosque enclosure, without the knowledge of these hereditary watchers. The story ran that the head of the family and other members had been paid by the excavators, but that one of the juniors, angry at being overlooked when money was in circulation, had betrayed his knowledge to the Government.

'Rumour and counter-rumour flew about Jerusalem. None was too gross, too improbable, to be believed. The English had been seeking the Ring of Solomon, in which was vested control of the spirits; had they obtained possession of it, they would have loosed the spirits and forced the whole world to their will. They had found and removed the Ark of the Covenant, the Censer, and other holy vessels, "which" (to quote an Arab newspaper) "no one knew about except God and these English, who came to our city and took our rare treasures. In truth, our loss is great, and the audacity of these English excavators is greater, and the greatest of all is the sin of certain sheikhs (chiefs) and officials in guarding and allowing them thus to excavate". "The English are a clever people", said the same paper in another place, "and everybody knows their acuteness." '

A crowd of at least 2,000 Muslims, Miss Blyth reported, 'townspeople and fellahin (peasants), clamoured at the serai (Government courts). They threatened to shoot the pasha and his whole family, to murder all the English, and so on. Undoubtedly the situation was very critical, and any lack of steadiness might well have precipitated the angry populace into action which they would have repented of only when too late. Christian and Jewish shopkeepers hastily put up their shutters, and the less furious amongst the people were glad to keep within doors and out of harm's way. It is not what has been done that counts with an Eastern crowd, but what it believes has been done or attempted; and when thousands are shouting and threatening, the still small voice of Truth is drowned in the general tumult. This was the only occasion upon which I saw Jews and Moslems making common cause together . . .

'It must be remembered that the Jews had been wounded in their tenderest religious feelings, equally with the Moslems. Every Eastern Jew believes that somewhere under that great expanse of the Mosque enclosure, upon which their wonderful Temple once blazed forth its glory to the world, are hidden the Sacred Vessels and the Ark, and that if a Jew should tread upon the spot under which these are hidden he would instantly be struck dead. No Jew would set his foot within the Mosque enclosure, had he been offered a handful of gold as reward. The Jews all believed that "these English", after bribing the no less hateful Moslem guardians of the place, had entered the sacred enclosure with sacrilegious intent. Nothing but a vital common hatred and a most vivid sense of injury, could have drawn together these two opposing elements of Moslem and Jew, who are usually so suspicious of one another's purpose and intention.'

Captain Parker fled the city. Through no design of his, some of his diggings were of value, especially with regard to the city's ancient water system. When he tried to return and continue his digging, the Turkish authorities would not allow him to land.

*

In 1913 the first archeological dig took place conducted by a Jew, at a primarily Jewish site. The funding was also Jewish, being provided by Baron Edmond de Rothschild. The site chosen by Captain Raymond Weill for his exploration was the City of David, the oldest of Jerusalem's built-up areas. It lay just to the south of, and below, the Temple Mount. It was after conquering this city 3,000 years ago that David purchased a threshing floor from a Jebusite woman, in order to build the Temple.

The impetus behind this Jewish archaeological activity had a national as well as a scientific aspect. The present excavator of the Herodian city near the Dung Gate and at the southern side of the Temple Mount, Dr Ronny Reich, has commented on this first Jewish dig of 1913: 'Unlike the archaeologists from other countries, Jewish archaeologists perceive themselves to have a direct link with the explorations of the distant past in excavations from the time of the First and Second Temples, or from the time of the Mishna and Talmud.' I was present in the summer of 1995 when Dr Reich himself, with the intense enthusiasm of a patriot, pointed out the massive stones from the Herodian Temple that had been hurled down by the Romans in AD70 and smashed on to the street far below – a street he was in the process of preparing for a new generation of tourists and sightseers.

*

The year 1913 saw the culmination of a fierce conflict among the modern Jews of Jerusalem: the question of language. Ought Hebrew to be the language of daily life, as Eliezer Ben Yehuda, David Yellin and their friends insisted, or would it make more sense in the twentieth century for German to be the language of education, commerce and social life? The German Government in Berlin looked to the German language as a means of increasing its own influence, and made efforts to swing the debate its way. Part of the battle was fought in the schools. It was exacerbated in June 1913 when it was reported, wrongly in fact, that the Hebrew Grammar School in the city had placed itself under French protection.

Two rival systems of Jewish education were in conflict: the Alliance Israelite Universelle schools, financed by French Jews, and the schools and colleges financed by the German Hilfsverein, an organisation founded in 1901 to channel German Jewish philanthropy to Palestine. To counter this influence, the educator David Yellin founded a Hebrew Teachers' Seminary in Jerusalem. On 15 June 1913, and again two days later, the German Consul-General in Jerusalem, Edmund Schmidt, suggested to Berlin that the Kaiser's Government should place the Hilfsverein schools and colleges under German protection. This, Schmidt hoped, would restrain the 'radical Zionists from Hebraising the Hilfsverein school'.

The Zionists proposed a compromise: exclusive use of Hebrew in the Hilfsverein schools, but with German to be the language of instruction in the colleges, except for one science subject, which was to be taught in Hebrew. The Hilfsverein rejected this. But in one of the schools they had taken over, the Laemel School in Jerusalem, Hebrew was already the language of instruction. This was as a result of the efforts of the Hilfsverein's own Director of Education, Ephraim Cohn-Reiss, who was the first person to introduce Hebrew as the language of instruction in a Jewish school in Jerusalem. Nevertheless, in 1913 Cohn-Reiss rejected a proposal made by the majority of his teachers to accelerate the process of Hebraisation in the schools under his authority.

The language controversy also had a political aspect. On 17 November 1913 the German Consul in Haifa, Julius Loytved-Hardegg, writing about the Zionists, warned Berlin: 'By excessive encouragement of a Jewish national language, they magnify the suspicions of the Arabs on the one hand, and weaken Jewry by this internal struggle on the other.' That internal struggle continued. On 10 December 1913 teachers and pupils demonstrated outside the Laemel School in Jerusalem in favour of Hebrew as the language of instruction in all Jewish schools. Windows were broken, and Cohn-Reiss called in the Turkish police to break up the protest. When the teachers were promptly dismissed, their pupils followed them out of the school building. The German Consul in Jaffa, Heinrich Brode, reported to Berlin that the Hebrew-language advocates were 'anarchist agitators'.

Elsewhere there were attempts at compromise. The headmistress of the Jerusalem Jewish Girls' School, Vera Pinczower, told the German Consul-General that, while Hebrew was the language of instruction in her school, German was strongly encouraged as a foreign language. The British Consul, P.J.C. McGregor, reported to the British Ambassador in Constantinople on 15 March 1914: 'The only Jewish educational establishment under British protection here is the Evelina de Rothschild School for Girls maintained by the Anglo-Jewish Association. This institution is a model of its kind and although placed under an ecclesiastical ban on account of its high standard of education, is conducted on the lines of orthodox Judaism. It is consequently in evil odour among the Zionists, who recently threatened to make things unpleasant for the Directress unless she gave a position of predominant importance to the Hebrew language, and I can only attribute the non-fulfilment of these threats to the fear of thereby compromising the scheme of obtaining British protection for their own undertakings, and also to the complete harmony prevailing between the Directress and her staff.'

Within a year the Zionist argument prevailed: that it was the Hebrew language that would best bring unity to a land where Yiddish, French and Ladino (the medieval Spanish spoken by many Sephardi Jews) were as much a part of daily Jewish life as German, if not more so, and where modern Hebrew was already established as the language of the Zionists both in their public work and in their private lives.

The German Government eventually accepted this. 'Germany would be sufficiently rewarded', a senior German diplomat wrote in March 1915, 'if, besides Hebrew, German would also be cultivated.' The defeat of Germany on the battlefield three years later finally ended the power of German officialdom to influence the debate.

*

The annual influx of Russian pilgrims was as great in 1914 as it had ever been. Stephen Graham, a London Scot who accompanied one such Russian group that Easter from the Russian Black Sea ports, wrote: 'It was amazing to me to see the extent to which the pilgrims sought in Jerusalem tokens for the clothing of their dead bodies, and how much their thoughts were centred on death and the final resurrection morning.' The pilgrims would take their silver and wooden crosses to the Church of the Holy Sepulchre, and to the site of the tomb of Jesus. 'They sanctified crosses at the grave, little ones to wear round their necks in the tomb, and larger ones to lie on their breasts; they brought their death shrouds and cross-embroidered caps to dip them in Jordan; they took Jerusalem earth to put in their coffins, and even had their arms tattooed with the word 'Jerusalem', and with pictures of the Virgin; so that they might lie so marked in the grave, and show it in heaven.' By such symbols and marks 'they felt they obtained a sort of sanctuary'.

For the Greek, Syrian and Arab Orthodox Christian pilgrim of 1914, the high point of the visit – the experience that gave all the travails and uncertainties, the inconvenience and the bewilderment, the crowding and jostling of the pilgrimage – its greatest meaning, was the ceremony of the Sacred Fire. Each Easter the city was transformed and electrified by the spectacle which took place on Holy Saturday at the Church of the Holy Sepulchre. Stephen Graham witnessed it while disguised as a Russian pilgrim. 'About two o'clock in the afternoon,' he wrote, 'the shouts and shrieks of the worshippers were hushed at the appearance of the Patriarch and his clergy and the commencement of the great litany. The Patriarch, twelve archimandrites, and four deacons were all dressed publicly in shining white by the servants of the church. That done, a procession formed of surpliced clergy carrying banners depicting Christ's sufferings, His crucifixion, burial, and glorious resurrection. These clergy walked in pairs and after them also in pairs came others carrying wonder-working crosses, then appeared a great number of clergy in pairs, many of them carrying sheaves of candles (thirty-three candles in a sheaf, one for each year of the life of Jesus).

'Directly the Sacred Fire appeared the clergy would light their sheaves of candles and distribute them to the pilgrims. Behind all came the Patriarch carrying his staff. Three times they went round the ark of the Grave with hymns, and then standing outside the door of the Sepulchre the Patriarch took off his mitre and all the emblems of his earthly glory before entering. A dragoman broke the seals with which the door of the Sepulchre was sealed and the Patriarch was allowed to go in. Before entering deacons gave him armfuls of candles to light when the fire should appear.

'The disrobing of the Patriarch before his entrance to the shrine of shrines is by way of protestation that he takes no chemicals – or at least the simple understand it so. He went into the chamber in a state as near to nakedness as decency permitted, and when he had entered, the door was immediately shut upon him again. The throbbing multitude was filled with a strange silence, and the minds of many people occupied with conjectures as to what was happening in the Holy of Holies into which the Patriarch had disappeared, and from which in a short while would appear the sign from heaven, the one slender sign for them of God's interference in a prosaic world.

'The suspense was awful, the outbreak of the heavy bells above us something unearthly. Every neck was craned just as every limb was squeezed and crushed in the great "passion towards the Sepulchre". In those minutes of "God's hesitation" there passed in the minds of the believers ages of exaltation mingled with doubt.

'At last from the wall of the north side of the ark of the Grave burst a great blaze of yellow light illumining the heads of the throng, and spreading with strange rapidity, as candle was passed to candle. From the interior of the ark sheaves of candles all lighted were handed out by the Patriarch, the sheaves having, as I said, thirty-three candles in each – the years of Jesus' life. Quick as thought, the years and candles were distributed, clutched, hung overhead on ribbons, dropped to the close-wedged crowd. On our faces and our clothes hot wax kept dropping, and now and then flames singed our ears. "Never mind," said one pilgrim to me, "the sacred fire cannot hurt any one for the first half-hour after it has come."

'Exalted Easterners took whole sheaves of lighted candles and plunged them into their bosoms to extinguish them; many wilfully applied the flames to their bare flesh and cried out in joy and ecstasy. Hundreds of pilgrims produced their black death-caps filled with sweet scented cotton-wool, and they extinguished the candles in them. These death-caps embroidered with bright silver crosses they proposed to keep to their death days and wear in the grave, cotton-wool and all. Other pilgrims carefully preserved their Sacred Fire, and getting out of the mob as quickly as they could carried it to the hostelry, protecting it from the wind with their open palms. Others, more provident, lit the wicks in their double lanterns.

'As for the crowd, as a crowd it was to all appearance mad with ecstasy as if under the influence of some extraordinary drug or charm. The people shouted, yelled, sang, danced, fought, with such diversity of manner and object, and in such a variety of dress and language, that the calm onlooker thought of the tale full of sound and fury told by an idiot and signifying nothing. There was one guiding cry, however, that one taken seemingly from the lips of the Patriarch, and repeated in every language of the Orthodox East – Kyrie eleison, Christos Voskrece, Christ is risen – and, as on Easter Eve in Russia, the happy Slavs kissed one another in rapture, finding themselves once more in the moment of revelation brothers and sisters in Christ and full of love for one another.

'It was the trial of their lives for the little khaki-clad Turkish soldiers, and it seemed to me from what I heard that they failed to keep the crowd back. When the Patriarch appeared to bless the people there was a regular stampede towards him, and despite the whir and crack of whips, and ungentle pounding from butt ends of rifles, the Orthodox Arabs burst through, and picking up the frail little greybeard of a Patriarch carried him in triumph to the altar. The crowd, however, began to move out, and few of us had any choice of road; we just walked in the direction in which we were pushed. I for my part was very glad to reach the hostelry again.'

Stephen Graham had experienced the most remarkable of all the scenes in Jerusalem's Christian calendar.

*

Wild rumours could circulate with ease in Jerusalem: in the summer of 1911 Albert Antébi, the director of the Alliance Israelite Universelle school in Jerusalem since 1900, told a friend that an Arab peasant had asked him if the Jews had really prepared a Jewish king for Jerusalem, and if this king would be a foreigner and speak Arabic. 'In all eyes,' wrote Antébi, 'the Jew is becoming the anti-patriot, the traitor prepared to plunder his neighbour to take possession of his goods. The Christian excels in these accusations, but the Muslim follows on his heels.'

In a further election to the Ottoman Parliament in 1912 the two Jerusalem Arabs elected, Ruhi Bey al-Khalidi and Uthman al-Nashashibi, were greatly angered when the new Governor of the Jerusalem district, Mahdi Bey, an Albanian by origin, expressed considerable sympathy for Zionist activity. As reported in the Jerusalem English-language newspaper *Truth*, Mahdi Bey offered to grant the Jewish colonies in the coastal plain the right of self-defence, and to help them with land purchase. He also said that he would allow the Jews 'a capacious Government Building which will serve as your central administrative premises'.

Repeated Arab protest, and the coming together of Ruhi Bey al-Khalidi and Uthman al-Nashashibi with some of the leading Christian Arabs in Jerusalem, helped speed up Mahdi Bey's dismissal.

Before a new governor could arrive, more land was sold to the Zionists in the plain. This led to more protests – one from the twenty-year-old Arif al-Arif, who wrote in the Arabic-language *Falastin* ('Palestine') on 25 January 1913: 'If this state of affairs continues, then the Zionists will gain mastery over our country, village by village, town by town; tomorrow the whole of Jerusalem will be sold . . .' Within a year of this warning, a group of Jewish workers had begun to farm land to the north of Jerusalem, at Atarot. It was a typical small farm, built on a stony hillside, where the farmers hoped in due course to produce the first fruits of their physical toil, a Zionist imperative. Yet the existence of the Atarot farm was a cause of agitation to the Arab villages through which the farmers had to travel on their way to the city.

As for the young Arif al-Arif, who so feared Jewish settlement, in 1920, as one of the leaders of the anti-Jewish riots in Jerusalem, he was arrested by the British, sentenced to death and, his sentence commuted, sent into exile. Later he worked as a British Mandate official, and from 1950 to 1955, under Jordanian rule, was Mayor of East Jerusalem.

*

During the spring of 1913 there was talk among the Palestinian Arabs of holding an anti-Zionist Congress. This idea was supported publicly by one of the leading Muslim Arabs in Jerusalem, Muhammad Salah al-Husseini. Although the Congress was never held, a society was formed, made up of notables from Jerusalem, Jaffa, Haifa, Gaza and Nablus, to buy up government land 'before it is done by the Zionists'. This was reported in *Falastin* on 12 July 1913.

At the end of that year the leading Russian Zionist Menachem Ussishkin made his third visit to Palestine. On his return to Russia he spoke publicly in favour not only of Jewish rural settlements but of 'Jewish towns, particularly Jerusalem – the heart of the nation and of the world'. In his speech, which was circulated in pamphlet form, Ussishkin argued that 'Jerusalem must be surrounded by a ring of Jewish settlements; various kinds of industry must be established there, as Professor Schatz has done with his "Bezalel". The shame and reproach must be removed from the holy and hallowed "Wailing Wall", which was surrounded by dirt.' The Zionist aim, Ussishkin said, was to establish 'a New Jerusalem, a Jerusalem of which a truly cultural nation can indeed be proud'.

For the Muslims and Christians of Jerusalem, such intentions were the cause of alarm. Khalil al-Sakakini, a Greek Orthodox Christian, wrote in his diary on 23 February 1914 that the Zionist 'conquest of Palestine' was as if it had conquered the heart of the Arab nation, because Palestine was the link binding the Arabian Peninsula with Egypt and Africa. A few days later he wrote that, although Palestine was not 'the cradle of Arab civilisation', it was not debarred from 'a share in it'. The Muslim holy places in Jerusalem, and Muslim schools, 'are eloquent signs that this country is Arabic and Islamic'.

The pace of Arab protests against Zionism was accelerating, and the protests were gaining in volume. The role of Jerusalem in this was central. The Arabs of Nablus had already publicly opposed the suggestion that their city be incorporated into the Jerusalem district, 'so as not to be infected with the Zionist germ'. The Zionist leaders followed these Arab protests carefully, but did not allow themselves to be deflected from their path. On 9 March 1914, a mere two weeks after Khalil al-Sakakini's first diary entry, the German-born Dr Arthur Ruppin wrote in his diary: 'Today I succeeded in buying from Sir John Gray Hill his large and magnificently situated property on Mount Scopus, thus acquiring the first piece of ground for the Jewish University in Jerusalem.'

Arthur Ruppin's purchase of the Englishman's house on the crest of Mount Scopus, overlooking the whole of Jerusalem, and with a view eastward to the Dead Sea and the distant Mountains of Moab, was decisive for the Zionist movement. The money needed to buy it had been sent to Jerusalem not only from a few wealthy Jewish philanthropists, but from tens of thousands of poor Russian Jews, who, inspired by Ussishkin, had contributed a total of 50,000 gold francs. Had it not been for the coming of war in 1914, a Jewish university might have opened its doors in Jerusalem in 1917 or 1918. The Turks had no objections.

Only six days after Ruppin's purchase of the British-owned house on Mount Scopus, P. J. C. McGregor reported to the British Ambassador in Constantinople that the Jewish 'nationalist spirit' was showing itself 'with increased vigour' in the Zionist schools in Jerusalem. At the same time, McGregor wrote, the hitherto strict Turkish restrictions on Jewish land purchase and immigration had disappeared. He put the responsibility for this on what he called the 'complacent attitude' of the Turkish authorities. The hope of the founders of the university, McGregor added, was that 'it must be British and it was hoped would be affiliated to one of the British universities'. A leading Zionist in the city had told him that the university site 'had cost £21,500 and must have foreign protection'.

*

Arab opposition to Zionist enterprise was strengthened in 1914 when new elections were held for the Ottoman Parliament in Constantinople. The Jews already had an influential Jerusalemite and Zionist in the Ottoman Parliament, David Yellin. The Arabs were determined to counter this. 'If I am elected as a representative,' Ragheb Bey al-Nashashibi, the Jerusalem District Engineer and a member of one of the city's most prominent families, told the Muslim Arab voters in 1914, 'I will dedicate all my energies, day and night, to remove the harm and danger awaiting us from Zionism and the Zionists.'

Ragheb Bey was elected with the largest majority of all the candidates. When the Zionist leaders in Jerusalem sought out the other successful candidate, Said Bey al-Husseini, and asked him why he was so strong in his denunciation of Zionism, he told them that it was only because of his desire for popularity 'and out of consideration for Arab public opinion'. The historian Yehoshua Porath has commented: 'These remarks seem to cast doubt on the sincerity of the speaker, but they certainly confirm the existence of anti-Zionist attitudes in Arab public opinion, which candidates for the Ottoman Parliament had to take into consideration if they wished to be elected.'

In a letter to Arthur Ruppin on 9 April 1914, a Jerusalem Jew reported that Muslims in Jerusalem had told him that Jewish immigration had become a special topic of discussion 'at the meetings of their secret societies'.

That month two leading Jews, Henry Morgenthau, the United States Ambassador in Constantinople, and Arthur Franklin from London, visited Jerusalem. The two men found themselves out of sympathy with both the ultra-Orthodox and the Zionist Jews, whose divisions were so marked. Commenting on this, P. J. C. McGregor wrote to his Ambassador in Constantinople on 26 April 1914 that Morgenthau, on his departure, 'appeared to be painfully disappointed by the irreconcilable spirit of the divers factions, and he advised Mr Franklin not to attempt too much. Mr Franklin stated to me that the English Jews whom he represented regarded both Zionism and anti-Zionism with indifference, their one bond of union with Jews throughout the world being their common faith and he told me that his object was to weld the Jews of Jerusalem into one solid body on that basis. He also hoped to pave the way for a better organisation of Jewish charities and a radical reform of the abuses prevalent in the Grand Rabbinate. I refrained from expressing surprise when Mr Franklin stated his ignorance of the actual lines of cleavage, viz., Zionism and free-thought versus Orthodox Judaism of the most conservative school, but I gave him the facts as I understood them and before his departure he reluctantly admitted that they were correct.'

As well as the conflict among the Orthodox and Zionist Jews of Jerusalem, Arab sensitivities had also been aroused by the continuing Zionist successes in the city. On 13 May 1914 one of Jerusalem's leading Muslim sheikhs, Abd al-Kadir al-Muzghar, told Dr Isaac Lévy, the Jewish manager of the Jerusalem branch of the Anglo-Palestine Company, that he was 'perturbed at attitudes held by Arab and Zionist youth, both of whom harboured extremely chauvinistic and potentially dangerous elements'. Two weeks later Isa al-Isa, the owner of *Falastin*, told one of the main Egyptian newspapers, *Le Journal de Caire*, that there was 'a very important movement afoot to put an end to the Zionist invasion'.

At the end of June 1914 (in the very week of the assassination of the Archduke Franz Ferdinand at Sarajevo, the catalyst for a war into which even Turkey was soon to be drawn), a pamphlet was distributed in Jerusalem. It was headed 'Beware of the Zionist Danger,' and signed 'A Palestinian'. The writer was angry at his fellow Muslims. 'Men!' he wrote, 'do you want to be slaves and servants to people who are notorious in the world and in history? Do you wish to be slaves to the Zionists who have come to you to expel you from your country, saying that this country is theirs? The Zionists desire to settle in our country and to expel us from it. Are you satisfied with this? Do you wish to perish?'

These questions presaged many decades of conflict to come. But before that conflict could break out, Jerusalem, like so many cities, was caught up in the turmoil and uncertainty of war.

CHAPTER THREE

War,
1914–1917

During the last days of July 1914 Europe seemed on the brink of a
general war. By chance, Jerusalem's Anglican Bishop since 1887,
Bishop Blyth, was leaving the city on July 21, 'by the midday train'
his daughter, Estelle, later recalled. 'The station was crowded with
affectionate and sorrowful faces,' she wrote. 'Representatives of the
various foreign consulates, the Eastern churches, and others were
there to bid him farewell, and amongst them the German Consul
and his wife, both of them very popular with all who knew them.
The German Consul, as he said goodbye, repeated several times, "I
have always striven for peace – I have always striven for peace!" My
Father could not understand his meaning at the time, but afterwards,
of course, it was clear.'

In Paris, a meeting had been fixed for August 1 at which Dr Chaim
Weizmann hoped to persuade Baron Edmond de Rothschild, one of
the main supporters of Zionist enterprise in Palestine, to give his
financial backing to a research institute that could serve as a nucleus
for a Jewish university in Jerusalem. Because of the diplomatic crisis
the meeting was postponed until August 8. Before it could take place
both Britain and France were at war with Germany, and the meeting
was cancelled. 'I have a foreboding that all the labour of the last
fifteen months for the University is lost,' Weizmann wrote. 'It breaks
my heart.'

For almost three months Turkey stayed outside the conflict, but
the German Kaiser and his advisers pushed the Turkish Government
forward, persuading the dominant figure at Constantinople, the Minister of War, Enver Pasha, that his country stood to gain a great deal
from participation in the war alongside Germany. In October, Enver
allowed two German warships, commanded by a German admiral
but flying the Turkish flag, to bombard the Russian Black Sea ports.

As a result, from 31 October 1914 the Ottoman Empire was at war with three European empires: those of Britain, Russia and France. Zionist Jews in Germany, where the Zionist movement was strong, hoped that a Turkish victory might lead to greater consideration of their desires. This seemed confirmed when the German Government exempted the Zionist representatives in Berlin and Constantinople from military service, so that they could continue with their Zionist work. Dr Ruppin was one of the beneficiaries of this exemption.

In Jerusalem, too, there was a sense in the first two months of the war that all would be well for the Jews of the city. Indeed, the Turkish Governor, Zakey Bey, went so far as to offer to sell the Jews the area in front of the Wailing Wall, known as the Moghrabi Quarter, consisting of about twenty-five Muslim Arab houses, in order to make a larger space for Jews who went to the Wall to pray. The sum asked was a large one, £20,000, to be used both to rehouse the Muslim families and to make a public garden in front of the Wall.

Unfortunately for the Jews of the city, they lacked the funds needed to make such a purchase. Nor could they count on the continuing goodwill of the Turkish authorities. When, in December 1914, the Chief Rabbi of Jerusalem complained at the expulsion of Jews from Jaffa, the Commander of the Fourth Ottoman Army, Djemal Pasha, threatened to remove him from office 'if he dared to meddle with matters that did not concern him'. A few months later, Muslim Arab pressure on the Turkish authorities in Jerusalem led to Jews being forbidden, by official decree, from placing benches or lighting candles at the Wailing Wall.

For centuries the Wailing Wall had been the place to which Jews went to remember in prayer the ancient days of the Temple. When the Temple had been finally destroyed by the Romans, the Wailing Wall, the western part of the Herodian structure above which the Temple had been built, was the last remaining trace. The Jews know it as the Western Wall. The ban on benches and candles at the Wall was a small but distressing vexation for religious Jews. Their case was taken up at the highest level by the Chief Rabbi of Ottoman Turkey, the Hacham Bashi, who, in a direct intervention in Constantinople, was able to have the ban removed. Later vexations at the Wall were not to be so easily overcome.

*

Throughout the First World War the future of Palestine, and of Jerusalem, were matters for considerable discussion among the

Powers ranged against Turkey. In March 1915 a member of the British Liberal Government, Herbert Samuel, a Jew but not a Zionist, proposed the establishment of a British protectorate over Palestine into which Jews from all over the world could settle. This was supported by one of the leading members of the government, David Lloyd George, soon to become Prime Minister, of whom a colleague wrote that he 'does not care a damn for the Jews or their past or their future, but who thinks it would be an outrage to let the Christian Holy Places – Bethlehem, Mount of Olives, Jerusalem etc – pass into the possession or under the protectorate of "Agnostic Atheistic France" '. Another member of the British Government, Jack Pease, recorded in his diary that March: 'Samuel made a caveat in Jewish interest that holy places should not go to the French. Damascus he was willing, but not Jerusalem.'

Another view inside British Government circles in early 1915 was the possibility, put forward by the Conservative Member of Parliament Sir Mark Sykes, an expert on the Near East, for 'the establishment of a special Russian administration in the region of Jerusalem, Bethlehem and Jaffa'. Russia, as Britain's ally, was thought to be in need of encouragement to continue at war.

In October 1915, when various territorial offers were being made to the Arabs of the Arabian Peninsula to encourage them to enter the war against Turkey, four districts in the Ottoman Empire were promised them to be part of their future territories. These districts were Damascus, Hama, Homs and Aleppo. Jerusalem was not mentioned in the letter sent to the leader of the Arab revolt, Sharif Hussein, in 1915: by then the British felt that they might want Jerusalem, and all Palestine west of the river Jordan (Transjordan), to be part of a British-controlled region.

Within a year of the outbreak of the war great privation had come to Jerusalem. The Turks had faced Allied landings at Gallipoli and in Mesopotamia, and were fighting in Eastern Anatolia against the Russian army. The Turkish authorities in Jerusalem, headed by a new Governor, Izzet Bey, felt vulnerable. A large British army was in Egypt, and a Turkish attempt to seize the Suez Canal had failed. The loyalties of both Jews and Arabs in the city were suspect. Many Jews were expelled to Egypt. Others lived in conditions of mounting hardship and hunger. The Bezalel art academy was among many recently established Jewish institutions that were closed down, and its founder, Boris Schatz, was among several leading Jewish figures in the city who were imprisoned. Those Arabs whom the Turks feared were deported to forced labour in Anatolian Turkey.

The small Hadassah clinic, with its two American nurses, Rachel Landy and Rose Kaplan, was among the Jewish institutions that suffered most as the war got into its stride. At the beginning of 1915 the Turkish authorities requisitioned all hospital buildings for their own use, all non-Ottoman doctors were deported from the city or went back to Europe to serve in their own armies, and all Allied citizens – French, Russians and Britons – were expelled. In January 1915 Rachel Landy wrote to her New York headquarters: 'Since the war began we are not having the usual luck with our infants. Quite a number are dying after a few weeks. Needless to say, it is all due to starvation.'

Rachel Landy was taken ill and returned to the United States. Later in the war Rose Kaplan died of cancer. The work which they had done was taken over by Dr Helena Kagan and three local Jewish midwives. Many years later Dr Kagan recalled how, as the war continued, she saw the population of Jerusalem dwindle, how starvation spread, how dead bodies lay in the streets, and how, desperate to keep the children under her care alive, she bought a cow to be able at least to give them milk. Her main helper was the Moravian-born Dr Albert Ticho, an ophthalmologist, who had come to Jerusalem in 1912, but he was eventually taken by the Turks to serve as an oculist in the Ottoman army. Helena Kagan contracted malaria, but she never gave up the medical work for children which had brought her to Jerusalem in the first place.

*

On 23 June 1915 Kamil al-Asad, a Syrian sheikh who had been informed of Arab plans for a revolt against Turkey which would begin in the Lebanese coastal towns, came to Jerusalem and told Djemal Pasha of what he had learned, and of who were the leaders. The main leader, Abd al-Karim al-Khalil, was at once arrested, charged with conspiracy, and hanged, as were other Arab nationalists, many in Beirut, some in Damascus and some in Jerusalem. Among those executed in Jerusalem were the Mufti of Gaza, Arif al-Husseini, and his son Mustafa, both of whom were hanged in public outside the Jaffa Gate.

After the war a British officer recorded the words of his Arab orderly about the Mufti of Gaza: 'He was a good man, greatly respected; therefore we all assembled to see him hang.'

*

On the outbreak of the war, Djemal Pasha had taken up residence in Bishop Blyth's house at St George's Cathedral. Later, after Djemal had moved his headquarters to the Anglican Mission houses, the bishop's house became the residence of the Governor of Jerusalem, Izzet Bey.

At the beginning of 1917 a large Allied army was gathered south of Gaza. It had twice failed to capture the port, but would undoubtedly try again. Many wounded Turks were taken up to Jerusalem where, that April, Djemal Pasha granted Bertha Vester, of the American Colony, permission to turn the Grand New Hotel, just inside the Jaffa Gate, into a hospital. 'The hotel was soon ready to receive the wounded,' she later wrote. 'It was neither Grand nor New, but filthy and full of vermin, and elbow grease had to fill in where soap and disinfectant were lacking.'

As the British Government contemplated the conquest of Palestine, it also moved, at the urging of the Zionist Organisation headed by Dr Chaim Weizmann, towards a commitment to establish a Jewish National Home in Palestine once it came under British control. William Ormsby-Gore, an expert on Turkey and the Near East, informed the British Cabinet Secretary on 1 April 1917 that 'the delivery of Jerusalem from the Turk would be hailed by every Christian, Jew and Arab', and would have a 'worldwide moral and political effect'.

*

A new British commander of the Egyptian Expeditionary Force, General Sir Edmund Allenby, was making his plans to capture Gaza. It was almost certain that his armies, among whom were British, Australian, New Zealand and Indian troops, would be able to approach Jerusalem from either the west, or from the south, or both, once Gaza fell. In early September there were several British bombing attacks on the German military headquarters at the Augusta Victoria Hospice. On September 7 Maggie Lee, a member of the American Colony then being used as a military hospital, wrote in her diary: 'Of all the bombs which were dropped on headquarters, only the church containing the Kaiser's and the Kaiserin's portrait was hit.'

At the end of September Allenby's army began military operations against Gaza and Beersheba. Were these two towns to fall, the way to Jerusalem would be open. Beersheba fell on the last day of October. On November 5 the former Chief of the German General Staff, General Erich von Falkenhayn, reached Jerusalem from Aleppo. He had been placed in command of the Palestine front. When he arrived he discovered that Djemal Pasha was incensed about a small group of Palestinian Jews, members of the 'Nili' group, who had been caught spying for the British; unknown to Djemal, one of them had passed on essential intelligence about the Beersheba region.

On November 7 Gaza fell to Allenby's troops. With Beersheba already under their control, the way was open for the advance on Jerusalem. Nor was there any letting up in Allenby's campaign. On the day after the fall of Gaza the rearguard of the retreating Turks was broken up and large numbers of prisoners, guns and ammunition were captured. On November 8 Djemal Pasha summoned the leading Jews of Jerusalem and Jaffa, to tell them that he regarded all Jews, not only the Nili members, as guilty of espionage. On being told of this ominous threat, a German member of the Reichstag, Oscar Cohn, asked the authorities in Berlin to restrain Djemal's vindictiveness. Von Falkenhayn, who was known to be friendly to the Jews, intervened. At a trial in Damascus, two members of Nili were sentenced to death and executed. Others were imprisoned. Those against whom no evidence was produced were released.

On November 9 the advanced units of the Australian and New Zealand Mounted Division had reached to within twenty miles of Latrun, the entrance to the Jerusalem hills from the west. From the south, an attempt was being made from Beersheba to reach Jerusalem through Hebron and Bethlehem.

That day, in London, the British Government made public a letter from the Foreign Secretary A. J. Balfour, sent to Lord Rothschild a week earlier, in which Balfour promised to use Britain's influence to establish a 'National Home in Palestine' for the Jews. At a 'thanksgiving meeting' held in the Royal Opera House, Covent Garden, on November 9, Herbert Samuel stressed that there must be 'full, just recognition of the rights of the Arabs who constitute a majority of the population of that country', as well as 'a reverent respect for the Christian and Mohammedan Holy Places which in all eventualities should always remain in the control and charge of representatives of those faiths'. He went on to speak of the Jewish dream of Jerusalem, repeating the words 'Next Year in Jerusalem' which are spoken each Passover as the climax of the annual celebration of the Exodus from Egypt.

Samuel told the assembled multitude: 'I see in my mind's eye those millions in Eastern Europe, all through the centuries, crowded, cramped, proscribed, bent with oppression, suffering all the miseries of active minds, denied scope, of talent not allowed to speak, of genius that cannot act. I see them enduring, suffering everything, sacrificing everything in order to keep alight the flame of which they knew themselves to be the lamp, to keep alive the idea of which they knew themselves to be the body; their eyes always set upon one distant point, always believing that somehow, some day, the ancient greatness would be restored; always saying when they met their families on Passover night, "Next Year in Jerusalem". Year after year, generation after generation, century after succeeding century, till the time that has elapsed is counted in thousands of years, still they said, "Next Year in Jerusalem".'

If that 'cherished vision is at last to be realised', Samuel continued, 'if on the hills of Zion a Jewish civilisation is restored with something of its old intellectual and moral force, then among those left in other countries of the world I can see growing a new confidence and a new greatness. There will be a fresh light in those eyes, those bent backs will at last stand erect, there will be a greater dignity in the Jew throughout the world. That is why we meet here today to thank the British Government, our own Government, that has made all this possible, that we shall be able to say, not as a pious and distant wish but as a near and confident hope, "Next Year in Jerusalem".'

Samuel spoke these last words in Hebrew. That 'near and confident hope' was very near indeed. On November 17 Allenby's infantrymen entered the Jerusalem hills. That same day General von Falkenhayn left Jerusalem for Nablus, the biblical Shechem, forty miles to the north, assuring the Turks that reinforcements would be sent, but leaving them to their own devices. Von Falkenhayn had no instructions to hold Jerusalem. Its defence was left to two Turkish officers, Ali Fuad Pasha, the commander of the Turkish forces in the district, and Izzet Bey, the city's Governor. The Spanish Consul in the city, Count Don Antonio Ballobar, later recalled how the German officers still in Jerusalem 'were quite indifferent to the fate of the City, and drank and laughed until the night before evacuation'.

To avoid any fighting in Jerusalem itself, Allenby launched his final attack to the north of the city, intent on cutting the Jerusalem-Ramallah road and breaking the Turkish lines of communications with Nablus and German headquarters to the north. By the morning of November 21 Allenby's men were fighting the Turks on the slopes of Nebi Samwil, the traditional site of the Tomb of the Prophet Samuel, from which could be seen the spire of the Russian Church of the Ascension on the Mount of Olives, and the tower of the former German military headquarters at the Augusta Victoria.

'We have had a very bad time,' the senior German Foreign Ministry representative with the Turks, Major Franz von Papen (later Chancellor of Germany), wrote to Berlin. 'The breakdown of the army, after having had to relinquish the good positions in which it had remained for so long, is so complete that I could never have dreamed of such a thing. But for this complete dissolution, we should still be able to make a stand south of Jerusalem, even today. But now the VIIth Army bolts from every cavalry patrol.'

The morale of the Turkish army was bad, von Papen reported. 'Single men fight very pluckily, but the good officers have fallen and the remainder have bolted; in Jerusalem alone we arrested 200 officers and 5,000–6,000 men deserters.' Von Papen also told the Foreign Office in Berlin that Enver Pasha, the Turkish Minister of War, was pressing 'very strongly to hold on to Jerusalem with all possible means, on account of the political effect. From a military point of view, it is a mistake, for this shattered army can only be put together again if removed from contact with the enemy and fitted out with new divisions. This, however, can only take place after the lapse of months. Now it is just a toss-up.'

Nebi Samwil was captured that evening. The army that was at last within sight of Jerusalem contained many Jewish soldiers, serving in two specially recruited battalions of the Royal Fusiliers, known as the Jewish battalions, or the Judaeans. The 38th Battalion had been recruited mainly in the United Kingdom, the 39th Battalion in the United States. Colonel Ronald Storrs, who was soon to be Military Governor of Jerusalem, recalled in his memoirs: 'A British General commanding one of the detachments which took Jerusalem told me at the time that the most reckless bravery he had ever seen was shown by a young Jewish lance-corporal of a London Regiment who, mounting over a ridge into sudden sight of Jerusalem, seemed to be transported and transformed, rushed alone against a Turkish machine gun, killed the entire crew, and captured the gun.'

Despite von Papen's pessimism, the Turkish troops did not melt away as the British continued to hammer them. Of this point in the battle the official British history stressed 'the immense recuperative power of Turks in strong defensive positions'. On November 22 the Turks made what the official British history called 'three formidable but fruitless counter-attacks' on Nebi Samwil. Heavy casualties were inflicted on both sides. A sudden cold spell, and the toughening of Turkish resistance, held up the British plan for a renewed offensive for more than a week. Then the Turks counter-attacked again, for four consecutive days, starting on November 27. Three British Yeomanry regiments, the Shropshire, Cheshire and Welch Yeomanries, beat the Turks back. Then, on November 30, the Australian Light Horse took the offensive against an attacking Turkish battalion, captured 200 men, and killed many more. The Turks began to fall back towards the city.

Inside Jerusalem the Turkish Governor, Izzet Bey, was determined to carry out a threat made earlier by Djemal Pasha that no Jews would be in the city to welcome the British. Forty Jewish residents with American nationality, and a number of Zionists of Ottoman nationality, were expelled. They were forced to go down to Jericho, and across the Jordan, on foot. Dr Curt Ziemke, who was on the staff of the German Consulate in Jerusalem, described how these Jews were driven out of the city 'like criminals, and beaten up'. Izzet Bey ordered a further, much larger, deportation to be carried out on December 9, in preparation for which hundreds of Jews were arrested, including the Austrian-born Dr Yaakov Thon, acting head of the Palestine Office of the Zionist Organisation.

*

On December 4 Allenby launched an assault on the Turkish positions all around Jerusalem. Advancing from the south as part of a flanking movement, British troops entered Hebron on December 6, but were prevented from any further advance by three days of almost continuous rain, when the Judaean Hills were covered in low-lying mist and the tracks turned into muddy torrents. The main attack came at dawn on December 8, when the strong Turkish fortified trenches just to the west of the city, at the village of Deir Yassin, were taken.

Heavy Turkish artillery fire prevented any further advance from the west. The ring was closing in, however, and that same morning cavalrymen who had earlier entered Hebron advanced northward through Bethlehem and were able to cut the Jerusalem-Jericho road, the city's only effective eastward supply and escape route. That morning the Turkish police warned all the inhabitants of Jerusalem who did not wish to be captured to leave at once. The official British history commented: 'The extent to which the Turks were prepared to clear the city is shown by the fact that out of the Armenian community of 1,400 souls, 300 received this notice. Djemal Pasha, when warned that vehicles were unavailable for the transport of the unhappy exiles to Shechem or Jericho, telegraphed curtly that they and theirs must walk. The fate of countless Armenians and many Greeks has shown that a population of all ages suddenly turned out to walk indefinite distances under Turkish escort was exposed to outrage and hardship which proved fatal to most of them; but the delay in telegraphing had saved the population, and the sun had risen for the last time on the Ottoman domination of Jerusalem, and the Turks' power to destroy faded with the day.'

In a tone that caught the historic importance of the moment, which affected all who participated in it, the official British history continued: 'Towards dusk the British troops were reported to have passed Lifta, and to be within sight of the city. On this news being received, a sudden panic fell on the Turks west and south-west of the town, and at 1700 [5 p.m.] civilians were surprised to see a Turkish transport column galloping furiously cityward along the Jaffa road. In passing they alarmed all units within sight or hearing, and the wearied infantry arose and fled, bootless and without rifles, never pausing to think or to fight. Some were flogged back by their officers and were compelled to pick up their arms; others staggered on through the mud, augmenting the confusion of the retreat.'

As for the situation inside Jerusalem: 'After four centuries of conquest the Turk was ridding the land of his presence in the bitterness of defeat, and a great enthusiasm arose among the Jews. There was a running to and fro; daughters called to their father and brothers concealed in outhouses, cellars, and attics, from the police, who sought them for arrest and deportation. "The Turks are running," they called; "the day of deliverance is come." The nightmare was fast passing away, but the Turk still lingered. In the evening he fired his guns continuously, perhaps heartening himself with the loud noise that comforts the soul of a barbarian, perhaps to cover the sound of his own retreat. Whatever the intention was, the roar of the gunfire persuaded most citizens to remain indoors, and there were few to witness the last act of Osmanli authority.'

Towards midnight the city's Governor, Izzet Bey, went personally to the telegraph office, discharged the staff, and himself smashed the instruments with a hammer. Then, as the official British history recounted, 'At 0200 on Sunday tired Turks began to troop through the Jaffa gate from the west and south-west, the anxious watchers, peering out through the windows of the Grand New Hotel to learn the meaning of the tramping, were cheered by the sullen remark of an officer, "Gitmaya mejburuz" ("We've got to go") and from 0200 till 0700 that morning the Turks streamed through and out of the city, which echoed for the last time to their shuffling tramp.

'On this same day 2,082 years before, another race of conquerors, equally detested, were looking their last on the city which they could not hold, and inasmuch as the liberation of Jerusalem in 1917 will probably ameliorate the lot of the Jews more than that of any other community in Palestine, it was fitting that the flight of the Turks should have coincided with the national festival of the Hanukah, which commemorates the recapture of the Temple from the heathen Seleucids by Judas Maccabaeus in 165BC. The Governor was the last civil official to depart. He left in a cart belonging to Frederick Vester, an American resident, from whom he had "borrowed" a hitherto unrequisitioned cart and team. Before the dawn he hastened down the Jericho road, leaving behind him a letter of surrender, which the Mayor, as the sun rose, set forth to deliver to the British commander, accompanied by a few frightened policemen holding two tremulous white flags.'

The last Turkish soldier was said to have left Jerusalem at about seven o'clock through the only gate on the eastern side of the city, St Stephen's Gate. 'But even later,' the official British history reported, 'armed stragglers were still trickling along the road just outside the north wall, requisitioning food and water at the point of the bayonet. This is no grievous crime on the part of defeated troops, uncertain of their next meal, but is recorded as the last kick of the dying Ottoman authority in a city where it had been supreme for four centuries.' Then, 'as the Turkish flood finally ebbed away into the shadowy depths of the Valley of Jehoshaphat the townsfolk roused themselves from the lethargy into which hunger and the Turkish police had plunged them and fell upon a variety of buildings, official or requisitioned for official purposes, and looted them, even stripping roofs, doors, and floors from the Ottoman barracks next to the Tower of David for firewood. It must be admitted that, as the government had furnished and maintained itself almost entirely by uncompensated requisitions, the crowd was only trying to indemnify itself.'

With those few hours of looting, the centuries-old story of Ottoman Jerusalem came to an end.

CHAPTER FOUR

The British Conquest, December 1917

On the morning of 7 December 1917, near the Arab village of Lifta, at the north-western entrance to Jerusalem, two British soldiers, Private H. E. Church and Private R. W. J. Andrewes, both of the 20th London Regiment (Blackheath and Woolwich), were up early in search of water. Their hope was to find some abandoned well, or a peasant willing to provide them with water. As the two soldiers reached the top of the hill they met a number or civilians who told them that a large group of people, bearing the flag of truce, was nearby.

The two privates at once reported this news to two sergeants, Frederick Hurcomb and James Sedgewick, of the 19th Londons, who, drawing closer to the city, saw coming towards them a motley group, some in civilian clothes, some in Turkish uniforms, carrying aloft a large white flag. It was the Jerusalem dignitaries, led by the Mayor of the city, Hussein Effendi al-Husseini, and the Chief of the Jerusalem Police, Haj Abd al-Kadir al-Alami, together with imams, rabbis and Christian priests, bearing with them the keys of the city. They were looking for a senior British officer to whom they could surrender Jerusalem. 'Surely there is something in keeping with the history of this city of "the Christ" who came to plead the cause of "the meek and lowly",' wrote a fellow-soldier, S. F. Hatton, 'that on this crystal-clear December morning, the keys of the citadel of Christendom should have been brought out on foot to two wandering and bewildered Cockney sergeants from Camden Town.'

It was eight in the morning. 'It was to these rather bewildered London laddies', Hatton wrote, 'that the keys of the city were offered and surrender made. They of course, immediately informed their officers, who hardly seemed to know what to do about it.' The two sergeants had found two Royal Artillery officers, Major W. J. Beck and Major F. R. Barry, who met the dignitaries and entered into conversation with the Mayor. The question in these two majors' minds was, could not a more senior officer be found to whom the city could be formally surrendered?

The two majors turned back to find someone of suitable rank, and chanced upon Lieutenant-Colonel Bailey; but he declined to take the surrender, not regarding himself as senior enough. The Lieutenant-Colonel then went in search of someone even more senior than himself. After a short while, he managed to find Brigadier-General C. F. Watson, commanding 180 Brigade. Watson at once rode forward on horseback to assure the Mayor that an even more senior officer would soon arrive. Watson then rode down the hill to Enab, where he found the commander of the 60th Division, Major-General J. S. M. Shea, to whom he explained that the Mayor of Jerusalem was waiting to surrender the city.

Major-General Shea, though by far the most senior officer so far in this chain, decided to seek instructions from his own superior, Lieutenant-General Sir Philip Chetwode, General Officer Commanding XX Corps. Meanwhile, Brigadier-General Watson had ridden forward along the Jaffa Road with a small mounted escort, followed by the Mayor in his carriage, to reassure the populace that there would be no more fighting. Watson was thus the first British soldier to reach the Jaffa Gate. It was half past nine. He at once posted British guards on the Turkish Post and Telegraph Office in the Jaffa Road, and at the Jaffa Gate.

North of the city, Sir Philip Chetwode had instructed Major-General Shea to accept the surrender on behalf of the Expeditionary Force. It was eleven o'clock when Shea, in a motor car, returned to the entrance of the city and drove along the Jaffa Road. At the Shaare Tzedek Hospital, built by the Jews just before the outbreak of the war, he received the formal surrender document. He then rode on to the Turkish Post Office just outside the Jaffa Gate, where he sent for the Mayor and the Chief of Police. As the official history records: 'These functionaries were informed that Major-General Shea accepted the surrender of the city in the name of the Commander-in-Chief, and Brigadier-General Watson was directed to make the necessary arrangements for the maintenance of order.'

*

The British had entered Jerusalem, and could enter the Holy City, without fighting. More than seven hundred years had passed since

Richard the Lionheart had reached almost the exact spot reached by Privates Church and Andrewes, to the north of the city, but the King had been unable to go further.

The Turks had not abandoned the Mount of Olives, and on the morning of December 9 they laid down an artillery barrage from nearby Mount Scopus on British and Indian troops who were spreading out across the city's northern suburbs. That afternoon an attack was made on the Turkish positions on the ridge, when, the official history wrote, 'they were dislodged from this at the point of the bayonet, leaving seventy dead'.

There was further fighting during December 10, when Turkish troops were finally driven off the Mount of Olives, and could no longer look down on the city or traverse it with their fire.

*

On December 11, following precise instructions laid down three weeks earlier in London, General Allenby entered Jerusalem. The official account described how the Jaffa Gate was opened, 'after years of disuse', to enable Allenby to enter on foot, and also 'to pass into the Holy City without making use of the gap in the wall made for the Emperor William in 1898'.

The official account continued with a description of the 'great crowd' that gathered to greet the new conqueror: 'They were themselves amazed, for during more than three years an assembly of more than three persons in one place was discouraged by the police by blows, fines, imprisonment, and even exile. Eye-witnesses of all three events state that the crowd gathered at the Jaffa Gate to greet the General was larger than that which met the Emperor William when on his fantastic political pilgrimage, and denser than the gathering which greeted the revival of the Ottoman Constitution when it was proclaimed, ten years later, at the Damascus Gate, where there is more space. Many wept for joy, priests were seen to embrace one another, but there were no theatricalities such as the hollow reconciliations which made the triumph of the Young Turks in 1908 memorable, and sicken the memories of those who know the horrors and calamities which that triumph was doomed to bring. The General entered the city on foot, and left it on foot, and throughout the ceremony no Allied flag was flown, while naturally no enemy flags were visible.'

Behind Allenby as he entered the Old City was the Turkish Clock Tower, built above the Jaffa Gate in the first decade of the century.

'An architectural monstrosity,' a British eye-witness, Basil Mathews, described it, 'a misbegotten atrocity in stone that makes one long that Allenby should have put just one shell on Jerusalem full in the face of the wedding-cake clock.' Mathews added that it was a 'grim irony' that Jerusalem, whose name meant 'the Abode of Peace, should be borne by a city that has never seen peace! Before ever General Allenby came to her, she had suffered sixteen sieges.'

Allenby took his place on the raised terrace at the entrance to the Citadel. 'Overhead,' Basil Mathews wrote, 'the aeroplanes droned, drawing upward the eyes of the curious onlookers.' Allenby listened as a solemn proclamation was read out. Order would be maintained in all the hallowed sites of the three great religions. These sites were to be guarded and preserved for the free use of worshippers. The proclamation was read first in English, then in French, Arabic, Hebrew, Greek, Russian, and Italian. 'When this was done,' the official record continued, 'the chief notables and ecclesiastics of the different communities who had remained in Jerusalem were presented to General Allenby. After this brief ceremony the Commander-in-Chief left the city by the Jaffa Gate.'

That day the Turks made a small counter-attack four miles north of the city, at Tel al-Ful, on the road to Ramallah, but were beaten back.

*

Allenby was elated by his victory, which redeemed for him three years of set-backs and stagnation on the Western Front. While in Jerusalem he acquired a fighting spider whose jaws could sever a scorpion's tail: he named it 'Hindenburg'. His giant charger was also named Hindenburg. Clearly the German Field Marshal whose trench lines Allenby had failed to breach on the Western Front, and whose armies were still unbeaten there, remained a dominant figure in his thinking.

The capture of Jerusalem caught the imagination of the Allied world. For Catholics, the Holy Places which had been lost when Saladin conquered the city more than eight hundred years earlier were once again under Western, and Christian, rule. In Rome, church bells rang out in triumph, as did the bells of London's Roman Catholic cathedral. Jews worldwide sensed a new dawn for their own national aspirations, which had been so recently supported by the Balfour Declaration, issued five weeks earlier, promising a Jewish National Home 'in Palestine'.

The Arabs were excited too: the name Allenby bore a close calligraphic resemblance to the Arabic word for prophet: al-Nabi. As he had come from Egypt, this seemed to fulfil an old Arab prophecy: 'When the waters of the Nile flow into Palestine, then shall the prophet (al-Naby) from the west, drive the Turks from Palestine.'

The Jews of Jerusalem had been fortunate that, on the eve of their planned deportation, the Spanish Consul had persuaded the Turkish authorities to release them from prison 'on bail'. By December 9, the date of their planned deportation, the Turks had fled the city. There was also among the Jews a feeling of gratitude that General von Falkenhayn had protected them from the wrath of Djemal Pasha. On December 15 Dr Yaakov Thon wrote to his Zionist Organisation colleagues in Germany: 'We would have suffered irreparable harm had the mighty hand of the German Government not protected us in the hour of danger. It was particularly fortunate that in the late critical days the supreme command was in the hands of General Falkenhayn. Had Djemal been responsible, he would, as he had so often threatened, have driven out the population.' In Dr Thon's view, von Falkenhayn had 'preserved the civil population from destruction'.

*

Allenby did as London told him: in order to show humility before the Holy Places, no Allied flags were flown over the city. 'It was seven centuries since a Christian conqueror had set foot in Jerusalem,' one of Allenby's officers, Major H. O. Lock, reflected soon after the victory. 'But there was now no gloating of the Cross over the Crescent. On the contrary, guards of Moslem troops from our Indian army were placed upon every building sacred to Islam, while Christian guards were mounted over those sacred to Christianity.' Major Lock added: 'Never before had Jerusalem fallen into the hands of conquerors so zealous for the safety of its populace or so concerned for the preservation of the city and all that it contained.' Self-congratulatory though these words might sound, they were true.

Although Jerusalem was firmly under British control, the front line was less than twenty miles north of the city. In mid-December the Turkish forces made two attempts to counter-attack towards the city, but were driven back. They then dug in for the winter. In Jerusalem, the British made strenuous efforts to recruit a battalion of Jewish soldiers for the struggle that lay ahead: the liberation of central Palestine and the Galilee.

In mid-December, a British officer, Major James de Rothschild, the son of the philanthropist Baron Edmond de Rothschild, and a cousin of the British Lord Rothschild, met the leading rabbis of the city to persuade them to support the recruiting drive. But the Orthodox Jewish community had long opposed the Zionists, believing that the return of the Jews to Jerusalem and Palestine would come through divine, not mortal or political, intervention. The Orthodox community deeply resented what it saw as the imposition of Zionist policies. Although the Orthodox Jews of Jerusalem tended to lead sheltered, often reclusive lives, with the main emphasis on prayer and study, they still outnumbered the secular and Zionist Jews of the city by four or five to one, and when disputes arose they never hesitated to point this out.

Major James de Rothschild's meeting with the rabbis was the first confrontation between Zionism and Orthodoxy under British rule. The meeting was attended by one of the leading, and most articulate opponents of Zionism in the city, Rabbi Yosef Chaim Sonnenfeld, known affectionately to his followers as Reb Chaim. According to Hillel Danziger, the rabbi's son-in-law and biographer, Major de Rothschild pleaded the case for Jewish recruitment 'ardently and eloquently', as did several other Jewish officers in the British army. 'They maintained that such volunteerism would greatly strengthen and lend substance to the Balfour Declaration, which was as yet a mere promise.'

When the officers finished speaking 'silence prevailed in the room. Even those rabbis who had previously expressed themselves in favour of the battalion now said nothing. Instead, all eyes turned to R'Chaim, with whom everybody knew the final decision rested. R'Chaim rose and succinctly but vigorously proclaimed his opposition to the idea. After R'Chaim finished speaking, no one else in the room cared to speak; the meeting was adjourned with no action taken and the participants filed out.' Major de Rothschild later remarked, 'In my personal struggle with Rav Sonnenfeld, I was defeated.'

The Orthodox Jewish community was to wage many such battles with the Zionists in Jerusalem, creating a bitterness in the city which re-emerged in every decade. Learning of this successful sabotaging of recruitment, Chaim Weizmann was indignant. Referring to the Orthodox community by a derisive term used for a small, often disorganised synagogue, he declared: 'As long as this "kloitzel" exists, there is no hope for our own institutions to achieve control over the country.'

Despite Orthodox opposition, the recruiting drive continued, and was so successful that, before Allenby renewed his offensive in 1918, the 40th Battalion, Royal Fusiliers, had been recruited entirely from Palestinian Jews, mainly from Jerusalem.

*

On December 12, a mere four days after the British arrival in Jerusalem, Dr Yaakov Thon convened a meeting of Jewish leaders in the city to discuss the establishment of a City Council of Jerusalem Jews. He was keen to ensure that the Zionist voice was fully represented once the British had established their own administrative system. The Orthodox community viewed this Zionist initiative with alarm. Of the fifteen delegates whom Dr Thon summoned to attend this inaugural meeting, only five were members of the Orthodox community. Another five delegates represented the Zionist 'Association of Officials and Teachers'. Three delegates were from the city's oriental, or Sephardi, community, descendants of Jews who had been expelled from Spain at the end of the fifteenth century, and who were Zionist in their feelings. Two further delegates classified themselves as 'unaffiliated'. The Orthodox Jews were outraged to find their views in a minority. They had been outmanœuvred.

*

'The fall – or rather the liberation – of Jerusalem has caused much emotion in this country,' Herbert Samuel wrote to his son from London on December 16. 'I have received dithyrambs from all sorts of people, mostly strangers.' That week the British Government appointed a Military Governor for the city: Colonel Ronald Storrs. Thirty-six years old, with ten years' experience of British administration in Egypt, and most recently a member of the War Cabinet Secretariat in London, Storrs reached Jerusalem on December 20. He noted in his diary the advice of an officer friend whom he met on arrival, that 'the only tolerable places in Jerusalem were bath and bed'. As to the currency situation in the city, Storrs wrote: 'As usual the Jews have cornered the small change, for which they extort a commission of five or six per cent. Surely here is a chance for Zionists to stop these filthinesses,' and he added: 'Town healthy, and only one VD case to date.' There were also no private cars or private telephones in the city. His own Governate had a 'fleet' of fourteen Ford cars.

Colonel Storrs visited the hotel he had stayed in before the war, Morcos' Grand New Hotel just inside the Jaffa Gate. It had been turned into a hospital, run by the American Red Cross. Inside the hospital Storrs talked to a Turkish officer 'whose shoulder had been shattered' in the recent fighting. The owner, Morcos, told him a sorry tale: the Turks had taken his electric generator, thirty beds, and all his cash. After a long day on December 22 visiting all the quarters, and also sightseeing, and having learned that the Turks had cut down more than 10,000 olive trees in the region to drive their trains – 'a barbarous gelding of this difficult soil' – Storrs wrote in his diary: 'The city is indeed quick with every time and kind of tragic memory, and has perhaps passed the age of its productivity, though surely not of its interest and attraction. Not the hopeless beauty of Venice, the embalmbed majesty of Thebes, the abandon of Ferrara, or the melancholy of Ravenna; but something past yet unalloyed and throbbing, that seems to confound ancient and modern, and to undate recorded history.'

During December 22 Storrs had spent more than an hour with the Mufti of Jerusalem, Kamel al-Husseini, the spiritual leader of the city's Muslims. His office overlooked the Haram. The Mufti was 'about forty-five years old,' Storrs wrote in his diary, 'with refined regular features and a pleasant address.' From time to time as he and Storrs talked 'litigants appeared, singly, always, before him, received what I took to be a sentence and noiselessly retired, without very much interrupting the course of our conversation.' The Mufti offered Storrs the services of one of his cousins to show him over the Haram, but when Storrs was about to go into the Dome of the Rock with his guide, the Indian Muslim soldiers on guard stopped them. In order not to offend Muslim sentiment, no British officer or soldier 'was on any account to enter the building'.

*

On December 23 Storrs was present at a gathering of Orthodox Ashkenazi rabbis. The religious élite from Central and Eastern Europe, or the descendants of Jews who had come from Europe in the previous two centuries, they had only just learned that the Zionists were determined to have a clear majority on the City Council of Jerusalem Jews.

Hoping to enlist Storrs's help in their struggle against the Zionists, the rabbis made him welcome. Some twenty of them, Storrs wrote in his diary, 'received me with much ceremony in the council chamber, a long commonplace room on the first floor (approached by an outside staircase) and quite unworthy of the Rembrandtesque fur-gowned, fur-hatted, ringleted Rabbis sitting on either side of me down a long deal table. The only tongue they all understood was an ultra-German Yiddish, though individuals spoke Arabic and French, and one self-elected speaker on my right hand very tolerable English. I asked them if they had noticed that the date of Allenby's entry coincided with the Maccabean feast of Hanukah, and received a roar of assent, together with the curious item that the news of the Great War reached Jerusalem on the 9th of Ab, the anniversary of its destruction by Titus.'

Storrs then taxed the rabbis about the Jewish coin-changing rates which had so annoyed him; they defended the rates by explaining that the merchants in the bazaars were refusing to accept Egyptian paper money, but would only accept 'hard coin' which was difficult to come by. 'At this juncture,' Storrs noted in his diary, 'jam, Richon le-Zion brandy, sugar and almonds were brought in for our enlivenment, and I was forced, in answer to toasts for the liberating Army, to raise my glass to the health and prosperity of the Jewish Community in Jerusalem. When I asked them if there were, as in Europe, any poets, artists, or musicians among them, one replied coldly that their thoughts and energies were chiefly concentrated upon religion, to which I rejoined that the Father of Solomon took a less narrow view of Life. (Murmurs of assent, but they are fanatics.) They rose to Zangwill, the Cattauis, Suares and Mosseris of Egypt and one Hornstein of Kieff.

'I left this remarkable and powerful Synod after about an hour, and seemed to breathe an easier atmosphere. The guide took us on an interminable walk to the remotest end of a distant Hebrew Colony, studded with Bukharis, male and female, in original Russian Ballet costumes, until, in the last house we intruded upon a mother, daughter and grandchild all sitting up in one bed; and waited in front of them whilst their chevalier dug from beneath it a distressingly coarse and ugly necklace upon the strength of which he had dragged us these weary miles. In the next house a beldam produced from under her bed with ominous chokings a couple of silk Bukhara petticoats, just not good enough to buy.'

Three days later, this 'remarkable and powerful Synod' took a decisive step in its dispute with the city's Zionists. At a City Council planning session on the day of the rabbis' meeting with Storrs, the balance of delegates was changed by the Zionist leaders so that the Orthodox had only eleven seats out of an enlarged council of forty-five. The Orthodox responded to this insult three days later by setting up their own 'Ashkenazi Community Council', with a determination to represent their needs direct to the British.

*

The first Christmas under British rule marked the first return of a Christian power to Jerusalem since the Crusades, more than 600 years earlier. Britain was still at war with Turkey, but the Holy City was no longer within range of Turkish guns. On December 26 Storrs went to the top of the Mount of Olives, where he stood for a while alongside two artillery batteries 'that were shelling towards Jericho'. The next day, from a vantage point on the Haram, he watched as 'the sunset struck the loftier buildings and the distant mountains of Moab with an exquisite burning glow as of pure fire.'

The beauty of Jerusalem had touched the heart of a new conqueror.

CHAPTER FIVE

British Military Rule, 1918–1919

On 28 December 1917 Colonel Ronald Storrs formally took up his position as Military Governor of Jerusalem. He had no official residence, but took rooms at Fast's Hotel, just outside the Jaffa Gate. His Governate was on the first floor of another hotel, Hughes' Hotel, a few yards up the Jaffa Road. There, he later wrote, 'I learnt what I could and, returning to Fast's for luncheon, heard in the hall a Major-General, complete with ADC, enquiring for the best rooms. Mr Fast regretted that these had been taken by the Military Governor. "I am the Military Governor," replied General Watson, who in his haste to report for duty from South Palestine had not received the telegram countermanding his appointment. I gave him the "suite" for the night, and took him round the City.'

When, on December 31, Storrs received New Year's greetings from all the city's communities, Muslim, Christian and Jewish, the Jewish greetings came with two separate delegations: the Zionist-dominated City Council of Jerusalem Jews, and the Orthodox Ashkenazi Community Council, whose members had entertained him eight days earlier. Storrs was rapidly gaining an insight into the fractious nature of Jerusalem politics. It was not only the Jewish community but also the Muslim and Christian communities that were divided into different, often fiercely quarrelsome sections, with each section equally determined to have its say.

Also on December 31, Storrs received an appeal from a Christian Arab which was, he wrote, 'clearly intended to combine a recognition of British conventions with a delicate personal flattery'. The appeal concluded: 'I do beseech Your Excellency to grant my request, for the sake of J. Christ, Esq.; a gentleman whom Your Honour so closely resembles.'

*

For many hundreds of British soldiers awaiting the next offensive against the Turks, a visit to Jerusalem was a moment of welcome relaxation. Lieutenant Robert Goodsall of the Royal Field Artillery recalled his visit in February 1918. Fast's Hotel had been taken over by the Army and Navy Canteen Board and was 'an excellent leave hotel for officers'. The streets of the Old City were disappointing, 'dirty, narrow, and covered in filth and garbage of every description'. A deluge of rain added to the discomfort. Of his guide on his first full day in the city he wrote: 'To what nationality he belonged I am unable to say, but he certainly seemed at home in the Holy City. He wore a tarboosh and a dirty overcoat which had seen better days, and carried a walking stick. He talked volubly and incessantly, but as his knowledge of English, "as she is spoke", was distinctly limited, fifty per cent of his conversation was unintelligible.' On 2 May 1918 the *Palestine News* informed its mainly military readers: 'You may be painfully aware that a Guide is weaving a web of fabrications for your edification, but if you hint that he is a stranger to the truth, his look of offended pride will almost make you wish you had not opened your mouth.'

Goodsall became entranced by Jerusalem. Recalling the moment when he reached the summit of the Mount of Olives, he wrote: 'Choosing the luxuriant shade of an aged olive tree, I sat down on the bank. Only then did I perceive the full beauty of the scene which lay before me. I looked out across the Holy City and all that is most revered in Palestine. It is difficult to analyse one's emotions on occasions such as this. Wonder, awe and a feeling of great peace all formed part; I was content merely to sit there, amid the great stillness and feast my eyes upon the view, conscious that it was a rare moment of enchantment.'

*

Jerusalem had welcomed its liberators. 'I think no one among the civil population was sorry to see the back of the Turks,' commented Lieutenant Goodsall. Although they were Muslims, the Turks had treated the Arabs, their fellow Muslims, with contempt, fearful that the strength of Arab nationalism, which had created an army against them, would topple their empire. The winter of 1917–18 was a time, Storrs later wrote, 'when the trace of a great fear was yet in men's eyes, and the gulp of relief still at their throats: when for friendship with the Allies, true or suspected, whole families of Christians had been exiled, at an hour's notice, into the interior of Asia Minor, a Moslem Kadi hanged at the Jaffa Gate, and a young Jewish girl tortured to suicide. But the Turk, when he struck his flag and the Camp in which he had bivouacked rather than settled for four hundred years, carried with him in his retreat money, records, registers, drugs and surgical instruments, much furniture, all food – and generally, everything that could be of the smallest use to the City or its liberators.'

Having become the leader of those liberators, Storrs's job was to make good those deficiencies, and to enable the city to flourish. Food, a stable currency, drainage and a constant supply of fresh water were among the achievements of his military governorship. Moving his headquarters into the St Paul's Hospice outside the Damascus Gate, a building whose sturdy structure had so impressed him on his visit to the city in 1910, he worked with the energy of a Trojan. One of his first acts was to authorise the rebuilding of the Ophthalmic Hospital of St John of Jerusalem, on the Bethlehem Road, which the Turks had used as an ammunition depot, and had blown up on the eve of their retreat. 'Nothing seemed to happen as quick as one wanted,' Storrs later wrote, 'for it took the best part of a week to clear it of exploded and unexploded cartridges,' and some months before it could be rebuilt 'and made ready to receive patients'.

*

The Christian Arabs and the Jews of Jerusalem both had the benefit of some help at least from their co-religionists in Europe. The Muslim Arabs had no such links. To remedy this Storrs persuaded the Muslims of Egypt to pay for the establishment of a free medical dispensary and a free soup kitchen. He had also to find food and shelter for more than 7,000 refugees, 'Armenian, Syrian, Latin, Orthodox, Protestant and Moslem suddenly flung into my hands' with 'a good deal of typhus' among them.

The most spectacular of Storrs's achievements concerned water. When British troops entered the city there were three sources of water supply: the rainwater stored in cisterns under houses, most of which the British considered unfit for human consumption; the water brought by a Turkish-laid pipe from Solomon's Pools to the south at the rate of up to 20,000 gallons a day; and the water from the Gihon Spring in the Kidron Valley brought into the city by vendors using unhygienic goatskins. The Gihon Spring water itself was, in the words of the official British military history, 'practically liquid sewage'.

The arrival of so many troops put an impossible strain on the city's cisterns and the Solomon's Pools pipe. Seeking to create a new water supply, Storrs began discussions with the army engineers, and on 11 February 1918 they put forward a plan which Storrs approved. An unusually harsh winter made it impossible to start work until mid-April, but once work began it was continuous, rapid and effective. 'The scheme proposed by the Engineers and successfully carried out is rich in historic and even romantic associations,' the official history of the Egyptian Expeditionary Force explained. 'It was based on a modification of the Herod-Pontius Pilate system. The ancient engineers of the Roman world had carried the water of the Wadi Arrub springs in rock-cut channels to a reservoir of four million gallons' capacity, and thence to Jerusalem by a masonry aqueduct via the Pools of Solomon. So now the rock-cut channels leading from the springs were thoroughly cleansed – they were blocked with an accumulation which can literally be described as "the dust of ages", including the remains of several individuals who may have belonged to almost any period. Next the ancient reservoir was repaired, pumps were installed, pumping water to a newly erected reservoir of 300,000 gallons' capacity at a point near the springs, whence water flowed by the force of gravity to a reservoir constructed on a high point west of Jerusalem, so that now it was possible for water-pipes to carry a supply to any point in the town itself.'

The official history went on to explain that although the British water system in Jerusalem 'was laid down primarily for immediate military necessities', and also 'to recoup the civilian population for the water stored in its cisterns and consumed by the army', the installation would be 'of permanent value to the city'. The construction work was begun on 15 April 1918. Nine weeks later, on June 18, water was delivered to the inhabitants through the new system. Gravity, which had earlier defeated the Turks, was the method of delivery. Twelve miles of pipeline had been laid to ensure this result. The daily supply was 280,000 gallons. When supply was plentiful in the early summer, storage cisterns were filled in Jerusalem for the bigger buildings. Commented the official history: 'Not since the days of the Romans has running water been so plentiful in the Holy City.'

*

The British military administration resembled no other in Jerusalem's history for its constructive work. Some seventy Armenian refugees, whom the American Red Cross had established as weavers, were provided with one of the most neglected and run-down areas of the Old City, the Cotton Market, which was restored and equipped for them. Early in 1918 a public Reading Room was set up in a house near the Municipal Gardens, where a regular bulletin of war news was posted, as well as newspapers and magazines in English, French, Arabic, Greek and Armenian. That spring Storrs founded a chess club, with himself as President, a Jewish Treasurer, a Latin Catholic Secretary and several Muslim members of the committee. In due course they held their first chess tournament, at which, Storrs recalled, 'the first four prizes were won by Jews and the fifth by the Military Governor' – himself.

Storrs also established a Jerusalem School of Music, persuading the army to release from front-line duties the distinguished violinist Tchaikov, who was then serving with the British forces at the Front. As the school's first professor, Tchaikov not only played in Jerusalem but travelled to Egypt to give concerts in Cairo and Alexandria to raise funds for the Jerusalem School of Music.

From the outset at least three-quarters of the professors and 90 per cent of the pupils at the school of music were Jews. 'I therefore sent for the Christian and Moslem members of the Council,' Storrs recalled, 'and warned them that, anxious as I was to keep the management and ownership of the School, as of my other enterprises, international and non-political – nevertheless, if their proportion of pupils were not materially increased in six months' time, I should present it to the Jewish community. After waiting six months without result, I duly handed it over.'

Storrs also did his utmost to provide the Muslim community with the support it wanted from the authorities. Each spring tens of thousands of Muslims left Jerusalem for a week to attend the celebrations overlooking the Jordan Valley at the traditional Muslim tomb of the Prophet Moses: Nebi Musa. The Turkish authorities had made this ceremony a focal point of their support for local Muslim sentiment. Storrs did his best to do the same. Each year under Turkish rule the Mufti and the Mayor had received the Sultan's representative in the festival tent on the Jericho Road. They then went to the Governate and handed the Turkish Governor the sacred Muslim banners, whereupon the Governor was escorted with great pomp to the ceremony on the Haram where the senior Muslim representative there, the Imam, formally proclaimed the start of the festival.

The Turkish Governor's duties, Storrs later wrote, 'I fulfilled myself; and the Army, entering into the spirit of the thing, not only produced the gun salutes (some at very trying hours) but paraded a regimental band for the hot, exhausting, and sometimes disorderly ceremony of the march.' This British participation in a Muslim event, Storrs noted, 'was more than justified by the intense satisfaction it gave to the population, Christian as well as Moslem; both of whom felt that the British were taking an interest in their traditions and were, generally, trying to do the right thing.'

Among the British visitors to Jerusalem in March 1918 was Queen Victoria's son the Duke of Connaught. On showing him the Old City, Ronald Storrs had cause to admire the Duke's memory. 'The interior of the Dome of the Rock struck him as looking brighter than on his previous entry, thirty-three years before. It had in fact been regilded by the Sultan Abd al-Hamid in 1890. He drew my attention to an Austrian Artillery sword, carried by an Arab Police officer, some thirty yards distant. Accustomed though he was to all permutations and combinations of military medals he did nevertheless indicate surprise when confronted with a Jewish policeman of his Guard of Honour who was wearing together (and had courageously won) the French *Croix de Guerre* and the German Iron Cross.'

*

In March 1918 the Colonial Office in London authorised the departure for Jerusalem of a Zionist Commission. Led by Dr Chaim Weizmann, the commission was to serve as a liaison body between the Jewish population in Palestine and the British military administration, which looked somewhat askance at the arrival of another layer of authority, albeit a subordinate one. Also uneasy was the Orthodox community, which three months earlier had been denied by the Zionists its numerical representation on the City Council of Jerusalem Jews. Hillel Danziger, the son-in-law of the Orthodox leader Rabbi Sonnenfeld, has written: 'Weizmann spent the first two weeks of his Jerusalem visit coaxing, threatening, cajoling, and almost succeeding in forcing the two sides to unify. In the end, however, the differences which had originally caused the rift remained unresolved and unification was not achieved.'

It was the Zionists who were to have the principal Jewish voice in all negotiations with the British authorities in the city. The ultra-Orthodox dislike of Zionism was not to prevail, nor were they to find anything like a majority of Jewish adherents for their belief that the Heavenly Jerusalem had to be created before the restoration of Jerusalem on earth.

*

On their arrival in Jerusalem, the members of the Zionist Commission had been invited to the Military Governate office. There, Storrs introduced them to the Mufti of Jerusalem, Kamel al-Husseini, the city's Muslim religious leader, to his cousin the Mayor, Musa Kazem al-Husseini, the municipality's chief administrator, and to other Muslim and Christian dignitaries. These included the Christian Orthodox Vice-Mayor, D. Salameh, the Muslim Director of Education for the city, Ismail Bey al-Husseini (another Husseini cousin), and the acting Armenian Patriarch, Thorgom Kushagian. 'The Jerusalem faces were unassuring,' commented Storrs.

Storrs later recalled that when Weizmann spoke, it was to try to give assurance. 'Let his hearers beware of treacherous insinuations that Zionists were seeking political power,' Weizmann said. 'Rather let both progress together until they are ready for a joint autonomy.' He added that the Zionists were following 'with the deepest sympathy' the struggle of both the Arabs and the Armenians 'for that freedom which all three could mutually assist each other to regain'.

According to Storrs, the Mufti was impressed, thanking Weizmann for allaying his fears which, 'but for his exposition, might have been aroused', and praying for 'unity of aim', which alone could bring prosperity to Palestine. The Mufti then quoted one of the traditions of the Prophet: 'Our rights are your rights, and your duties our duties'. But the more the Zionist Commission worked to establish Jewish institutions in Jerusalem, the more the Arabs came to feel, as Storrs expressed it, that it was 'the thin end of the wedge, the beginning of a Government within a Government'. This feeling was exacerbated when, three years later, the members of a Palestinian Arab delegation to London were told by the Colonial Office that they must take up their points with the Zionist Commission.

From the start of the work of the Zionist Commission, the Arabs were ill at ease. They resented the subsidy that the commission had begun to pay to the wages of Jewish municipal policemen and clerks, railwaymen and telephonists. This was done because the commission wanted Jewish wages to be closer to the familiar European than the local Arab standard. The Arabs were also resentful when the date of the King's Birthday Parade in Jerusalem was postponed so that it would not fall on the Jewish Sabbath.

Arab contact with members of the Zionist Commission became something of which to be wary. Storrs writes that 'between anxieties and suspicions, the pitch of good relationship was being irreparably queried'. As an illustration, he tells of the time when Weizmann suggested to him 'that he should present the Mufti with a Koran. I procured him a magnificent example from Cairo. The Mufti, preferring a private presentation, elected to accept the great manuscript unattended in his Office at the Moslem Law Courts. By that evening, Arab Jerusalem had decided that the box taken into the room had in reality contained hard cash.'

*

Weizmann hoped to secure his various aims by goodwill, by negotiation and by compromise, but from the outset he found that Muslim sensitivities were impossible to overcome. Anxious to enable Jews to go to the Wailing Wall unmolested, he offered £75,000 to the Muslim custodians of the area if they would transfer to the Jews the small area in front of the Wall, with its two dozen houses, most of them in a ruinous state. The £75,000 would include the rehousing of the Muslim occupants of the houses. A similar attempt had been made in 1914 to secure a Jewish presence in the area in front of the Wall.

The British military authorities approved of Weizmann's offer. Storrs was excited because he was certain that some of the £75,000 could go to improve Muslim education. To make the offer less difficult for the Muslims to accept, Storrs decided that it would come best from him rather than from the Zionists. At first it seemed that all might go well, but then the negotiations broke down on Muslim reluctance. Storrs later wrote: 'Even if the Mufti had been willing himself, he would have had to reckon with the quivering sensitiveness of his own public (quite apart from their growing fear of Zionism) over the slightest rumour of interference even with the ground adjoining the outside wall of the Haram al-Sharif.'

Looking back two decades later, Storrs reflected: 'The acceptance of the proposals, had it been practicable, would have obviated years of wretched humiliations, including the befouling of the Wall and pavement and the unmannerly braying of the tragi-comic Arab band during Jewish prayer, and culminating in the horrible outrages of 1929.'

Storrs tried to be even-handed as between Arabs and Jews, and at the same time to take firm steps whenever he felt that a conflict was imminent. The Zionists had prepared thousands of light-blue and white flags and banners, with the Shield (also known as the Star) of David as their centre-piece, to be flown from houses or waved in processions: a joyful manifestation of national enthusiasm. But the flags were seen by the Muslims as a provocation. 'Almost immediately,' wrote Storrs, 'they provoked such a commotion that their use had to be virtually prohibited.'

Seventy years later, the Government of Israel was to forbid the flying of the Palestinian national flag in Jerusalem; but with changing times all rules can change, and in 1995 the Palestinian and Israeli flags both flew in Jerusalem unmolested. Sometimes, when joint meetings are being held, as in the summer of 1995 between groups of Arab and Israeli students, those flags fly side by side.

*

The most senior member of the Zionist Commission, after Weizmann, was the Russian Jewish leader Menachem Ussishkin. Unlike the other members of the commission, he decided to stay in Jerusalem, and to put his Zionist ideals into practice in *Eretz Israel*, 'the Land of Israel'. On his third visit to Jerusalem, just before the outbreak of the European war, he had been upset at the lack of Jewish settlements in the vicinity of the city: only one, Motza, existed at that time. He therefore made, as his first task in 1918, the purchase of a tract of land on a rocky hillside eight miles west of Jerusalem. A small village was built there, known as Kiryat Anavim, 'Vineyard City' (or 'Raisin Town' as Hachette's guidebook called it). Ussishkin brought the first pioneers to the village. They cleared the stones, restored the ancient terraces, and established a kibbutz on the lines of those that had been established in the Galilee before the war. The vineyards, fruit orchards and dairy cattle of Kiryat Anavim provided Jewish Jerusalem with by far its nearest non-Arab source of food.

*

After Storrs had been Military Governor for six months, a more senior British officer, Major-General Sir Arthur Money, reached Jerusalem as Chief Administrative Officer of Occupied Enemy Territory. Although Storrs remained Military Governor of the city, some of his authority was, for a while at least, eclipsed. Looking back on his first six months, he later wrote of his power as Governor:

'As there were no lawyers, judges or courts, it was the only law. Better still for Palestine then, there were no newspapers. Legally and

70

journalistically we lived in a State of Innocence. To be able, by a word written, or even spoken, to relieve distress, to right wrong, to forbid desecration, to promote ability and goodwill is to wield the power of Aristotle's Beneficent Despot. When for instance the Jews wished to rename Fast's Hotel *King Solomon* and the Arabs *Sultan Sulaiman* (the Ottoman Soliman the Magnificent), either of which would have excluded half Jerusalem, one could order it, without appeal, to be called the *Allenby*. Technical illegalities may have been committed, but the advantage of being able to execute by a stroke of the pen obviously needed reforms, which can later be amended or abolished, is very great.'

Storrs's most lasting achievement was in the sphere of town planning. On 8 April 1918 he issued a proclamation, posted in English, French, Arabic and Hebrew, that 'No person shall demolish, erect, alter, or repair the structure of any building in the City of Jerusalem or its environs within a radius of 2,500 metres from the Damascus Gate (Bab al-Amud) until he had obtained a written permit from the Military Governor.' Shortly after this ordinance Storrs issued another, forbidding the use of stucco and corrugated iron within the Old City. The object of these two orders was to prevent any new building or structure being put up unless it were faced in stone. Concrete and wood façades were also banned. Thanks to Storrs's vision, the particularly pleasing impact of several thousand buildings all built of Jerusalem stone was to be preserved. This ordinance has remained in effect since then: it is now in its eighth decade.

*

On 12 May 1918 the sound of verbal and intellectual strife echoed through the Jewish section of the city. At a meeting with Jerusalem's rabbis that day, Dr Weizmann sought to persuade the Orthodox leaders to accept a more modern curriculum in their religious schools, the yeshivas. The Orthodox leader Rabbi Sonnenfeld refused to attend this meeting with the 'secular heretic', as did another champion of Orthodoxy, Rabbi Yitzhak Yerucham Diskin. But thirty-five rabbis and heads of the yeshivas did attend, and listened to Weizmann's criticism that they were not in touch with modern life. 'He portrayed himself,' wrote Rabbi Sonnenfeld's son-in-law Hillel Danziger, 'as the concerned benefactor of the impoverished teachers of the yeshiva system and announced his intention to alleviate their plight, provided only that some "minor" adjustments be made in the curriculum to bring it more in line with the spirit of the times.'

Weizmann had with him the funds which Russian Jewry had sent through the Zionist Organisation to subsidise the yeshivas. But he was determined to get the yeshivas' support for those modern aspects of Zionist ideology that were hitherto anathema to them, including the use of Hebrew not only as the holy tongue but as the language of daily life. He was not successful. One of the yeshiva heads, Rabbi Avrahom Aharon Prague, whose students were all young boys not yet in their teens, rose to denounce the doctor's proposals. 'We have been entrusted by God and the parents with the souls of these children,' he declared, 'and they do not desire any changes. Are we to violate our sacred trust for the sake of our personal welfare? I propose that we vote a unanimous "no"! We will continue to guard our trust, even at the cost of our personal welfare, to our last breath. And if we are fated to die of hunger, then let us die as courageous men and not sell ourselves for money.'

Rabbi Prague's appeal was successful. No change would be made in the Orthodox curriculum. Weizmann was defeated. When he returned two months later and took his case direct to Rabbi Sonnenfeld he was equally unsuccessful. 'They were enclosed in a self-imposed medieval ghetto, stronger than any ever imposed by an enemy,' Weizmann later wrote. 'We did everything in our power to break through to them, but we know that we did not succeed very much. Moreover, it became shockingly apparent to us how wide a gulf separated us even after half a year of extended, vigorous efforts.'

Jerusalem's Orthodox Jewry was determined not to change. Black-garbed, black-hatted, its womenfolk covered in the most modest of dresses and head scarves, its Sabbath finery resplendent in the styles and furs of late-medieval Poland, it survived the efforts of the dynamic Weizmann to change its ways, and has guarded them to this day.

*

The war was not yet over. On 15 July 1918, 500 German and Turkish prisoners-of-war were marched through the city. Yet even while the Turks were still in control of all of Palestine north of Jerusalem, British rule brought a vision of future growth to the city. On July 22 a town-planning scheme, devised by William MacLean, the City Engineer of Alexandria, whom Allenby had brought from Egypt to Jerusalem, was approved by the Commander-in-Chief. The plan envisaged, over a ground area more than four times that of the Old City, a road plan within which streets and boulevards, municipal and residential buildings, parks and gardens, would create a modern town as far west as the hill beyond the Monastery of the Cross (that hill is now the site of the Israel Museum).

British rule also liberated the Jews of Jerusalem from the restrictions and hardships imposed by the Turks after the outbreak of war. On 24 July 1918, while Allenby's armies and the Turks still faced each other in their trenches just north of Ramallah, Allenby and Weizmann were among those who laid the first twelve foundation stones on Mount Scopus for a future Hebrew University. Each stone was for one of the Tribes of Israel. One of those present at the stone-laying ceremony, the nineteen-year-old Edwin Samuel (Herbert Samuel's son), later recalled: 'While General Allenby and Weizmann laid their stones in the midst of a vast crowd that had streamed on foot up the mountain, we could hear the British and Turkish guns faintly booming out some fifteen miles to the north. That ceremony was an act of faith indeed.'

It had long been a Zionist dream that a university in Jerusalem would become a centre of academic learning and research for Jews from all over the world. 'Here, out of the misery and desolation of war,' Weizmann declared, 'is being created the first germ of a new life. In this University we have gone beyond restoration. We are creating, even during the war, something which is to serve as a symbol of a better future. In the University, the wandering soul of Israel will reach its haven.'

*

In September 1918 Ronald Storrs established the Pro-Jerusalem Society, one of his most imaginative achievements. Its aim was to encourage the most attractive repairs, construction and development of the city, within an approved and aesthetic framework. British officials, and Muslim, Christian and Jewish leaders, all joined and participated. 'The official language found to be most convenient was French, in which the Minutes were also kept,' Storrs later wrote, 'but animated asides – sometimes almost broadsides – were discharged in Arabic, Turkish, Hebrew, and even Armenian.' Even the city's merchants, Storrs wrote with understandable pride, 'realising how greatly the future prosperity of Jerusalem depended upon its preservation as Jerusalem (and not an inferior Kieff, Manchester or Baltimore), subscribed liberally to our funds'.

Storrs raised money from banks in Palestine and outside it, and from wealthy Britons and Americans. He appointed an official Town

Planner, William MacLean, and also a Civic Adviser, C. R. Ashbee. The aim of the Society was described in its prospectus as 'the protection of and the addition to the amenities of Jerusalem, the provision and maintenance of parks, gardens and open spaces, the protection and preservation . . . of the Antiquities, the encouragement of arts, handicrafts, and industries'.

Storrs later described some of the Pro-Jerusalem Society's work and achievements: 'We repaired, cleaned, and cleared of many hundred tons of modern Turkish barrack rubble, the Citadel, generally known as the Tower of David, which crowns the lower courses of the Hippicus and Phasael towers recorded by Josephus. Much desecration we averted, but sometimes we were too late, and could only prosecute. The Roman staircase at Siloam was saved, but already a building contractor had stolen some twenty tons of Roman stonework which he carried off by night on the backs of donkeys. He was fined £50 and had to return the stones, but they could never be put back in the exact positions from which they had been taken.

'The severe winter of 1917–18 had a deplorable effect upon the wind racked north-west façade of that utmost fulfilment of colour, rhythm, and geometry: the Dome of the Rock. The brilliant tiles were constantly falling from the walls, and frequently to be found for sale in the City. I was fortunate enough to enlist for a technical Report on the interior as well as the exterior of the Mosque, Ernest Richmond, once architect to the Egyptian Wakfs, then eating out his heart in the Imperial War Graves Commission.'

Ernest Richmond joined MacLean and Ashbee, and the Dome was restored to its earlier splendour. In the course of his work, Richmond discovered the furnaces and kilns in which the original Dome of the Rock tiles had been fired many centuries before. A 'Dome of the Rock Potteries' was established, not only to replace the damaged and lost tiles, but to provide skilled work and the commercial production of tiles, bowls, ewers, goblets, beakers and plates, which Storrs later noted with pride were on sale as far away as Edinburgh, Cape Town and New York.

*

On 20 September 1918 Allenby renewed the British offensive which had effectively come to a halt with the capture of Jerusalem almost a year earlier. A week later the Turks were driven out of the Galilee, von Falkenhayn being forced to flee Nazareth in his pyjamas. More than 30,000 Turkish soldiers were taken prisoner. At the end of

September a British officer wrote from Jerusalem: 'Prisoners, war material, etc keep pouring through the City all day long and only yesterday I saw about twenty German lorries coming in driven by their own German drivers with an escort of about six Britishers all told.'

With Allenby's troops poised to enter both Damascus and Amman, Colonel Storrs later recalled how, in Jerusalem, he celebrated the despatch of the Turks from Palestine 'by playing upon my Steinway a medley of "Vittoria" from *La Tosca*, Handel's Marches from *Jephthah* and *Scipio*, Parry's "Wedding March" from the *Birds* of Aristophanes, the Pilgrims' Chorus and the Entry of the Gods into Valhalla'.

On 30 October 1918 the Ottoman Empire signed an armistice, ending in defeat and ignominy the hostilities it had begun with such confidence four years earlier. For the Jews of Jerusalem, with the Balfour Declaration having promised them a National Home in Palestine, it seemed that a bright future was in prospect, under the benign eye of the British military authorities. Amid great enthusiasm, as the war in Europe clearly looked as though it would soon be ended, the Zionists in Jerusalem celebrated the first anniversary of the Balfour Declaration. That day, November 2, a training school for Jewish nurses, financed by the Hadassah women's organisation in the United States, was dedicated, and the first student nurses were enrolled. That same day the Zionist Commission held a parade in the city. In the evening there was dancing and singing. But, while the Jewish community rejoiced, the Arabs were angry, fearing Jewish predominance in Palestine with British support.

According to popular belief among the Arabs of the city, the German and Austro-Hungarian Empires, surely among the most powerful the world had ever seen, had been brought to their knees only because they had failed to do the bidding of the Jews. The same was true of the Russian Empire. The British would not risk their empire by refusing to do the bidding of the Jews. The Arab leaders did not intend to remain silent, however; immediately after the Balfour Day celebrations they organised a petition protesting against Zionist policy.

The petition was taken to Storrs by a delegation of senior Arab citizens, headed by the Mayor, Musa Kazem Pasha al-Husseini. It was signed by a hundred leading Jerusalem Arabs and sheikhs from the surrounding Arab villages. Although Storrs refused to speak against the fixed policy of his Government, this pattern of Arab protest was to continue, and to intensify: against Zionism, and against Jewish immigration which was an integral part of both the Zionist ideal and the British promise.

*

On 11 November 1918 the First World War ended, when Germany, the last of the Central Powers still at war, agreed to an armistice. The Kaiser, who in 1898 had ridden in triumph into Jerusalem, slipped away from his headquarters in Belgium to exile in Holland. The news of Germany's surrender reached Jerusalem on a day of torrential rain. Major-General Money and his staff were at their headquarters in the Kaiser's own creation, the Augusta Victoria Hospice on the Mount of Olives. Storrs was later told that the exuberant officers 'had rushed into the Chapel, sung three verses of God Save the King, consumed a fair amount of champagne and rung the bells of the Hospice; inaudible to the ears of the City'. A Royal Air Force unit managed to send some flares into the grey and louring sky 'which came down so slowly that I thought for an instant they must be stars'.

*

The first months after the ending of the First World War saw a determined effort by Dr Weizmann and his Zionist colleagues to break the monolithic opposition to Zionism of Jerusalem's Orthodox community. On 15 December 1918 these efforts were crowned with success at the founding meeting of a group of senior rabbis, who, in defiance of Rabbi Sonnenfeld and the ultra-Orthodox, set up a Joint Sephardi-Askenazi Council, which called itself, to Sonnenfeld's anger, 'the religious representative of Palestinian Jewry and the supreme court of religious appeal'.

The new council, wrote Sonnenfeld's son-in-law Hillel Danziger, created the first breach in the Orthodox community's 'strong and united opposition to Zionist institutions'.

*

Shortly after the ending of military hostilities Major-General Money went on leave for four weeks, and Colonel Storrs was appointed Acting Chief Administrator of Occupied Enemy Territory with the rank of Brigadier-General. He also remained Military Governor of Jerusalem. On 26 February 1919 he saw one of his earliest projects come to fruition when General Allenby opened the reconstructed Ophthalmic Hospital 'in formal state before representatives of every language and community'.

Less formal was Storrs's habit of taking footballs with him when he visited the outlying police posts of the city. On one occasion a special football match was arranged to celebrate his arrival. The police commandant, in his letter of thanks, told Storrs: 'The Teams were composed of Moslems, Christians and Jews, captained by (a) Sgt Shwili (Jew) and (b) Police Constable Badawi (Moslem), and it is of interest to note that utmost harmony prevailed throughout fifty minutes of play.'

On a visit to the Russian Church of the Ascension on the Mount of Olives, whose six-storey tower, with its 214 steps, still dominates the Mount of Olives today, Storrs brought with him the four parts of the opening chorus of *Die Meistersinger*. This he had copied out by hand, and, conducting the music with a walking-stick, 'did my best to impart its beauties to the elderly Russian nuns'.

The Christians in Jerusalem, whether European or Arab, had cause to be displeased with Storrs. 'The Christian Communities have no idea of allowing Jerusalem to lose any of its prestige as the centre of the Christian religions,' he wrote in his diary in 1919, 'and are far from sympathetic to my efforts to place the Jews in every way upon an equality with the others.' Yet the Jews also often saw Storrs as an enemy, and accused him of frustrating their designs: he was publicly accused of having intentionally caused the Wailing Wall negotiations to break down. 'The ardent Zionist from Pinsk or Przemysl,' he wrote, 'between the bitterly hostile Arab and the coldly impartial British official, always recalled to me Theocritus' description of Ptolemy, "Recognising his friend, but his enemy even better"; sometimes indeed confusing the two.' As an example, Storrs wrote twenty years later, 'Jewish Doctors would alienate the Public Health Department even where their talents were most admired.'

*

Among the services that were restored in the first years of British rule was that of a daily Hebrew-language newspaper, the pioneering effort embarked upon by Eliezer Ben Yehuda in 1910 having been forced to close by the Turks five years later. In 1919 a second Hebrew-language daily newspaper reached the streets, *Hadashot Ha Aretz*, 'News of the Land'. For four years it struggled under a number of editors, before seeking greater economic security in Tel Aviv, becoming one of Jerusalem's earliest casualties to Tel Aviv's slow but steady growth into a modern city.

A Christian newspaper also made its appearance in Jerusalem in 1919, the *Jerusalem News*, the motto of which was 'Jerusalem news is good news.' It was produced by a small American religious group, evangelical Christians known as the 'Cementers', led by Mrs Ulysses Grant McQueen and William McCracken. Their success was less than their enthusiasm, and within a year they had returned to the United States.

*

On 1 February 1919, under the watchful eye of the British military administration, the First Congress of Muslim-Christian Associations began its deliberations in Jerusalem. These associations had been set up by the Arab leaders in Jerusalem as a direct response to the Balfour Day celebrations held in Jerusalem by the Zionist Commission three months earlier. The congress had to discuss a matter of central concern to the whole future of Palestinian-Arab nationalism: were the Palestinian Arabs and their future to be dependent upon Greater Syria, and to be part of Greater Syria, or were they to seek a purely Palestinian outlet for their national aspirations? Was Jerusalem to be subordinate to Damascus, or independent of it?

The first act of the Congress of Muslim-Christian Associations was to issue a long memorandum rejecting Zionism; on this, it seems, pro-Syrian and pro-Palestinian, Muslim and Christian, Jerusalemites and those from other towns, were all agreed. Twenty-five delegates signed the memorandum. Only four did not (one of the four was later revealed as having been working both for the French and for the Information Office of the Zionist Commission).

When the congress voted in favour of the Greater Syria policy, two of the four Jerusalem delegates, the pro-British Yakub Farraj and the former Turkish general Arif Pasha al-Dajani, managed to persuade the two Haifa delegates and the two Gaza delegates to renounce their earlier support for unity with Syria. On 9 February 1919 these six delegates issued a statement which set out both the primacy of Palestinian-Arab nationalism and their determination to oppose Zionism. Issued in Jerusalem, their statement set the tone for the future of Arab-Jewish political and physical confrontation in the capital. 'Palestine should have a constitutional autonomous government,' they declared, 'independent for its home internal affairs, based on the wishes of its inhabitants, able to promulgate special laws . . .

78

provided that the British Government would defend Palestine from the Zionist immigration.' A third leading Jerusalemite, Ismail Bey al-Husseini, supported this anti-Syrian and anti-Zionist resolution. Palestinian-Arab nationalism had come of age, with Jerusalem as its centre.

*

Whatever Jews or Arabs might hope to achieve in Jerusalem, the victorious powers, who would be allocating the Palestine Mandate to Britain within a year or two, also had their views. On 28 August 1919, on the initiative of President Woodrow Wilson of the United States, a report was presented to the Paris Peace Conference by two distinguished Americans, Henry King and Charles C. Crane. They recommended the joining of Palestine to Syria, an end to the establishment of a Jewish National Home in Palestine, and an international and interdenominational committee to supervise the Holy Places. The King-Crane Report made the specific point that Jews were 'unacceptable' to both Christians and Muslims as guardians of the Holy Places.

King and Crane returned to the United States. Their report was abandoned a few months later, when the Senate voted to oppose the Versailles Treaty altogether and to withdraw the United States from all responsibilities with regard to Europe and the Near East.

*

In December 1919 a British official reached Jerusalem who was to remain in the city until almost the end of British rule twenty-nine years later. Edward Keith-Roach began his career in Jerusalem as Public Custodian of Enemy Property, and ended as District Commissioner for Jerusalem. He remembered when he arrived being entertained by Miss Annie Landau, the headmistress of the Evelina de Rothschild School for Girls. 'We used to meet in each other's houses,' Keith-Roach later wrote, 'to play, sing and recite. There was no other form of amusement – the military cinema had been blown down in the piercing winter winds.'

On his first walk in the Old City, Keith-Roach was struck by the extraordinary range of colours. 'The steps were hemmed in on either side by vegetable shops aglow with colour,' he later wrote. 'Purple aubergines and red radishes, huge cauliflowers, lemons and golden oranges. Butchers' shops alongside, selling goats' meat and mutton with very naked fat tails, were festooned with intestines and tripe. Flies were rampant. Laden camels passing up and down caused as much disturbance as a motor lorry passing along an English lane.' As to the denizens of the bazaar, 'stout, bow-legged Kurdish porters, with huge burdens carried on packs fastened across their shoulders, brushed past coffee-sellers clashing their brazen saucers. Muslim townswomen enveloped from head to ankles in coarse white winding sheets, with figured muslin or black veils hiding their faces, passed their unveiled Arab countrywomen with tattooed chins and lips wearing dresses of Damascus spun stuffs surmounted with short coloured velvet jackets embroidered with gold thread. Most of Jerusalem – Arab, Jew and European – appeared to be in the overcrowded thoroughfare. Gesticulating, haranguing, expostulating, they went from shop to shop, accompanied by little Arab boys with baskets strapped across their shoulders, turning over, choosing or rejecting the produce ... There were no carts within the city walls, nor were there streets wide enough to take them.'

The bustling visual images of the Old City were those which most frequently appeared in travellers' tales and European letters home. But behind the chaos and the colour were many serious political purposes, some in harmony but most in conflict.

CHAPTER SIX

In Search of Equilibrium, 1920–1921

The British military administration in Jerusalem, headed by Brigadier-General Ronald Storrs, was proud of its efforts to maintain a peaceful equilibrium between the Jews and Arabs in the city. But there were stirrings in the air which constituted bad omens. 'In politics,' Storrs later wrote, 'Jerusalem was growing more difficult and less agreeable. Arab resentment against the Balfour Declaration was now louder as well as deeper.' As more Jews came to Jerusalem to live, and to participate in the growing Jewish life of the city, that resentment threatened to boil over into physical action.

The Mayor of Jerusalem since March 1918 was Musa Kazem Pasha al-Husseini, the brother of the wartime Turkish Mayor, and a cousin of the Mufti. As the British saw it, Musa Kazem's task as Mayor was to represent all three communities impartially: Muslim, Christian and Jewish. But as the head of one of the leading Muslim families of the city, he emerged, as tensions rose in Jerusalem, as the leader and spokesman of Muslim opposition both to the British Mandate, and to Britain's pledge to allow the Jews to come to Palestine from all over the world, and to make it their National Home.

'I had met him one afternoon', Storrs later wrote, 'marching before a rabble to demonstrate against the Zionist Offices, and bade him take them and himself home lest trouble should arise. That evening I warned him that he must make his choice between politics and the Mayoralty.'

Forcing the Mayor to make this choice was a shrewd move. For some, it bore out Storr's reputation for oriental deviousness: he was nicknamed 'Oriental Storrs' after a notoriously cheating commercial establishment in Cairo. A similar choice, politics or administration, was put to the other leading anti-Zionist figure of that time, Arif

Hikmat al-Nashashibi, the General Administrator of the Muslim Religious Foundation. Both men chose administration, effectively silencing their voices as leaders of Arab dissent. But there were many voices forecasting a troubled future. On 10 February 1920 C. R. Ashbee wrote in a letter home of the remarks of the Deputy Mayor, a Syrian Greek, who told him: 'You English are doing so much here, planning such a wonderful city, showing us the way to so many new and strange things, that I suppose in twenty years' time we shall be wanting to turn you out.'

Musa Kazem remained Mayor, but there were others who took up his mantle as the leader of Arab protest, most notably Arif Pasha al-Dajani, leader of the large and influential al-Dajani family. Arif Pasha, like Musa Kazem Pasha, held the rank of General in the former Turkish Army. Feeling in the Arab sections of the city against the Zionists intensified. On 27 February 1920 the Officer Administering the Government of Palestine, Major-General Louis Bols, issued an official proclamation that the British Government intended to carry out the Balfour Declaration. There were immediate Arab protest demonstrations, with 1,500 Arabs marching in Jerusalem. Shops were closed down, and petitions were presented. There was no violence that day. But further protest demonstrations on March 8 led to several Arab attacks on Jewish passers-by and shop owners. The British authorities were alarmed at the violent tone of the Arab protests, in which calls to kill the Jews were heard alongside the popular slogan 'Palestine is our land and the Jews are our dogs'. On March 11 an order was issued by General Bols, prohibiting further demonstrations in Jerusalem.

That Easter, on 4 April 1920, the serenity of the city was violently endangered. It was once more the time of the Muslim feast of Nebi Musa, the third such celebration under British rule. 'The pilgrims not being expected to arrive at the Jaffa Gate until after midday,' Storrs recalled, 'I went with my father and mother to Easter Matins at St George's Cathedral, ordering a member of the staff to warn me there as previously, so soon as the procession was within half an hour of Jerusalem. He forgot. As after the Service I was walking with my parents the three hundred yards to the Governate, my orderly Khalil murmured softly behind me in Arabic: "There has been an outbreak at the Jaffa Gate and a man has been wounded to death." It was as though he had thrust a sword into my heart.'

Writing sixteen years later Storrs commented: 'Even now the mere memory of those dread words brings back the horror of the shock.' Elias Epstein, a Jewish journalist who arrived at the railway station while the riots were taking place, wrote two days later: 'A hush seemed to be over everything; immediately we saw signals being flashed from the station to a point in the city, as in wartime. Few carriages met the train and none would go near the Old City. To our query, "What has happened?" they looked at us blankly and hurried off.'

In the Muslim Quarter of the Old City, wall posters appeared with the words 'The Government is with us, Allenby is with us, kill the Jews: there is no punishment for killing Jews.' In the Jewish Quarter, Arabs ransacked the Torat Hayim religious seminary; its students survived by hiding in the cellar. As the fighting continued, a group of some 600 Jews, led by the Russian-born Vladimir Jabotinsky, who had served with the British forces at Gallipoli, formed a self-defence group, the Hagannah ('Defence').

As Arab attacks on Jews continued inside the Old City, a Hagannah squad marched down the Jaffa Road to the Jaffa Gate, intent on coming to the aid of those who had been attacked. The would-be defenders were quickly dispersed by British soldiers. In two days, five Jews and four Arabs were killed, and more than 200 Jews were injured. When the fighting was over, Jabotinsky and nineteen others were arrested. Jabotinsky was sentenced to fifteen years' penal servitude, the rest to three years.

To avoid Jewish protest demonstrations in Jerusalem, the British military authorities decided to send the prisoners to the Sudan, to serve their sentences there, but Allenby, who was then governing Egypt, would not let them cross the Egyptian border for fear of protests by the Jewish community in Egypt. They were therefore brought back to Palestine and imprisoned in Acre, on the coast.

*

The conflict that had erupted in Jerusalem on 4 April 1920 was the first of many future days, and weeks, and even months of violence that were to curse Jerusalem in the following seventy years and more. There were to be many lulls and some periods of hope, but violence in its streets was to mar some of the brightest days of a city whose blue skies have always been a spur to civic pride and the warmth of community life.

As the riots flared, it looked to Storrs as if 'all the carefully built relations of mutual understanding between British, Arabs and Jews seemed to flare away in an agony of fear and hatred.' Zionism, he added, 'had at least united (for the first time in history) Arab Moslems and Christians, who now opposed a single front to the Mandatory'. For it was not only against the Jews that the rioters fumed: British rule was just as much the target of their curses and their fury.

The 'immediate fomenter of the Arab excesses,' Storrs wrote, and an official commission of inquiry later confirmed, was Haj Amin al-Husseini, the younger brother of the Mufti and a cousin of the Mayor. Storrs commented: 'Like most agitators, having incited the man in the street to violence and probable punishment, he fled.'

'I regret to say,' the British Secretary of State for War, Winston Churchill, told the House of Commons at the end of the month, 'that about 250 casualties occurred, of which nine-tenths were Jewish.' Not only had Vladimir Jabotinsky been sentenced to fifteen years for arming the Jews in self-defence, two Arabs had also been given fifteen-year sentences, for raping two Jewish women. Following protests in the House of Commons, Jabotinsky's sentence was reduced to one year.

*

During the riots, the Mayor of Jerusalem, Musa Kazem Pasha al-Husseini, had declined to use his influence with his fellow Muslims to stop the violence, or to persuade his cousin Haj Amin to moderate his incitements. 'He became first intractable and then defiant,' Storrs later wrote, 'and I informed the Administration that I proposed to dismiss and replace him forthwith.' This was done, and another leading Muslim, Ragheb Bey al-Nashashibi, from the main rival family to the Husseinis, was appointed in his place. Ragheb Bey had been a deputy in the Ottoman Parliament in Constantinople before the war, and an active opponent of Zionism even then.

Following the riots there was an incident at the Wailing Wall. According to the Muslim custodians of the Haram above it, the upper courses of the Wall were in need of repair. The Jews, for whom the Wall is a particularly holy site, the last standing wall of the platform on which their ancient Temple stood, and who came daily to pray at its lower courses of 2,000-year-old stone, had not been consulted about the repairs. The Muslims said that the high wall had become dangerous. The Zionist Commission, the main Jewish authority in the city, wrote to Storrs in protest. 'Why has this danger become so suddenly apparent – just at a moment when the minds of the inhabitants are disturbed by political events? Was there a need for these repairs to proceed on Saturday – when hundreds of Jews stand in prayer near the Wall? Are the religious feelings of the Jews entitled to no consideration whatsoever?'

Storrs knew that the Wakf, the Muslim authority on the Haram, had the right to repair the Wall where, at its upper level, it served as the roof and wall of the Haram itself. It was by their 'method of exercising a hitherto uncontested right,' he wrote, that they had been 'guilty of a piece of unwarrantable and calculated bad manners'. For the Jews, this attempt to harass them while at their prayers was an ill omen.

Storrs sent his Civic Adviser, C. R. Ashbee, a distinguished architect, to inquire. After speaking below to the Jewish representatives, and to the Arabs above, and examining the site, he concluded that while it was imperative to repair the Wall to a depth of several metres from the top, it was 'unnecessary and undesirable for work to be done during the hours of prayer, as fragments must inevitably fall on the heads of the worshippers'.

On Ashbee's suggestion orders were given that 'No work of any sort is to be done during the hours of prayer' and that the stone cleaning and pointing 'is not to be carried out below a distance of three metres from the top of the roof until the matter has been gone into more carefully'. This decision to limit the Muslim right of repair to the upper courses of masonry evoked, as Storrs recalled, 'a sharp protest from the Mufti'.

*

On 24 April 1920, at the San Remo Conference of the League of Nations, the British Prime Minister, David Lloyd George, accepted a British Mandate for Palestine. The Mandate would be held in trust under the League of Nations, to which the British authorities would submit each year an account of their rule.

A British civil administration was set up in Palestine on 1 July 1920, with its headquarters in Jerusalem. The first British Government House was the German-built Augusta Victoria Hospice, with its view across the whole city. The first High Commissioner, Sir Herbert Samuel, travelled by train to Jerusalem on 30 June 1920. On reaching the station, he was welcomed by the new Mayor, Ragheb Bey al-Nashashibi. Driving up to the Augusta Victoria, he was greeted by a seventeen-gun salute fired from the nearby grounds of Sir John Gray Hill's house on Mount Scopus. At the porch of Government House the Mayor read a second address of welcome.

That afternoon a reception was held for all the leading citizens of

Jerusalem. Among those present was Dr Arthur Ruppin. 'The scene,' he wrote in his diary, 'which lasted from four until about five o'clock, made a deep impression on all the Jews, including even myself, though generally I am not as impressionable as other Jews. Until now, pronouncements about a Jewish National Home and the decisions at San Remo had only been words on paper; but now they rose before us embodied in the person of a Jewish High Commissioner. The King's message that the Jewish National Home was to be established by stages in Palestine, delivered by Samuel in this banquet hall in the presence of the highest officials and dignitaries from all ranks of the population, sounded like a fanfare to wake the dead. Many of the Jews present had tears in their eyes.'

Samuel himself was deeply moved when, on his first Sabbath in Jerusalem, after walking from the heights of the Augusta Victoria to the Hurva Synagogue in the Jewish Quarter, he read from the portion of the Book of Isaiah for that day, beginning with the words 'Comfort ye, comfort ye my people, saith your God. Speak ye comfortably to Jerusalem, and cry unto her, that her warfare is accomplished, that her iniquity is pardoned.' In his memoirs, Samuel recalled how 'the emotion that I could not but feel seemed to spread throughout the vast congregation.' A young civil servant, Max Nurock, who was present, later wrote of 'the rich carpets spread for this Prince in Israel by ecstatic spectators over the cobblestones of the Jewish Street, the flowers strewn in his path'.

*

Several senior British politicians looked askance at Britain's commitment to govern Palestine and at the same time to try to satisfy Zionist aspirations. But Lloyd George was determined to make the Mandate work. One of the doubters, Lord Curzon, wrote in a private letter in August 1920: 'The Prime Minister clings to Palestine for its sentimental and traditional value, and talks about Jerusalem with almost the same enthusiasm as about his native hills.'

Considerable effort was put by Britain into the smooth, or hoped-for smooth, administration of Palestine, and of Jerusalem. At the Jerusalem District Headquarters, situated in the St Paul Hospice just outside the Damascus Gate, were six district officers: two British Christians, three Jews, and one Muslim. Among the Jews was Herbert Samuel's son Edwin. At his wedding in December 1920 some 800 guests were assembled in Government House and its bells were rung for the first time since the British occupation.

The home to which Edwin Samuel took his bride that winter was one of the stone cottages built by the German Templars just before the First World War, and from which the Germans had been expelled when the British arrived. 'There was no central heating,' he later wrote. 'We had to burn olive wood in locally-made sheet-iron stoves. There was no bathroom: we bathed in a galvanised hip bath in a stone outhouse. There we heated up water in a cauldron and mixed it with cold water from the pump: it was quite an operation. As there was no electricity – or gas – everyone used kerosene lamps which invariably smoked at the worst possible moments (as at Ramallah, on our wedding night). Cooking was done on a patent "Primus" stove, using vaporised kerosene under pressure from an air-pump. But we were happy in this cottage. It had a small garden with shady trees.'

A pioneering Jewish agricultural enterprise came to Jerusalem in 1920, with the establishment of an Educational Farm to the south of the city, on a path leading eastward from the Convent of the Poor Clares to the biblical Hill of Evil Counsel. The aim of the farm was to grow saplings of trees adaptable to the climate of Palestine, with which the Jewish-owned areas could be reafforested. Later a vegetable garden, a vineyard and a poultry farm were added.

Modern communications were also making their way to Jerusalem: in July 1920 the first telephone service was opened in the city. There were eighty subscribers. Within a decade there were to be more than 3,000.

*

That winter saw a phenomenon not usually associated with Jerusalem by those who have not been there, but all too familiar to its citizens. 'The winter of 1920–21', Estelle Blyth later recalled, 'saw another unusually heavy fall of snow, so heavy, indeed, that some of the older houses in Jerusalem collapsed under the weight, and people going to and fro were glad to walk on the tops of the high stone walls that bordered the invisible roads. The winters, though shorter than our own, are felt a good deal, for absolutely no provision is made for warming the houses, and the small stoves of iron or porcelain do little more than warm the corner of the big room in which they are. The people suffer, too, and creep about looking exceedingly miserable and only half alive; they have an odd way of covering up their heads and leaving their legs bare to the weather, but it seems to suit them quite well.'

Every winter, Miss Blyth added, 'we used to hear of deaths from their dangerous custom of sleeping in a room hermetically closed to every breath of air, with a kanoon, or charcoal brazier, burning all night. The unfortunate fate of those who were found dead in the morning was greatly lamented by their surviving friends, but it never seemed to occur to any one that it was quite a preventable tragedy. Sharp and comfortless as the winters were, they had one great beauty which ours at home have not. After torrents of rain, and after heavy snow, the sun would blaze forth in perfect beauty, and the effect of the bright sunshine on the wet roads, with blue skies overhead, or on the unbroken sweep of the snow-covered hills around Jerusalem, was a sight never to be forgotten, and never to be seen too often.'

*

In March 1921 Winston Churchill, who had just been appointed Secretary of State for Colonial Affairs in Lloyd George's Government, travelled to a still chilly Jerusalem from Cairo. In Cairo he had been presiding over a conference to settle the boundaries and constitutions of Britain's mandated territories in the Middle East. While he was in Jerusalem he stayed with the High Commissioner at Government House, the Augusta Victoria.

On Sunday March 27 Churchill went to the nearby British Military Cemetery on Mount Scopus, where he attended a service of dedication. After the service he made a short speech, which was reported in the *Egyptian Gazette* two days later: 'The Colonial Minister said that he spoke with a full heart, especially as he thought of the place where they stood, on the Mount of Olives, overlooking the Holy City. It was a company of many people and diverse faiths which had met to commemorate the victorious dead, who had given their lives to liberate the land and to bring about peace and amity amongst its inhabitants, but there remained the duty and responsibility on those who were present to see that the task was completed.'

Churchill went on to tell the assembled dignitaries, of all three faiths: 'These veteran soldiers lie here where rests the dust of the Khalifs and Crusaders and the Maccabees. Peace to their ashes, honour to their memory and may we not fail to complete the work which they have begun.' The ceremony ended with three volleys fired by a guard of honour, and the sounding of the Last Post.

A stone inscription at the entrance to the war cemetery states that the land on which it stands was 'the free grant of the people of Palestine, to whom it was given by the municipality of Jerusalem, for the perpetual resting place of those of the Allied armies who fell in the war 1914–18 and are honoured there'. From the gate of the cemetery, visible in the distance across the valley of the Upper Kidron, were the well-known features of the Old City, the Dome of the Rock, the domes of the Church of the Holy Sepulchre, and the dome of the main Jewish synagogue, the Hurva. Within the ranks of graves were 2,180 soldiers and airmen from Britain, 143 from Australia, 51 from South Africa, 40 from the West Indies, 34 from New Zealand, and 65 men so badly mutilated by shell fire or grenade that their identity was never established. Also buried in the cemetery were three nursing sisters, one from South Africa, one from the West Indies, and one from New South Wales; and sixteen German and three Turkish prisoners-of-war who had died in British captivity.

The Hindu and Muslim soldiers from India were buried elsewhere, in a small garden to the south of the city, in what was soon to be the new Jewish suburb of Talpiot, with a view to the distant Dome of the Rock. Not individual graves but stone-carved inscriptions in Hindi and Urdu mark their last resting-place.

*

Churchill's visit to Jerusalem was to bring to the fore the main arguments of both sides of the Arab-Jewish divide. On March 28 the Executive Committee of the Haifa Congress of Palestinian Arabs presented him with a 12,000–word memorandum protesting against Zionist activity in Palestine. 'The Arab', they declared, 'is noble and large-hearted; he is also vengeful, and never forgets an ill-deed. If England does not take up the cause of the Arabs, other Powers will. From India, Mesopotamia, the Hedjaz and Palestine, the cry goes up to England now. If she does not listen, then perhaps Russia will take up their call some day, or perhaps even Germany.'

As to the voice of Russia, the Arabs warned, it 'is not heard in the councils of the nations, yet the time must come when it will assert itself'. They also warned Churchill that the 'unnatural partitioning' of their lands must one day disappear. Britain must befriend the Arab cause, for the Arabs were 'the key' to the East. 'They possess its doors and passes. Arabia, on the Red Sea and the Persian Gulf, is the way to India, and Palestine, on the Mediterranean, holds today the balance between the Powers.'

The Arab memorandum sought to prove 'that Palestine belongs to the Arabs, and that the Balfour Declaration is a gross injustice'. As for the Jewish National Home: 'For thousands of years Jews have

89

been scattered over the earth, and have become nationals of the various nations amongst whom they settled. They have no separate political or lingual existence. In Germany they are Germans, in France Frenchmen, and in England Englishmen. Religion and language are their only tie. But Hebrew is a dead language and might be discarded. How then could England conclude a treaty with a religion and register it in the League of Nations? Nay, rather, how could the Jews themselves agree to this treaty? For if there exists a Jewish Power and a Jewish nation, what is the status, amongst others, of those high Jewish officials who are serving England today? Are they Jewish nationals or English nationals, for it is obvious they cannot be both at the same time?'

'Jews have been amongst the most active advocates of destruction in many lands,' the Arab memorandum continued, 'especially where their influential positions have enabled them to do more harm. It is well known that the disintegration of Russia was wholly or in great part brought about by the Jews, and a large proportion of the defeat of Germany and Austria must also be put at their door. When the star of the Central Powers was in the ascendant Jews flattered them, but the moment the scale turned in favour of the Allies, Jews withdrew their support from Germany, opened their coffers to the Allies, and received in return the most uncommon promise.

'The Jew, moreover, is clannish and unneighbourly, and cannot mix with those who live about him. He will enjoy the privileges and benefits of a country, but will give nothing in return. The Jew is a Jew all the world over. He amasses the wealth of a country and then leads its people, whom he has already impoverished, where he chooses. He encourages wars when self-interest dictates, and thus uses the armies of the nations to do his bidding.'

In their memorandum the Palestinian-Arab leaders concluded with an appeal to Churchill to agree to five specific requests, 'in the name of justice and right'. These were the abolition of the principle of a National Home for the Jews; the creation of a National Government 'which shall be responsible to a Parliament elected by the Palestinian people who existed in Palestine before the war'; putting a stop to Jewish immigration 'until such a time as a National Government is formed'; annulling all laws framed 'after the British occupation', and creating no new laws 'until a National Government comes into being'; and finally, not separating Palestine 'from her sister States'.

These five requests had been circulated in the form of a mass petition before Churchill's arrival in Palestine. The petition was now handed to Churchill by the President of the Haifa Congress, the former Mayor of Jerusalem, Musa Kazem Pasha al-Husseini.

Churchill replied at once, telling the Palestinian-Arab deputation that there were in the Arab memorandum 'a great many statements of fact which we do not think are true'. He then set out his own view of the Arab appeal: 'You have asked me in the first place to repudiate the Balfour Declaration and to veto immigration of Jews into Palestine. It is not in my power to do so, nor, if it were in my power, would it be my wish. The British Government have passed their word, by the mouth of Mr Balfour, that they will view with favour the establishment of a National Home for Jews in Palestine, and that inevitably involves the immigration of Jews into the country. This declaration of Mr Balfour and of the British Government has been ratified by the Allied Powers who have been victorious in the Great War; and it was a declaration made while the war was still in progress, while victory and defeat hung in the balance. It must therefore be regarded as one of the facts definitely established by the triumphant conclusion of the Great War.

'Moreover, it is manifestly right that the Jews who are scattered all over the world, should have a national centre and a National Home where some of them may be reunited. And where else could that be but in this land of Palestine, with which for more than 3,000 years they have been intimately and profoundly associated? We think it will be good for the world, good for the Jews and good for the British Empire. But we also think it will be good for the Arabs who dwell in Palestine, and we intend that it shall be good for them, and that they shall not be sufferers or supplanted in the country in which they dwell or denied their share in all that makes for its progress and prosperity. And here I would draw your attention to the second part of the Balfour Declaration, which solemnly and explicitly promises to the inhabitants of Palestine the fullest protection of their civil and political rights.'

Churchill pointed out that it was not the Arabs of Palestine who had overthrown the Turks. 'It has been the armies of Britain which have liberated these regions. The position of Great Britain in Palestine is one of trust, but it is also one of right. For the discharge of that trust and for the high purposes we have in view, supreme sacrifices were made by all these soldiers of the British Empire, who gave up their lives and blood.' On the road to Government House, he added, was the graveyard of more than 2,000 British soldiers, 'and there are many other graveyards, some even larger, scattered about in this land'.

At the end of his reply, Churchill told the Arab deputation: 'If instead of sharing miseries through quarrels you will share blessings through co-operation, a bright and tranquil future lies before your country. The earth is a generous mother. She will produce in plentiful abundance for all her children if they will but cultivate her soil in justice and in peace.'

The Arab deputation withdrew, its appeal rejected and its arguments rebutted. A Jewish deputation followed in its place. It too presented a memorandum, signed by the executive of the recently established Jewish National Council. The Jewish memorandum expressed gratitude to the British for helping to rebuild 'the National Home of Israel' and pointed out that the Zionist programme 'lays special stress on the establishing of sincere friendship between ourselves and the Arabs'.

The Jewish leaders stressed that the Jewish people, 'returning after 2,000 years of exile and persecution to its own homeland, cannot suffer the suspicion that it wishes to deny to another nation its rights'. The Jewish people had 'full understanding of the aspirations of the Arabs with regard to a national revival, but we know that by our efforts to rebuild the Jewish National Home in Palestine, which is but a small area in comparison with all the Arab lands, we do not deprive them of their legitimate rights. On the contrary, we are convinced that a Jewish renaissance in this country can only have a strong and invigorating influence upon the Arab nation. Our kinship in language, race, character and history give the assurance that we shall in due course come to a complete understanding with them.'

In his reply to the Jewish deputation, Churchill began by explaining that he had already told the Muslim deputation 'quite plainly' that there could be 'no question of our departing from the principles enunciated by Mr Balfour in his declaration'. As for his own view of the Jewish National Home: 'I am myself perfectly convinced that the cause of Zionism is one which carries with it much that is good for the whole world, and not only for the Jewish people, but that it will also bring with it prosperity and contentment and advancement of the Arab population of this country.'

Churchill concluded his remarks to the Jews: 'I earnestly hope that your cause may be carried to success. I know how great the energy is and how serious are the difficulties at every stage and you have my warmest sympathy in the efforts you are making to overcome them. If I did not believe that you were animated by the very highest spirit of justice and idealism, and that your work would in fact confer blessings upon the whole country, I should not have the high hopes which I have that eventually your work will be accomplished.'

One of the Jewish delegation, Dr Arthur Ruppin, recorded in his diary that Churchill's remarks 'made a great impression on all present, as we had been afraid that he had been influenced against us by the Arabs'. That night Churchill was Ruppin's guest at a reception given in his honour by the leading Zionists in Jerusalem. Ruppin's Russian-born wife, Hannah, prepared as lavish a banquet as was possible in their home in Ethiopia Street.

Among those who had come to Jerusalem for talks with Churchill was the new ruler of Transjordan, the Emir Abdullah. At noon on March 29 Abdullah visited the Haram. Outside the Dome of the Rock he tried to speak to a large crowd of Muslim Arabs who had gathered to see him, but he was interrupted repeatedly by shouts of 'Palestine for the Arabs' and 'Down with the Zionists'. The protesting crowd then marched to the main post office to demonstrate against the Balfour Declaration. They were dispersed by the British police.

That same afternoon Churchill visited the site on which the Hebrew University of Jerusalem was being built. This was a project which had long been a part of Zionist aspirations. It was already three years since Dr Weizmann had laid one of the first twelve foundation-stones. Churchill's visit to the site was intended as a landmark in the university's progress. Although the visit had been arranged only the night before, all Jewish shops in the city had closed, and Jewish shopkeepers mingled with Jewish boy scouts and girl guides in the throng. On his arrival at the site, Churchill was greeted by one of the leading Zionists, Nahum Sokolow, who told him, in words which were spoken with a deep passion: 'The Jews are not content to live on terms of peace with the Arabs, but must live on terms of cordiality and fraternity.'

Churchill was then asked to plant a tree. Before doing so, he was given a Scroll of the Law, the Old Testament as read each Saturday in synagogues throughout the world. After receiving the gift, he declared: 'Personally, my heart is full of sympathy for Zionism. This sympathy has existed for a long time, since twelve years ago, when I was in contact with the Manchester Jews. I believe that the establishment of a Jewish National Home in Palestine will be a blessing to the whole world, a blessing to the Jewish race scattered all over the world, and a blessing to Great Britain. I firmly believe that it will be a blessing also to all the inhabitants of this country without distinction of race and religion.'

Churchill then spoke of his hopes of a Jewish initiative. 'This last blessing depends greatly upon you,' he said. 'Our promise was a double one. On the one hand, we promised to give our help to

Zionism, and on the other, we assured the non-Jewish inhabitants that they should not suffer in consequence. Every step you take should therefore be also for the moral and material benefit of all Palestinians. If you do this, Palestine will be happy and prosperous, and peace and concord will always reign; it will turn into a paradise, and will become, as is written in the scriptures you have just presented to me, a land flowing with milk and honey, in which sufferers of all races and religions will find a rest from their sufferings. You Jews of Palestine have a very great responsibility; you are the representatives of the Jewish nation all over the world, and your conduct should provide an example for, and do honour to, Jews in all countries. The hope of your race for so many centuries will be gradually realised here, not only for your own good but for the good of all the world.'

Churchill ended with the words: 'I am now going to plant a tree, and I hope that in its shadow peace and prosperity may return once more to Palestine.' This speech too made a profound impression on those present. An English Zionist, the former journalist Harry Sacher, who had recently set up a law practice in Palestine, was a witness to the tree-planting ceremony. He was critical of the way in which it had been arranged, writing to a friend in England: 'It was characteristic that Churchill was asked to plant a tree on the University site. As they were handing it to him the tree broke, and there was not even a reserve. They had to hunt about for a measly palm, which of course won't grow there, while Churchill looked annoyed and Samuel said "disgusting".'

Harry Sacher was worried about whether the British Government really would remain in Palestine and abide by the pledges of the Balfour Declaration. 'Churchill spoke very plainly in reaffirming the Balfour Declaration, both to the Jews and the Arabs,' he wrote to his friend. 'But he also told the Jews that they must do their bit, and he enlarged upon the pressure of the taxpayer, and the anti-Zionist critics in Parliament. The Arabs were angry, and there was a bit of trouble in Haifa, where a demonstration was dispersed by force, perhaps too much force. I am not happy about the Arab position. I am still more troubled by doubts as to whether the British Government may not finish by dropping the whole thing and clearing out, for financial reasons. I really don't know whether England today can afford such a luxury as a foreign policy, with or without Mandates. Perhaps,' Sacher added, 'we ought to discover oil here quickly, and so rope in the Admiralty.'

Oil has yet to be discovered in Palestine, and the British did eventually weary of trying to hold the ring, at considerable financial expense as well as public obloquy, between Arabs and Jews. But, as Churchill left the city, the British rulers in Jerusalem were confident of their abilities to work out an acceptable system whereby Jews and Arabs could live in the same country, and in the same city, with Britain maintaining law and order, national security and municipal prosperity.

*

Under the Muslim Turks, even in peacetime, the Muslim Arabs of Jerusalem had felt that their national aspirations were being ignored, and their lives subordinated to Constantinople and the Ottomans. The Christian British, led by a Jewish High Commissioner, were determined to change this. Herbert Samuel and his officials worked strenuously to give the Muslims their rights and to enhance their lives. With considerable pride, Ronald Storrs wrote: 'The northern façade of the Dome of the Rock was saved by no Arab initiative, but by British application for a British architect; and when funds were needed to extend the repairs to the Mosque of al-Aksa (after Mecca and Medina the most sacred shrine in Islam) the leaders of Arab agitation were not only permitted, but encouraged and assisted by the generous liberalism of the High Commissioner to make collections throughout the Moslem world (his honourable confidence was justified). Under British rule every piastre of the Moslem religious endowments was now used exclusively for Moslem purposes in Palestine, instead of being largely diverted to Constantinople; and certain wealthy endowments, sequestered by the Turks eighty years before, were returned to the Wakf authority.'

The most decisive act in what was thought to be the interest of all the Muslims of Jerusalem, and indeed of Palestine, was Herbert Samuel's decision to appoint as Mufti Haj Amin al-Husseini, the man who had been held responsible for the 1920 riots. Haj Amin was a cousin of Kamel al-Husseini, the Mufti who had died two months earlier, and whose family was one of the most prominent in Jerusalem.

Haj Amin, whose opinions and actions were to dominate the Muslim Arab scene for the next two decades, had been born in Jerusalem in 1893. He was educated first in Jerusalem, at a Turkish government school, and then in Cairo at the school of Sheikh Rashid Rida, where the basis of study was Islamic philosophy. He never went to university, but instead, in 1913, made the pilgrimage to Mecca and Medina, thus adding the title 'Haj' to his name.

War came shortly after Haj Amin returned to Jerusalem. He joined the Turkish army and served as an officer in Smyrna. Returning to Jerusalem after the defeat of Turkey, he was a clerk in the office of the Arab Adviser to the British Military Governor. Later he became a tutor in the Rashidiyeh School, just outside Herod's Gate. He began to write strident nationalistic articles and to excite large crowds with his oratory. One of the Mufti's biographers, Maurice Pearlman, a Jew who emigrated from England to Palestine, wrote of Haj Amin: 'He quickly achieved a place in Arab public life through family connections and the vigour and forthrightness of his tongue and pen. He also showed considerable organising ability and a certain ruthless courage. From the very outset he was frank and open in his views.'

Haj Amin made no secret of his hatred of the British and the Jews. His appointment as Mufti by Sir Herbert Samuel, a Briton and a Jew, has long been the subject of controversy. In July 1920 Haj Amin had been one of the very few people who was excluded from the High Commissioner's amnesty. But in September that year he had received a special pardon, and returned to Palestine. His cousin the Mufti died five months later. Haj Amin put himself forward as his successor. In the Muslim elections that followed, on 12 April 1921, he came fourth. Only the first three were eligible for selection by the High Commissioner. One of the three stood down. Haj Amin's name went forward with the other two. He was chosen, and the Muslim voice in Jerusalem began to adopt a harsher tone.

Of the many controversies stirred up in Jerusalem during the Mandate years, the appointment of Haj Amin as Mufti is perhaps the deepest. That Herbert Samuel, an exponent of law and order in the British administration, and a Jew, should have been the person to put in place the future standard-bearer of disorder and anti-Jewish feeling has appeared inexplicable. But on the eve of the appointment, the annual Nebi Musa celebrations had taken place. In 1920 they had led to bloodshed. In 1921 they were calm. This welcome change was attributed to the influence of Haj Amin, and was a major factor in his subsequent appointment.

The appointment of Haj Amin was not unopposed. In the family rivalries which dominated so much of the Jerusalem Arab scene, the al-Nashashibis felt so aggrieved at the prospect of another al-Husseini as Mufti that the Mayor, Ragheb Bey al-Nashashibi, not only campaigned against the appointment but stated publicly that he would oppose it at the highest level. On 8 May 1921 Haj Amin was told, by word of mouth, that he had been appointed Mufti. He at once pressed Samuel for confirmation in writing, but this was never forthcoming, nor was his appointment ever officially gazetted.

Haj Amin was not satisfied to inherit his cousin's title of Mufti of Jerusalem: he wanted to be the spiritual leader of all the Muslims of Palestine. A previously unknown title became attached to him, that of 'Grand Mufti', and with this he established his primacy in the hierarchy of towns throughout the area of the Mandate. Following this elevation, Haj Amin pressed for a higher salary from the British than that given to his fellow (or former fellow) Muftis. This was granted.

In an attempt to reassure the Muslims that they could control their own religious affairs, the British Government set up a Supreme Muslim Council. The authority of the council was wide. It was given charge of the Muslim Religious Trust, the Wakf, as well as of the administration of all Muslim social services, all mosques, and all teaching and preaching appointments throughout Palestine. Among the council's income was revenue from land leased to tenant farmers and a Government subsidy. The council was made up of five members, headed by a President. The President was to be elected by fifty-three representatives from the different regions of Palestine – the same regional electoral college as had elected the representatives to the Ottoman Parliament before the war.

With the active support of Mandate officials, and the 'knowledge and blessing of Samuel', as Samuel's biographer Bernard Wasserstein has written, the newly-styled Grand Mufti was elected President of the Supreme Muslim Council in January 1922. His appointment was opposed by Ragheb Bey al-Nashashibi, but Ragheb Bey was outvoted. At its first meeting, the Council confirmed Haj Amin's position both as 'Head of the Muslim Community in Palestine' and as 'Head of Islam in Palestine'.

*

On 1 May 1921 Arab riots broke out in Jaffa against the continuing Jewish immigration. Several Jewish settlements in the coastal plain were also attacked. Although the riots did not reach Jerusalem, the extent of the looting of Jewish homes caused consternation among the Zionists in the city. Their fears were underlined by the report of a British commission of inquiry, headed by a distinguished British judge, Sir Thomas Haycraft, that 'the looting and wreckage of furniture and household effects was appalling in its savage thoroughness.'

The commission's report added: 'It has been said that what the Arabs really want is loot, that when there is trouble they take advantage to pillage, that this love of pillage is at the bottom of every anti-Jewish movement. It is true that, when Arabs fight they also loot.' In the riots of 1921, the report pointed out, 'the looters were almost exclusively Arab, the victims almost exclusively Jews.'

It was not looting alone that gave cause for concern. The Haycraft Report also took note of what it described as 'that sudden excess of violence which characterises the Arab when roused to anger by some actual or supposed wrong or provocation', in this case the fear of an eventual Jewish majority in Palestine. Hoping to calm Arab agitation, Herbert Samuel ordered an immediate suspension of all Jewish immigration. Some Jews already at Jaffa waiting to disembark were refused permission to land. When immigration was restored a few months later it came with a condition, that it should never exceed 'the economic capacity of Palestine to absorb new immigrants' – a phrase and a policy which pleased the Arabs and alarmed the Jews.

By the end of 1921 a total of 8,000 Jews had been allowed to enter Palestine as immigrants within twelve months. Denunciation of Jewish immigration in the mosques led to a riot in Jerusalem that November, when an Arab mob attacked the Jewish Quarter of the Old City. The Jews were no longer as ill-prepared as they had been a year and a half earlier. The Jewish self-defence group, the Hagannah, established during the riots of 1920, was able to drive the attackers away. Nevertheless, four Jews were killed and twenty injured. The riot took place on November 2, the fourth anniversary of the Balfour Declaration. That day was meant to be graduation day for the first nurses to have completed the three-year course at the Hadassah nursing school. The ceremony was postponed. Two Zionist leaders, Montague David Eder and Arthur Ruppin, disagreed about what form the funeral of those killed should take. 'Dr Eder wanted to have the four dead buried quietly this evening, in order not to provoke new disturbances,' Ruppin wrote in his diary on November 3. 'I was against it and demanded a public and dignified funeral by daylight; it seems to me that we owe this to our national dignity. My demand has been accepted.'

On November 4 the Hadassah nurses and their teachers took part in the solemn funeral procession which left the Rothschild Hospital on the Street of the Prophets, formerly the Street of the Consuls, for the Jewish Cemetery on the Mount of Olives. The Jewish community declared a month of mourning. The nurses' graduation ceremony was further delayed.

*

Despite this second outbreak of bloodshed in two years, Herbert Samuel felt that he had an ally in the Grand Mufti. 'The Mufti and his personal friends', Samuel told a Cabinet Committee in London two years later, 'are always active in times of political crisis – and we have them every month or two – in preventing people getting too excited and too violent.'

Samuel intended to find ways of linking all groups in Jerusalem with the British flag. On 7 November 1921 His Beatitude Yeghiché Turian, the former Armenian Patriarch of Constantinople, was enthroned as Patriarch of Jerusalem. The formal approval of King George V had been obtained in advance. 'This was the first instance', commented Cook's *Traveller's Handbook*, 'in which a British sovereign officially approved the election of an Eastern Patriarch.'

The postponed graduation ceremony for the Jewish nurses finally took place on December 7. The graduation address was delivered by Dr Eder. A distinguished British Jew and member of the recently established Zionist Executive, Eder spoke in English. Hardly had he finished his first sentence than Dr Eliezer Ben Yehuda, the veteran pioneer of modern Hebrew, walked out in protest. Each community in Jerusalem might be in dispute with its neighbours, but within each community the rumbles of disagreement could be almost as loud.

CHAPTER SEVEN

The First Six Years of the British Mandate, 1922–1929

On 1 March 1922 a baby boy was born in Jerusalem whose life and death were to make their impact on the city. His father, Nehemia Rubitzov, was a Russian-born Jew who had emigrated to America shortly after the turn of the century, and in 1918 had enlisted in the British army as a private soldier in order to go to Palestine, which he did. He and his wife had met when they volunteered to defend the Jews of the Old City against Arab attack in 1920. Their son Yitzhak, who later took the surname Rabin, was born in the Shaare Tzedek Hospital on the Jaffa Road, a few minutes' walk from the spot where the city had surrendered to the British five years earlier.

A sense of calm and normality had begun to enter the streets of Mandate Jerusalem. That March, the Muslim celebrations at Nebi Musa passed without incident, unlike in the previous two years. One of those who witnessed them was a British traveller, Philip Graves, who was impressed by the procession of the men from Hebron to the Jaffa Gate. 'As they entered the Old City,' he wrote, 'the enthusiasm of the crowds reached its highest intensity. Men with the set blank stare of extreme excitement danced round and round, bareheaded, their long locks flying wildly as they revolved. Last came the green banner of Hebron surrounded by a guard of ten horsemen. Proudly they walked with their flag, till they came to where the narrow Street of David plunges down into the labyrinth of the Old City. For the last time they whirled their bright blades above their heads and disappeared into the shadows of the streets.'

It was a scene of normal exuberance, a sign that the British rulers could cope with the moments of religious devotion that could also be moments of tension and conflict. On 24 July 1922 the Council of the League of Nations approved the Mandate for Palestine as entrusted to Great Britain. Thomas Cook's handbook commented:

'And thus a new phase begins in the history of the world's most sacred city, which comes again out of years of bondage, from the darkness of bad government – if indeed it was government at all – to the light of Freedom and Progress. Perhaps it is no longer the Jerusalem of Solomon or of Herod, of Hadrian, or of Godfrey de Bouillon – the hill on which it stands is higher for its vicissitudes; but none the less it is the city more universally intimate than any other in the world.'

A second decision by the League of Nations, made on 16 September 1922, was to establish in Jerusalem one of the city's most enduring organisations, the Jewish Agency. The agency was authorised to act in 'concert' with the British Mandate authorities with a view to 'facilitating Jewish immigration and fostering intensive settlement of Israelites on the soil of the country'. The officials of the Jewish Agency were in constant contact with the British, while at the same time setting up departments that supervised Jewish education, health and welfare on a growing scale. Two other Zionist organisations had their headquarters in Jerusalem, the Keren Kayemet (the Jewish National Fund), originally founded in 1901, in charge of land settlement, the draining of swamps, irrigation, the clearing of stones, farming and afforestation throughout Palestine; and the Keren Hayesod (the Palestine Foundation Fund), founded in 1921, the financing and fund-raising arm of this country-wide Zionist activity.

The constructive work of the Mandate authorities in Jerusalem focused in its early days on repairing old buildings and creating a new municipal centre, the 'New Town'. The philosophy of this work was expressed by C. R. Ashbee, the Civic Adviser from 1919 to 1922. 'The real work', he wrote, 'is, after all, not the drawing of the city plan on paper, nor the description of it in a book, nor the comments on it in an office file, nor even the making of a picture of it for the walls of the Royal Academy. The real work is to administer it intelligently and towards the shaping of a more or less ideal end. The only test of this is the beauty and comeliness of the city itself.'

Impressive repair work was done to restore the eroded stone pinnacles of the Damascus Gate, the victim of time and neglect. The equally neglected structure of the Dome of the Rock was carefully repaired. David's Tower and Citadel at the Jaffa Gate, structures dating back to the time of Herod, were restored, and the much-despised Turkish clock tower, set up at the Jaffa Gate at the end of the nineteenth century, was taken down. A walkway was cleared along the Old City ramparts, on the top of the city walls built by Suleiman the Magnificent in the sixteenth century. Repairs to the

Street of the Chain inside the Old City proved impossible to start, however, as the Wakf was reluctant to see British activity in what was largely its own property.

The New Town, or New City as it soon came to be called, was an even more ambitious project. It involved the creation of a garden zone around the city walls, the planting of more than 3,000 trees, the establishment of three Jewish garden cities, the creation of an extensive new municipal centre in which the British, Jews and Arabs could build their official structures, and, a blessing for those who had to live in or visit Jerusalem old or new, the naming of 130 streets, complete with ceramic tiles on which the names were emblazoned in English, Arabic and Hebrew.

The names chosen by the Pro-Jerusalem Society, of which Storrs was President, were 'so full of history, poetry and folklore', Ashbee has written, that they were 'well worth careful study'. Among the street names chosen for the Old City were 'Feather Lane', 'Water Melon Alley', 'Blacksmiths Lane', 'Stork Lane', and 'Dancing Dervish Street'. The New City could boast among its eighty new names the 'Street of the Prophets', 'Herod's Way', 'Street of Josephus' and 'Isaiah Street'.

A major project of the Pro-Jerusalem Society was the furnishing and decorating of the former Augusta Victoria Hospice to make it suitable as Government House, the centre of the administrative and social life of the Mandate. At first it was felt that the work could best be done by bringing out expert craftsmen from Britain, using a well-established firm such as Maple or Waring. But Herbert Samuel decided to use only local materials and local labour. Ashbee, who was put in charge of the work, later commented: 'The experiment was not purely aesthetic; it was also human. I think that all constructive ventures in the crafts have their human side, and may be submitted to a human as well as a merely aesthetic test; for it is a fact daily growing clearer to us that in these days of the industrial helot state, with its infinite subdivisions of mechanical labour, we often get better value for our money from work produced among groups of men working happily and humanly together, and conscious of their own personal creation, than from work produced in an impersonal factory.'

It was a noble vision, carried out in Government House by forty to fifty craftsmen all working on the site: stonemasons, ceramic-tile-makers and painters, carpenters, blacksmiths, cabinet-makers, wood-carvers, upholsterers, weavers and even glass-blowers. Mount Scopus soon bustled with their activities. The stone they used was local Jerusalem sandstone and marble, the glass came from Hebron. The wood had to be brought mostly from India, due to the Turkish destruction of the Jerusalem forest, but was carved on the site. The only artisan work done outside Jerusalem was making the silks, which, for lack of good local weavers, were woven in Cairo.

It was not, however, the rare materials that were the greatest challenge. 'The chief difficulty,' Ashbee wrote, 'and it is the difficulty familiar to every administrator in Palestine, was labour co-ordination. How were all these different races and religions, with their various traditions and customs, to be got to work together? In Jerusalem we had not only every variety of race and language as a natural condition, but on the top of it all the disorganisation of the war, and the chronic confusion which industrialism has introduced into the crafts, a condition that is now rapidly disintegrating the traditional methods of the East, as it has long ago destroyed those of our western workshops.

'But craftsmanship and the love of craftsmanship – the cunning of a man's own right hand – were found here to be, as so often before in the human story, a great amalgam; and it was interesting to observe how all these different work-people, Moslems, Christians, Jews; English, French, German; Greeks, Armenians, Syrians, Poles, and Russians, with no common language, and who when the machine-guns of the Mandatory Power patrol the streets are ready to be at each others' throats, were working, jesting, and in the end banqueting harmoniously together. Of my four foremen, one talked Greek, Arabic, and French; the second Arabic, French, and Armenian; the third German and Arabic; and the fourth Arabic and Turkish. Among the Jewish carvers, upholsterers, and seamstresses the languages were Yiddish, Polish, Russian, and there may have been a dash of classic Hebrew and American Bowery English. Whatever the aesthetic merits of the work may be which this polyglot community produced, it was an object-lesson in the futility of political methods as set beside the cohesive power of the arts and crafts when practised rather than talked about.'

Pro-Jerusalem was dependent for most of its funding on public subscription. Storrs had cast the appeal widely, as was clear from the list of subscribers. Among them were the Anglican Bishop in Jerusalem; a leading Arab scholar, George Antonius; the founder of modern Hebrew, Eliezer Ben Yehuda; a Catholic cardinal; the National Bank of Egypt; the American department-store owner, Marshall Field; a distinguished Egyptian Jew, Sir Victor Harari; and the widow of the painter Holman Hunt, who had painted spectacular scenes of the Judaean Desert in the late nineteenth century. Also subscribing were two British Prime Ministers, David Lloyd George and Andrew Bonar Law, as well as a Sikh regiment stationed in the city (the 51st), and the arms manufacturer Sir Basil Zaharoff.

The work of the Pro-Jerusalem Society dovetailed closely with that of the Palestine Land Development Company, a Zionist enterprise headed by Dr Arthur Ruppin. The company's aim was to build Jewish suburbs outside the New Town, on high ground, with particular attention to parks and gardens. The most ambitious scheme was for the garden suburb of Talpiot, an empty area to the south of the city, just above the Bethlehem Road.

Eight hundred houses were to be built in Talpiot, each in its own plot of land, as well as a hotel and a synagogue. Ten per cent of the area was to be parks and woodland. There were also to be three substantial public buildings, though lack of funds eventually made these impracticable outside the city centre: a hospital, an academy and a theatre. Ashbee commented: 'The planning and the dream are symbolic of Zionist activities. One must admire the enthusiasm and the hope.'

One such area of Zionist hope was unexpectedly challenged in the summer of 1922. At a time when progress was proving very slow in setting up a Hebrew University in Jerusalem, Ronald Storrs proposed in its place, as one of his very last initiatives before leaving Jerusalem, what was referred to by its supporters and critics alike as an 'English University'. Storrs wanted the new university to contain both a Hebrew and an Arabic Department. First he set up a Council for the Establishment of a Palestine University. He then invited three leading Zionists, Eliezer Ben Yehuda, David Yellin and Dr Joseph Klausner, to be in charge of the Hebrew Department.

Klausner later wrote: 'It was not difficult to see in an English University a serious rival to the Hebrew University, and there was reason to fear the effect of an alien culture on the Jews of such a Government institution'. Yet both Ben Yehuda and David Yellin accepted Storr's invitation. It was only after considerable pressure from Menachem Ussishkin, then Chairman of the Zionist Executive in Jerusalem, that they withdrew, much to Storrs's anger. Not content with foiling what he saw as a challenge to the essentially Jewish character of the long-awaited university in Jerusalem, Ussishkin also appointed a Special Committee for the 'prompt establishment' of the Hebrew University.

Would such a university ever come into being? It was decided, largely on Ussishkin's insistence, that the new university should be first and foremost concerned with teaching; and that research would develop from teaching, not the other way round. Planning was put in the hands of a recently arrived American Jewish rabbi, Judah L. Magnes, whose pacifism during the First World War had alienated him from the New York Jewish community of which he had been a leading light. Magnes moved forward rapidly; in 1923 the first teaching institute of the Hebrew University, the Institute of Chemistry, was opened in a building on Mount Scopus. The university library was also opened that year, and amalgamated with the Jewish National Library, which had been established thirty years earlier, in Turkish times. The librarian of the Hebrew section of the new library was the distinguished German-Jewish scholar Gershom Scholem, who had just arrived in Jerusalem from Berlin.

In his memoirs, Scholem recalled the general scepticism about whether the full university would ever come to pass. 'In Jerusalem,' he wrote, 'there was a committee of a few notables who carried on fruitless discussions about the coming university and its professorships. For the rest, no one in the country believed that the project which had been decided upon as early as 1913 and for which a symbolic cornerstone had been laid in 1918 (before the war's end) would come to fruition in the foreseeable future. Nor was there any lack of sceptics and opponents. After all, in those days there was a sizable Jewish academic proletariat, and if the designation of "doctor" as a "Jewish forename" was very much in fashion at that time, this was by no means intended as flattery. Was the number of unemployed Jewish intellectuals to be augmented even further by opening an institution that would issue diplomas? Many people shuddered at such a prospect. Besides, as I have already said, the Zionists had no money, even though they liked to use the idea of a Hebrew University in Jerusalem as propaganda at meetings. But things took an unexpectedly favourable course.'

As the Institute of Chemistry and the library carried on their work, the wider concept was coming to fruition. The turning-point was the visit to Jerusalem in April 1924 of the German-American philanthropist Felix Warburg, who, on leaving Palestine, handed Dr Magnes a letter containing a cheque for the establishment of an Institute of Jewish Studies. The institute was opened that December, during Hannukah, the Festival of the Maccabees. The language of instruction, for research as well as teaching, was to be Hebrew, and the Institute was to be open, Magnes declared, 'to men and women without distinction of religion, race or creed'.

In 1922 a distinguished archaeologist, Professor John Garstang, appealed for funds to begin the systematic excavation of the oldest part of Jerusalem, David's City, on the spur below the Temple Mount. Within a year the money was raised and work began under R. A. S. Macalister. Within two years Macalister had made a series of remarkable discoveries, uncovering a large section of the pre-Davidian Jebusite wall, and a later wall built by David's son, King Solomon. These structures were more than 3,000 years old.

New structures were being built as rapidly as old structures were being uncovered. Small in area, Jerusalem was busy with construction in the early years of the Mandate. In 1922 the Greek Orthodox Patriarchate sold, to the Jewish Agency's land-purchasing commission, a large tract of sloping land in the centre of the New City on which were built the shops, hotels and cafés of Ben Yehuda Street. In 1923 an imposing Jewish Talmudic academy, the Porat Joseph Yeshiva, was completed in the Jewish Quarter of the Old City. It had been the pre-war vision of a distinguished Jew from Calcutta, Joseph Abraham Shalom, who had begun the building in 1911. War had forced all such construction to cease, but Shalom persevered as soon as British rule was established.

Shalom's aim was to restore in Jerusalem, where Ashkenazi Jews had been in the ascendant for almost a hundred years, the finest of the Sephardi traditions. As well as an attractive synagogue, whose dome was held aloft on marble pillars, the yeshiva had eight classrooms, a library, lecture halls and study rooms, offices and dormitories, as well as spacious flats for the teaching staff. Shalom set up a trust fund to maintain the entire student body and academic staff: the fund survived the ravages of inflation for almost twenty years. The academy itself, with its commanding position at the edge of the Jewish Quarter, eventually became a British military outpost, then a battleground, and finally, in 1948, a ruin.

*

Under the Mandate, Jerusalem was filled with British officials, and bustled with all the building activities of a capital city. The officials included several British Jews, who devoted themselves to the impartial working of the Mandate. One of the most senior Jews in the government was Albert Hyamson, an Orthodox Jew from North London and a former British civil servant who had worked for the

British Post Office. He became head of the Immigration Department, responsible for applying the regulations for the admission of Jews into Palestine.

Another Jewish official was Norman Bentwich, the Attorney-General to the Mandate Government. Like Hyamson, he strove for fairness. The Arabs were discontented, however, that a man who was the son of a leading Zionist pioneer, and had written a sympathetic study of Zionism, should be in such a senior juridical position. For their part, many Zionists resented what they regarded as Bentwich's excessive moderation in cases involving Arab disturbances. Unable to satisfy either group of those whose interests he worked so hard to sustain, Bentwich left the British administration.

*

Having become Mufti in April 1921, and head of the Supreme Muslim Council nine months later, Haj Amin al-Husseini worked with great energy and skill to enhance the status of Jerusalem throughout the Muslim world. His principal effort, which he understood to be a crucial one, and in which he succeeded, was to make the Dome of the Rock and the al-Aksa Mosque far more prominent than they had been hitherto in the minds of Muslims everywhere.

In October 1923, in a first effort in that direction, Haj Amin sent a mission to India, to seek funds for the restoration of both the dome and the mosque. A considerable sum was raised, £22,000 in all, of which £7,000 came from one of India's most prominent rulers, the Nizam of Hyderabad. In the following year Haj Amin sent further missions to the Hedjaz, Iraq, Kuwait and Bahrain, raising a further £64,000.

Using this money, Haj Amin organised an impressive restoration. The dilapidated façade of the al-Aksa Mosque was repaired, and the Dome of the Rock was plated in gold. The historian Yehoshua Porath has written: 'The above restoration project was of immense significance. It enhanced the value and importance of the two Jerusalem mosques, both in the eyes of Muslims in Palestine itself, and also in the eyes of Muslims in other countries. The fund-raising drive throughout the Muslim world had attracted international attention, which became focused in turn on Jerusalem and the rest of Palestine. This fitted in well with Haj Amin's efforts to achieve recognition as a Muslim personage of world standing.' Also, as Haj Amin intended, it put a stronger focus on Jerusalem in Muslim eyes than the city had ever had before.

*

Murder of an unusual kind came to the streets of Jerusalem in 1924. The victim was a Dutch-born Jew in his early forties, Yaakov Yisrael De Haan. Once a secular Jew, he had turned to Orthodoxy and become a disciple of the ultra-Orthodox Rabbi Sonnenfeld. With Sonnenfeld he had travelled to Transjordan for talks with the Emir Hussein, when the Emir was visiting his son Abdullah. The Zionists were distressed by the links between the strongly anti-Zionist Sonnenfeld and the Arab leaders.

De Haan was to head an ultra-Orthodox delegation to London to explain to British politicians the Orthodox community's opposition to Zionism. The delegation was to argue that the Orthodox Jewish community should not be subject to the authority either of the secular Zionist institutions or of the Chief Rabbinate, with which the ultra-Orthodox had also quarrelled. Three days before the delegation was due to depart, news of its mission leaked out into the newspapers. On the following evening, 30 June 1924, De Haan was at prayer in the synagogue of the Shaare Tzedek Hospital. He then left by a small side entrance into the Jaffa Road. After he had taken a few steps, three shots rang out. He had been shot in the heart. The police were called and went in pursuit of the killers, the police detachment being led by a Jewish officer, David Tidhar.

De Haan's funeral was attended by 20,000 members of the ultra-Orthodox community. The community was convinced that De Haan had been murdered by the Zionists. Rabbi Sonnenfeld, in his funeral oration, described the murder as having been perpetuated 'by the descendants of Jacob employing the tactics of Esau in order to still the voice of Israel and Jacob', and he added: 'See the abysmal depths to which the Zionist leadership has fallen, and call out in a strong voice, "Separate yourselves from this evil community." '

Many Zionist leaders and thinkers condemned the crime. A police inquiry headed by David Tidhar, the policeman who had led the chase, was inconclusive. When, at the demand of the Orthodox, Tidhar himself was questioned, the only fault found in his activities that day was that he had earlier replaced the Arab officers in the precinct with Jewish ones. Several extreme Zionists suggested that De Haan had been murdered by the ultra-Orthodox themselves in order to win the sympathy of Jews worldwide.

The De Haan case caused anguish among the Jews of Jerusalem. The suspicion that he was murdered by a Jew was painful, even horrific. Forty years were to pass before the mystery was resolved. It had been the Zionist self-defence group, the Hagannah, set up four years earlier to combat Arab terrorism, that had done the deed. The head of the Hagannah, Yosef Hecht, had asked Zahariah Urieli, the Hagannah commander in Jerusalem, 'to eliminate the traitor'. Urieli asked for volunteers. Two Jewish police officers, both of them immigrants from Russia, volunteered.

What had been De Haan's crime? The editor of the official history of the Hagannah has written, from the Hagannah perspective: 'Were it not for De Haan the Orthodox would have organised their own small community devoid of any political or communal significance. De Haan used his connection to move the struggle into the realm of international politics. He aspired to establish a political organisation to rival the Zionist movement, which was still in its infancy and not yet fully established – this was the danger of De Haan.'

When the truth about De Haan's murder was first made public, in an Israel radio broadcast in 1970, Jerusalem was once more troubled. Forty-six years after the event, David Tidhar was unrepentant about his part in the murder. It had been decided by the Hagannah, he recalled, not to allow De Haan to travel to London. 'If he would have continued to live, he would have caused trouble. I regret that I was not chosen to liquidate him. My job was to protect those who did. Naturally I appeared on the scene immediately. Since I knew in what direction the gunmen had to escape, I directed the police to pursue them in the opposite direction.'

The repercussions of the broadcast lasted for many months. One of De Haan's strongest public opponents at the time of his murder, A. J. Brawer, subsequently a noted historian and biographer, wrote to the newspapers that, although he still felt that De Haan's activities has posed a threat to the Zionist efforts to establish a Jewish National Home, 'no one has raised the question of whether De Haan's threat could have been neutralised in some less drastic fashion'. Whatever experts might decide, Brawer wrote, about whether De Haan's murder 'was something necessitated by the times, or a tragic error, I for one am afraid that the stain of murder will not be eradicated from the judgement made by future historians'.

The murder of one man in a Jerusalem street had stirred, and disturbed, the conscience of many.

*

Whatever the disturbances on the streets of Jerusalem, the city was always a magnet for tourists. In 1924 Cook's *Traveller's Handbook* for *Palestine and Syria*, edited by the Assistant Governor of Jerusalem, Harry Luke, contained a description of the Old City that is timeless and endearing. 'Among these streets, and the hundred and one narrow lanes and byways that are tributary to them', it told the traveller, 'there is endless passage of camels, donkeys, sheep, goats and the picturesque natives of the city; small native cafés and bazaars lie thickly piled along either side, and modern wretchedness frequently jostles medieval ruin. The city throughout testifies to its universal character – churches, mosques, synagogues, convents, belfry towers and soaring minarets, dark hovels and wide courts, Lipton's tea and sherbet, tourist and Bedouin. A small, and at first sight, unprepossessing city covering only 210 acres; but nevertheless a city of perpetual interest – an ethnographical museum, a bazaar of antiquities and curiosities, and, above all, the holiest place in Christendom.'

As for the New City, the guidebook commented: 'Cafés, or similar establishments of a reputable character, are not abundant in Jerusalem. Restaurants are attached to the leading hotels, some of which make a feature of *Thés Dansants* and weekly balls. The Bristol Garden Restaurant in the Jaffa Road can be recommended. The Municipal Gardens (with tea-rooms, band etc,) are patronised in the afternoons and evenings.' Shops were not yet 'on a level' with European establishments but were 'rapidly improving'.

In the spring of 1924 the archaeologist R. A. S. Macalister, who had first entered the Jaffa Gate before the Kaiser's breach in it, his carriage being obliged to make use of the 'narrow and dangerous right angled passage', walked through the gate before returning home to Ireland. 'A huckster had established his stall under its shelter,' he wrote. 'Among the goods which he was offering for sale I noticed an Arabic translation of *Tarzan of the Apes*. Thus is Europe holding out a helping hand to the East, sharing with her the blessings that she herself enjoys!'

On 9 December 1924, the seventh anniversary of the conquest of Jerusalem by the British, a fine new street was opened in western Jerusalem. King George V Avenue linked the Jaffa Road with the railway station in a broad sweep from north to south, passing to the east of the new Jewish garden suburb of Rehavia. The Zionist leader Dr Arthur Ruppin, who had built the first Jewish stone house in Rehavia, noted in his diary that day that the road was 'a real achievement' for the Mayor, Ragheb Bey al-Nashashibi. 'The entire appearance of the town has changed,' Ruppin commented, 'and the new road has become its centre. It is the first street wide and long enough to invite one to walk here.'

*

One of the recurring aspects of Jerusalem's history in the twentieth century is the concern of outsiders at the situation in the city. More criticisms must have been levelled from afar at aspects of life in Jerusalem than at any other city in the world. There was an example of this at the beginning of 1925, when the Jerusalem correspondent of the Vatican newspaper *Osservatore Romano*, the mouthpiece of Catholic concerns in Rome, deprecated the quality of the recent Jewish immigrants. A few of these were Zionist idealists, he wrote. Some were Jews escaping from persecution in Poland and Russia, and were 'without any religious feeling'. But the largest group were 'parasites hoping to make a livelihood on the assistance of the special Zionist funds'.

The correspondent had nothing to say about the growing municipal and institutional efforts of the Jews in the city from which he was writing. Yet the previous year had seen considerable Jewish efforts in Jerusalem in every sphere. Cafes and restaurants were becoming one of the more charming features of daily life: the Bristol Garden Restaurant offered 'cuisine and cellars and orchestra, the best in Palestine'. Light industry was flourishing. Among the factories and workshops to be found in the city in 1925 were manufacturers of table salt, macaroni, soda water, carpets, socks and stockings, parchment, leather goods, stationery, bookbindings and paper bags.

To the north of Jerusalem, the year 1925 saw the expansion of Atarot, the small Jewish farming settlement which had been established just before the First World War, into a substantial and flourishing community. From its dairy, Jerusalem was furnished with fresh milk daily. Fruit and vegetables were also provided. For their water supply, the farmers dug a pool in which the winter rains could be collected and stored.

*

Most significant of all the Jewish developments in Jerusalem in the early years of British rule was the opening of the Hebrew University on Mount Scopus in the spring of 1925. This had been a Zionist aspiration from before the war. But when it was announced that Lord Balfour would be coming to open the university, the Arabs declared that they would hold a strike. Judah L. Magnes, the President of the new university, noted in his diary: 'Relations with Arabs, Muslim world, whole Near East, exacerbated.' He had been given a report that Egyptian scholars were 'definitely hostile'.

When Balfour reached Jerusalem, such hostility confirmed Magnes's fears that the university was being seen by the Arabs not as an educational and intellectual development, but as a political one. 'Balfour will be leaving soon,' Magnes wrote three days before the inauguration ceremony. 'The excitement will be over. What will be left? In the mind of the outside world – the fact that the Jews rejoiced and the Arabs struck. In the Arab-Moslem mind, increased bitterness and resentment. In the Jewish mind outside Palestine – increased inflation. Among the Jews of Palestine, increased difficulties with their neighbours.'

The inauguration ceremony took place on 1 April 1925. It was held in a specially constructed amphitheatre overlooking the Judaean Desert. 'The setting was impressive,' Arthur Ruppin wrote in his diary, 'but the speeches suffered from their length, and from the cold, which was rather noticeable.' Balfour told the 7,000 invited guests of the great future he envisaged for the new university. The Hebrew national poet, Chaim Nachman Bialik, also spoke. The Zionist youngsters who were working the land, he said, 'elevate crude physical labour to the level of supreme holiness, to the status of a religion. We must now light this holy flame within the walls of the building which is now being opened on Mount Scopus. Let these youngsters build with fire the lower Jerusalem while we build the higher Jerusalem. Our existence will be recreated and made secure by means of both ways together.'

Among the Zionist leaders on the platform at the opening ceremony, were Dr Weizmann and Menachem Ussishkin, for whom the university was such a central part of their concept of Jewish national renewal. Many foreign academic dignitaries were also present. 'In scarlet robes, in splendid academic gowns,' the journalist Elias Epstein wrote in the London Zionist magazine *New Judea*, 'each brought a message of tribute from his seat of learning to the new shrine dedicated that day. Oxford and Cambridge, Columbia and Johns Hopkins, Egypt and Athens, which each sent its rector to greet Jerusalem, they were grouped on a raised dais.'

Jerusalem's Muslim and Christian dignitaries, resplendent in their robes, were also present on that dais at the opening ceremony. But the growing Arab discontent at all aspects of Jewish activity in the city had been reflected in the Arab refusal to allow Balfour, during

1. Ottoman Jerusalem, inside the Jaffa Gate, looking towards David Street and the Old City bazaar. On the right (the building with four large windows) is the Austrian Post Office. On the left, the German Palestine Bank. *(Keren Hayesod photographic archive)*

2. ABOVE The first decade of the century, Bezalel art students at an open-air art class. *(Central Zionist Archives)*

3. LEFT Jewish troops in the Austro–Hungarian Army among the worshippers at the Wailing Wall during the First World War. *(Jewish Agency Archives)*

4. General Allenby entering Jerusalem on foot, as a mark of respect to the city, December 1917. The breach in the Ottoman wall, made in 1898 so that the German Kaiser could enter on horseback, is in front of the mounted officer. The Turkish clock tower, a recent construction, was thought by the British to distort the line of the wall, and was taken down. *(Imperial War Museum)*

5. Turkish prisoners-of-war are brought in to Jerusalem, 1918, watched by British troops. *(Imperial War Museum)*

6. Two British soldiers of the 40th Battalion, Royal Fusiliers, with their most recent Jewish recruits, 1918. *(Central Zionist Archives)*

7. The British war cemetery on Mount Scopus, overlooking the Old City, a photograph taken in 1919. The wooden crosses were later replaced by stone headstones. *(Elia Photographic Service)*

8. Herbert Samuel, the first British High Commissioner to Palestine, accompanies Winston Churchill to the Hebrew University tree-planting ceremony in March 1921. Jewish girl guides line the route. *(Central Zionist Archives)*

9. King Abdullah of Transjordan, Herbert Samuel and Winston Churchill at Government House. Behind them are James de Rothschild (left) and Ronald Storrs (between Samuel and Churchill). *(Central Zionist Archives)*

10. British soldiers look at the Crusader portals of the Church of the Holy Sepulchre. *(Imperial War Museum)*

11. Muslim soldiers from the British Indian Army present arms outside one of Islam's holiest places, the Dome of the Rock, as the Kadi of the Haram looks on. *(Hanna Safieh photographic archive)*

12. The Nebi Musa festival: the marchers from Hebron reach the Jaffa Gate with their banners. It was during the Nebi Musa festival in April 1920 that the first anti-Jewish riots broke out in Jerusalem. *(Jewish Agency Archives)*

13. A British Indian soldier searches a Greek Orthodox priest. *(Hanna Safieh photographic archive)*

14. Haj Amin al-Husseini, a member of one of Jerusalem's leading Muslim families, and Mufti of Jerusalem from 1921 until he fled from the city in 1937. *(Hanna Safieh photographic archive)*

15. The Wailing Wall, until 1967 reached by a narrow lane in the Muslim Moghrabi quarter. At the top of the Wall is the Temple Mount, known to Muslims as the Haram al-Sharif (the Noble Sanctuary), on which are the Dome of the Rock, the al-Aksa Mosque, and several Muslim places of prayer and study. A fifteenth-century minaret overlooks both the Wailing Wall and the Haram. *(Jewish Agency Archives)*

his stay in the city, to listen to the Christian Arab choirboys at St George's Cathedral, or to enter the precincts of the Haram. Before the First World War the Russian Jew Mendel Beilis had been welcomed to the Haram as a hero; eleven years later a former British Prime Minister and Foreign Secretary was being boycotted as a protest against Jewish immigration.

Among the many non-dignitaries at the opening ceremony was a Jewish agricultural labourer, Eliahu Epstein. Together with a group of fellow labourers he had walked forty miles from the coastal plain in order to be present. Arriving on Mount Scopus, he and his friends had found all the seats occupied by the many thousands of invited guests. He therefore climbed a pine tree at the edge of the amphitheatre, and watched the inauguration ceremony of the institution of which, forty years later, he was to become President.

Another of those who had come to the ceremony was an elderly Jew from Haifa, Hayim Schwartz, whose son Reuven had been executed by the Turks in 1917 as a Nili spy. Not having the money to travel by horse-drawn carriage, Hayim Schwartz was on his way by foot from Haifa when he was seen by his niece and her husband, who were also on their way, by carriage, to the ceremony. They took him along. Seventy years later that niece's son, Menahem Milson, a distinguished Arabist, was Dean of the Faculty of Humanities.

Only two small research institutes were added to the existing Institutes for Jewish Studies and Chemistry at the time of the opening ceremony: one for chemistry research and the other for research in microbiology. The latter was headed by Professor Saul Adler from England. But funds for the university building programme, including several more research institutes and a considerable expansion of the library, were soon acquired through the philanthropy of Jews worldwide. Among the principal benefactors in the first five years were Jews from Prague, Vienna, Berlin, Frankfurt, Stuttgart, Cracow, London, New York, Detroit and Sydney.

*

'Now the Jewish element in Jerusalem is about ten times what it was then,' Canon Hanauer wrote in his 1926 guidebook, recalling that in 1846 there were an estimated 8,000 Jews there. 'The city is, to a great extent, Jewish,' Hanauer added. 'This is especially noticeable on Saturday, the Jewish Sabbath, when Hebrew shops are closed; and as the peasantry do not find it worth their while to bring their farm produce to market on that day, the public thoroughfares generally regain the quiet Sabbath-air brought about originally by the influence of Nehemiah' – 2,372 years earlier.

That same year, 1926, Jerusalem saw a strange development: the establishment of a kibbutz within the municipal border. It was created by left-wing Zionists, pioneers of a self-proclaimed Labour Legion. The site they chose was Ramat Rahel, on a hilltop at the southern extremity of the city, from which one could see the Jaffa Gate, the Dome of the Rock and the Mount of Olives. Archaeological digs subsequently revealed that the hilltop had been inhabited at the time of Solomon, 3,000 years earlier. The discovery of a pagan statuette on the site raised the intriguing possibility that this might well have been the hill on which Solomon built the palace for his non-Jewish wives. According to legend, he had married one of these, Pharaoh's daughter, on the day on which, on the Temple Mount, he had dedicated the Temple.

The remains of a Roman fortress were also uncovered at Ramat Rahel, together with a Roman bathhouse. There were also the foundations of a fifth-century Christian church: according to Byzantine tradition, Mary, the mother of Jesus, had rested on this hilltop on her way to Bethlehem to give birth. It is not only the walls of Jerusalem to the north, but the town of Bethlehem to the south, that can be seen from the kibbutz gardens.

The members of the kibbutz had little or no time for the legends of the past. They had to create, on a bare and often fiercely windswept hilltop, living quarters, a communal dining-room, orchards and a farm. Their achievement survives to this day, enhanced by one of Jerusalem's most popular swimming-pools, complete with water slide.

*

In the summer of 1926 a young American scholar, Jacob Rader Marcus, spent three months at the Hebrew University. Before leaving, he wrote to Dr Magnes with his impressions and suggestions. He was troubled by what he regarded as too narrow a focus in the fledgling Hebrew University. 'I wish that this new school would be filled with the social spirit and the finer nationalism that is so true of the better American colleges,' he wrote. 'The University dare not be an academic factory; it must not only produce students, but also Jews who are conscious of their social obligations to the Jewish people and its cultural traditions.' It would also provide the 'authority' needed by world Jewry. 'Good God, with what it costs to establish a group of Jewish colonies about the size of a North Dakota farm we could build up a University here that would revolutionise World Jewry and start the blood pounding through its veins.' This was a vision of what a thinking, imaginative, constructive, cultured Jewish world could become with Jerusalem at its centre. But Dr Marcus had also seen the problems of Arab-Jewish relations. 'I find the Arabs very nationalistic,' he wrote. 'I despair of any working agreement between the two groups, particularly since England will always be able to exercise – to the detriment of Arabic-Jewish concord – her traditional policy of a "balance of power".'

Dr Magnes was more confident that a way could be found to bring Arab and Jew together.

*

On 7 May 1927 Field Marshal Viscount Allenby, as General Allenby had become, returned to Jerusalem for the unveiling ceremony at the British Military Cemetery on Mount Scopus, henceforth known as the Jerusalem War Memorial Cemetery. He was also to lay the foundation stone of the Hospice and Church of St Andrew, the Scottish Church. This church commemorated Robert Bruce, King of Scotland, who had wanted his heart to be buried in Jerusalem, in redemption of his unfulfilled vow to visit the Holy City. After Bruce's death in 1329 a fellow Scot had set out with the embalmed heart but was killed fighting the Moors in Spain. The heart was returned to Scotland and buried at Melrose. Allenby now spoke of his pride at the 'heroes from Scotland' who had been among the liberators of Jerusalem in 1917. To this day the St Andrew's Cross flies above the church.

Several new Jewish suburbs were under construction in 1927, including Sanhedriya to the north of the city and Mekor Hayim to the south. The Franciscans were building the Terra Sancta College, and the Jesuits the Pontifical Biblical Institute, both in western Jerusalem.

That year the destructive forces of nature affected old and new buildings in Jerusalem when, on July 12, the city was shaken by an earthquake. One man and two women were killed. One of the worst affected buildings was Government House, the former Augusta Victoria Hospice. Other buildings which suffered damage were the Hebrew University on Mount Scopus, the Church of the Holy Sepulchre, the Abyssinian Palace, the Bezalel School of Arts and Crafts, and the al-Aksa Mosque, almost all of whose magnificent columns were seriously weakened, as were its central ceiling, the eastern transept and the stone floor. The process of renewal took time. It was not until 1938, following a second serious tremor, that the columns of al-Aksa were replaced: Benito Mussolini, the Italian dictator, provided the Carrara marble as a gift from the Italian people.

One of the Jewish buildings destroyed in the earthquake was the Beit-el Yeshiva, one of the oldest religious seminaries in the Jewish Quarter. It had been founded nearly 200 years earlier, in 1737, by Rabbi Gedalia Hayon, who had come to Jerusalem from Turkey to teach cabbala, the mystical aspect of Jewish study. The yeshiva was rebuilt almost immediately.

An Earthquake Relief Fund was set up, which raised nine million Egyptian pounds. Five million came from a single donor, the American Jewish philanthropist Nathan Straus, who stressed that his donation was to go 'to destitute persons of all races and creeds'. Others who gave generously were two intellectual leaders on opposite sides of the Arab-Jewish political divide: the Christian Arab writer George Antonius and the Zionist writer Harry Sacher. It was Sacher's wife, Miriam, who had been the moving force, three years earlier, for the establishment of the Jerusalem Baby Home, a residential home for abandoned and neglected babies, the first such home in the Middle East. She also established a school for nursery nurses. Under the auspices of the Women's International Zionist Organisation (WIZO), of which her sister Rebecca Sieff was a founder, the Baby Home became a focal point of care and support for infants who would otherwise almost certainly have perished.

In 1925, the year after the establishment of the Jerusalem Baby Home in Jewish Jerusalem, Bertha Vester, the daughter of the founder of the American Colony, founded the Spafford Centre, just inside the Damascus Gate, as a training-centre and clinic for Muslim girls. Among those who helped her, and also helped the Jerusalem Baby Home, was the Russian-born Jewish paediatrician, Dr Helena Kagan, who had begun her own nursing work in Jerusalem under the Turks.

*

On 5 March 1928 Herbert Samuel's successor as High Commissioner, Field Marshal Viscount Plumer, a distinguished First World War commander, opened Jerusalem's first Arts and Crafts Exhibition. It was held in the Citadel at the Jaffa Gate. 'All goods are bona fide productions of the people of Palestine,' the invitation read, 'and all districts and all sections of the population are represented.' The

Tower of David was reserved for crafts from Jerusalem, Bethlehem and Ramallah. Elsewhere in the citadel were the wares from Haifa, Gaza and Beersheba. According to the official record of the occasion: 'Ladies volunteered to serve in different stalls, where objects could be sold or ordered, and tea was served each afternoon.'

It was in 1928 that the British began one of their most ambitious projects for Jerusalem – pumped water. That year a water-pump was installed at the Ayin Farrah spring in the Wadi Kelt, several hundred feet below the city on the eastern side, towards Jericho. The pump meant that the city no longer depended on the flow of gravity from Solomon's Pools in the hills south of Bethlehem. Over the next seven years, two more pumps were installed in the Wadi Kelt, at the Ayin Fawwar and Ayin Kelt springs. Then, in 1936, an eighteen-inch-diameter pipe was laid to bring water from the other side of the Judaean Hills, from Ras al-Ayin on the edge of the coastal plain. The nearly 2,000-foot rise was made possible by four pumping-stations along the forty mile route.

The garden cities that were being established in Jerusalem were models of urban planning. The builders of Rehavia, the first homes of which were built in 1922, had a regulation that at least two-thirds of every building plot 'must be sacrificed for gardens and fresh air, and between every two houses a good space must be allowed'. Two kindergartens, and two tennis courts, had also been constructed in Rehavia. Education, culture, music, friendship, all found a fertile soil in the new suburbs. Over these civilised developments, however, a General Muslim Conference, meeting in Jerusalem on 1 November 1928 under the presidency of the Mufti, cast a dark shadow. After establishing a Society for the Protection of Muslim Holy places, the conference issued an ominous statement warning of 'the danger which threatens the Mosque owing to the ambitions of the Jews to expropriate it from the hands of the Muslims'. No such danger existed, but the authority of the Mufti was proof to many Arabs in the city that the danger was a real one.

*

When, on 19 November 1928, the music-loving Austrians celebrated in Vienna the centenary of Schubert's death, so too did the European-born Jews of Jerusalem. Alexander Baerwald, a state architect of Berlin, and the London-born Thelma Yellin, were among those who played at the Schubert concert given that evening in Jerusalem.

Thelma Yellin, who had married into a leading Jerusalemite family, was responsible for setting up the first of the two kindergartens in Rehavia. She was also a cellist of distinction. Under her inspiration, weekly chamber-music concerts were given in Jerusalem – the Saturday Evening 'Pops'. But the joys of music were soon to be overshadowed by even greater disturbances than before, as riots and death returned to the streets of Jerusalem in the late summer of 1929.

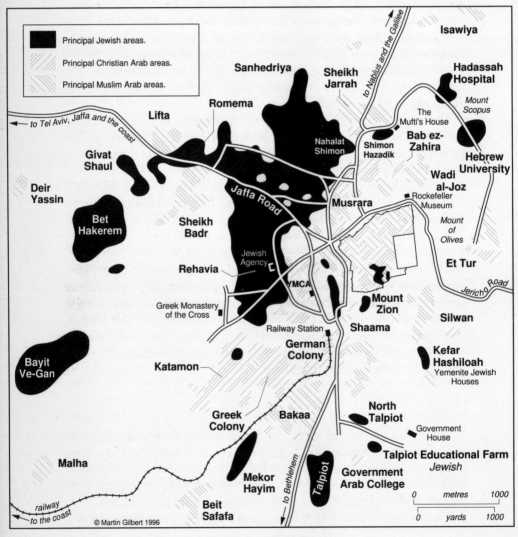

Jewish and Arab neighbourhoods by 1929

CHAPTER EIGHT

The Riots of 1929

In the autumn of 1928 there had been an ill omen of political dissension to come in Jerusalem. On September 23 that year, the eve of Yom Kippur, the Day of Atonement, religious Jews put up a screen to divide men from women at the Wailing Wall. A physical division between the the sexes was imperative according to Jewish religious law. Every Orthodox synagogue, large or small, separates the women worshippers from the men. The screen was simply intended to give physical recognition to that fact. But the Muslim religious officials in the city at once declared that the screen was a construction that altered the British-sponsored 'status quo' at the Wall. They also said that it obstructed a right of way, even though the short alleyway where the screen stood led nowhere, and was exclusively a Jewish place of worship, and an intensely holy one at that. As a result of these protests, British police constables were instructed to have the screen removed.

The constables arrived during services on the following day, the most solemn in the Jewish calendar. No Jewish police officer was present, as would normally have been the case, because it was the Day of Atonement and they had all been excused from duty. The officer in charge at the Wall that day, Police Inspector D. V. Duff, asked the worshippers to remove the screen. The worshippers, men and women, pointed out that they were in the middle of a particularly holy prayer. Duff then ordered the constables to remove the screen. The men and women resisted, and several were hurt. The screen was torn, and then taken away.

The Muslim Arabs were jubilant that the screen had been taken down. They also wanted to warn of dark Jewish plots. Speaking in the name of the Supreme Muslim Council, the Mufti declared: 'The Jews' aim is to take possession of the Mosque of al-Aksa gradually.'

At the instigation of the Mufti, the Arabs changed the cul-de-sac in front of the wall into a thoroughfare, by knocking down an old wall at one end of it. They also organised noisy Muslim calls for prayer from a nearby rooftop. Nor were these the only provocations. Even more inflammatory, faked photographs were circulated to the Muslim faithful showing the Jewish flag, with the Star of David at its centre, flying from the top of the Dome of the Rock – something which had never happened.

To the distress of the Jews, the British authorities endorsed the transformation of the cul-de-sac into a thoroughfare, and took no steps to minimise the irritation caused to Jewish worshippers by the deliberately loud Muslim calls to prayer. It was a situation fraught with danger. The following summer, on 15 August 1929, a group of young Jews responded with provocative action of their own, marching to the Wailing Wall through the Muslim Quarter of the Old City waving Jewish national flags and singing patriotic Zionist songs. On the following day, by way of retaliation, a huge Muslim protest demonstration was held, not on the Haram, the usual site of such gatherings, but at the Wailing Wall itself. The few Jewish worshippers present were forced to flee and hide, the beadle in charge of the Wall was assaulted, and Hebrew prayer books were torn up and burned.

A day later a Jewish boy, Abraham Mizrachi, inadvertently kicked a football into an Arab garden. When he went to get it back, he was set upon and stabbed. He died in hospital three days later. On the morning of August 23, following the boy's funeral, Jewish vigilantes marched towards the Jaffa Gate, intent on attacking the Muslim Quarter. They were prevented from entering the Old City by the police, and twenty-four of the youths were injured. There was an air of growing tension throughout the city. At noon several thousand Muslims poured from the Haram after morning prayers and made for the Old City gates.

Edwin Samuel, then serving as private secretary to the Officer Administering the Government, was working in his office just outside the Damascus Gate. 'The first we knew that anything was wrong', he later wrote, 'was a faint and distant shouting, like the ominous buzz of bees. Looking out from the balcony, I could see small groups of men running out of the Old City through the next exit, the New Gate, and pouring down the hill to the Damascus Gate. Other Arabs came running out of the Damascus Gate itself and attacked any Jewish passers-by they happened to meet. I could see in the sunshine the flash of daggers that most peasants carried. Some Jews ran and escaped: others took refuge in nearby Arab houses and were mostly saved; some were attacked indoors and killed.

'A few Arab mounted police with long staves arrived and tried to drive the crowds back into the Old City; but ten times their number could not have restrained the mob. Egged on by shouts from agitators, the crowd grew more excited by the minute: the noise of the crowd out for blood is truly frightening. The Commandant of the Palestine Police Force, Colonel Alan Saunders, arrived to take personal charge of the situation. But, by then, it was already out of hand, and he came into the office, hot, dusty, spattered with blood, to telephone for reinforcements.'

Just beyond the Damascus Gate was a row of houses (they are still there today) built before the turn of the century by a group of Jews who had come from the Georgian region of the Caucasus. Theirs was a small community that had lived in harmony with its Arab neighbours for three decades. That harmony was swiftly broken. 'There was simply a massacre,' the English-language *Palestine Bulletin* reported. 'The mob broke into houses and slaughtered the inhabitants, the Jewish population in this section being too small to resist.'

With considerable courage, several prominent Muslim Arabs, among them Fakhri Bey al-Nashashibi, came out into the street near the Jaffa Gate and appealed to the mob to desist, but they were swept aside. That afternoon and evening there were attacks on Jewish houses in all the outlying suburbs, including Kiryat Moshe and Romema at the entrance to the city, and Bet Hakerem and Bayit Vegan to the west. So fierce was the attack at Bayit Vegan that the suburb had to be evacuated. In the attack on Bet Hakerem, as the Arab mob looted and burned house after house, the residents gathered in the recently built Teachers' Seminary building, where they sheltered for three nights, terrified of trying to return to their homes.

In the Jewish suburb of Zikhron Moshe a synagogue was burned down. In response, Jews from Zikhron Moshe began to vandalise a nearby mosque that contained some Muslim tombs. They were dispersed by the Jewish civil authorities in the city, who then posted a Jewish guard at the mosque until the position could be secured by the police.

At seven o'clock that evening a band of Arabs, armed with rifles, attacked the Jewish garden suburb of Talpiot. The defenders gathered in one of the houses and, armed with a single rifle and a few pistols, drove the attackers off. The attack was renewed in the early hours of August 24, when one Jew was killed. Among those helping the defenders were three Englishmen, students at Oxford University who were among a group of forty spending that summer in Jerusalem.

*

The British authorities were ill-prepared and their forces ill-equipped to deal with rioting on such a scale. The number of British policemen in the city was small – less than 200. Most of the uniformed police were Arabs, who were reluctant to open fire on their fellow Arabs. On August 23 the Deputy District Commissioner of the Jerusalem Division, Edward Keith-Roach, issued a three-part order intended to halt the rioting. All places selling intoxicating liquor had to close after six in the evening. Police officers were 'to disperse any assembly whatever in any public place' and to arrest without warrant 'any person in such assembly refusing or delaying to disperse, or reassembling after dispersal'.

The third part of Keith-Roach's order read: 'Any person found in any public place in possession of any knife, stick, bludgeon, iron bar, stone or weapon of any sort or description which in the opinion of the Police Officer he is carrying for the purpose of assisting in a disturbance, or is likely to use in case of a disturbance, and any person inciting others to assemble either by word or by writing or by other means, and any person singing a song or making use of words or gestures which in the opinion of a Police Officer are likely to lead to a breach of the peace may be arrested without warrant and is liable to fine and imprisonment.'

These were strong words, but their effect was not immediate. On August 24 the attack on Talpiot had become so persistent and so fierce that by late afternoon all women and children were sent to the New City for safety. After their departure the men were concentrated in three houses. At half-past six a British armoured car arrived and the officers ordered the defenders to move some way down the street, to the house of a noted biblical scholar, Mordechai Caspi. The armoured car then left. The *Palestine Bulletin* reported the sequel: 'Immediately the Arabs descended on the vacant houses, looted them, stripped them entirely of all their belongings, and broke what furniture they could not carry with them.'

Sixteen houses were looted. 'Much of the loot was scattered about neighbouring Arab villages,' the *Palestine Bulletin* reported, 'and some of it was offered for sale at ridiculous prices in Bethlehem.' Two precious libraries, that of Joseph Klausner, Professor of Hebrew

Literature at the Hebrew University, and that of the author S. J. Agnon, were completely destroyed. Among Agnon's literary treasures had been 3,000 rare documents relating to the history of Palestine over the past three centuries.

Despite Keith-Roach's proclamation, August 24 saw a series of attacks in Jerusalem and outside it. During the day an Arab mob attacked Jewish worshippers and passers-by at the Wailing Wall. A Jew was assaulted at the American Colony. In the Old City, a Russian Christian who was mistaken for a Jew was severely beaten. At Motza, five miles west of the city on the Tel Aviv road, Arabs broke into the home of the Maklev family. Five members of the family were murdered, as were two Jews from Tel Aviv who were staying with them for the summer, eighty-five-year-old Rabbi Shach and sixty-eight-year-old Mr Glaser. Several houses near the Maklev home were also looted and burned. The attackers had come from the nearby Arab village of Kolonia.

Also attacked by the rioters was Kibbutz Ramat Rahel. One member of the kibbutz was killed, and after the others had been driven away the rioters laid waste to the three-year-old settlement. In the Arab village of Deir Yassin, just to the west of Jerusalem, an Arab gunman shot dead a British Immigration Officer, E. T. Best. He was to have been married that very week.

Further from Jerusalem there were further killings, including the massacre of fifty-nine Jews in Hebron, eighteen miles away. Five rabbis were among the dead, as were eight American students studying at a religious seminary there. Most of the Jews in Hebron who escaped owed their lives to the protection of Arab friends.

*

On August 25 fifty British troops arrived by plane from Egypt to take up positions in Jerusalem. By the time the riots were over, thirty-one Jews had been killed by Arabs in the city, and more than 100 wounded. Not only the death toll but the large number of injuries, and the destruction of hundreds of Jewish homes, sharpened the divide between the Arab and Jewish communities. More than 300 Jews had been injured by Arab rioters. Nearly 4,000 Jews were forced to leave their homes.

Hundreds of Jewish refugees from abandoned suburbs and villages came to Jerusalem for safety and succour. Hundreds of wounded were brought to the Hadassah Hospital in the Street of the Prophets. On a visit to the hospital, Mrs Corrie, the wife of the Senior British

Judge, wept on seeing the wounded, many of whom had been mutilated by the rioters. Among the wounded was Mr Viney, one of the
Oxford students who had come to the aid of the Jews in Talpiot.

*

The Muslim Arab leaders wanted to make sure that the purpose
of the riots was understood, and in a memorandum to the High
Commissioner they set out their demands: the disarmament of the
Jews, the establishment of a parliament in Palestine, and the withdrawal of the Balfour Declaration. Throughout the Muslim world it
was falsely stated that the Jews had provoked the disturbances by
'desecrating the Mosque of Omar'. Chief Rabbi Kook at once invited
the most prominent Muslim representatives 'of religion and science'
to come to Jerusalem and verify the truth: the Dome of the Rock
was intact.

The Mufti, Haj Amin al-Husseini, issued his own statement: 'Jews
have given continual provocation since August 15 when a Zionist
demonstration walked unauthorised through Moslem streets to Al
Burak (the Wailing Wall), which is purely a Moslem property, where
the Zionist flag was illegally hoisted. Moslems were insulted there,
and subjected to individual attacks by Jews. This was the immediate
cause of the trouble.'

The question of the Wailing Wall was taken up in a letter to *The
Times* in London by the British Zionist, Harry Sacher, who had
recently returned to England after eight years in legal practice in
Palestine. His letter was published on August 29. 'The Wailing Wall
is not a part of the western wall of the Mosque of Omar,' he wrote,
in an attempt to answer Muslim allegations. 'It is a considerable
distance from the Mosque structure. The area adjacent to the Wall
is not Moslem public property, but is private Wakf, "a kind of entail
with only a formal semblance of piety about it". So little sanctity do
the Moslems attach to this area that they are in the habit of driving
donkeys laden with dung across the pavement immediately in front
of the wall where Jews pray.

'The practice of Jews praying in front of the Wailing Wall goes
back for many centuries, and in the 10th Century, before all the
buildings now in existence in the Haram area were constructed there
was a Jewish sanctuary at the Wailing Wall, within the Haram area,
for which a Jewish vizier devoted large sums of money. In the White
Paper issued by the Colonial Office in 1928, the Jewish right of
public worship at the Wall is specifically and repeatedly acknowl-

edged. Article 13 of the Mandate guarantees to Jews and to other sects in respect of the Holy Places free access thereto and the free exercise of worship. These rights are further guaranteed in articles 14, 15 and 16 of the Mandate.

'In the White Paper already referred to, the Secretary of State declared that: "Public opinion in Palestine has definitely removed the matter from the purely religious orbit, and has made it a political and racial question." In bringing about that transformation, with all the unhappy consequences, now visible, no one has been more active than the Mufti of Jerusalem.'

*

News of the riots in Jerusalem had made headlines throughout the world. On August 30 a telegram from Reuters news agency was telegraphed to all its subscribers: 'Jerusalem has now been a city of death for eight days during which work has ceased and people are starving. Hundreds are receiving bread rations. Everywhere it is deadly quiet, and everyone is very nervous.'

Amid all the intensity of conflict, several examples of life-saving cooperation were made public. On September 3 an article in the *Palestine Bulletin* told of four Jewish workers at the Rockefeller Museum building works 'saved from death by Arab comrades who bravely opposed a large Moslem mob'. The paper also told the story of a group of Georgian Jews living in the Mendel Rand Quarter who, excited by the massacre of the Georgian Jewish Quarter, wanted to kill an Arab servant. The Arab was saved by local Jews, while other Jewish residents nearby hid his property in their houses for safety. The paper also reported: 'A Jewish milkman in the Schneller Quarter employed three Arab women servants. Jews wanted to kill them but some members of the self-defence organisation opposed them with revolvers and prevented the murder. They escorted the women to their village.' Jews had protected Arabs from Jews.

The attacks on Jews had not ended. On September 3 a group of Arabs on horseback attacked Talpiot, but were driven off by British troops. Six days later two Jewish homes were looted in Bet Hakerem. That day, in a second public statement, the Mufti declared: 'Jewish ambition and greed are deliberately responsible for provoking the Arab attack, in order to gain the support of the whole world.'

Less than three weeks after the start of the riots, Arab hostility to the Jews expressed itself in calls for their destruction. On September

11 the Muslim Orphanage Press, the official publication house of the Supreme Muslim Council, issued a printed proclamation, a students' 'appeal to the sons of the Fatherland' which began: 'You Arab, cut off your commercial relations with the Jews!' The proclamation urged Arabs not to do business with the Jews, 'who killed your innocent Arab brethren with weapons purchased with the money you paid in buying his goods, and which he intends to utilise for the acquisition of the land remaining in your hands in order to drive you away from your Fatherland'.

In buying anything from the Jews, the pamphlet warned, 'you will yourself work for the extermination of your life and your country with your own hands, and will betray your Fatherland and religion'. Arabs should buy nothing from Jews except land, and should sell everything to the Jews except land. The proclamation pointed out that there was a religious basis to the economic boycott of Jewish goods, the words of the 'upright' Caliph Omar Ben Khutab: 'The foreigner shall overcome you in trade which is one third of domination.'

The Palestinian-Arab proclamation continued: 'O Arab! Remember that the Jew is your strongest enemy and the enemy of your ancestors since olden times. Do not be misled by his tricks for it is he who tortured Christ, peace be upon him, and poisoned Mohammed, peace and worship be with him. It is he who now endeavours to slaughter you as he did yesterday. Be aware that the best way to save yourself and your Fatherland from the grasp of the foreign intruder and greedy Jew is to boycott him. Therefore boycott him and support the industry of your Fatherland and God.'

This Arab boycott of Jewish goods took place four years before a similar boycott was enacted in Berlin. At the time, it was inconceivable to the Jews of Jerusalem that their troubles would be mirrored, and soon massively overtaken, by anti-Jewish actions in one of the great centres of western civilisation. There was nothing but pity among the half-million Jews of Germany during 1929 for the plight of their half-million fellow Jews in Palestine.

Could the gulf between Jew and Arab be bridged? 'We are convinced,' wrote the head of the Palestine Zionist Executive, Colonel Kisch, on September 12, 'that were it not for the fact that through the circulation of deliberately false reports calculated to stir up their feelings – such as the allegations that the Mosque of Omar had been bombed, looted or burnt – the Arabs of Palestine would have continued to live in peaceful relations with their Jewish neighbours, as is still the wish of the overwhelming majority of the Arab population'.

That same day, the day after the Arab pamphlet called for a boycott of Jewish goods, Harry Sacher told the Zionist General Council in London: 'The Arab question should be treated respectfully and seriously. Every Palestine Jew should try to get on human and friendly relations with the Arabs.' This was also the view of the President of the Hebrew University, Judah L. Magnes, who, following the riots, called for Jewish-Arab harmony both for the building-up of the country and for the sake of the Jewish spirit. At the opening of the new academic year on Mount Scopus, he told the teachers and students: 'One of the greatest cultural duties of the Jewish people is the attempt to enter the promised land, not by means of conquest as Joshua, but through peaceful and cultural means, through hard work, sacrifices, love, and with a decision not to do anything which cannot be justified before the world conscience.'

With Jerusalem's two dozen Jewish and Arab suburbs intertwined, the chance of harmony seemed difficult, if not impossible. This was made clear on 26 October 1929, when a Palestinian-Arab Women's Conference was convened in the city, at the home of Tarab Abdul Hadi. An executive committee of fourteen was created, drawn mainly from the principal Arab families of Jerusalem, and as their first act they visited the High Commissioner, to demand the rescinding of the Balfour Declaration and a halt to Jewish immigration.

Once again the British found themselves confronted by demands which they were determined not to countenance, with regard both to Britain's promises to the Jews and to its treatment of Arab rioters. In addition to a halt to Jewish immigration, the women demanded the repeal of the British administration's Collective Punishment Ordinance, whereby a whole family and even a whole village could be punished for a riotous act by one of its members. They also demanded a drastic improvement in the treatment of Arab prisoners. These demands having been rejected, the women decided to demonstrate in the streets. In a move which exploited to the full the patriarchal nature of Arab society, the High Commissioner persuaded the men who headed the main Palestinian families to caution their womenfolk not to take to the streets.

Yet the national aspirations of many Palestinian-Arab women led them to break the taboos and restrictions imposed upon them by their social position as women. To this day, the names of Matiel Moghanon, Zlikha Shihabi and Zahiya al-Nashashibi are remembered in East Jerusalem for having broken the social mould of female passivity, and for having raised aloft the banner of the Palestinian national cause. Through the Arab Women's Association, they did undertake women's demonstrations in the streets. They also raised funds, made contact with women's organisations in Europe, and continued to confront the British officials with their demands.

Relief for the poor, a reduction of taxation, an ending to the discrimination against Arabs, and an improvement in the treatment of Palestinian-Arab prisoners were among the main causes espoused by the Jerusalem women activists. Within a decade, however, their unity of purpose was broken, when, as a result of the rivalry between the al-Husseini and al-Nashashibi families, the Arab Women's Association split in two. They had nevertheless been pioneers in the assertion of Arab women's rights, and in their fight for Palestinian-Arab nationalism.

CHAPTER NINE

The Search for Normality, 1930–1936

In January 1930 a thirty-three-year-old German doctor, Julius Kleeberg, left Frankfurt for Jerusalem. He had been invited to become Chief Physician at the Bikur Holim Hospital in the city. Between the arrival of his invitation and his departure from Germany the riots had broken out. 'But I disregarded such matters as riots and financial stringency,' he later wrote. 'I assumed that this new environment would pose all kinds of exciting medical problems unknown in Germany. Perhaps I could make some important research discovery? I was certain that there would be few physicians in Palestine with qualifications to match mine; I had studied medicine, pathology, anatomy and chemistry. Finally, perhaps most important of all, I was motivated by my desire for adventure; I longed to see a new and fabled part of the world. The name "Jerusalem" was like a magnet; was it not the most famous and most hallowed city in the world? So my motives were not at all Zionistic; they were a mixture of romanticism and ambition. Of course, I assumed that I would be provided with a well-equipped laboratory and a substantial budget for research, such as all heads of departments had in Germany. I planned to apply modern scientific methods to vanquish medical problems as old as time. For years I had lived in an ivory castle; I had no idea what was waiting for me in Jerusalem.'

Dr Kleeberg found a hospital, and a medical system, with far fewer facilities than even a below-average hospital in Germany. But the will to improve was enormous in Jerusalem: two of the most active forces for higher standards were Dr Albert Ticho, the ophthalmologist whose treatment of the Arabs was so remarkable that the word 'ticho' entered the local Arabic language as 'ophthalmologist', and Dr Helena Kagan, the paediatrician who had come to Jerusalem from Russia during the Ottoman time.

*

It was in 1930 that one of the most impressive buildings in the New City was built; the King David Hotel. It was commissioned by two Egyptian Jews who owned the already famous Shepheard's Hotel in Cairo, and was designed for them by two Swiss architects, Emile Vogt and G. A. Hufschmid. The decorations inside the hotel were remarkable even for Jerusalem. The motif which they chose for the lobby was Assyrian, for the lounge Hittite and for the dining-room Phoenician. 'Tall Sudanese waiters, each attired in white pantaloons and a red tarboosh, slid silently along freshly waxed marble floors carrying precious trays above their heads,' Nitza Rosovsky wrote half a century later, 'trays laden with pots of tea blended in India and Ceylon, buttered toast that always stayed warm, exotic jams, starched linen napkins. Those elegant days are gone for ever.'

It was not only elegant houses and hotels that were going up in Jerusalem in 1930. Impressive civic buildings were also being constructed. One was a new municipality building, which was to serve successive mayors of the city, from Ragheb Bey al-Nashashibi to Teddy Kollek, for more than sixty years. Another was the nearby Generali Building, designed by the Italian architect Marcello Piacenti, and named for the Italian insurance company which owned it. The roof was adorned by a winged lion carved in stone.

Throughout 1930 the Jews of Jerusalem worked to rebuild the houses and suburbs damaged during the riots. The village of Motza was rebuilt, and a new section, Upper Motza, was founded by professional Jews working in Jerusalem, who at the same time embarked on small-scale farming and nursery gardening. Rebuilding was also in process at Kibbutz Ramat Rahel, which had been completely laid waste only three years after its pioneers had begun it. During the rebuilding, however, an ideological debate broke out which was as fierce as the pace of reconstruction – so much so that a split developed between those members who wished to follow a socialist philosophy and those who were more attracted by Soviet Communism.

Tragically for those involved, the ideological split was not to be healed by debate. Some Communist kibbutzniks from elsewhere in Palestine had already returned to the Soviet Union, and were given a large farm in the Crimea on which to practise their pure ideology. Eighty Communist members of Ramat Rahel decided to join them, and made their way to the Soviet Union, leaving only forty to work their Jerusalem fields.

In Russia, Stalin's regime welcomed the Jerusalem kibbutzniks as returnees from a 'capitalist hell', even though, as one of them, Shira Gorshman later recalled, there was a lack of food, clothing and shoes. Within five years, many of those who had returned were caught up in Stalin's purges and sent to Siberia. Some of them died there, including their leader, Menachem-Mendel Elkind. Others joined the Red Army at the time of the German invasion of Russia, or made their way to Moscow and other cities. When the German armies reached the Crimea in 1942 a local peasant informed the Germans of the existence of the remnants of a Jewish collective farm. All the remaining Jews, mostly women and children, were rounded up and thrown alive into a deep well, where they perished.

Only after the death of Stalin did a handful of the survivors of Ramat Rahel's exodus emerge from their grim experiences in the Soviet Union and, in due course, make their way back to Jerusalem.

*

Since the first years of British rule, the population of Jerusalem had grown faster than at any time in the city's history. Britain's 1922 declaration, subsequently enshrined in the League of Nations Mandate, that the Jews were in Palestine 'of right, and not on sufferance', affected Jerusalem as much as any other part of the country. By 1931 the city's population had grown from 91,272 in 1922, the first year of the Mandate, to 132,661. Jewish immigration accounted for an extra 20,107 inhabitants. But the British census reports show that an even larger number of Arabs, 21,282 in all, took advantage of the increased amenities of the city – amenities which were Britain's great contribution: paved streets and pleasant suburbs, piped running water, effective municipal services, and enhanced commercial activity. Jerusalem was a capital city for the first time since the crusades.

The British census returns gave the country of origin of all the city's new inhabitants. In some cases the numbers of Jews and Arabs were quite similar. Thus 365 Jews and 443 Arabs came to Jerusalem from Egypt. The figure for Turkey was 1,039 Jews and 2,367 Arabs. The largest numbers of Jewish immigrants were from Poland (5,714), the Soviet Union (4,413), Iraq (2,670), Persia (2,076) and Britain (1,650). There were Jews who came from every country in Europe, as well as from India (48). The Arab immigration also included India (31). From the United States 358 Jews and 21 Arabs had emigrated to Jerusalem in that nine-year period. Thirty-two Jews and one Arab had come from Australia.

On 6 December 1931 a World Islamic Conference opened in Jerusalem. This initiative by the Mufti marked the culmination of his ten years' work to gain prominence, and indeed predominance, for Jerusalem throughout the Islamic world. In this he had succeeded, creating a heightened Muslim awareness worldwide of the sanctity of the city. He had also succeeded in characterising the Jews as the enemy of Islam in Jerusalem.

To the dismay of many Jewish Jerusalemites, the conference organisers decided that, owing to the attitude taken by Jews 'in persisting to misrepresent all Moslem or Arab affairs, no Jews will be admitted'. As the conference continued its meetings, the focus of press attention was on the disputes among the Palestinian-Arab delegates, some of whom were strongly opposed to the Mufti's strident anti-Jewish leadership. On December 7 the Mufti rejected compromise proposals put forward by two fellow Palestinian Arabs, Shawkat Ali and Dr Abdul Hamid Said, and persisted in his refusal to allow several of his leading Jerusalem Arab critics, including Hassan Sidki Bey al-Dajani, Fakhri Bey al-Nashashibi and Mohammed Sameh al-Khalidi, to enter the conference at all.

On December 9 the Mufti's supporters distributed to the delegates photographs showing Jews with machine-guns attacking the Dome of the Rock. The photographs were fakes. Among many of the delegates, the *Palestine Bulletin* reported, 'great resentment is expressed over this disgraceful and discredited propaganda being foisted on the Conference'. So hostile were many leading Muslims to the Mufti's attitude that they held a protest meeting in the King David Hotel on December 12, presided over by the Mayor, Ragheb Bey al-Nashashibi, and passed a vote of no confidence in Haj Amin. But in the Supreme Muslim Council, consisting of five members, the Mufti retained a majority of one – his own casting vote.

One of the decisions of the Mufti's conference, which ended on December 17, was to deny Jews access to the al-Aksa Mosque. Another was to set up an international Muslim organisation, the Islamic Congress, with the Mufti at its head and its headquarters in Jerusalem. Its aim was to maintain the sanctity of the Haram in its widest political context. To achieve that aim it would challenge at every possible opportunity the work of the Zionists. In his speeches inside Palestine, and in his messages to the faithful throughout the Muslim world, the Mufti continued to accuse the Zionists of wishing to control the mosques of Jerusalem, and above all the Haram.

Seeking greater autonomy within the predominantly Jewish areas of Jerusalem, and greater security in the face of such Muslim hostility, on 7 January 1932, in a letter to the High Commissioner from the head of the Political Department of the Jewish Agency, Chaim Arlosoroff, the Zionists proposed that the municipal region of Jerusalem should be divided into two boroughs: West Jerusalem, the newer part of the city, which was mostly Jewish, and the Old City, which was largely Arab. Each would have a council of its own, which would raise taxes to sustain and operate municipal services and development. A United Municipal Council would supervise all wider interests. The Holy Places were already excluded from all Palestinian court jurisdiction, coming, since 1924, directly under the High Commissioner.

The British rejected Arlosoroff's proposal. 'The Government views with disfavour any proposal for the partition of Jerusalem,' was its formal response. At the same time, the Jewish suburbs grew in area and population, increasing the number of electoral wards within the city boundary. The Mandate authorities 'balanced' the ratio of the two communities by adding Arab villages outside the boundary, among them Lifta, to the municipal roll.

The Mufti continued to denounce Jewish immigration, and to blame the British for allowing it. In an effort to find a point of contact with moderate Arab opinion, and to counter the Mufti's efforts at dividing the two communities, a number of leading Jewish figures, among them the President of the Hebrew University, Dr Magnes, and the former senior British Mandate official Norman Bentwich, had formed a group called Brit Shalom, the Covenant of Peace. Among its initiatives were courses in Arabic for Jewish Jerusalemites. The aim of Brit Shalom was to reconcile Arabs and Jews and to bring about economic, political and social cooperation. This was strongly opposed by the New Zionist, or Revisionist, Party led by Vladimir Jabotinsky, which wanted Jewish statehood throughout Palestine.

When, in February 1932, Bentwich accepted the Professorship of International Peace at the Hebrew University, his first lecture as professor was on the theme 'Jerusalem, City of Peace'. At the end of his first sentence, he later recalled, 'there was noisy and persistent interruption. I "should go and talk peace to the Arabs and the Mufti of Jerusalem". After a long hubbub I continued; immediately the uproar started again, this time accompanied by stink bombs and the throwing of sheaves of pamphlets. The attempts of the University staff to restore order failed; and a few British policemen, who were on Scopus to direct the traffic, were called in. The disturbers were ejected, the public remained in the hall, and guarded by men with fixed bayonets I continued my lecture on "Jerusalem, City of Peace".'

The 'disturbers' had been Jews, members of the Revisionist Party, among whom were extremists for whom even physical violence was to become a means of asserting their political views: it was a Jewish extremist who was to murder Chaim Arlosoroff on the beach in Tel Aviv in 1933.

*

Modernity reached Jerusalem later than many places, but in 1932 the first cinema opened its doors: the Edison Film Theatre. It showed European and American films, with Hebrew subtitles projected at the side of the screen. Among the most popular early films was Sergei Eisenstein's *Alexander Nevsky*. One of those who went to the films in those days, Shaul Nahum, later the Edison's manager, recalled: 'We would put a big bag of sunflower seeds on our laps, buy a couple of drinks, and have a great time. Every week there would be a new film. People used to fill the theatre, even on Saturday night. There wasn't anything else to do.'

*

Hitler's coming to power in Germany in January 1933 brought hostility, isolation and persecution to the Jews of Germany. Within a few months several thousand university teachers, schoolteachers, scientists, doctors and lawyers had been driven from their professions. Jerusalem was to be transformed as a result of this distant event. The influx of Jews fleeing persecution in Germany, beginning in the first months of 1933, affected every aspect of life in Jerusalem. The German Jews brought with them their secular, civilised, cultured way of life, their love of German music and literature, and their modern ideas in medicine and the arts, architecture and town planning.

At the Hebrew University on Mount Scopus, the new German immigrants strengthened alike the teaching and student bodies. Some German immigrants went to work on the kibbutz at Ramat Rahel, so recently depleted by the departure of many of its members to the Soviet Union. Among the services provided by the renewed kibbutz were a laundry and a bakery service for the city. Perhaps the most important single contribution of the German Jews was to medicine. Among those who came in the first year of Hitler's rule were Bernard Zondek, one of the Germany's most distinguished gynaecologists, and Professor Ludwig Halberstaedter, a dermatologist and radiation therapist.

The Arab fears of an eventual Jewish majority could not be assuaged even by their own substantial immigration. The new immigrants from Hitler's Germany seemed an added threat. During a meeting in the King David Hotel on 8 April 1933 between the leading Arab sheikhs of Transjordan and the Zionist leaders Dr Weizmann and Chaim Arlosoroff, the sheikhs expressed their hope of cooperation with the Jews to develop their country. The Palestinian Arabs, however, had no such public enthusiasm for Jewish enterprise west of the river Jordan.

Daily life in Jerusalem was not always overshadowed by the political storm clouds. At noon on the day after the Weizmann-Arlosoroff meeting with the sheikhs, the first telephone link was established between Jerusalem and London. At a ceremony in Government House the voices of the first speakers, the Secretary of State for the Colonies, Sir Philip Cunliffe-Lister, and the High Commissioner, Sir Arthur Wauchope, were heard through loudspeakers in the ballroom for the benefit of the press. That afternoon the Sixth Egyptian Medical Congress, meeting at the newly-built Jerusalem YMCA, was entertained to tea at the King David Hotel by the Mayor. In the evening the Congress devoted its session to a standardisation of Arabic medical terms.

On April 9, Palm Sunday, the solemn procession from Bethfage to Jerusalem, commemorating Jesus' triumphal entry into Jerusalem when he wept over the impending destruction of the city, was resumed for the first time since 1563, under the auspices of the Latin Patriarch Barlassina. All the walkers carried palm or olive branches. The Salesian Boy Scouts, and the Catholic Associations of Young Men and of Girls, brought their flags and insignia. As the procession made its way down the Mount of Olives, past Gethsemane and through St Stephen's Gate to the Basilica of St Anne, hymns were sung in Latin, Arabic, Syriac and French.

The Jews of Jerusalem were celebrating the Passover festival that week, commemorating the Exodus from Egypt, and the synagogues were filled to overflowing. So were the hotels. 'Complaints are made on all sides', commented the recently established *Palestine Post*, 'that the hotels, particularly the moderately-priced ones, are unable to cope with the record crowds.' At the Edison Film Theatre, Mae Marsh, who had come to fame in 1915 when she was the star of *The Birth of a Nation*, was appearing in *Over the Hill*. At the Zion Hall, Buster Keaton was appearing in *The Passionate Plumber*. In its newspaper advertisements that week, the Levant Agency was offering the latest models of Humber and Hillman cars and Commer trucks. In its patisserie in the Street of the Prophets, Patt's was offering 'delicious home-made Passover cakes'. Thomas Cook's had 'special rates' for those who stayed in its camp at Petra, in Transjordan.

On the morning of April 13, Field Marshal Viscount Allenby arrived at Jerusalem railway station, where a large crowd of spectators had gathered to catch sight of the man described in the newspapers as 'the Conqueror of Palestine'. He had come for the formal opening of the magnificent YMCA building on the following day, but on the afternoon of his arrival he was present at the dedication of the Hebrew University's new open-air theatre. During the theatre ceremony the Palestine Oratorio sang Handel's *Judas Maccabaeus*.

In his speech of dedication, the President of the university, Judah Magnes, warned that 'the great Jewry of Germany, which has contributed to the culture both of the German people and of Judaism, is in danger of systematic extermination. But we, in Jerusalem, should have no scruples. At this moment of destruction in Germany, we are endeavouring to build here; and building means for us not only the creation of miles of brick and stone, but also the creation of our culture and civilisation.'

The immigration from Germany accelerated. So, too, did Arab protests at Jewish immigration. On 13 October 1933 the Arabs declared a general strike throughout Palestine. A planned Arab protest demonstration in Jerusalem was banned by the Government, but went ahead after Sheikh Said al-Khatib, in his sermon at al-Aksa, described the 'dangers' of Jewish immigration and called on the faithful to 'do their duty'. The service over, 2,000 worshippers, led by the Chairman of the recently-established Arab Executive, Musa Kazem Pasha, and chanting '*Allahu Akbar*' ('God is the Greatest'), marched from the Haram to the Damascus Gate, then turned westward to the New Gate. There the police prevented them for reentering the Old City. The roads into the New City were also blocked. When stones and bottles were thrown at the police, the first baton charge was made, and the crowd was forcibly dispersed. Six Arabs, and five policemen, were injured.

Nine days after the Arab demonstration, the Palestine Government reduced the numbers of certificates to be issued to Jewish immigrants over the following six months from 6,500 to 5,500. This was not because of the Arab protests, but because of the number of German Jews who were estimated to have entered the country illegally in the previous six months, and whose numbers were being docked off the quota. 'In view of the situation of the German Jews,' David Ben-Gurion, the Chairman of the Jewish Agency Executive, told the High Commissioner on October 22, 'this drastic curtailment was a serious and bitter blow for world Jewry.' It was not, however, a sufficient curtailment from the Arab perspective, and on October 28, as Arab rioting spread once more throughout Palestine, violence broke out again in Jerusalem. It was aimed not only at the Jews but also at the British. The police dispersed the crowd by opening fire. Five Arabs were killed, including one who had come from Hebron and one from Transjordan.

Riots did not deter tourism in Jerusalem. In 1934 the sixth edition of Cook's *Traveller's Handbook to Palestine, Syria and Iraq* was published. It gave descriptions of some of the most recent buildings, including 'the handsome new buildings of the Jewish Agency' on King George V Avenue, the new General Post Office still under construction on the Jaffa Road, the magnificent YMCA completed a year earlier, and the Rockefeller Museum under construction at the north-east corner of the city wall. This museum was made possible by a $2 million grant from John D. Rockefeller. The grant included funds for a library, laboratories and research. 'The building is now (1934) about complete,' commented the handbook, 'so that it has taken just as long to build as Solomon's temple.' The handbook added: 'It has been well worth waiting for; and will be found to be not only an interesting example of adapted Arab architecture, of a style in perfect harmony with the best traditions of the locality, but an admirably designed museum with the lighting, sunshine, and other technical problems, carefully considered.' On a less exalted level, the three establishments appearing in the 'Restaurant and Cafes' section of the handbook were the Deutsches Restaurant, the Vienna Café and the Café Europa – all in the Jaffa Road.

In October 1934 the cornerstone was laid in the Hadassah Medical Centre on Mount Scopus, just north of the Hebrew University buildings. The head and inspiration of the proposed new hospital was the seventy-four-year-old Dr Henrietta Szold, an American Zionist leader who had spent more and more time in Palestine after 1920, directing medical and nursing work, and, following the rise of Hitler, Jewish youth resettlement. Dr Szold was determined that Hadassah should leave its 'historic but inadequate' premises in the pre-First World

War Rothschild Hospital on the Street of the Prophets. The aim was more than a change of location. 'Stark modern science,' she declared in her address at the stone-laying, 'must be clothed in modern vestments'. So the work of building the new centre began: it was hoped to open the new hospital within five years. The Nursing School began work on Mount Scopus only two years after the stone-laying.

To the south of the city, the Jewish Educational Farm established on the road to the Hill of Evil Counsel in 1920 was turned into a training-farm for Jewish girls who wished to devote their lives to agricultural work. A hundred yards east of the farm the British High Commissioner took up residence in a new Government House, from whose windows the whole city could be seen stretching to the north. That the new centre of Mandatory government should be located on the Hill of Evil Counsel was a source of considerable merriment among the inhabitants of Jerusalem. In 1935 the Government set up an Arab College on the approaches to the same hill.

Visible on the horizon north of the Hill of Evil Counsel, across the deep cleft of the Kidron Valley, the Hebrew University on Mount Scopus was receiving an influx of books from its German-Jewish refugee teachers and scholars, many of them leaders in their respective fields of study. These books significantly enhanced the holdings of the university library. A German-Jewish publication, the *Philo-Lexicon Encyclopaedia of Jewish Knowledge*, issued in Frankfurt in 1936, noted with pride that there were 278,000 books in the Hebrew University and National Library.

*

Edward Keith-Roach, the Jerusalem District Commissioner, prevailed upon the Jerusalem Municipal Council to build a public lavatory for men and women just off the Jaffa Road, near Zion Square. It was designed and constructed according to the most modern sanitary and artistic considerations of the day. Keith-Roach tried to persuade the Mayor, Dr Hussein al-Khalidi, to open it with a ceremony at which, amid brass bands and due ceremonial, the Mayor would, as happened in French municipalities, inaugurate it by using it. 'His worship beat a hasty retreat.' Keith-Roach later wrote. 'For once a public building was opened without speeches.'

The public lavatory remained an adornment to the New City for more than fifty years. When I went to photograph it for this book, I discovered that it had recently been taken down. The Mayor lasted less long than the edifice: in 1937 he was one of six Arab leaders deported to the Seychelles, in the Indian Ocean, for his part in fomenting Arab unrest. But that still lay in the future when, on 30 March 1936, a few minutes' walk from Keith-Roach's useful structure, the High Commissioner inaugurated the Palestine Broadcasting Service. From Jerusalem there now went out music, sport and news of international events in a world where the activities of Hitler's Germany and Mussolini's Italy were by then in the headlines almost daily.

The aim of the broadcasting authority was to balance the interests of both Arabs and Jews. The first day's programme set the tone. Musical item number one was Arab players on Arab instruments, followed by Hebrew poetry and songs, followed by Arab songs, and then more Jewish songs. But within a month of this hopeful development, and within only three years of the most recent riots, violence was to return yet again to the streets and suburbs of Jerusalem.

CHAPTER TEN

The Riots of 1936 and Their Aftermath

The riots of 1936, although they began slowly, were far to exceed in their violent impact the riots of 1929. The violence began in Jaffa on April 19, when sixteen Jews were killed by Arabs. In Jerusalem all was quiet until April 22, when several Jews were threatened by Arabs in the street, and a Jewish merchant in the Old City was beaten up, but there were no fatalities. With the support of the Mufti, an Arab Strike Committee was set up, which called for the closing of all Arab businesses. Some Arab merchants refused to close their stores, and would not be intimidated by the groups of Arab youths who demanded that they obey the strike call. By the last day of April, however, three Christian-Arab schools, Terra Sancta, Bishop Gobat's and St George's, had been closed down as a result of Muslim Arab intimidation.

On May 3 a number of Arab vegetable-sellers from the village of Lifta were attacked by other Arabs as they sold their wares in the Mahane Yehuda Jewish market. But it was the murder not of a Jewish Jerusalemite but of a Jew in Poland that was the front-page 'After Midnight' item in the *Palestine Post* on May 4, a reminder of the growing storm in Europe. The victim was twenty-six-year-old Jacob Selig, who had been killed during anti-Jewish excesses in Poland that were to take more than 100 Jewish lives that year.

On May 5 the leaders of the Arab Strike Committee were arrested in Jerusalem by the British and detained. On the following day the Arab Higher Committee issued a statement, signed by its General Secretary, Auni Bey Abdul Hadi, that 'under no circumstances' would the Arabs 'consent to "Judaise" the Holy Land'. Among those signing this statement was Dr Hussein al-Khalidi, the Mayor of Jerusalem. On May 8 the Supreme Muslim Council, presided over by the Mufti, passed a resolution that no Arab would pay taxes until Britain halted

Jewish immigration, stopped the sale of land to Jews, and formed a National Arab Government. Four days later the High Commissioner went to the studios of Jerusalem Radio and broadcast a strong warning. 'I wish all law-breakers to know,' he said, 'that the Government will suppress all outbreaks of lawlessness and punish the perpetrators.' That midnight Kassim Eissa, an Arab from Transjordan who was serving as a watchman at a Jewish-owned quarry at Kiryat Anavim, was shot dead by fellow Arabs. He had refused repeated Arab demands to join the strike and to abandon his post. He was the first Jerusalem fatality of the new disturbances.

Violence suddenly flared throughout the city. On the morning of May 14 two Jews were shot dead at point-blank range in the Jewish Quarter of the Old City. One of them, forty-six-year-old Rabbi Reuben Kloppholtz, left a widow and eight children. The other, the seventy-year-old Kehat Cohen, who lived in an old-age home, was shot through the mouth and died instantly. There were no expressions of regret from the Arab leaders. Instead, on a visit to the coastal town of Acre, the Mufti of Jerusalem declared: 'The Jews are trying to expel us from the country. They are murdering our sons and burning our houses.'

On May 16 death came to the centre of the New City when an Arab gunman opened fire inside the Edison Film Theatre. Three Jews were killed. One of them, twenty-three-year-old Alexander Polonsky, had emigrated a year earlier from Poland and was studying at the Hebrew University. Another, Dr Zvi Szabchoski, was a skin specialist who had come from Poland only three months earlier. His widow was expecting their first child. The third, Isaac Yolovsky, was a baker. He had been married only six weeks earlier.

On the following day, the day of the funeral of the three victims, Jewish Jerusalem came to a halt. Workshops stopped their machines, offices dismissed their staffs, and the university closed down for the day. 'Innocent blood has once more been spilled on the stones of Jerusalem,' Yitzhak Ben-Zvi, Chairman of the General Council of Palestine Jews, told the enormous crowd of 10,000 mourners, while Arthur Ruppin wrote in his diary: 'This crime in the midst of the Jewish sector of Jerusalem, committed in such a strikingly bold manner, has aroused an unprecedented uproar among the Jews.' Under the heading 'War of Extermination?' the *Palestine Post* declared: 'The Jews have shown restraint. This restraint has been acknowledged and tributed in the highest places. Their moral repugnance for murder has overcome their instinct for self-defence. They hold life dearly, and the life even of their sworn enemy is dear to them. But who can now guarantee that Jews, outraged to their depths, will not undergo a change of outlook on the sacredness of human life?'

Jewish restraint held, but the killing of Jews went on. At Kibbutz Ramat Rahel, where one member had been killed in 1929, three were killed in 1936 and much property was again destroyed. Inside the Old City many institutions which had been attacked in 1929, among them the Torat Hayim religious seminary which had been built just before the end of the century on the Via Dolorosa, were abandoned after a new outburst of violence against them. In a desperate attempt to preserve their spiritual treasures, the Torat Hayim seminarists asked the Arab janitor if he would keep the building locked and preserve it as best he could from looting. This he did – an act of considerable courage.

The riots brought many moments of pain for the Hebrew University. Among the staff members who were murdered was Lewis Billig, a teacher from England whose expertise was medieval Islam. Billig believed that Jewish and Arab aspirations could be reconciled if each side knew something of the other's history and culture. On the night of his murder he was at his desk in the small garden suburb of North Talpiot, preparing an edition of a ninth-century Arab text by the Shiite author al-Saffar al-Qummi. The text consisted of a collection of Shiite traditions mainly describing the merits of the religious leaders of the early Shiite community.

In addition to Alexander Polonsky, four other Hebrew University students were killed during the summer of 1936: Rachamim Kalantorov, Gershon Masheioff, Baruch Gurevitz and David Nishri. University teaching had not been disrupted, however. According to a report published a year later: 'The disturbances had no effect upon university life, and in spite of various difficulties the Departments continued their ordinary work fully, and the summer term was completed in the ordinary course of events.'

*

In the aftermath of the riots the British Government decided to set up a Royal Commission to examine the working of the Mandate and to make proposals for the future. The commission was headed by Lord Peel, a former Secretary of State for India. Its second most senior member was a former British Ambassador to Berlin, Sir Horace Rumbold, who had been in Berlin when Hitler came to power. The choice of commissioners had been made on the basis that, while all of them were distinguished public servants, they had 'no previous association with Palestine, and no past either on the Jewish or Moslem side'.

The commissioners reached Jerusalem on 11 November 1936, Armistice Day, arriving in time to attend a ceremony at the British Military Cemetery on Mount Scopus, overlooking Jerusalem. 'No one in the circumstances,' the commission wrote in its report, 'could help reflecting that the peace which followed the Armistice of 1918 had been an even less real peace in Palestine than in Europe. Something like another war, however minute in scale, had recently been waged, and something like another armistice had been concluded.

'The more we saw and the more we heard in the days that followed, the clearer it became that the Armistice was only a suspension of hostilities not a preliminary to peace. The Arab leaders had refused to co-operate with us in our search for a means of settling the dispute. It was believed in many quarters that another outbreak might occur at any moment. Several isolated murders or assaults occurred during our stay, and at one time acts of brigandage were reported almost every day. It was impossible not to feel the sense of tension at Jerusalem, and of pessimism. In neutral circles the task we had undertaken was regarded as well-nigh impossible.'

While in Jerusalem, the commissioners stayed at the King David Hotel. They took evidence at the nearby Palace Hotel, which had been built six years earlier as a financial venture by the Mufti's Supreme Muslim Council. An attempt to persuade the Palestinian-Arab leaders to give evidence was made on November 22, by the Emir Abdullah, who came to Jerusalem for that purpose. Staying at the King David Hotel, the Emir broke the Ramadan fast with the Mufti, but failed to convince him to participate in Lord Peel's deliberations. Two days later the Jerusalem Arab daily newspaper *al-Liwa* demanded that the Royal Commission should reach only one conclusion: 'a National Arab Government' throughout Palestine.

Because the Mufti declined to put the case against any further Jewish immigration, it was Dr Weizmann who spoke first, on November 25, putting the case for immigration. Speaking of what he called Jewish homelessness in Poland and the territories that were formerly part of the Russian Empire, and of Central and Eastern Europe, he told the commissioners: 'It is no exaggeration on my part to say that there are about six million Jews in this part of the world – I am not speaking of the Oriental Communities whose Jews are inarticulate – condemned to live in a place where they cannot live and in places which do not want them.'

So impressive was Weizmann's speech that the Arab Higher Committee, after what the *Palestine Post* described as a stormy session, decided, while still boycotting the commission, to send one of its most senior members, Ragheb Bey al-Nashashibi, the former Mayor of Jerusalem, to meet the commissioners unofficially the following week in Amman, where they would be on a brief visit.

*

In Jerusalem the Peel Commissioners worked at full stretch. On December 4 the *Palestine Post* gave an account of their day. They rose at 6.30 each morning. After breakfast they reviewed the material which was to form the basis of the evidence of the next witness. Witnesses were then examined from 10.30 until shortly after 1.00. In the afternoon the commissioners met again to discuss the evidence which had been presented. 'The strain was great,' wrote the *Palestine Post*, 'and rumour has it that one or two of the Commissioners are beginning to feel the effects of such continuous and arduous work.' On January 15 Sir Horace Rumbold wrote to his son: 'Peel and I are finding some of our colleagues rather difficult to manage. They complain that we have been driving them too hard but as we ourselves are always prepared to work they really have no case.'

Among the Jews whom the commissioners examined on December 30 was the Russian-born Dov Hos, who, while an officer in the Turkish army, had been sentenced to death by the Turks for defending Jewish settlements in the Galilee against Arab attack. In 1918 Hos had escaped from Palestine and joined the British army. He was a senior member of the General Federation of Jewish Labour. At one point in the questioning, speaking about the work of the Jewish institutions in Palestine, he told the commissioners that, where the Jews established hospitals and schools, 'that is relieving Government from the responsibility and expense connected with them'.

Rumbold took this as a criticism of the Mandate for being unwilling to take responsibility or incur expense. 'Now let me tell you this,' he expostulated, 'Lord Cromer was in Egypt for twenty-five years and he took over a country which was in a very bad way indeed. It took him nearly twenty-five years to restore that country to prosperity. My impression is that the task here is more difficult than that which Lord Cromer had, because not only was this country completely derelict when the Mandatory Power took over, but the Mandatory has had to develop the country having regard to the unique experiment, the injection of an alien race into the body politic of this native race.'

There was an outcry at Rumbold's remark: Jews were outraged to be called an 'alien race'. The Jews would describe themselves not as an alien race, Dov Hos replied, but as 'children returning to their country, to the country where they lived or to a country where they are going to have their home'. Jewish immigration, he added, carried with it not only 'enthusiasm and devotion to the work, but the actual possibilities of development which were not inherent in this country, which did not exist here before the arrival of the Jews'.

Rumbold's use of the phrase 'alien race' was much criticised. 'Perhaps nothing will so have depressed the Jews of this country and abroad', declared the *Palestine Post* on 1 January 1939, 'as the epithet which fell from the lips of Sir Horace. He really leaves the Arab Committee little to say.' At the commissioners' next public session, on January 5, Rumbold explained that what he meant by 'alien race' was 'a race having different characteristics from the Arab race. That seems to me quite the obvious interpretation.'

Rumbold had become an object of Jewish scorn. That New Year's Eve the King David Hotel held a dance for 500 Jews which went on long into the night. As the Secretary of the Peel Commission, John Martin, wrote in a private letter home, while Rumbold was asleep a young woman who had been at the dance burst into his room carrying a small trumpet, which she blew until he woke up. She then declared that Rumbold 'was the ugliest member of the Commission, and told him various other home truths while he cowered helpless beneath the counterpane'.

*

A death took place that winter that was unconnected with the riots. In October, Lady Genevieve Watson, an eighty-two-year-old widow, had been knocked over by a donkey in the Old City, breaking her thigh. She died at the end of the year. After her husband's death in the First World War she had been offered a suite of rooms in Hampton Court Palace by King George V. She declined, deciding instead to give up her home in London when the war was over and settle in Jerusalem.

An active member of the Order of St John of Jerusalem, and a patron of its hospital, Lady Watson bought a house in the Old City which, on her death, she left to the Order. She was also a patron of the archaeological work being done by the Palestine Exploration

Society, and had co-authored a book on Jerusalem in a series on medieval towns. She was buried in the Protestant cemetery on Mount Zion, her coffin being borne by six British police officers who had received their first training at the St John Hospital.

*

On 30 December 1936, while the Peel Commissioners were still trying to persuade the Palestinian-Arab leaders to end their boycott of the commission, the commissioners attended a concert which attested to the new Jewish life in Jerusalem. 'The most important musical experience in its history,' was how Arthur Ruppin described it in his diary. 'Ancient Jerusalem came of age musically last night,' was the comment in the *Palestine Post*.

The occasion was the visit to Palestine of the world-famous conductor Arturo Toscanini. He was conducting the newly formed Palestine Orchestra, many of whose players were former members of the leading German orchestras, forced to abandon their musical careers in Germany because they were Jewish. Rumbold, who had been British Ambassador in Berlin from 1928 to 1933, recognised on the stage several of the leading players of the Berlin Philharmonic Orchestra. The music played was mostly that of the German Romantic period. It included music by Mendelssohn, whose work had been banned in Germany by the Nazis.

On 4 January 1937 Toscanini conducted in Jerusalem for the second time. The works were all by Beethoven. 'Once launched,' the *Palestine Post* reported, 'the programme was conducted more like a religious revival than a musical recital.' The newspaper's music critic concluded his report: 'May the Maestro leave us with the knowledge that, though all the world may appreciate his worth, there is probably nowhere that so much sincere honour and love are being laid at his feet as here.'

*

A week after Toscanini's second concert, a memorial meeting was held at the Hebrew University for the six university victims of the riots. 'Six worlds have been destroyed wantonly,' a student leader, J. Shaked, told the gathering. 'But the sacrifices have not been in vain. Another world will be perpetuated, that of Israel and the people of Israel.' That day an Arab armed with a shotgun opened fire on the Jewish farm settlement at Atarot, on the Jerusalem-Ramallah road. A Jewish police corporal in charge of the settlement's defence forced him to stop shooting, and no one was hurt.

The Arabs finally agreed to end their boycott of the Peel Commission. Their first witness was the Mufti, who had established the Arab Higher Committee at the start of the riots, with himself as its head, to 'control and manage the strikes of Arabs in Palestine'. The Mufti told the commissioners that the Balfour Declaration was 'extremely prejudicial to the interests of the Arabs. The Jews were enabled to acquire large areas in the most fertile of Arab lands. Every hope which the Arabs had of attaining independence was frustrated.' The 'ultimate aim' of the Jews, said the Mufti, was the reconstruction of the Temple of Solomon on the ruins of the Muslim Holy Places in Jerusalem. 'The Jews had various means of securing their aims, wide means of propaganda, their relations with British statesmen and others. What can Arabs do? Who could prevent the Jews from making such claims to Moslem shrines?' When Rumbold asked the Mufti if he thought the Jews would be able to remove the Mandatory Power, the Mufti replied: 'What I can see, and my experience up to now, shows that the Jews can do anything as far as Palestine is concerned.'

During his evidence the Mufti insisted that the Balfour Declaration be annulled and Palestine made over to a sovereign Arab body. When he was asked whether Palestine could 'assimilate and digest' the 400,000 Jews already there, he replied in a single word: 'No.' When asked if he would have preferred Turkey as the Mandatory Power, he replied that the Arabs would prefer 'complete independence'. Whatever the weight of his opinions, the Peel Commission publicly condemned the Mufti and the Arab Higher Committee for having been 'responsible for extending and protracting the strike' and for never having condemned 'the acts of sabotage and terrorism which became more frequent as the strikes continued'. The Mufti 'must, in our view, bear his full share of responsibility for those disorders'.

*

The Peel Commission's recommendations were as revolutionary as they were unexpected: Palestine should be partitioned into two separate, independent States, one Jewish and one Arab. The Jews would rule on the coastal plain and in the Galilee. The Arabs would rule on the West Bank of the Jordan, in the Gaza District, and in the Negev Desert. But for both Jews and Arabs there was also disappointment: Jerusalem, and a corridor linking Jerusalem to the sea, were to be excluded from both the proposed States.

The Arab Higher Committee, determined to have only one State in Palestine, an Arab State, rejected the Peel proposals. The Jewish Agency, exhilarated at the prospect of Jewish statehood for the first time in 2,000 years, prepared a map on which they drew a line around the Jewish suburbs of Jerusalem, and asked that these should be included in any Jewish State. In order to make their map more acceptable, the Jewish Agency excluded several outlying Jewish suburbs, including Mekor Hayim, Talpiot, Arnona and Ramat Rahel, which lay beyond the Arab suburbs of Katamon, Talbiyeh and Bakaa, from the hoped-for 'Jewish Jerusalem'. The Agency also excluded the Jewish Quarter of the Old City, which it was assumed would be part of a protected zone for all the Holy Places.

This Jewish willingness to compromise was to no avail: neither the Peel Commission plan nor the Jewish Agency's maps and proposals for a variation on Partition came into effect. Arab determination to see no State in Palestine but an Arab one, and to halt Jewish immigration altogether, led to renewed violence, and the breakdown of dialogue. Jewish extremism also threatened to exacerbate the violence, as the violence itself intensified. On 18 March 1937, after several Jews had been murdered in the Galilee in the previous week, a bomb was thrown by an Arab in the Jaffa Road, seriously injuring three Jews. An hour later, Jewish extremists, members of the recently formed Revisionist Party's military wing, the Irgun Zvai Leumi (or IZL), threw two bombs at two Arab cafés in Jerusalem, killing one Arab and wounding at least twenty. Arthur Ruppin commented in his diary: 'The Jews are pleased that at least they are not the only ones to be attacked and injured, as they were in 1936.' The Jewish Agency at once condemned the reprisals, however, and urged the Jewish community to have no part in them.

*

The conflict between Jews and Arabs in Palestine was not to be resolved by Britain to the satisfaction of either side. When, in November 1936, the Secretary of State for the Colonies decided not to suspend Jewish immigration altogether, but to limit it to certain carefully defined categories, the Zionists were deeply distressed by the limitations, and the Palestine Arabs equally distressed by the continuation of any immigration at all. When the London representative of the Arab Higher Committee, Emile Ghory, transmitted the

British proposals to Jerusalem, there was, reported the magazine *Palestine* on November 11, 'profound disappointment' among the Arab leaders.

In August 1937 the Arab Mayor of Jerusalem, Hussein al-Khalidi, went on leave. The Deputy Mayor, Daniel Auster, a Jew, became Acting Mayor in his place. Short periods when Jews acted as Mayor were not uncommon. But when Hussein al-Khalidi returned at the end of the month he was arrested by the British as a member of the Arab Higher Committee, which had been declared illegal following the riots of 1936, and deported to the Seychelles in the Indian Ocean. Auster remained Acting Mayor, to the considerable anger of the city's Muslims. As another of the six Arab councillors, Ibrahim Darwish, was also arrested, there was, for the first time, a Jewish majority on the city council. The four remaining Arab councillors at once boycotted the meetings, paralysing the administration of the city. After many months of argument and near-chaos, the High Commissioner intervened, and on 1 October 1938 a Mandate High Court judge, Mustafa al-Khalidi, a cousin of the exiled Mayor, was appointed Mayor in his place, while another Muslim, Hussein abu Saud, was appointed councillor to replace the imprisoned Darwish.

*

The British were monitoring the activities of the Mufti as closely as they could. On 16 July 1937 he had made contact with Herr Dohle, the German Consul-General in Jerusalem, and a convinced Nazi. During their conversation the Mufti expressed his sympathy for the 'new Germany' and hoped it would support the Arabs and oppose Zionist aims in Palestine. He also asked Dohle to maintain contact with his confidential agent, a local Arab, who would go to Berlin. On the following day British police entered the Supreme Muslim Council office outside the Old City to arrest a man whose incitement to violence was clear from all the documents at their disposal. But the Mufti managed to evade arrest, and to seek sanctuary on the Haram. Police guarding the gates of the city were given orders to arrest him should he try to leave. With supreme confidence, the Mufti worked each day in his office on the Haram, and even gave an interview to a correspondent of the London *Daily Telegraph*.

The correspondent's account was published on July 29. 'With light eyes which periodically break into a merry twinkle,' the correspondent wrote, 'he has such an attractive, disarming personality, one could not believe that this smiling, soft-speaking, somewhat languid

Sheikh, has been officially held responsible for most of the troubles of the past year. The Mufti now never leaves the enclosure. His only distraction is to promenade within the walls of the area, or to watch the world from his private rooms overlooking the Wailing Wall.'

Encouraged by the 'somewhat languid Sheikh', the violence against the British continued. On September 26 the British District Commissioner in the Galilee, Lewis Andrews, was murdered there. In retaliation, on October 1 the Mufti was deprived of his positions both as President of the Supreme Muslim Council and as Chairman of the General Wakf Committee responsible for all Muslim religious property. On the following day a protest demonstration by Arab youth forced all Arab shopkeepers in the Old City to close their shops.

Still the British hesitated to enter the Haram, for fear of exacerbating Muslim sensitivities worldwide. Then, on the night of October 14, the Mufti slipped away, disguised as a woman. To conceal his absence from prayers at the al-Aksa Mosque it had been given out that he had tonsillitis. Making his way to the coast, he was taken by boat to Beirut. He was never to return to Palestine. From afar he remained active, fomenting anti-British agitation and encouraging the murder of his Arab opponents.

Another Arab leader who escaped arrest and fled from Palestine at the same time was Abdul Khader al-Husseini. A graduate of the American University in Cairo, he had led the Arab revolt in the Hebron region. Five years later he emerged in Iraq, together with the Mufti, to give support to Rashid Ali's wartime revolt against Britain.

The killings continued. On October 23, nine days after the Mufti's flight, Avinoam Yellin, an officer in the Mandate Government's Education Office, and the son of the distinguished Jerusalemite Jew David Yellin, was shot dead as he left his office. Avinoam Yellin was the author of a standard textbook on the teaching of Arabic, which he had co-authored with Lewis Billig, a fellow student at Cambridge in the early 1920s. Billig had been murdered a year earlier.

Members of the Irgun wanted to carry out reprisals for the killing of Jews. The Jewish Agency condemned such talk and called publicly and continually for restraint. In the second week of November 1937 five Jewish manual labourers were murdered by Arabs while working in the quarry at Kiryat Anavim, just outside Jerusalem. A few days later, on November 14, seven Arabs were murdered by Irgun extremists in and around Jerusalem. There was outrage among the great majority of Jews in Jerusalem at these killings carried out by Jews, on what became known as 'Black Sunday'. The Jewish Agency Executive met in emergency session that same day. 'All the members expressed their disapproval of these acts of terrorism on the part of Jews,' Arthur Ruppin wrote in his diary, 'strangely enough with the exception of Rabbi Fishman, who even defended them with quotations from Maimonides.'

The Roumanian-born Judah Leib Fishman, who had lived in Palestine since 1913, was emphatic that every Jew had the right to bear arms 'in his own defence'. He was later to give evidence on behalf of Irgun prisoners, and to oppose the efforts of the Jewish Agency to suppress the Irgun.

*

During three years of violence throughout Palestine, between 1936 and 1939, 500 Jews and 150 Britons were killed by Arabs. By far the largest number of deaths, however, was that of the Arabs themselves. More than 3,000 were killed – at least 1,000 of them by their fellow Arabs because they supported some form of compromise with the British or with the Jews. Almost all the others were killed by British soldiers. Ten years later the Anglo-American Committee of Inquiry commented: 'By July 1938 the Arab gangs had become thoroughly organised. Rebel courts were set up, rebel stamps were issued, and the Old City of Jerusalem became a rallying point of bandits, from which acts of violence, murder and intimidation were organised and perpetrated freely and with impunity.'

In October 1938 Fakhri Bey al-Nashashibi, one of the leading moderate Palestinian-Arab leaders, told a British newspaper, the *Yorkshire Post*: 'I accuse Haj Amin al-Husseini, the former Mufti of Jerusalem, of diverting the noble Arab revolt to his own selfish ends. I also accuse him of using funds collected for the relief of Arab sufferers in Palestine to buy arms and ammunition to further his own ambition. Haj Amin's fifteen years' tenure of office in Jerusalem proved his destructive tendencies.'

As these 'destructive tendencies' escalated, a death warrant was issued for Fakhri Bey by Palestinian Arabs who accused him of collaboration, and of treason to the national cause. The warrant was published in a Damascus newspaper. Three years later, while he was in Baghdad, Fakhri Bey was shot dead by a Palestinian Arab. On that very day the Mufti was on his way by air from Rome to Berlin for an audience with Hitler, to whose cause he had committed himself. On the day after reaching the German capital the Mufti broadcast over Radio Berlin: 'The enemies of the Mufti will not escape their fate.'

The British Government made it clear that the Mufti was an enemy with whom there could be no compromise. On 17 May 1938 it was announced from London by the Colonial Secretary, Malcolm MacDonald, that the Mufti would be excluded from Palestine 'indefinitely'. This was because he was not only 'the head of the organisation held responsible for the campaign of terrorism and the assassination of British and Jews', MacDonald explained, 'but also the head of a faction which for many months past had pursued a similar campaign against large numbers of Arabs'.

*

On 9 May 1939 a peaceful event took place of great practical significance for the Jews of Jerusalem, and for the aspirations of Zionists everywhere. This was the opening of the new Hadassah Hospital, School of Nursing, and Medical School on Mount Scopus, on land adjacent to that of the Hebrew University. For several years the Zionist dream had been to move the hospital out of the New City and on to this mountaintop. After the foundation-stone had been laid in 1934, money for the construction had been raised all over the Jewish world, in particular by the Hadassah Women's Zionist Organisation in the United States.

The opening of the three new buildings was of similar importance to the opening of the Hebrew University building fourteen years earlier, but the celebrations were very different. 'Owing to the present political situation,' the *Jewish Chronicle* correspondent reported to London two days later, 'an elaborate ceremony was dispensed with, but, in the words of the official account, the actual dedication "was most deeply impressive by its modest character, which contrasted so forcibly with the size and importance of the accomplishment".'

When the Hadassah Hospital moved from the Rothschild Hospital building on the Street of the Prophets to Mount Scopus, there moved with it twenty-four Jewish and Arab men and women who had been severely wounded in the earlier riots, and who still required hospitalisation. A further sixty-five wounded were given treatment at the Hadassah clinics. 'After the disturbances had subsided,' the hospital's report for 1939 noted, 'there was an increase in the number of non-Jewish patients who applied to the hospital.'

The transfer of the Hadassah Hospital to its new premises brought about many improvements in the medical services that could be provided by all its departments, institutes and laboratories. In the hospital, the number of beds available for patients increased from just over 100 to more than 300, with the possibility of doubling even that number. In the School of Nursing there was also accommodation for eighty student nurses and five graduate nurses. In the Medical School there were five operating-theatres, each with an observation gallery for students, and the latest medical apparatus, together with improved facilities for both diagnosis and research.

The new hospital served Arab as well as Jewish patients: indeed, on its new site, it became more accessible to Arabs from the many outlying villages to the north and north-east of Jerusalem. This widening of the catchment area brought to the hospital for treatment diseases that were rarely found in Jerusalem itself, including malaria and dysentery. Also considerably increased at the new location, as a result of the great improvement in facilities, were the number of gynaecological cases brought from afar, even from beyond the boundaries of Palestine. Between May and December 1939 there were 1,269 deliveries.

The journey up to the Hadassah Hospital from Jerusalem led through the Muslim Arab neighbourhood of Sheikh Jarrah. This was a particularly nationalist area, and from time to time cars on their way up to the hospital, and doctors and nurses making their way there, were shouted at or stoned. But this did not affect the scale or quality of the work that was being done. Under the energetic leadership of Dr Chaim Yassky, the hospital flourished in its new location, while the research done by its doctors was recognised throughout the Middle East, and beyond.

*

A series of Nazi laws had subjected German Jews to indignity and fear. Polish Jews were also being confronted before 1939 with many manifestations of anti-Semitism. Jerusalem provided a haven for both groups. But not every Jew persecuted or harassed in Europe was prepared to make the journey to Palestine. A Jerusalem teenager, Yigael Sukenik (later the archaeologist Yigael Yadin), recalled, in conversation with the author, how he was taken by his mother to the Polish cities of Lodz and Bialystok, where, fearful of what lay in store for the Jews of Poland, she tried to persuade their many relatives to leave Poland for Palestine. The teenager was shocked to hear his relatives say that going to Palestine would merely be going 'from the frying-pan into the fire'. Jerusalem born and bred, the young Sukenik knew that, despite the riots, life in the city was full of warmth and richness; that Jerusalem was not only a haven for Jews but a place where Jews could walk in the streets with pride and contentment.

Even though many Jews hesitated to leave Europe, the Jewish population of Jerusalem rose between 1931 and 1939 by a further 26,000. Many of the individuals and institutions that had for many years graced Berlin and Vienna came in the late 1930s to Jerusalem. In April 1939, following the compulsory closing-down of the Jewish Institute of the Blind in Vienna, its Jerusalem counterpart became, as the *Palestine Post* reported, 'the only Jewish home of its kind in the world'. The Arab immigrant population of Jerusalem also grew in the 1930s, by 15,000, with Muslim immigrants mostly from Syria and Transjordan, but also from Egypt and Iraq.

By early 1939 the British Government was under considerable Arab pressure to restrict, and even to halt, Jewish immigration to Palestine. This pressure came principally from five independent Arab States: Egypt, Iraq, Transjordan, Saudi Arabia and Yemen. While Jerusalem had retained a Jewish majority for almost a century, in Palestine itself the Jews were still in a substantial minority – under half a million Jews but more than a million Arabs.

Unwilling to exacerbate Arab hostility in the Middle East while the German danger loomed in Europe, on May 18, only nine days after the opening of the new Hadassah Hospital on Mount Scopus, the British Government issued a White Paper setting out a new policy. This particular White Paper, a statement of Government intentions, was known to the Jews of Palestine as the 'Black Paper'. It stipulated that future Jewish immigration would be limited, during the next five years, to 75,000. After that, the majority then in Palestine, that is to say the Arabs, would have the right to veto any further immigration if they chose to do so.

The Jews knew that an end to all further Jewish immigration was exactly the Arab leaders' intention, and were devastated by the White Paper proposals. In Jerusalem, after a day of peaceful protest, a riot broke out as several hundred Jews converged on Zion Square. 'There must have been among them not a few who had decided that the day should not pass without violence,' commented the *Palestine Post*. Shop windows were smashed, and telephone boxes and lampposts were destroyed. A section of the crowd, reaching the government offices which contained the immigration and citizenship records, set part of the building on fire. In repeated police baton charges, more than 100 Jews were injured. Then shots were fired from the crowd, and a British policeman, Constable Harold Lawrence, was killed.

On May 19 the General Officer Commanding the British troops in Palestine, Lieutenant-General Haining, summoned the Jewish leaders, among them David Ben-Gurion, Bernard Joseph and Yitzhak Ben-Zvi, to his headquarters in Jerusalem, and warned them: 'There must be no more rioting in Jerusalem. But if blood is shed that blood will be on the head of the Jews.' When a crowd of 1,000 Jews gathered in Zion Square on the following evening, Ben-Zvi, as Chairman of the General Council of Palestine Jews which had earlier condemned the murder of Constable Lawrence, successfully urged the crowd to disperse.

On the morning of May 23, after two more days of street marches and demonstrations, including one by Jewish women, the Jerusalem District Commissioner, Edward Keith-Roach, told members of the Jerusalem Jewish Community Council, who had also helped disperse the rioters on May 20, that there were to be no more processions in or around the Jaffa Road, and that 'any breach of the peace will be met with force'. The council members promised to do their utmost to restrain the passions that had been roused by the White Paper. That same afternoon Jewish Special Constables, wearing khaki, with brown berets, were keeping order in the Jaffa Road and on King George V Avenue.

*

Speaking in the House of Commons on 23 May 1939, Winston Churchill, then a Conservative Member of Parliament at odds with his party, opposed the new policy of enabling the Arabs to exercise a veto on all Jewish immigration after five years. He knew, that since the publication of his own White Paper in 1922, more Arabs had emigrated to Palestine than Jews, despite that White Paper's declaration that Jews could enter Palestine virtually without restrictions. Emphasising this point, Churchill declared: 'So far from being persecuted, the Arabs have crowded into the country and multiplied till their population has increased more than even all world Jewry could lift up the Jewish population. Now we are asked to decree that all this is to stop and all this is to come to an end. We are now asked to submit, and this is what rankles most with me, to an agitation which is fed with foreign money and ceaselessly inflamed by Nazi and by Fascist propaganda.'

Churchill put his plea for Jewish immigration into the context of the rapidly growing German dominance of Central Europe, and the effect of that dominance on the Jews. In March 1938 Hitler had annexed Austria. In March 1939 he had entered Prague. With each German territorial advance, large Jewish populations immediately fell under the full force of his anti-Jewish legislation.

When the vote was taken Churchill was supported by more than eighty fellow Conservatives. But the Government had such a huge majority that it could ignore this protest vote, even when it was joined by the Labour members. That same day, the White Paper policy was passed by 268 votes to 179. It was put into immediate effect. Fewer and fewer Palestine certificates were issued by British Passport Control Offices in Europe, while off the coast of Palestine British naval vessels began intercepting Jews who tried to land, illegally, on its shores. Among the Jews of Jerusalem there was deep anger, manifested by protest marches and demonstrations against the 'perfidious betrayal'. In front of his whole congregation, Rabbi Isaac Halevi Herzog, the Ashkenazi Chief Rabbi of Palestine, dramatically tore up the White Paper and cast its fragments to the ground.

In the immediate aftermath of the new British restrictions on Jewish immigration, Jewish terrorism intensified. Although it was denounced by the Jewish Agency, and by the mass of the Jewish community in Palestine, it was devastating in its impact on Jewish-British relations. The terrorist targets were British government servants and public institutions and utilities. One early victim of a Jewish terrorist attack was himself a Jew, Police Corporal Arieh Polonsky, who had emigrated to Palestine from Poland ten years earlier. He died of his injuries on May 29. Two time bombs which were set off by Jewish terrorists in the Rex Cinema that day badly injured two British police constables, three Arab constables, and ten Arab cinema-goers. Also on May 29, Jewish terrorists opened fire on Arab buses in the neighbourhood of Romema, at the entrance to the city, and also on the Rehavia-Katamon route.

The British authorities responded by arresting several members of the Revisionist Party, who rejected the mainstream Zionist policy of cooperation with the British, and by imposing two collective punishments: an evening curfew on all cafés and restaurants in the city centre, and the closure for two days of the main Jewish bus lines. The King David, Fast and Eden Hotels successfully petitioned to have their facilities kept open. At the Eden Hotel the Palestine Jewish Medical Association was holding its twenty-fifth annual conference, the first having been held in Jerusalem on the eve of war in 1914. Many of the speakers were recent immigrants from Germany and Austria.

Arab terrorism as well as Jewish was in evidence in the last week of May. Despite the fact that the new White Paper was so much to the Arab national advantage in the long term, it had been denounced by the exiled Mufti, who urged his supporters to call for immediate Arab independence throughout Palestine. On May 26 a thirty-two-year-old German Jew, Marcus Ansbacher, who had reached Jerusalem from Germany only seven weeks earlier, having emigrated immediately after his release from the concentration camp at Dachau, was shot dead in the street by an Arab attacker. When, on May 30, a delegation of senior members of the Arab National Defence Party, among them Ragheb Bey al-Nashashibi and Fakhri Bey al-Nashashibi, went to see the High Commissioner, to announce their support for the White Paper proposals, they also condemned Arab terrorism.

*

There was mourning of a different sort among many of Jerusalem's Jews in the last week of May, when one of the city's most respected religious leaders died. Rabbi Jacob Meir had been elected Chief Rabbi of the Sephardi community in the city in Turkish times, but, as the Ottoman Government feared that he was 'too advanced in thought', the Sultan had refused to ratify his appointment, and he had served in Salonica instead. The British welcomed him back to Jerusalem, and from 1919 he was a source of considerable liberalism of thought among the religious Jews of the city. 'He became a popular leader,' one of his obituarists wrote, 'genial, broadminded, and with a keen sense of humour.' He was fluent in Hebrew, Arabic, French, Spanish and Turkish. His keenness to unite the Sephardi and Ashkenazi communities, a feat in which he succeeded in Jaffa, was to be unsuccessful in Jerusalem. But as a measure of the respect in which he was held by the British authorities he had been appointed a Commander of the Order of the British Empire.

*

On the morning of June 2 Jerusalem was shocked by a Jewish act of terror which killed nine Arabs in the Arab melon market outside the Jaffa Gate. Once more the Irgun had defied the Jewish Agency's calls for restraint. The dead included an Arab police-corporal, Awad Mahmud al-Abed, whose body was thrown thirty feet into the air by the force of the explosion. Most of the other Arab dead were from Hebron. As a collective punishment the British suspended three more Jewish bus routes in the city, making it necessary for two-thirds of the 25,000 Jewish passengers who went to work by bus each day either to walk through Arab sections of the city on their way to and from work, or to stay at home. Within hours of the explosion the Jewish Community Council issued a statement condemning acts of terror. 'The methods of combating the White Paper policy are determined by the superior organs of Palestine Jewry,' it declared. The responsible Jewish institutions 'oppose and denounce the shedding of innocent blood.'

That same evening Jewish terrorists exploded three bombs placed deliberately in telephone-cable manholes in the centre of the city, cutting off almost half of the Jerusalem urban telephone system. Five days later, on June 7, a Jewish terrorist shot and killed an Arab vegetable-seller, Fatoub Itzhak al-Naji, as he entered the Jewish market at Mea Shearim. The Military Commander of Jerusalem, Major-General Richard O'Connor, issued an angry notice. 'The murder took place close to, and in full view of, a number of other Jews who took no steps to stop the murderer and have since refused to give any evidence to the police with regard to his identity or movements,' the notice read. It continued: 'Lip service to non-violence is useless, if the Jewish community does nothing to check its criminal members or to assist the authorities in their efforts to maintain public security.' Once more a collective punishment was imposed on Jewish Jerusalem: the closure of all cafés and restaurants after four o'clock in the afternoon. That evening was to have been the first on which they reopened after the previous closure.

There was a moment of pageantry amid these sombre events when, on June 8, Jerusalem celebrated the King's Birthday. At the High Commissioner's residence on the Hill of Evil Counsel there was what the *Palestine Post* called 'the customary picturesque gathering, the attire ranging from the khaki of Army officers to the sober black of priests and monks, the colourful full-dress uniform of the Black Watch pipers and drummers, to formal morning coats of Consuls, officials and other notables, interspersed with the summer frocks of the ladies'. Several leading rabbis were present, and several leading members of the Muslim-Arab community, but no representatives of the national or local Jewish bodies. For them, the White Paper was too hated an instrument to permit social courtesies.

The violence in the streets did not deter overseas visitors to Jerusalem. Throughout June 7 and 8 a young American, John F. Kennedy, the second son of the American Ambassador to London, was in Jerusalem, seeing the many devotional places of Roman Catholic interest. On the evening of June 8, as the future President of the

United States spent his last night in Jerusalem before leaving for Lebanon and Syria, there were fourteen explosions throughout the city, as Jewish terrorists immobilised the electricity grid, cutting off electricity to almost all Jerusalem.

Kennedy left Jerusalem on the morning of June 9. On the following evening, as Edward Keith-Roach later recalled, 'an extremely ingenious time bomb, worked by acid and touched off by the hour hand of a watch, was pushed into the letter box of the new main hall of the General Post Office, completely wrecking the lovely green marble walls and counter. The British armourer sergeant was sent for to examine another bomb, which had failed to explode. It went off, and he was blown to bits. I saw his brains scattered over the ceiling while his lacerated body lay all over the floor.'

Jewish terrorists also managed to take a bomb into the Palestine Broadcasting Building. It exploded, killing two British army officers. A bomb was also thrown at the immigration offices in the city. 'A mine buried in the ground near my office', Keith-Roach later wrote, 'was attached to a long electric wire and touched off by a bell push. I saw the mutilated bodies of two British police inspectors being picked up in baskets.'

That summer, as both Arab and Jewish terrorist attacks continued in Jerusalem, many wounded Jewish civilians were brought to the new Hadassah Hospital on Mount Scopus. There was also, that summer, a most unusual obstetrical emergency. In the words of the official report: 'A woman in the ninth month of pregnancy was injured by bomb splinters. As the heart-beats of the embryo could not be clearly distinguished, it was feared that the uterus had been injured. The patient was operated on, and it was found that the uterus had been torn by a splinter, and that its cavity was filled with blood. The infant had swallowed some of the blood and developed asphyxia pallida. He was resuscitated, and the uterus did not have to be removed. In this case the baby saved his mother's life. Had she not been pregnant, the splinters would have entered her intestines. Both mother and child are well.'

*

The danger of war in Europe was impinging on Jerusalem. In June the fortnightly German News Agency bulletin was suspended in the city. With the coming of war in September 1939, both Arab and Jewish terrorism waned. War brought military controls to Palestine and Jerusalem, as to all the Allied and Axis capitals. Censorship of the mail was instituted. War also brought many personal privations, as German and Italian forces dominated much of the Mediterranean, and the sea supply route through the Strait of Gibraltar was cut off.

For the Jews of Jerusalem, war also brought a unifying sense of patriotic endeavour. Hitler was persecuting the millions of Jews who were falling under his control. The defeat of Hitler, to which Britain was committed, became also a Jewish goal. In Jerusalem, as elsewhere in Palestine, the enlisting of Jews in the army, support for the British war effort, and prayers that Britain herself would not be invaded, became part of the pattern of daily life.

For the Arabs of Jerusalem there was less fervour for the Allied cause. Denied the possibility of returning to Palestine, the Mufti of Jerusalem began to turn his powers of intrigue and agitation to the support of the Axis.

CHAPTER ELEVEN

The Second World War,
1939–1945

From biblical times Jerusalem had been a city of refuge, as well as a city of pilgrimage. Three years before the outbreak of the Second World War, the Emperor of Abyssinia, Haile Selassie, had arrived in Jerusalem as an exile, having been driven from his kingdom by the Italians. Among his titles was that of 'Lion of Judah'; his presence in the City of Judah inspired many of his followers to see his exile as an act of providence, and proof of his divinity. With the German conquest of Yugoslavia and Greece in April 1941 two more royal exiles reached the city: King Peter of Yugoslavia, whose government's defiance of the Germans had led to a savage bombing raid on Belgrade on Easter Monday, and King George II of Greece, who set up his first government-in-exile there.

As Nazi rule spread over Europe, those few Jews who were able to escape the Gestapo net and reach a neutral port also sought entry to Palestine. Help in obtaining the necessary entry documents for them came from an unexpected quarter: a senior Mandate official, Rashid al-Nashashibi, an official in the Palestine Government's Immigration Department in Jerusalem. When the wife of Dr Kleeberg, a physician who had joined the Hadassah Hospital on Mount Scopus, asked Rashid al-Nashashibi for help, he issued the documents that enabled five German-Jewish families to reach safety. 'Although he was a fervent Arab patriot,' Dr Kleeberg later recalled, 'he was nevertheless a humane man who could sympathise with the plight of refugees.'

Despite the active volunteering of Jewish Jerusalemites to serve in the British army and fight against Hitler, in the first week of March 1940 there was a series of street demonstrations in Jerusalem against British policy towards Palestine. On the last day of February the British Government had published regulations restricting land purchase by Jews throughout the country. No Jewish land purchase was to be allowed in the Jerusalem Corridor. The anger of Jerusalem's Jews was considerable. But they were guided in their actions by David Ben-Gurion's dictum, that the Jews of Palestine would fight the White Paper policies as if there was no war, and would fight the war as if there was no White Paper. The flow of volunteers to serve in the British Army was continuous.

Jerusalem itself was in danger in 1941, as Crete and Greece fell to the Germans. For a moment the Jewish-Arab dispute was suspended. On 8 August 1941 the former Mayor of Jerusalem, Ragheb Bey al-Nashashibi, gave a garden party. 'It was, I think, the first time in four or five years at which Jews, Arabs and Englishmen attended a social occasion together,' Arthur Ruppin wrote in his diary.

At the beginning of 1942 Rommel's desert army came within striking distance of Cairo and the Suez Canal. General O'Connor, the former Military Governor of Jerusalem, commanded several successful actions in the Western Desert, before being captured by the Germans. Thousands of Jewish Jerusalemites were already serving with the British forces in Egypt. Thousands more hastened to volunteer. Recruiting was particularly high among the students at the Hebrew University. Dr Judah Magnes, the university's President, asked: 'If the men of the Hebrew University do not realise the urgency of this hour, who will?' A Committee of Public Safety was set up, in case the British had to withdraw from Jerusalem: it was headed by the three leading Jerusalemites – Dr Magnes, Jamal al-Husseini and the Anglican Bishop of Jerusalem.

The danger to Jerusalem receded when Rommel was defeated at Alamein in October 1942 and driven back across the Western Desert towards Tunisia. But another anxiety quickly loomed: the fear of Jerusalem's Jews for the fate of the millions of Jews in Europe whom Hitler had sworn to destroy. During 1942 it had become known that hundreds of thousands of Jews had been confined in ghettos in German-occupied Poland. Hundreds of thousands had been massacred in the fields and ditches of German-occupied Russia. Hundreds of thousands had been deported from cities in Western Europe and from Poland to camps where they had been murdered.

Towards the end of November 1942 news reached Jerusalem of several horrific aspects of the Nazi Holocaust, including what were described as 'poison gas chambers' in which Jews had been killed. This news was brought by sixty Jews who had been exchanged for Germans living in Palestine. These men and women, who had reached Palestine by rail through Turkey, had experienced the Nazi occupation of Poland at first hand. In the same week, the Polish Government in London, which contained two Jewish Cabinet Ministers, issued a statement describing the atrocities of which it had been informed by Jan Karski, a courier who had managed to make his way out of German-occupied Poland. The *Palestine Post* published details from this statement on November 25, under the heading 'Mass-Butchery of Poland's Jews'. Two days later the Jewish Agency declared three days of official mourning, to begin on November 29 and culminating in a day of fasting on December 2.

From noon until midnight on December 2 all shops and businesses were closed throughout Jewish Jerusalem. All musical concerts and dances in cafés and restaurants, and all cinema performances, were cancelled. At the Wailing Wall, the *Palestine Post* reported, 'Famous rabbis stood shoulder to shoulder with porters and workmen' reciting psalms for divine intercession on behalf of Europe's Jews. In every school that morning teachers devoted the nine o'clock lesson to telling their pupils 'the tragic story of enslaved and tortured European Jewry'. At the end of the fast the Jewish Agency issued a special Recruiting Appeal, calling on all Jewish men and women who had not done so to enlist in the British forces.

On December 17 the mass murder of the Jews of Europe was denounced in the British House of Commons as a 'bestial crime'. Henceforth, every one of the thousands of Allied soldiers who came to Jerusalem on leave, from Egypt and North Africa, was seen as part of the avenging army that would overthrow Hitler and rescue those who managed to survive his evil intention. In the ghettos and concentration camps, men and women who were marked out for death clung tenaciously to life. For many of them, Jerusalem remained a part of their prayers and longing: no longer a distant spiritual aspiration, but a desperate hope of eventual redemption.

*

It was during 1942 that the ten-year-old Atara Mintz, then living at Ness Ziona in the coastal plain, made her first visit to Jerusalem. 'It was a tradition in those days,' she later recalled. 'All school children went to Jerusalem. It was a "must". Three classes went, we slept in the Laemel School. We spent the days walking. It was part of our upbringing. There was not a single poem about Jerusalem that was not taught in school. We were educated to regard Jerusalem as the centre of the world. During that visit I went to Mount Scopus to see the National Library. One of the directors there had brought my mother from Poland in the twenties. My father was then in the British Army. As we hadn't heard from him for so many months, I went to the Wall. I put, like every good girl, a note in the Wall. As my father came home on leave three weeks later, I was sure it was because of me.'

By a strange coincidence, when Atara Mintz's father was wounded in the Western Desert, he was brought back for hospitalisation to Jerusalem, to the Augusta Victoria Hospice, which in the First World War had been the German military headquarters, then British Government House, and in the Second World War was a British military hospital. So the young Atara Mintz returned to Jerusalem, to see her father.

At the nearby Hadassah Hospital, a Muslim Arab prince, Prince Feisal (later King of Saudi Arabia) was admitted with an undiagnosed disease that had led him to make the long journey by ship and train from Arabia. He was looked after by Dr Kleeberg and, having been diagnosed, spent four weeks at Hadassah being treated before returning home. Dr Kleeberg later recalled: 'The hospital presented its bill to the prince's secretary on the day that the prince was due to be discharged, and the secretary paid it. But shortly afterwards the secretary came into my office, looking rather distraught, and said that the prince wanted to know what my special fee was, for the brilliance of my diagnosis and treatment, which had certainly saved his life. I explained that medical ethics and my contract with Hadassah prevented my charging him anything over and above what the hospital charged. The secretary went away, clearly dissatisfied. He returned shortly afterwards carrying a package. He explained to me that I might have my medical ethics, but the prince also had his system of royal ethics as befitted a prince of Arabia. He said that the prince had decided that it was unthinkable that I could give him the inestimable gifts of life and health without his giving me some gifts, trifling in comparison, in return. The secretary then handed me his package. I opened it, and I found that it contained a large sum in bank-notes, a beautiful brown burnous and a golden keffiyeh. There was no way out, without mortally offending the prince, but to accept the gifts. I told Dr Yassky, the director-general of the hospital, about it, and handed over the money to Hadassah – he allocated it to my department for us to use for our research – and, with Yassky's permission, I gave the burnous and keffiyeh to my wife.'

Another story of reward in wartime Jerusalem was recalled by Edwin Samuel, head of the wartime Imperial Censorship in Palestine.

There was, he later wrote, 'a madman in Jerusalem who kept on writing begging-letters to God, always asking for ten (Palestinian) pounds to save him from starvation. After censorship, the letters were put in the "dead letter office" as undeliverable. These piteous pleas always went to the same examiner and eventually got her down. She took a five pound note out of her purse and sent it anonymously to the writer of the letters. By the next post came the following: "Dear God, Thank you so much for the ten pounds; but those bastards in the censorship stole half of it." '

*

On 19 March 1943 Haj Amin al-Husseini, the exiled Mufti of Jerusalem, broadcast from Rome to the Arab world. It was the birthday of the Prophet, and Haj Amin used the occasion to try to stir up anti-Jewish hatred. 'The Jews have a dangerous aim,' he declared, 'by which they challenge four hundred million Muslims, and that is their express wish to occupy the holy Islamic institutions including the al-Aksa Mosque in Jerusalem, under the pretext that this Mosque is the Temple of Solomon.' Arabs should remember, the Mufti added, that they had never fought the Jews without the Jews being 'the loser', and he then read out a pledge from the German Foreign Minister, Joachim von Ribbentrop, that 'the obliteration of what is called the Jewish National Home' was 'a basic tenet of German policy'.

Four months after the Mufti's broadcast, a British Cabinet Committee, meeting in secret in London, proposed the partition of Palestine into a Jewish State, an Arab territory, and the State of Jerusalem, this latter to remain under British 'supervision'. The area of the State of Jerusalem was to be extensive: the city itself, Bethlehem to the south, Ramallah to the north, Lydda and Ramleh in the coastal plain, the water source at Ras al-Ayin, and an outlet to the sea just south of Jaffa. All this would have to wait, however, if it were even to be discussed, until the end of the war.

The arrival in Palestine of sixty Jewish youngsters who had escaped the Nazi net, and had made their way across Russia and through Iran, created a sense of joy in Jerusalem. The first of several more, much larger groups, they were sent to youth villages to recuperate, and to learn the language and ways of Palestine Jewry. To help them in their new life, Henrietta Szold, who since 1933 had been in charge of Jewish youth resettlement in Palestine, had the idea of taking sixty boys and girls from the Old City, where girls were usually kept at home, and where living conditions were harsh, and mixing the two groups together. So it was that young Yemenite, Kurdish, Georgian and Moroccan Jews had a chance to experience village life, and to live in much more agreeable surroundings than those of the narrow alleyways to which they were accustomed. This was the start of an experiment which was to be continued on a much larger scale after the war, a tribute to Henrietta Szold's vision.

*

Among the thousands of British and Commonwealth soldiers stationed in Jerusalem in the war, not to police Palestine but to guard the whole region, was Peter Peirson. Before the war, as a student, he had been a witness of the Nazi occupation of Czechoslovakia. As the officer in charge of civilian labour in and around Jerusalem, he had to oversee the work of 10,000 Jews and Arabs. His office was in the Allenby Barracks, on the road to Bethlehem. 'The officers were billeted in long wooden huts, each divided into four,' he later recalled. 'Between them were strips of grass and beds containing shrubs, the haunt of chameleons. Our quarters were bare and spartan: the floors were concrete and there were few facilities – just a hard bed, an uncomfortable wooden folding chair, and some cupboards. Washing and toilet amenities were minimal and primitive.' In the Officers' Mess 'we had a dining room, a lounge, and a bar, with two NCOs in charge, but the food left much to be desired'.

Peirson's recollections continued: 'The local climate affected life and business far more than I realised at first. Most of the time it was warm, very warm, or hot, especially when the *khamsin* was blowing (at least, when it reached Jerusalem it sat on the top of the hills motionless, depriving the air of freshness, so that one felt lethargic beyond all belief, sapped of all will-power or desire). In HQ units, therefore, no work was carried out in the afternoon, whereas those units, whose outdoor labour force could not work at night, had to work in the afternoon, which meant that we had to carry on through the hottest hours. In the summer it was difficult to keep alert and to concentrate on work in the office. It was then that I discovered the efficacy of hot tea to cool one down. There was an Indian NAAFI in the next compound, and a steaming pint mug of good Indian tea would be brought to me in the sweltering heat of the Palestine afternoon; it was a job to drink it really hot, but I soon found myself cooling off after it! One class of men did not work during the day – the night watchmen.'

Wartime brought rationing to Jerusalem, as it did to all the Allied and belligerent cities. In the first week of June 1944 the egg ration was three eggs per child per week. Two weeks later adults were entitled to a single egg each week. In view of the shortages of so many foodstuffs, the inhabitants of the city were encouraged to eat potatoes. A special booklet was issued by the Food Controller, entitled '101 potato recipes', and an official Food Demonstration was held in thirteen different towns in Palestine, including Jerusalem, featuring 'the use of potatoes as main dishes, sweets, bread and cakes'.

*

The Allied landings in Normandy on 6 June 1944 electrified Jerusalem. At ten o'clock that morning the *Palestine Post* distributed a handbill in the streets, and pasted it up on walls. Animated crowds gathered to discuss the news. A second handbill was distributed at noon. At the request of the Chief Rabbinate, prayers were offered in the synagogues for 'the success of His Majesty's and Allied Forces in the liberation of all enemy-occupied territory'. Thousands of people went to the Wailing Wall to offer up their prayers. On June 11, in a special parade, 300 khaki-clad Auxiliary Transport Service women marched through the city. There was a 'general feeling', wrote the *Palestine Post*, 'that these girls were part of the forward march of the United Nations on the path of liberation'. So great was the crowd of onlookers in Ben Yehuda Street that the marching girls 'were almost forced to fight their way' down the street.

*

Inside Jerusalem, the British military authorities were waging a battle against the Jews of the Stern Gang, the 'Fighters for the Freedom of Israel', known from its Hebrew acronym as 'Lehi'. Named for their dead leader, Avraham Stern, they were a tiny but intensely active break-away terrorist group of the Irgun. Most of their victims were British soldiers, but they had also killed an Arab taxi driver near St George's Cathedral. A bomb left at the Cathedral with the intention of killing the High Commissioner had been discovered before it could go off. On June 19 two Stern Gang members were sentenced in the Jerusalem Military Court to long prison terms. Six days later it was announced that a home-made bomb workshop had been discovered in the Nahalat Shiva Quarter.

On 24 August 1944, as the Allied armies were about to drive the Germans from Paris, the issue of Jerusalem impinged on the outside world with the death of the city's Arab Mayor, Mustafa al-Khalidi. The Jews, with their substantial majority in the city, immediately demanded that al-Khalidi's successor should be a Jew. The population of Jerusalem was then almost 61 per cent Jewish, 21 per cent Muslim Arab and 18 per cent Christian Arab. The Muslims objected to a Jewish Mayor. This position had been held by a Muslim, they pointed out, ever since the British had arrived, even though there had been a Jewish majority then.

No decision was reached, and the Deputy Mayor continued in office as Acting Mayor. The Deputy, as was often the case, was a Jew, Daniel Auster. After much secret correspondence between the High Commissioner and the Colonial Office in London, the British proposed an annually rotating mayoralty, the first Mayor being either Jewish or Arab and the third (a new concept this) British. The Jews accepted this, provided that the rotation was every two years, not one, and provided also that the first Mayor under the new system was a Jew. The Arabs rejected this and held a protest strike throughout the city on 24 March 1945.

Daniel Auster remained Acting Mayor. The Arabs immediately boycotted all municipal council meetings, and business there was paralysed. On 11 July 1945 the High Commissioner issued a decree winding up the Jerusalem municipality. In its place he appointed a committee of six British officials to administer the city. This committee continued to supervise all municipal administration, and to maintain municipal services, for almost three years, until the end of the Mandate.

*

The declaration of Victory-in-Europe Day on 8 May 1945 was an electric moment for Jerusalem, although the city lay in Asia. Hardly a family of Jerusalem's Jews had not had a member fighting in the Allied armies, or relatives trapped, and in many cases murdered, in German-occupied Europe. That morning, outside the King David Hotel, surrounded by senior civilian and military personnel, the new High Commissioner, Field Marshal Viscount Gort, who had won the Victoria Cross in the First World War, saluted the hoisting of the Union Jack and the flags of the other Allied nations.

As the flags rose to the top of their poles the band of the Palestine Police Force struck up 'God Save The King'. The High Commissioner then proceeded to St George's Cathedral for a noonday service. Later that day, 'in token of the overwhelming victory won by His Majesty's Forces and the forces of our gallant allies in their fight to liberate Europe from oppression', Lord Gort granted an amnesty for a number of political prisoners, both Jews and Arabs. Then the citizens of Britain's most troubled Mandate celebrated the victory.

'Gaiety broke bounds late in the afternoon,' the *Palestine Post* reported. 'Hundreds of flags and pennants and bunting flying from most of the buildings in the centre of the town and decorating the squares sprang into life in the cooling breeze. Cars and buses and trucks, also beflagged, sounded their horns, and suddenly the empty streets were jammed with crowds.' On the steep slope of Ben Yehuda Street, wine flowed freely where, 'out of three huge barrels, servicemen passing the Carmel Mizrahi shop were served free drinks. By 6.30, 8,000 glasses had been poured.' A cyclist delivering bread was so inebriated after pausing to celebrate that he had to give up the rest of his bread round.

Although most British soldiers joined in the celebrations 'they could not help feeling their homesickness more keenly on the great day,' wrote the *Palestine Post*, 'and many of them were heard to say, 'What a time I would be having if I were in Blighty now.' '

*

On May 9, Jerusalem's VE-Day celebrations turned into two conflicting demonstrations. At the Jewish Agency building, to which a large crowd of Jews marched that afternoon, the *Palestine Post* reported that 'the Zionist colours were draped and bordered in black in mourning for Jews murdered in Europe'. Many in the crowd were discharged soldiers of the war that had just ended. Others were veterans of the First World War. Their slogans, 'which drew prolonged cheers from the watching crowds', demanded an end to the immigration restrictions of the 1939 British Government White Paper and free immigration to Palestine 'of the Jews of Europe'. Late that night an Arab demonstration formed up at the city's Jaffa Gate, and the marchers, 'shouting nationalist slogans', marched through the commercial centre of the city.

There was no bloodshed in Jerusalem on May 9, merely separate assertions of priorities. Both demands were quickly to be frustrated: the British refused repeated Jewish requests to allow 100,000 survivors of the concentration camps into Palestine, and tens of thousands of survivors who made their way 'illegally' to the Palestine coast were interned in camps in Cyprus. Arab national demands for immediate Arab majority rule likewise remained unfulfilled.

The war that had so shaken the equilibrium of Europe was over. But the coming of peace in Europe did not bring peace to Jerusalem. The conflict that had twice led to bloodshed in the decade before the war was about to re-emerge with renewed intensity.

CHAPTER TWELVE

A City in Turmoil, 1945–1947

The coming of peace in Europe and the Far East left Jerusalem stranded like a beached whale on the shore of conflict. Unhappy at the idea of denying Jews and Arabs a part in the municipal running of Jerusalem, the High Commissioner, Viscount Gort, asked Sir William Fitzgerald, the Chief Justice in the Mandatory administration, to carry out an independent inquiry into how the city should be run.

On 28 August 1945, two weeks after the surrender of Japan and the ending of the Second World War, the British Mandate Government published the Fitzgerald Plan. Cynics, with whom Palestine and Jerusalem abounded, could be forgiven for throwing up their hands at the thought of yet another British blueprint for Jerusalem. Yet as a search for the depoliticising of Jerusalem, it was a masterpiece. Two boroughs would be created, one Arab and one Jewish, each with six wards. The two boroughs would be self-governing.

Each borough would also send four representatives to the city's Administrative Council, where they would be joined by two other members, nominated by the British High Commissioner. The Administrative Council would have special control over the Holy Places, and over the Old City, which was to be excluded from the borough system.

Terence Prittie, an Irish Anglo-Catholic and a lover of Jerusalem, later commented: 'In case it should be thought that this was the brainchild of an insular Briton, it should be mentioned that Sir William was an Irishman, from County Limerick.' Writing in 1980, Prittie added: 'The best feature of the plan was its simplicity. The only flaw was extraneous; the plan presupposed that Britain would continue to supervise it. This basic assumption was already in doubt, and the plan – like so many others – was shelved. But the concept may not be dead.'

On 6 March 1946 the members of yet another commission to Palestine, the Anglo-American Committee of Inquiry, reached Jerusalem. One of them, Richard Crossman, a Labour Member of Parliament, described in his diary their first night in Jerusalem. 'The atmosphere of the King David Hotel is terrific,' he wrote, 'with private detectives, Zionist agents, Arab sheikhs, special correspondents, and the rest, all sitting about discreetly overhearing each other.'

*

In the immediate aftermath of the Second World War Jewish terrorism intensified. It was to cause the Anglo-American Committee considerable anger. Two organisations were involved, the Irgun Zvai Leumi (Etzel), or 'National Military Organisation', and the breakaway Stern Gang, the 'Fighters for the Freedom of Israel' (Lehi). Although their attacks were strongly and repeatedly condemned by the Jewish Agency, as well as by the vast majority of Jerusalem Jews, the bombing and killing were savage and relentless.

Hatred of the British had been inflamed among these two groups by the refusal of the British to allow survivors of the concentration camps into Palestine. The Jewish terrorists, who included two future Israeli Prime Ministers, Menachem Begin and Yitzhak Shamir, believed that by 'blood and fire' they could drive the British out of the country, and establish a Jewish State. Their most devastating attack was made on 22 July 1946, when members of the Irgun, disguised as Arabs, brought explosive charges in milk-churns into the hall outside the Regence Café in the basement of the King David Hotel. Above the café, the south wing of the hotel, five floors in all, was being used as the British administrative headquarters. An anonymous woman telephoned the switchboard operator at the hotel to say that the hotel must be evacuated as there would be an explosion 'in a few minutes'. Her warning was ignored.

At 12.37 the explosives went off. Five floors and twenty-five rooms collapsed into rubble. Ninety-two people in the wing were killed: Britons, Arabs and Jews. Among the dead were military and civilian officials, soldiers, clerks, typists, cleaners, drivers and messengers. The British dead included the Postmaster-General of Palestine, G. D. Kennedy, a veteran of the retreat from Mons in 1914. One of the Arabs killed, Jules Gress, a senior assistant accountant with the Secretariat, was a Catholic. He had been an officer in the Turkish army in the First World War, when he was taken prisoner by the British.

While at his bank that morning he had asked to be served quickly, so as not to be late for a Secretariat meeting. Commented the *Palestine Post*: 'He hurried back to his duty and his death.'

Among the Jews killed were Julius Jacobs, a senior Mandate official and secretary of the Jerusalem Music Society, who had served in the 2nd Jewish Battalion under Allenby; Dr Wilhelm Goldschmidt, a refugee from Hitler's Germany in 1933 who had risen to be an assistant legal draftsman to the Government of Palestine; and Claire Rousso, a nineteen-year-old telephone operator in the Secretariat. One of several drivers killed was an Armenian, Garabed Paraghanian. Twenty British soldiers were also killed, among them Sergeant Staples from Hull, Private Trebble from Totnes and Private Cole from Farnham. One of the Arab dead, Badr Abdul Fattah Abu Lahab, an official driver, was at the wheel of his parked car outside the hotel, waiting for his boss, when the explosives detonated. Another of those killed was a passer-by who had been walking in the street outside the hotel: he was struck by a large iron safe, hurled from the building by the force of the blast.

The Jewish Agency denounced what it called 'the dastardly crime' perpetrated by a 'gang of desperadoes', and called upon the Jews of Palestine 'to rise up against these abominable outrages'. The Sephardi Chief Rabbi, Ben Zion Uziel, spoke of his 'loathing and abhorrence' at the crime. The Jewish Community Council warned of the 'abyss opening before our feet by irresponsible men' who had carried out a 'loathsome act'. Watching the Jewish mourners at one of the many funeral processions, the *Palestine Post* commented: 'The faces were set and expressionless, as though they were burying not only our countrymen, but cherished hopes.' At the Muslim Cemetery, the Arab burials took place with military honours.

On the afternoon of July 23 all work and traffic stopped in Jewish Jerusalem at three o'clock, in mourning for the dead. 'Jerusalem is a small city,' David Courtney wrote in the *Palestine Post* on July 24, 'and a deed like this encompasses it. The cortèges yesterday moved off from no one house and no one quarter, and the lamentations were in many tongues: their burden was pitifully the same. The streets were still, but behind the shuttered windows pain rocked and moaned.'

On 1 March 1947 the Irgun blew up a wing of the British officers club in Jerusalem. No warning was given, and twelve British officers were killed. A month later, on 2 April, the British Government, weary of the struggle of governing the ungovernable, informed the United Nations that it would ask the General Assembly, due to open in five months' time, to make recommendations 'concerning the future government of Palestine'. Britain had decided to give up its Mandate. At Britain's request, a United Nations Special Committee on Palestine, UNSCOP, known also as the Palestine Committee, was set up to make proposals for the future of the country, and of the Jewish National Home. It published its report on 31 August 1947.

Under UNSCOP's proposals, Palestine was to be partitioned into two sovereign States, one Jewish and the other Arab. Both States would have to be democratic in character, and would have to safeguard the rights and interests of minorities. There would be an economic union between them, to ensure joint economic development. Jerusalem would be given to neither State, but would form a demilitarised and neutralised city with international trusteeship and a governor under the United Nations.

UNSCOP proposed that its plan should come into being by 1 September 1948, and that until then the British could continue to administer Palestine under the control of the United Nations. The plan was discussed by the United Nations at Lake Success, just outside New York, and was to be put to the vote on 29 November 1947. The Jewish Agency for Palestine accepted the plan, although the proposed Jewish State excluded Jerusalem. From early November the Agency lobbied with great energy to persuade a majority of the voting nations to vote for statehood. The resolution as eventually passed included the sentence 'The City of Jerusalem shall be established as a *corpus separatum* under a special international regime and shall be administered by the United Nations.' This was accepted by the Jewish Agency as the price to be paid for statehood elsewhere in Palestine. Under the United Nations plan, Jerusalem's governor was to be neither an Arab nor a Jew, nor a citizen of the new Arab or Jewish States in Palestine. A special police force, likewise neither Jewish nor Arab, would protect the Holy Places.

Under the United Nations plan, a referendum was to be held after ten years to seek the views of Jerusalem's residents as to whether the international regime should continue, or be modified. At the time of the United Nations vote, the population of the Jerusalem municipality was 99,320 Jews and 65,000 Arabs. But the borders of the *corpus separatum* were drawn from a far wider area than the municipal ones, to include many Arab towns and villages outside the municipal border, among them Bethlehem, in such a way as to tilt the balance away from the Jewish majority in Jerusalem itself to a figure of 105,000 Arabs and 100,000 Jews. As a result of this redrawn map, the Arabs would have a majority when the time came for a referendum.

Although the partition resolution was welcomed by the Jews, who had already, a decade earlier, accepted a similar plan put forward by the British, the Arab Higher Committee, supported by three outside Arab States, Iraq, Saudi Arabia and Syria, refused to accept the partition of the country even under a plan which gave the Arabs a State with considerably more land than the Jews. The Arab Higher Committee demanded instead a 'unified, independent Palestine' under Palestinian-Arab rule, from the Mediterranean to the Jordan.

*

Life in Jerusalem while waiting for the United Nations to decide on the future of the city and the country was conducted under the eye of the British army. 'Jerusalem is thick with barbed wire and barricades,' Zipporah Borowsky (later Zipporah Porath), who had just come from the United States on a scholarship to the Hebrew University, wrote to her parents on 22 October 1947. 'I registered at the American consulate and had to go through the business of British-controlled security zone passes and identity inspection. I still haven't gotten used to the idea of being frisked every time I go into a public building, even the Post Office.' The British had established three security zones in the centre of the city, Zones A, B, and C, known to the Jews as Bevingrad. Within these zones, behind barbed wire, the administration carried out its daily tasks. From the zones, and from their barracks in different parts of the city, British army patrols set out to maintain order, and to arrest troublemakers.

Was it inevitable that Britain's withdrawal would lead to bloodshed between Jews and Arabs in the city where their lives and quarters were so intermixed? On October 29 Judah Magnes used the opportunity of the ceremony at the Hebrew University to mark the opening of the academic year to speak out, on Mount Scopus, against the growing divisions in the society, and against the terrorism that had begun to divide Jew from Jew. He had not seen the terrorists 'called by their right name,' he said – 'killers, brutalised men and women within whose soul some savage beast was at prey. They are in truth dissenters – dissenters from the commandments of Judaism.'

Five days after Magnes spoke, three of those Jewish 'dissenters', members of the Stern Gang, shot dead Corporal Shalom Gurewitz, a Jewish member of the British Criminal Investigation Department, at his home in Jerusalem.

On 29 November 1947, at Lake Success, the United Nations voted on the partition resolution. A dramatic, tense call of votes, country by country, resulted in the resolution being passed with thirty-three votes in favour, thirteen against, and ten abstentions. One nation, Thailand, which could not make up its mind even to abstain, stayed away altogether. The abstainers included Britain, the Mandatory power. The opponents of partition included six Arab and four Muslim states, as well as the newly independent India. Both the United States and the Soviet Union voted in favour.

Because of the difference in time zones, the news of this endorsement of Jewish statehood reached Jewish Jerusalem after midnight. Throughout the early hours of November 30 the streets filled with singing and dancing. 'The moonlit blue night slipping into the red of dawn seemed unnoticed by the teeming tireless throngs in Jerusalem who had begun their celebrations about 2 a.m. yesterday,' the *Palestine Post* reported on the following day. 'The marching and singing and dancing continued past the time when shops and offices would normally have started their day's work. Many did not open.'

'With the dawn,' the *Palestine Post* account continued, 'the Zionist flag could be seen draped from buildings, strung to lamp posts, and fluttering from cars and trucks. Lorry-loads of singing youngsters careered through the streets. In the cafés, during the morning, there were celebrations in which Jew and Briton joined. Many of the soldiers and policemen had been on duty all night, but had discarded their guns to sample the revelry.'

Not revelry but violence was the reaction of some Arabs to the United Nations vote. During November 30, Arab riflemen fired shots at an ambulance on its way to the Hadassah Hospital on Mount Scopus. No one was hurt. That same day, a bus travelling from the coast to Jerusalem was attacked, while still in the coastal plain, by three Arabs with a machine-gun and hand grenades. Four Jews were killed. Two of those killed were Jerusalemites, Hirsh Stark and Hanna Weiss. Another of the dead, the twenty-two-year-old Shoshana Mizrachi Farhi, had been on her way to Jerusalem to get married.

A second bus, also bound for Jerusalem, was attacked half an hour later at almost the same spot, again with hand grenades and automatic fire. One passenger was killed, Nehama Hacohen, a pathologist at the Hadassah Hospital. Later that day a twenty-five-year-old Jerusalemite, Moshe Goldman, was shot dead at the Jaffa-Tel Aviv boundary.

*

In spite of these tragic events, the Jewish rejoicing at statehood, even with Jerusalem excluded, continued throughout December 1. That afternoon, long lines of boys and girls in Scout uniform made their way down the Jaffa Road and into King George V Avenue, led by a drummer and three buglers, on their way to the Jewish Agency Building. Police armoured cars made their appearance. They did not, as had become usual every time the British intervened, seek to control the crowds or to push them back, but instead 'took on their loads of cheering boys and girls and flew the Zionist flag'.

That day, as the Jews of Jerusalem celebrated the prospect of Jewish statehood, the Arabs of Jerusalem, who had also been offered statehood, but whose leaders rejected any form of Jewish sovereignty anywhere in Palestine, were bystanders to the Jewish rejoicing, in which dancing the horra, an exhilarating dance in the form of a rapidly whirling circle, was a main feature. 'In Zion Square,' reported the *Palestine Post*, 'groups of Arab youths watched a horra, while Arab hawkers were seen as usual with their vegetables and fruit in the Jewish quarters. There was no dwindling in the Arab attendances at matinee cinema performances in the Jewish area, and a number of Arabs came as usual to do their shopping in Ben Yehuda and other main streets.' During the afternoon an Arab Legion truck 'manned by silent men with fingers on triggers, drove slowly through the Jaffa Road crowds, some of whom banged good-naturedly on the side of the vehicle.' But while Jewish Rehavia 'spilled over with people', Arab Talbiyeh was 'quiet'.

That quietness was a brief lull before the storm. Notices put up by the Arab Higher Committee throughout the Arab areas of Jerusalem on December 1 called for a three-day general strike to begin on the following day, together with a complete boycott on the purchase of all Jewish goods. On December 1 the Committee declared that November 29 was henceforth to be 'a day of mourning' and that it marked the start 'of the struggle against Partition'. Even with British rule still in place, and British troops and policemen still the ultimate arbiters of law and order, Jerusalem's 99,000 Jews, 40,000 Muslim Arabs and 25,000 Christian Arabs were entering a period of disintegration. Unknown to them, the British, who could have stayed in Palestine until September 1948, had decided to leave in May.

*

The Arab reaction to the suggestion of any form of Jewish State in Palestine cast a pall of apprehension over Jewish Jerusalem. On December 1 groups of Arabs hurled stones at the consulates of two of the countries which had voted in favour of partition: Poland and Sweden. The Czechoslovak Consulate was also threatened. On the following day, in the Old City, three Jews were shot dead through a break in the wall separating the Jewish and Arab quarters. That same day about 200 Arabs, mostly youngsters between the ages of ten and twenty, marched towards the centre of Jerusalem, from Mamilla Street to Princess Mary Street, making for Zion Square, chanting 'Death to the Jews!' A line of British police barred their way. The mob then turned back down the hill to the Commercial Centre below the Jaffa Gate, forcing their way into many textile and other shops. Forty shops were looted, and large quantities of textiles were set on fire.

When Jews tried to reach the Commercial Centre in order to repel the attacks, British forces prevented them from doing so. Against the Arab attackers, however, the British forces did not intervene. Some soldiers were even photographed looking on while the attackers continued to loot. Although no Arabs were apprehended, sixteen Hagannah members were arrested for bearing arms some distance from the scene of the violence. That evening the Hagannah commanders decided that in any such similar circumstances in future the Jewish forces would open fire.

Throughout the city there were violent episodes on December 2. As the Arab attack on the Commercial Centre was in progress, a crowd of Jews gathered in Zion Square and proceeded to attack Arab shops on Queen Mary's Avenue. At the same time they set fire to an Arab garage in Nahalat Shiva. Hagannah volunteers hurried to the scene, and, helped by British police, drove the Jews back up the Jaffa Road.

That evening the drivers of a Jewish bus company expressed their thanks to a British Police Inspector and his men. The Britons had protected five Jewish buses and their passengers on their way from the city to Mekor Hayim and Talpiot when they were attacked by an Arab mob. Three Jews, including one of the drivers, had been hurt.

In anguish, the columnist David Courtney wrote on December 3 in the *Palestine Post*: 'The Arab goes out, and stones a bus, stabs a poor Jew. He is got together in a crowd and worked up to a desire to break, burn, loot, kill. He is persuaded that to do so is to be a patriot. He is persuaded that to do so is to serve Freedom. He cannot surely be persuaded that to do so is to ensure for himself and his family, bread, work, good wages, the produce of his labour in the fields, a better standard of life, and peace, without which, what is the substance or use of freedom?'

*

There was resentment among Jews everywhere in Palestine, but particularly in Jerusalem, that the city's 99,000 Jews, and many Jewish public institutions, including the Hebrew University, were to be excluded from the Jewish State under the United Nations plan. Almost one-sixth of all the Jews in Palestine lived in Jerusalem: all of them were to be outside the Jewish State. The city would also, according to the United Nations, be 'permanently dependent' on the new Jewish and Arab States 'for its power, water and food supplies'.

Working out the details for an international Jerusalem was a high point on the United Nations agenda. A six-nation working-group had been set up at Lake Success to formulate detailed plans. The nations were the United States, Britain, France, China, Mexico and Australia. One area of encouragement for Jewish Jerusalem during the discussions of the working group was that, provided money was found to establish new industries, Jewish immigrants would be allowed to settle in the city and find employment there.

*

Following the attack on the Commercial Centre on December 2 the British imposed a curfew on Jerusalem's Arab quarters. But on the following morning, as Jewish workers were evacuating undamaged goods from the the Centre, a group of Arabs attacked them. The workers withdrew on a truck, but one of them, Yitzhak Penzo, slipped and fell off. He was immediately set upon and killed. At about the same time, three Jews were attacked and injured in the Old City. An Armenian who was nearby, Artin Dargumian, died of fright.

Later in the day there was further violence throughout Jerusalem. A group of Arabs who gathered on Mount Zion to attack Jewish homes in Yemin Moshe were fired on by British police and driven off. Forty Jews employed at the Post Office workshops near the Government Printing Press were stoned as they made their way back to western Jerusalem. A Jewish veterinary surgeon, Dr O. Kahane, returning by car from calling on an Arab client in Abu Tor, was stoned near the station. In the Old City, Arabs attacked one of the synagogues in the Jewish Quarter, but were driven off. That same day, eight Jews living in a house in the Musrara Quarter outside the Damascus Gate were forced to leave their homes. As the *Palestine Post* reported, they 'were warned that the house would be fired by Arabs if they did not evacuate. They reported to the Police and a British officer and a squad of British constables went down to assist them to move out.'

In Musrara, and in the Old City, there then began what was to become a frequent sight in Jerusalem: the movement of Jews and Arabs from their homes, to places of safety. This was particularly noticeable during December 3, as Jews living in Muslim areas of the Old City, and Arabs living in the Jewish Quarter, packed up their belongings and left. Each hoped to be able to return when the violence was over. The Jews who remained in the Jewish Quarter felt isolated and vulnerable. They were only a small community by 1947: some 2,500, compared with the Old City's 24,000 Muslim and 5,000 Christian Arabs. And they were separated from the Jews of western Jerusalem by gates, roads and quarters controlled by the Arabs.

On the morning of December 5 the Jewish Agency announced the call-up of all men and women between the ages of seventeen and twenty-five for national service. The Hagannah, although not legally armed, would take over responsibility for the defence of Jews against attacks. An Arab who walked through Zion Square that morning, and was believed by the Jews to be armed, was attacked by a group of Jews in full view of several British policemen, who made no effort to go to his aid. He was rescued by Jewish policemen and Hagannah members, who escorted him out of the area. Also that morning, Hagannah guards caught three Arabs pilfering damaged shops in the ruined Commercial Centre: they were handed over to the British police.

Buses and cars coming from Tel Aviv and the coast to Jewish Jerusalem were now travelling mostly in convoy.

*

To prevent Muslim Arabs who might come to pray on the Haram from being incited to violence, the British imposed a curfew on the Jerusalem-Ramallah and Jerusalem-Hebron roads. The road to Tel Aviv continued to be the scene of sniping. On December 7 a convoy of eight buses on its way to the coast was fired on while still in the Jerusalem hills. One girl was killed, nineteen-year-old Pessia Lev. She was being trained as a nurse in Jerusalem, and was on her way home for the festival of Hanukah. It was the thirtieth anniversary of the British army's victorious march to Jerusalem through those same hills.

On December 8, in violence throughout Palestine, fourteen Jews, three Arabs and two Britons were killed. One of the Jews was a senior Hagannah officer, Yehoshua Globerman, shot when his car was stopped by Arabs at Latrun, on its way from Jerusalem to Tel Aviv. He had been travelling in a convoy, but drove on when the convoy was stopped at a British checkpoint but he was allowed to proceed. The convoy passed his body a few minutes later.

Almost all movement in and out of Jerusalem was now made by convoy. Among the supplies brought safely to Jerusalem on December 8 were 60,000 eggs. On December 10 three convoys left Jerusalem for Tel Aviv, and two from Tel Aviv to Jerusalem. A single stoning and one person injured made it seem an almost uneventful day. Three convoys also made the journey southwards that day to and from the Jewish settlements of the Etzion Bloc, ten miles south of Jerusalem.

An uneasy pattern of life fell on Jerusalem. Almost every day one or two Jews were killed, mostly by stabbing. Almost every day gangs of Jews stoned Arab vehicles. After one such attack, on an Arab truck carrying vegetables, the *Palestine Post* reported: 'The driver escaped but the vegetables were destroyed.' On December 11 there was a concerted Arab attack on the Jewish Quarter of the Old City, where 2,500 Jews were living. For six hours Hagannah members fought them off. Three Arabs were killed, among them Issa Moham-med Iraqash, believed to be one of the leading inciters of violence in the Old City. Also killed, the *Palestine Post* reported, were Abed Ibrahim Abdul and his fifty-six-year-old mother, who died 'of bullet wounds as she ran to him'. Three Jews were injured in the fighting. A Red Shield ambulance which went to the Old City for the Jewish wounded was fired on, but succeeded in taking the men to the Hadassah Hospital. The Red Shield was the symbol – a Star of David – of the Jewish equivalent of the Red Cross, known in Hebrew as the Magen David Adom (Red Shield of David).

Also on December 11 ten Jews were killed when their convoy, carrying food and water to the Etzion Bloc settlements, was ambushed just south of Bethlehem. A rapid-firing Bren gun was believed to have been used in the attack. Red Shield ambulances brought the dead and wounded back to Jerusalem.

*

It was increasingly dangerous for Jews to reach Jerusalem from the coast. On December 12 a British Overseas Airways truck being driven by an Arab from Lydda Airport to the city was stopped by an Arab gang, who ordered the Arabs on board to scatter. Three Jews on the truck were then taken down and shot. Two were members of the BOAC staff at the airport, Yitzhak Jian and David Ben Ovadia; the third was a cook at the airport restaurant, Joseph Litvak.

An extra element in the fighting that December was the dramatic increase in activity of the Irgun and the Stern Gang. Both groups still regarded terrorism as the most effective method to be used against both British rule and the Arabs. They were also still repeatedly denounced by the Jewish Agency, and opposed by the Hagannah. Although remaining small in numbers and secretive in method, they made a cruel mark on the city. On December 13 several Irgun members, driving in two cars near the Damascus Gate bus station, hurled two bombs into the crowd, and opened fire with automatic weapons. Five Arabs were killed, including a fourteen-year-old boy, Ahmed Amin Hamma, from the village of Et Tur on the Mount of Olives. Forty-seven Arabs were injured. That evening, grenades were thrown at the offices of the al-Husseini newspaper, *al-Wahda*, in Nahalat Shiva, and four Arabs were injured.

*

After two weeks of violence throughout Jerusalem and on the roads around it, the death toll was 74 Jews, 71 Arabs and 9 British. As Arab attacks intensified, the Hagannah began to shell buildings in which they believed armed Arabs were gathering as a prelude to an attack. Among the buildings shelled were a flour mill in Beit Safafa and a soda-water factory near Romema. Also shelled was the Supreme Muslim Council headquarters near the American Colony. No one was killed.

With sniping, stabbing and stoning becoming daily occurrences in the city, the Jews took steps to prepare for a long struggle. It was not yet clear whether, when the British eventually withdrew, several armies from Arab States outside Palestine might attack. They might even move into Palestine before the British left. The Associated Press reported in the second week of December that the Prime Minister of Iraq, Saleh Jabr Pasha, had spent three days in Amman trying to persuade King Abdullah to allow Iraqi troops to pass through Transjordan on their way to Palestine. The King was said to have resisted the Iraqi pressure, but to have been warned by Saleh Jabr: 'You will lose your throne, unless you wholeheartedly join the Arab people.'

The Jews of Jerusalem prepared for the worst. On December 17 a blood bank was opened. It had a target, which it surpassed within two months, of 1,000 doses of plasma. Dr Bernard Joseph (later Dov Joseph), who was in charge of all emergency measures in Jerusalem, later recalled: 'When the thousandth donor, a woman, was offered the not inconsiderable gift in those days of a bottle of kerosene and an egg, she refused and felt insulted.'

The water supply to the city presented, as always, the gravest of problems. This water came from the coastal plain through three pumping-stations, any one of which the Arabs could disable. On December 19 a secret request was sent to all Jewish householders with unused cisterns, asking them to clean them out in preparation for water storage. Forty Jewish engineers examined the cisterns, and helped to make them good. It was calculated that, if the water supply from the coast was cut off, the cisterns, together with the water in the Romema reservoir at the entrance to the city, would provide a ration of ten litres of water per person per day for drinking, cooking and washing – sufficient, it was calculated, to withstand a 115-day siege. If the ration was cut to five litres per person, the city could hold out for 250 days.

The municipal water engineer, Zvi Leibowitz, arranged for some of the water that was being pumped in freely for the daily needs of the city, and for the British, to be diverted to the cisterns. When the British complained to the municipal water authority that they were not getting their full regular supply, there was genuine mystification: Leibowitz had not let his British superiors into his secret.

*

On December 27 Golda Meyerson (later Golda Meir), the head of the Jewish Agency's Political Department, was among those travelling to Jerusalem by convoy when the Arabs attacked in force. She herself was unharmed, but seven Jews were killed. Among the dead was Hans Beyth, who for many years had been at the centre of the help given to newly arrived German-Jewish and other immigrant children. Beyth had just come from welcoming a group of European Jewish children, survivors of the German concentration camps, who had just been released by the British from detention camps in Cyprus. On the day after this attack, ten people were killed in Jerusalem: five of them were Jews and five were Arabs. This was the highest number of daily killings since the beginning of the disturbances a month earlier.

The five Arabs were killed when a group of Jewish youths, members of the Stern Gang, forced their way into an Arab home in Romema and opened fire on the men inside. One of the Jews who was killed was stabbed to death near the Damascus Gate on his way to a funeral. Another of the Jews, Miriam Meir, the mother of six children, was hanging up her washing on the roof of her house in the Jewish Quarter of the Old City when she was shot dead by an Arab sniper. Another Jew, Dr Hugo Lehrs, a British Government medical officer at the Beit Safafa Government Contagious Diseases Hospital, was walking with an Arab doctor and an Arab nurse from one hospital building to another when three armed Arabs approached. 'Which is the Jew?' they asked. The Arab doctor and nurse then stood aside, shots were fired, and Dr Lehrs was killed.

During the day there was also firing from Deir Yassin into the Jewish suburb of Givat Shaul. Later that day the Arab Mukhtar of Deir Yassin and a number of his villagers went to Givat Shaul to apologise for the shooting, which, they said, had been carried out by strangers. 'They wanted peace with their Jewish neighbours.'

On the morning of December 29 Moshe Rembach, a Jew who had been working at Barclays Bank since it first opened in 1918, was on his way to work when he was offered a lift in a friend's car for safety's sake. He refused the lift, telling his friend: 'The Arabs know me, nothing will happen to me.' A few minutes later, almost at the entrance to the bank, he was shot and killed.

Rembach's was not to be the only death in Jerusalem that day. Four hours later, three members of the Irgun struck for a second time at the Damascus Gate bus station. Riding in one car, they threw out a single bomb as they sped past. Fifteen Arabs were killed, among them a ten-year-old boy, Suaal Amashe, and an eleven-year-old girl, Namal Shamaa. Shortly after the explosion, two Jews, a father and daughter, and two British policemen were shot dead by Arab gunmen.

Because of the Damascus Gate bomb, the funeral processions of the Jews killed on the previous day, including that of Dr Lehrs, had to be turned back on security grounds as they made their way through eastern Jerusalem to the Jewish Cemetery on the Mount of Olives. At about the same time, five Jewish doctors, returning to the city by car from the Hadassah Hospital, were attacked at Sheikh Jarrah. They managed to find refuge in a Jewish home in the nearby Shimon Hatzadik Quarter. Their car was set on fire. On the following morning a bus making its way to Mount Scopus with hospital workers was attacked near Sheikh Jarrah, and fourteen passengers were wounded, four of them seriously.

Killing, wounding and setting fire to cars had become a daily feature of life in Jerusalem. There seemed no end to the permutations that the killing could take. On December 30 yet another funeral of victims of the violence was held at the Jewish Cemetery on the Mount of Olives. Ten Jews were to be buried that day, seven of them men and women who had been murdered. These included Dr Lehrs and the others whose funeral procession had been turned back at the Damascus Gate on the previous day. A British police escort accompanied the funeral bus on its second journey in twenty-four hours. As the burials began, Arab gunmen opened fire from the direction of Et Tur. Members of the Burial Society, which was in charge of the actual burials, took cover in a ditch and behind a wall. The police guarding the funeral fired back at the attackers.

For two hours the firing continued back and forth. One Arab, one British policeman and one Jew, a member of the Burial Society, were killed. The bodies of those who had been about to be buried, and the bodies of those newly killed, were taken back in the bus to Jerusalem. As the bus drove through Et Tur it was fired on, and one man wounded.

The year 1947 ended with two religious festivals being celebrated throughout the world: the Jewish Hanukah and the Christian Christmas. Both were overshadowed in Jerusalem by a violence and bitterness that had no precedent in the history of the city in modern times, or at any time in the past since the Jewish revolt against the Romans nearly 2,000 years earlier.

CHAPTER THIRTEEN

The Last Four and a Half Months of British Rule, January-May 1948

Although British rule still had four and a half months to run, the road from Tel Aviv to Jerusalem had become precarious for all Jews making the journey to or from the city. For much of its thirty miles the road went through Arab-controlled areas. Inside the Jerusalem municipal boundary several Jewish suburbs lay beyond Arab suburbs and could be cut off from the centre by Arab snipers. The Jewish Quarter of the Old City could be reached only through Arab areas, and was effectively besieged by January 1948, despite British promises that convoys of food and other essential supplies could drive to it through the Jaffa Gate.

From the Arab suburb of Katamon, in the south-west of the city, fire was continually being directed into the Jewish suburbs around it. Hoping to halt this fire, on the morning of 5 January 1948 the Hagannah launched a military operation against Katamon. The attack took place during a ferocious thunderstorm. The main target was the Semiramis Hotel, a meeting place for young Arabs active in the fighting. The Hagannah detonated a bomb in the hotel. At least eleven Christian Arabs living in the hotel were killed. Another resident who was killed was the Spanish Vice-Consul. The hotel had indeed been a meeting place for Arab insurgents, but they usually gathered there in the evening. The bomb went off in the morning.

The Jewish Agency leaders were outraged by the Semiramis Hotel bombing. Golda Myerson, the Director of the Agency's Political Department, complained angrily that it had been carried out without her knowledge. The Chairman of the Jewish Agency, David Ben-Gurion, summoned before Lord Gort's successor as High Commissioner, General Sir Alan Cunningham, appeared to Cunningham to be 'clearly upset' by the attack, which Ben-Gurion called 'entirely wrong'. A few hours later Ben-Gurion removed the Hagannah officer responsible for the bombing, Michael Shechter, from his post as Deputy Commander in Jerusalem.

Some days later David Courtney wrote in the *Palestine Post*: 'A week or two back the Jewish Hagannah, in a rash and misguided moment, put a bomb in a Katamon hotel, which, it was believed, had become an important post of the enemy. That tragic act killed innocent people. When communities, or nations, or groups of nations are set against each other in violent conflict, the innocent die along with the others. The guilty, in all wars, are few and well hidden and not always recognisable. But the Jews put the bomb in a small hotel, which blew the hotel up, and killed innocent people.'

The wider impact of the Semiramis Hotel bomb was immediate, as most of the Arabs living in Katamon, and all the women, children and old people, left the suburb in panic, abandoning their homes and most of their belongings. Some went south to the predominantly Christian Arab village of Beit Jalla, near Bethlehem. Others went to the Muslim and Christian Quarters of the Old City. Those with the means to do so went to Amman, Cairo, Beirut or Damascus.

*

Bombs had begun to replace bullets in the battleground that was once a bustling city. On January 7 the Irgun planted a bomb at the Arab National Guard outpost at the Jaffa Gate, through which no food was being allowed to pass to the Jewish Quarter. The bomb killed fourteen Arabs and wounded forty. As the Irgun men drove off, the British police vehicle which they had commandeered for the attack broke down. They continued to flee on foot, but three of them were shot dead by British police. On January 9 a British police driver, Wally Thorley, was killed when his armoured car hit an Irgun roadblock. On the following day another Palestine policeman, Inspector J. C. 'Taff' Taylor, a senior member of the Jerusalem Operational Patrols, was killed in a clash with Arab gunmen at Ramat Rahel. That day the British released figures showing the number of dead in Jerusalem in the previous six weeks. It was a real war, with the heaviest death toll for such a period in the city's history; 1,069 Arabs, 769 Jews and 123 Britons killed: an average of forty-six people killed every day.

Mid-January saw a second exodus of Arabs from their homes, only six days after the Semiramis Hotel bomb had created panic among the Arab residents of Katamon. On January 11 the Hagannah blew up the home of Suleiman Hamimi, the village elder of Sheikh

Badr, a small Arab village at the entrance to the city. There had been sniping from Sheikh Badr against Jewish convoys making their way out of the city towards Tel Aviv. In a second Hagannah raid on Sheikh Badr two days later, twenty Arab houses were damaged. The nearby mixed suburb of Romema and the two nearby Arab villages of Kerem as-Sila and Lifta were already under Hagannah and Irgun attack. The Arab owner of the petrol station at Romema, who was suspected of informing the Arab irregular troops in the area about the departure of convoys to Tel Aviv, was attacked by a Hagannah unit and killed.

As the fighting intensified around the entrance to the city, the Jewish residents of Romema, where there was an Arab majority, wanted to leave, but the Hagannah ordered them to stay. It was the Arab residents of Lifta, Kerem as-Sila, Romema and Sheikh Badr who fled from their homes that week, abandoning most of their belongings. Their empty homes were soon the prey to the unscrupulous. On January 16 Sheikh Badr was looted by a Jewish crowd. Four days later the commander of the Hagannah in Jerusalem, Israel Zablodovsky, informed Ben-Gurion that 'the eviction of Arab Romema has eased the traffic situation', while in the centre of western Jerusalem the predominantly Arab suburb of Talbiyeh 'is also increasingly becoming Jewish, though a few Arabs remain'.

It was not only Arab families caught up in Hagannah and Irgun attacks who were fleeing from Jerusalem. Many Arab leaders had decided to sit out the fighting away from Palestine altogether, and to return after the British had left and all Jerusalem was, they assumed, in Arab hands, as a result of the fighting that others would do on their behalf. On January 10 a member of the Arab Higher Committee, a former Mayor of Jerusalem, Dr Hussein Fakhri al-Khalidi, complained to an Arab merchant, Abu Zaki, about his committee's departure: 'Everyone is leaving me. Six are in Cairo, two are in Damascus. I won't be able to hold on much longer. Jerusalem is lost. No one is left in Katamon. Sheikh Jarrah has emptied, people are even leaving the Old City. Everyone who has a cheque or a little money is off to Egypt, off to Lebanon, off to Damascus.'

*

On Mount Scopus, the Hebrew University and the Hadassah Hospital were isolated from the centre of the city by Arab snipers who had taken up positions in the deserted Arab quarter of Sheikh Jarrah. It was only possible for teachers and students to get to the university in cars or trucks that had been fitted with armoured plates. On the last day of 1947 the Hebrew University had been forced to end all courses and close its doors.

It was to secure the road to Mount Scopus, and in particular to the Hadassah Hospital, that the Hagannah launched an attack on Sheikh Jarrah on January 13. Sheikh Jarrah was captured, but then the British intervened, and it was handed over to British control. The British promised not to permit armed Arabs into the area. Forty-eight hours later, British forces handed over the area to Arab control.

Attacks on those going up to the hospital were a daily occurrence. When, in the middle of January, a student nurse was killed, Dr Chaim Yassky, the Director-General of the hospital, wrote to the Hadassah organisation in New York: 'If we regarded complete security as an essential condition for our work in Palestine, we would have to give up all ideas of nationhood.'

*

Each of the dozens of isolated incidents that month had a different twist to it. Two such were reported in the newspapers on January 15. On the previous day a British civilian employed by the army, Thomas Berry, and his Jewish wife, Tikva Shitreet, decided that it was too dangerous for them to continue to live in the German Colony, scene of repeated Arab attacks. The couple had met when they were both serving with the British army in Cairo. They decided to move away, but while walking along the main street of the German Colony that very day they were shot at by two Arabs in full daylight. Berry was killed outright. His wife died as she was being taken by car to the Hadassah Hospital. Later that day, in the looted Commercial Centre, a Jewish woman, Sarah Friedman, the owner of a beauty salon in Julian's Way, was removing some of her goods from one of the damaged buildings when an item of furniture fell off the truck. As she went to pick it up an Arab approached her, dragged her back into the Commercial Centre, then shot her in the head and knifed her in the face. She survived, but with the loss of one eye.

Some sort of daily life went on; in the same newspapers that reported these two violent incidents were advertisements for a 'special sale of ready-made shoes', 'hot water boilers – British made', and 'high grade materials for coats, dresses, costumes – at very low prices'. Restaurants and cafés remained open, though at the Corso Café in King George V Avenue six customers were wounded when a grenade was thrown in on January 17. In spite of the 'holding up of the city's administrative, municipal and commercial life by gunmen', the *Palestine Post* wrote three days later, 'the Jews, as far as possible, have kept about their normal affairs'. The Arabs did likewise. But the killings went on without respite.

*

On the night of January 18 an attempt was made by thirty-five Hagannah volunteers to make contact with the isolated Jewish settlement of Kfar Etzion, ten miles to the south, which had been under constant Arab attack for more than a month. Each of the volunteers was trained in patrol techniques and in night fighting. On the second night they were ambushed by several hundred armed Arabs. All thirty-five were killed. Among the eleven Arabs killed was Sheikh Haj Salman al-Atram Ibn Said, a leading figure of the Negev Bedouin.

'Jerusalem's face was sad today,' Zipporah Borowsky wrote to her parents on January 19. 'It isn't easy to accept the fact of death, and even harder when you know personally many of those who died. But *thirty-five boys* is heartbreaking, all young wonderful people.' One of the thirty-five was Moshe Pearlstein, 'the first American to be killed here. The American group here is grieved. Moshe was a great guy.'

An added and deep dimension to the ill-feeling that now festered between the Jews and the British in Jerusalem was caused that January by the clandestine help given to the Arabs by members of the British police, and also by British army deserters. More than 200 British soldiers had disappeared from their barracks and were known to be participating on the Arab side or, for reasons of their own, acting directly against the Jews.

*

On the night of February 1 there was an explosion in the centre of the city which completely destroyed the building in which the *Palestine Post* was printed. One of the paper's journalists, Ted Lurie, recalled leaving the building a few minutes earlier for a coffee break at the Café Atara just down the street. As he approached the cafe a blast knocked him off his feet. He tried to telephone the paper from the cafe to find out what had happened, but could not get through. Then he saw flames in the sky and hurried back to the building. It appeared that an army-type car filled with dynamite had been parked outside. It was widely believed, not only by Jews, that British army deserters had carried out the attack.

No one was killed outright in the *Palestine Post* explosion, but twenty people in the building were hurt by the blast and flying glass, and four of those injured died later of their injuries: Haim Farber, a printer who worked at the paper; Yehoshua Weinberg, the building's watchman, who had been a partisan in Europe during the Second World War; sixty-year-old Deborah Daniel, who lived in a flat in one of the adjacent buildings; and seventy-five-year-old Binyamin Meyuohas, who also lived in a flat next to the printing press.

The *Palestine Post* went to press on the night of the explosion in borrowed office space, reporting on the following morning: 'The last injured man to be brought out of the press, when it was thick with smoke and dust and stiflingly hot, was rescued by Mr John Donovan, the Jerusalem correspondent of the NBC, who was on his way to the *Palestine Post* when the explosion occurred. Another foreign correspondent who helped in the rescue work was Mr Fitzhugh Turner of the *New York Herald Tribune*, who climbed the stairs into the burning building in search of victims, together with three British constables.'

Many of the tenants in the damaged buildings reached safety in their night clothes. Others, the *Palestine Post* reported, 'wandered aimlessly about the nearby streets until taken in by friends and hotels'. Also destroyed in the blast was the irreplaceable documentation of the life and personalities of North African Jewry that had been collected over many years by Abraham Almaliah.

The attack on the *Palestine Post* building had been ordered by Abdul Khader al-Husseini, the leader of the Arab irregular forces around Jerusalem, and a cousin of the exiled Haj Amin. The bomb had been prepared by Abdul Khader's explosive expert, Fawzi al-Kutub, helped by a Christian Arab, Abu Khalil Genno (also known as Aboud Jonkho) and by two British deserters, Corporal Peter Marsden and Captain Eddie Brown. They had originally intended to bomb the Zion Hall Cinema, but, according to Genno, who discussed the bombing with Ted Lurie in Ramallah after the 1967 war, they had arrived at the cinema too late, after the film had ended and the audience had left, and so their vehicle headed for the only building nearby that was still lit up.

Genno was assassinated thirty years later by an Arab gunman, as part of the campaign against those who, at that time, were accused of working, as Genno had done, in business partnership with Israelis. His funeral service was held in the Church of the Holy Sepulchre.

*

Violence and counter-violence escalated. On the day of the *Palestine Post* bomb, the Stern Gang blew up the homes of two Arab families in Katamon from which sniper fire had been directed on the Jewish suburb of Rehavia. In a Hagannah raid on an Arab gang which had penetrated the Jewish suburb of Mekor Hayim, eight Arabs were killed. In the Jewish Quarter of the Old City, Arabs had thrown bombs near the Nissim Bek Synagogue. On February 2 a British constable was wounded and a Syrian Arab, Mustafa Sarah, was killed when rifle fire was directed on the Jaffa Gate. Four days later, in the Old City, a Jewish sniper killed Haj Abed Khaled al-Yamani, the leader of one of the Arab gangs that had been most active in attacking the Jewish Quarter.

*

The Arab exodus from the western part of Jerusalem had continued since mid-January. Within three weeks it had altered the population pattern of the city. The facts of demographic change reflected personal hardship on a substantial scale. On February 5 Ben-Gurion ordered the new Hagannah commander in the city, David Shaltiel, to conquer more Arab districts and to settle Jews in the abandoned and conquered areas. At a meeting of his party leaders in Tel Aviv two days later, Ben-Gurion told them that 'from your entry into Jerusalem through Lifta-Romema', on down the Jaffa Road to King George V Avenue, there were no 'strangers' but '100 per cent Jews', and he added: 'Since Jerusalem's destruction in the days of the Romans, it hasn't been so Jewish as it is now. In many Arab districts in the west one sees not one Arab. I do not assume that this will change.'

Arab gangs were particularly active near the railway station. A British soldier, a gunner with the 48th Field Regiment, Royal Artillery, was near the station on February 7 when he heard shouts of 'Kill the Jew.' He ran forward to where a Jew was lying on the ground being kicked and beaten by a number of Arabs armed with knives and pistols. The soldier used his rifle butt and fists to push the Arabs away. When they tried to force the Jew into a passing Arab taxi, the soldier told the driver to drive on, or he would shoot. The occupants of a passing army vehicle saw the episode and called up reinforcements. The Jew was saved, and the soldier returned to his unit.

For Jews, although it was now possible to leave western Jerusalem without sniper fire at the entrance to the city, the journey to and from the coastal plain remained hazardous. On February 8 Hans Lehman, a driver in a convoy of trucks on its way from Tel Aviv, was killed in an ambush near the Arab village of Mughar. The convoy guards gave chase, and seven of the Arab attackers were killed. That day a group of Arabs destroyed part of the Jewish-owned Ford Automobile Agency in Julian's Way, in the centre of the New City. At the same time, another group of Arabs destroyed a Jewish-owned wool shop near the Government Printing Press, only a few yards from the railway station. Elsewhere in the city, Arab gangs opened fire on Yemin Moshe, opposite the Jaffa Gate, on the southern Jewish suburbs of Talpiot, Arnona and Ramat Rahel, and on Upper Motza, to the west of the city, injuring a child.

From that February, in an attempt to prevent such attacks, Jewish Civil Guards, wearing special blue uniforms, operated roadblocks, which were reinforced with stones and iron stakes, on all roads and lanes leading from Jewish quarters to Arab areas, and controlled traffic between them.

*

On February 9 the Stern Gang blew up two Arab-owned buildings, one in the Commercial Centre below the Jaffa Gate and one in the Arab suburb of Katamon. Sustained rifle fire from these buildings had earlier been directed on Jewish homes. In a Hagannah attack that day on the Arab village of Sur Bahir, from which rifle fire had been directed repeatedly against Talpiot, two Arab snipers were wounded and a sixty-year-old Arab man was killed. In a letter to the *New York Times*, Dr Magnes wrote that, while the Arabs were the aggressors in the struggle, 'we are now confronted day by day with reprisals on one side and on the other'. Magnes wanted the United Nations Security Council to invite both Jews and Arabs to lay down their arms 'so that all possibilities for a peaceful solution may be canvassed'.

It was becoming more and more difficult for Jews to reach the Jewish Quarter of the Old City. Large quantities of flour, rice and sugar, which the British administration had allocated to the Jewish Quarter, were accumulating in stores in the New City. Various volunteer groups in Jewish Jerusalem were collecting newspapers, books and radio sets, in order to send them into the Jewish Quarter, which was effectively besieged. As the Jaffa Gate was virtually sealed off by Arab snipers, special convoys were having to make the journey through the Zion Gate.

On February 10 a large gang of armed Arabs, some from the Old City and some from Hebron, launched a ferocious attack on the Jewish suburb of Yemin Moshe. They were met by a strong Hagannah defence, and for six hours there was heavy and prolonged shooting. Seven of the Arab attackers were killed, as was a Jew, Shmuel Tolsik, who was bringing food for the schoolchildren of the quarter. At the last moment, British troops intervened and drove the Arabs off; but one British soldier was killed by the Arabs as they fled. In the Jewish area of Nahalat Shimon, facing Sheikh Jarrah, Arabs blew up what they thought was a Jewish house. It was in fact one of the few houses in Nahalat Shimon belonging to an Arab. Its owner was a member of the Barakat family, leading traders in the city.

*

British rule still had three months to run. Sometimes, in a limited, local context, it was effective, as when on February 11 a British army detachment took up position below the Jaffa Gate and prevented a further attack by Arabs on Yemin Moshe. That day the British police swore in thirty Jewish municipal policemen, and were busy enlisting a parallel Arab force, both groups to be uniformed, and both to be armed. Their duty was to patrol and operate the roadblocks which now straddled all the roads between the two communities.

The existence of roadblocks did little to lessen the intensity of the conflict in the dividing areas between the two communities. On February 12, under covering fire, Hagannah units entered the village of Beit Safafa, on the southern edge of Jerusalem, and blew up four houses from which firing had been directed on Mekor Hayim. One of the houses that was destroyed belonged to Mahmoud Sheikh Jaber al-Omari, a leading Arab commander, who was buried under the debris. His funeral the following day was attended by Dr Hussein Fakhri al-Khalidi, Secretary of the Arab Higher Committee.

Also on February 12, after a Jewish woman had been wounded by gunfire in the Arab suburb of Talbiyeh, a Hagannah loudspeaker van drove through the suburb ordering the remaining Arab residents to leave, or they and their property would be 'blown up'. The British seized the van and arrested its occupants, but those Arabs still living in Talbiyeh took the warning seriously and left.

Arab families were also leaving from two mixed Jewish-Arab areas along the divide between western and eastern Jerusalem, Musrara and Schneller. With their departure, western Jerusalem had become completely Jewish, and eastern Jerusalem, with the exception of the Jewish Quarter of the Old City, completely Arab. In the centre of he New City most Jews had left their offices because of the dangers on their way to work and back. On February 13 the Jewish staff members of the Reuters Office in Princess Mary Street left, never to return. A Christian Arab woman was the only member of staff left. Reuters asked its London office to send out two British staff members.

*

There was bitterness among the Jews at what they saw, and denounced, as a British bias against them. On February 13, British soldiers who had arrested four young Hagannah men in a Jewish suburb took them on foot, not to the nearby British police station, but to an entirely Arab neighbourhood near the Damascus Gate. There, the sergeant-major in charge released them, unarmed, in the middle of an Arab mob. All four were murdered.

Jewish anger at the British was intensified nine days later, on the morning of February 22, when a British police armoured car and three British army trucks, driven by British deserters wearing army uniforms, parked on one of Jewish Jerusalem's main thoroughfares, Ben Yehuda Street. The truck-drivers then drove off in the armoured car. A few moments later the three vehicles blew up, destroying a six-storey building and damaging many others. Fifty-two Jews were killed. Two months later a British soldier at Arab Legion headquarters, almost certainly one of the deserters, told a *Life* photo-reporter, John Phillips: 'I pulled Ben Yehuda,' and then complained to Phillips that the Mufti had 'refused to pay me the five hundred pounds he had promised'. Two of the drivers were later identified as Eddie Brown and Peter Marsden, who had also participated in the *Palestine Post* bombing three weeks earlier.

One of the buildings most seriously damaged in the Ben Yehuda bombing was the Atlantic Hotel, owned by a Christian Arab. Among the dead were the four-year-old Ita Morodestsky and her eight-month-old brother Elimelech.

As a reprisal for the Ben Yehuda bombing, members of the Irgun and the Stern Gang went on the rampage looking for British soldiers: they killed ten and wounded twenty. In the resultant crossfire, a ten-year-old Jewish boy, Yitzhak Deutsch, was also killed. That night the Jewish Agency negotiated with General Cunningham that British troops should no longer enter the Jewish parts of the city, which would in future be guarded entirely by Jewish Home Guard units.

The days that followed the Ben Yehuda bombing saw a spate of killings in the streets of Jerusalem, mostly by Arab sniping. On February 24 Vita Melamede, the wife of the Assistant Accountant-General, was killed by a sniper's bullet as she was leaving her house in Rehavia. Next to her when she was shot was the widow of a Jew who had been killed in the King David bombing.

*

Like the Arabs before them, Jews also began to leave the city in some numbers, 'each on a different pretext', Yona Cohen noted in his diary on March 5. 'It is thought that of some 100,000 Jews living in Jerusalem before the partition resolution, about 70,000 or less left,' he wrote, mostly to Tel Aviv. 'Many leave by virtue of their positions in government and public institutions, for the State is being "prepared" there. Numbers of people go because they are afraid of a siege or because they wish to live in a Jewish State and not an international city. Public figures in Jerusalem note with pain that everything is being transferred to Tel Aviv, the offices, the workshops, the factories and the industries. All the meetings of Jewish organisations, people and institutions and of the new bodies currently being established are held there, in Tel Aviv. Jerusalem bleeds and looks enviously and anxiously towards Tel Aviv, which is developing and growing both qualitatively and quantitively. Lip service is paid to Jerusalem and every article and speech abounds with high-flown phrases about "the heart of the nation" and "the eternal capital", but Tel Aviv is the capital in practice.'

*

On March 11 a further act of terror intensified the agony of Jewish Jerusalem. A car belonging to the United States Consulate General, flying the Stars and Stripes, was driven into the well-guarded courtyard of the Jewish Agency. The car was known to the Agency guards, who did not search it but waved it in. It was driven by Anton Daoud, a thirty-seven-year-old Christian Arab who was also known to the guards. Daoud parked the car, and slipped away. Soon after he had gone the car blew up. A section of one of the wings of the building was destroyed, and thirteen people were killed. Among the dead was a veteran Zionist leader, seventy-one-year-old Dr Leib Jaffe – one of only five men still alive who had been delegates to the first Zionist Congress of 1897. Also killed was Alice Lasker, who had gone to Jerusalem from England when the Jewish Agency had transferred there in 1929. She was sixty-two. Among those cut by flying glass were Edwin Samuel, then Director of Broadcasting in Palestine; Walter Eytan, the Jewish Agency liaison officer with the United Nations, to whom Samuel was talking; and Reuven Zaslani, who in the Second World War had helped organise the Jewish parachutists sent behind German lines. A thirteen-year-old messenger boy, Chaim Polotov (his first name means 'Life'), was also killed. Daoud, the driver of the car, was next heard of in Venezuela.

The wounded were driven out of the Jewish Agency courtyard in trucks and tenders. As one tender went by, Malkah Raymist, a Jewish journalist, later recalled how she 'saw a friend of mine stretched on its floor with another man supporting him by the shoulders. His head was lolling helplessly and he was bleeding profusely from a head wound. The sun shone brightly on his wavy golden hair. That, more than anything else, brought home the tragedy to me. The tender passed before I could ask about him. Stunned, I kept repeating foolishly, like a broken record; "Such beautiful golden hair . . . such beautiful hair . . . full of blood . . ." '

*

That week, Pablo de Azcazarte, a Spanish diplomat who had just been appointed Secretary to the United Nations Truce Commission, which was about to be set up, reached Jerusalem. He was at once struck by the total lack of British control. The various foreign consulates, he later wrote, had already, 'in actual practice, established relations with, on the one hand, the Arab Higher Committee and, on the other, the Jewish Agency, in place of their former relations with the British authorities. Whenever incidents arose which involved citizens of European countries (a frequent occurrence), the respective consuls took up the case not with the British Authorities, but with the Jewish Agency or the Arab Higher Committee, according to whether the incident occurred in the Jewish or the Arab zone. The same thing happened when the consular corps, represented by its doyen the French Consul, thought it necessary to protest against the restrictions placed on the admission of consuls to the Jewish zone after the attack on the Jewish Agency, which was carried out, as we have seen, by means of the American Consul's car. The laborious negotiations to which this incident gave rise were conducted by the

French Consul, in the name of the consular corps, and the Jewish Agency, without the British authorities having any knowledge of, or share in the matter; and this occurred two months before the termination of the Mandate!'

On March 13 members of the Stern Gang entered the Arab suburb of Katamon and blew up two houses from which Arab snipers had been firing at Kiryat Shmuel and Rehavia. That evening Arab attacks on Yemin Moshe and Ramat Rahel were driven off by the Hagannah.

*

British rule had scarcely two months to go. For the Arabs of Jerusalem the imminent withdrawal of the British seemed a remarkable opportunity. 'We have always maintained that the British withdrawal from Palestine is to be regarded as a purely Arab victory,' the Arab newspaper *Falastin* declared on March 21. 'The little that will be left to the Jews afterwards could easily be eliminated. In their political immaturity, the Jews keep on bragging that it is they who have forced the British to give up what they have held for the last thirty years. Be that as it may, the British withdrawal gives the Arabs the longed-for opportunity to stamp out Jewish dreams once and for all.'

This hope of an Arab victory received a set-back a week later, when the Arab Higher Committee, which had hitherto controlled and inspired its followers from its headquarters in Jerusalem, decided to move to Damascus. Not one of the committee members remained in Jerusalem at the very moment when the struggle for control of the city was about to begin. This was a grave tactical error for them. A second error was to announce that on May 15 a provisional Arab government for Palestine would be set up, under the presidency of Haj Amin, with its capital in Jerusalem or, if that was not possible, with its capital in Nablus. The introduction of Nablus seemed to suggest that the leadership was not confident of retaining control in Jerusalem.

*

The road from Tel Aviv to Jerusalem was under constant Arab attack. Fewer and fewer Jewish food convoys were able to get through to Jerusalem. Towards the end of March a food convoy failed, for the first time, to get through at all. One food convoy that did get through in March had taken ten days to do so. Food and fuel were in desperately short supply. By the end of the first week of April there was only enough flour in Jewish Jerusalem to last for thirty days. The bakeries had only enough flour to bake a third of a loaf of bread per person per day. Meat, fish, milk and eggs were unobtainable, except, in small quantities, for children. The shortage of vegetables was such that children were sent into the fields to collect a weed which was growing in profusion as a result of the heavy winter rains: known as *halamith*, it tasted somewhat like spinach, and could be made into soup.

The domestic aspects of coping with the siege were overshadowed on April 9, when an Irgun and Stern Gang attack on the Arab village of Deir Yassin threw the whole country into turmoil. Before the attack, on learning what was intended, two senior Hagannah officers had tried to dissuade the Irgun and the Stern Gang leaders from their course. They failed to do so, and the attack went ahead. 'Fighting which should have taken an hour went on all morning,' wrote Bernard Joseph. 'The attackers were incompetently directed and a few Arab marksmen in one house held them up for a long time. Women and children had not been given enough time to evacuate the village, although warned to do so by loudspeaker, and there were many of them among the 254 persons reported by the Arab Higher Committee as killed.' Another Jewish Jerusalemite, Harry Levin, wrote in his diary: 'None of the barbarities the Arabs have committed in the past months can excuse this foul thing done by Jews. Most Jews I have spoken with are horrified.'

Among the dead at Deir Yassin were two uniformed Syrian soldiers. Four of the Irgun and Stern Gang attackers were also killed.

*

The killings in Deir Yassin gave the Arabs a powerful rallying call against the Jews. The killings also brought fierce Jewish criticism down upon the Irgun and the Stern Gang. Bernard Joseph later recalled how the terrorists 'earned the contempt of most Jews in Jerusalem, and an unequivocal public repudiation by the Jewish Agency'. Following an emergency meeting of the Jewish Agency Executive, a statement was issued expressing 'horror and disgust' at the massacre, while the *Palestine Post* declared: 'Nothing can condone the action of the Jewish dissident organisations in entering the Arab village of Deir Yassin and killing many of the inhabitants, men, women and children. No explanation, no excuse, can wipe out the stains. Deir Yassins may or may not strike terror into the hearts of the Arabs. They bring horror into Jewish hearts – that is the twofold crime.'

There was further distress among most Jerusalem Jews when, on the morning of April 10, the Irgun and the Stern Gang paraded groups of captured men, women and children from Deir Yassin, including the village elder and his family, in open trucks through the streets of Jerusalem. As the shameful parade was in progress, the Hagannah intervened, taking the prisoners from their captors and releasing them into British custody.

*

The battle for the Jerusalem-Tel Aviv highway continued. On April 10, after a week of heavy fighting, Jewish soldiers, led by two young commanders, Uzi Narkiss and Yitzhak Rabin, finally drove the Arabs from the hill at Kastel, from which they dominated the road to the coast. During the battle, Abdul Khader al-Husseini, the charismatic commander of several thousand Arab irregular troops and Iraqi regulars, was killed. He had only just returned from Damascus after 'military consultations' with the Arab Higher Committee members there. His death demoralised most of his followers, who returned to their villages, providing unexpected relief for the Jewish forces trying to gain control of the city's lifeline.

Only five weeks earlier a British Government spokesman in the House of Commons had described Abdul Khader as 'very difficult to catch'. Aged forty-two, he was the son of Musa Kazem Pasha al-Husseini, one of the leading Palestinian-Arab nationalists of the inter-war years. And it was Abdul Khader's son, Feisal al-Husseini, who would lead the Jerusalem Palestinians in their political struggle in the 1990s. After Abdul Khader's funeral on the Haram, attended by 30,000 Muslim Arabs, a large Arab crowd attacked the Jewish Quarter of the Old City, but was driven off. Following Abdul Khader's death, one of Iraq's senior military commanders, Fadel Bey Abdullah Rashid, was sent with Iraqi reinforcements to take command of the Kastel area and to try to regain Kastel. Two weeks later Abdul Khader's command was taken over by Emile Ghory, a forty-year-old member of the Arab Higher Committee, and a graduate of the University of Cincinnati.

Following the capture of Kastel, all the village houses not needed by the Hagannah as defensive positions were blown up. But the nearby Arab village of Kolonia, most of whose inhabitants had fled during the fighting for Kastel, was occupied by armed Arabs who were using it as a base to attack traffic on the Jerusalem-Tel Aviv road. On April 10, commando detachments of the Hagannah – the Palmach – occupied Kolonia. One of those who accompanied the Palmach on that attack was Harry Levin, who described in his diary leaving Jerusalem after dark and making his way to the outskirts of the village.

'Our men tightened their belts and waited,' Levin wrote. 'At the order they advanced, moving across the slope to approach from the given angle. Suddenly the village seemed to erupt. Our mortars started it, and at once came a bedlam of answering fire. We saw the summer-lightning flashes of their guns and the shots passing over-head. They fired wildly, to all points of the compass – except to where our men were crawling forward almost as fast as they had walked. All the time, the hissing rain of machine-guns poured down on the village. Suddenly an explosion that seemed to rip open the hillside: shrieks of terror. Our shock troops and sappers had reached the houses.'

Many of the houses were empty. 'Others continued to spit fire, but not for long. I saw grim resistance from one house. More of our men came up and attacked it from three sides. Maybe the machine-gun ended its resistance, maybe the hand-grenades flung through the windows. In half an hour it was over. Most of the Arabs had fled into the darkness. I counted fourteen dead, but there were more.'

The battle for Kolonia over, Harry Levin returned to Jerusalem. 'When I left,' he wrote, 'the sappers were blowing up the houses. One after another the old stone buildings, some built in elaborate city style, exploded and crashed. Within sight of Jerusalem I still heard the explosions rolling through the hills; and in between, some-where in the lonely distance, still rose the half-hearted barking of the village dog.'

Kolonia was never rebuilt. Following a decision that April by Ben-Gurion and the Hagannah High Command, any captured Arab village in the Jerusalem Corridor was levelled to the ground. A new policy was in operation: to clear the Jerusalem corridor of its Arab homes. After Kolonia, the villages of Biddu and Beit Surik were largely destroyed, followed immediately by the village of Khulda, which was bulldozed to the ground. In the eight-hour operation at Biddu and Beit Surik, every one of the hundred houses was levelled to the ground. Only the two mosques were untouched.

The only exception to the new policy of clearing the Jerusalem corridor of all its Arab villages was Abu Ghosh, whose inhabitants had never attacked the road, and were well-disposed to the Jews.

This was, and remains, the only surviving Arab village in the Jerusalem corridor: today it is a flourishing town.

*

On April 10 Ben-Gurion called an emergency meeting in Tel Aviv to discuss what should be done to alleviate the food shortage in Jerusalem. The head of the Jerusalem Emergency Committee, Bernard Joseph, later recalled his journey to the meeting. 'We travelled in an armoured bus which was fired on by Arabs. At one point, the bus and the convoy stopped, and through the peepholes I could watch our armed escort climbing the hillside to drive off an Arab band which was attacking us.'

At the meeting, Ben-Gurion gave Bernard Joseph full powers to requisition food and to conscript both drivers and vehicles. Within Jerusalem, the first Arab shells fell on the Jewish areas that same day. From then on, the shelling was continuous. Remote suburbs such as Atarot, to the north of the city, were also subjected to heavy machine-gun fire, while rifle, machine-gun and mortar fire were directed at four other Jewish suburbs: Rehavia, Kiryat Shmuel, Neve Shaanan and Mekor Hayim. 'I entered the house of a peaceful, cultured family,' a Jewish Jerusalemite, Pauline Rose, wrote in her diary on April 13. 'A woman was in tears. "My son", she said, "was killed last night." '

During a spate of Arab shelling of the Jewish Quarter on April 13 a kindergarten was hit and more than twenty children were injured. Efforts were made to counter the daily barrage. A young Jewish engineer, David Leibovitch, invented a home-made weapon, a makeshift mortar, using a six-inch drainpipe and a bomb of nails and metal scrap. Its explosive charge was not great, but its incredible noise gave it a power out of all proportion to its physical impact. In honour of its inventor, it became known as the 'Davidka'. The name also recalled the boy David's slingshot against the giant Goliath.

*

The Hadassah Hospital, to which the injured of every day's shelling were taken, although still cut off from Jewish Jerusalem, was fortunate to have a personal assurance from the High Commissioner, and also from the Secretary of State for the Colonies in London, that medical and civilian traffic going up to Mount Scopus would be protected by British soldiers and police.

On April 14 a convoy made up of ten vehicles – two ambulances, three armoured buses, three trucks with food and hospital supplies, and two small escort cars – set off at 9.30 in the morning for Mount Scopus, after receiving an assurance from the British officer in charge that the road was clear. The vehicles, containing doctors, nurses, patients (including an Irgun man injured in the attack on Deir Yassin), and Hebrew University staff, were clearly marked with the insignia of the Magen David Adom – the Red Shield Society – the Jewish equivalent of the Red Cross.

Shortly after passing through the suburb of Sheikh Jarrah while moving up the hill to the corner known as Karm al-Mufti, the convoy struck a mine. It had been placed there by an Arab tailor, Mohammed Neggar. The lead escort vehicle, whose occupants were armed, nego-tiated the crater and tried to act as cover for the rest. The ambulance immediately behind it and two of the buses were damaged and could no longer move. The six vehicles in the rear, including one whose driver had been shot in the face by an Arab gunman, were able to turn around and return safely to the city.

The escort vehicle, the immobilised ambulance and the two buses were then hit by a barrage of rifle and grenade fire from Karm al-Mufti, and by Molotov cocktails. Firing continued throughout the morning. Except for those in the escort vehicle, no one in the convoy was armed; that had been a British condition for allowing the doctors and nurses to proceed. The commanding general of the British forces in Jerusalem, General Gordon MacMillan, happened to pass the bottom of the hill in a car fifteen minutes after the attack began. Although his car was caught in some crossfire, he was under the impression that the attack was ending. But it was still continuing in the early afternoon, the doctors and nurses being pinned down by gunfire.

The British military post responsible for the safety of the road was less than 200 yards away. Its commanding officer, Colonel Jack Churchill, the second-in-command of the Highland Light Infantry battalion in Jerusalem, was a veteran of the Dunkirk evacuation of 1940 and the Sicily landing of 1943. In 1945 he had led a commando mission behind German lines that had ended, for him, with intern-ment in Dachau. Summoning a half-track with a machine-gunner to accompany him, Colonel Churchill drove in his own armoured car to investigate. As he reached the scene, armed Arabs were arriving from every direction, shooting at the convoy and chanting over and over, in cries of hatred: 'Deir Yassin! Deir Yassin!'

Colonel Churchill reached the last of the trapped vehicles, one of the armoured buses, and tried to persuade those inside it to transfer to his own armoured car and drive back with him to the security of his barracks. But they preferred to wait, they said, for the arrival of the Hagannah. Churchill radioed to British military headquarters for permission to shell the houses from which the Arabs were firing, but his request was refused. Then, as he was making a final effort to persuade at least some of the bus passengers to go with him, his gunner, Cassidy, was hit in the neck by an Arab rifleman. Churchill left the besieged convoy with Cassidy, and went in search of medical help, but Cassidy died. He was the first victim of the Hadassah convoy ambush.

The director of the hospital, Dr Chaim Yassky, with whom Colonel Churchill had dined only a week earlier, was among those with the convoy. Twice, at 1 p.m. and again at 2 p.m., he tried to flag down British military cars that passed by, but neither of the cars stopped. Between these two events, at 1.45 p.m., as the shooting continued, the university President, Judah Magnes, who was at his home in the city, telephoned the British Commander-in-Chief, General MacMillan, to ask permission for a Hagannah detachment to be sent to the scene. MacMillan said that he was trying to get there himself, 'but the difficulty was that a major battle was going on'.

When asked if Hagannah units could be allowed to go to the scene, MacMillan replied: 'The arrival of the Hagannah will only inflame the situation and increase the danger.' The army had the situation in hand, and would extricate the convoy. This reply was repeated several times, as a number of urgent Jewish Agency requests were made to the military command.

By three o'clock that afternoon the two buses were on fire. Most of the passengers who had not yet been killed were being burned alive. At a quarter past three Dr Yassky turned to his wife with the words, '*Shalom* my dear, it's the end.' At that very moment a bullet passed through the slit in the front armour of the ambulance, and Yassky was killed. Fifteen minutes later, at 3.30, following further requests from Colonel Churchill, troops of the Highland Light Infantry, commanded by Brigadier C. P. Jones, launched an attack on the Arabs surrounding the convoy. Within an hour the Arabs were driven off. Twenty-eight Jews, twenty of whom were wounded, were rescued. Seventy-seven Jews had been killed.

During the British intervention forty Arabs had been killed, among them a fifty-five-year-old journalist, Shukri Kuteineh, whose son had been killed several months earlier during fighting in the Old City. Two British soldiers were also killed, as well as an elderly Arab who, walking into the city with his donkey, was shot dead when he was caught in the crossfire.

*

The dead in the Hadassah convoy included several leading members of the Faculty of Medicine, among them Dr L. Doljansky, head of the Cancer Research Department, and one of his assistants, Dr Boris Miszurski. Several people going up to the hospital for surgery were also killed. The deaths of two of those on the convoy created particular distress – 'two pioneers of healing' as the *Palestine Post* described them. Dr Doljansky, who had emigrated from Russia to Palestine as a youth, had been a leading cancer researcher in Berlin before Hitler came to power. Arrested by the Gestapo, he was released on the intervention of the British Consul and returned to Palestine. 'He was full of plans for future work when a cruel death overtook him,' the *Palestine Post* wrote. 'Apart from music (he was an excellent pianist) Doljansky lived entirely for his work. He took no part in any social or political activities except for expressing his conviction of the importance of Arab-Jewish friendship.' Dr Yassky, who had come to Palestine from Russia as an ophthalmologist in 1921, was a doyen of medicine in Palestine. During the course of his career he had treated several thousand Arabs for trachoma. In the words of one of his obituaries, 'He both preached and practised medical help for the Arab population.' He was fifty-one years old.

'The whole city is in mourning,' Zipporah Borowsky wrote to her parents in the United States. 'So many friends, so many doctors, nurses, patients, university scientists, administrative staff, such a heavy loss, so damn much of everything. All Jerusalem is walking around asking itself: "Is there no end to it?" '

*

After the Hadassah convoy attack, the Arab Higher Committee issued a statement. The attack had been commanded, it said, by an Iraqi officer. His had been a 'heroic exploit'. The British were condemned for their belated intervention. 'Had it not been for Army interference,' the Arab Higher Committee pointed out in anger, 'not a single Jewish passenger would have remained alive.'

The Hebrew University, only twenty-three years since its foundation, was in mourning. Its plans to expand fourfold in numbers and in area along the crest of Mount Scopus – plans which included the purchase of the Augusta Victoria, and the building of substantial residential dormitories, a sports ground and a stadium designed by the Jerusalem architect Richard Kaufmann – had to be shelved. Nor were Kaufmann's imaginative drawings ever to leave his architectural drawing-board. To learn whether they would be able to return to their studies and lecture halls, all the university teachers, among them Gershom Scholem, Professor of Jewish Mysticism, and the archaeologist E. L. Sukenik, would have to wait for the outcome of a battle that was gaining in intensity with every day, as the date for the British withdrawal drew near.

'Such deeds as Deir Yassin and the butchery on the road to the Hadassah Hospital are in themselves unbearably tragic,' the *Palestine Post* wrote on April 14; 'they are staggering in their relation to the constituted Authority of this land, which, in the purpose of the Government of the United Kingdom, stands by helpless and humiliated.' Slowly and steadily British authority was being officially withdrawn. In mid-April the judicial system in Jerusalem was divided into Arab and Jewish sections, each with its own courts. Roads in the Jewish and Arab areas were likewise under the control of the respective communities.

On April 15, as a consequence of the Jewish occupation of Kastel, a convoy of 131 trucks, carrying more than 500 tons of food, reached Jerusalem unhampered. It had been seven hours on the road. It was followed two days later by a convoy of 280 trucks. This convoy was attacked on the way, and thirty trucks were forced to give up the attempt. The rest got through. Bumper to bumper, they had been spread out along six miles of road. They brought with them 1,000 tons of supplies, including flour, sugar, milk, fruit and vegetables.

This second convoy reached the city on the Sabbath, when Orthodox Jews do not drive or work, but on its arrival it was blessed by an elderly rabbi, who called out: 'These men hallow heaven and earth!' Religious Jews, coming from synagogue still in their prayer-shawls, helped to unload the trucks – work that in normal times would have been a desecration of the Sabbath.

A third convoy that followed on April 20 was also attacked. Its 300 trucks were fired on at Bab al-Wad, the entrance to the gorge leading up to the city, and for a whole day they were under fire. Three Jews were killed. Some of the drivers volunteered to try to drive the Arabs away, and were successful. Thirty Arabs were killed in the battle, as was the Jewish commander, Maccabi Mosseri, a member of one of the leading Jewish families of Egypt. A total of 294 trucks got through to Jerusalem. Only six had to be abandoned.

Their rusted frames lie at the side of the highway to this day, as a memorial.

The Arab forces returned to Bab al-Wad when the third convoy had passed, and no more convoys were possible. Some 280 drivers from the third convoy were unable to return to their families at the coast. Jerusalem was both cut off and besieged. On April 24 an attempt was made to drive the Arab forces from their base at Nebi Samwil, the tomb of the prophet Samuel, which was both a Muslim and a Jewish Holy Place. This was one of the main sources of the attacks on the Jerusalem road. The assault was a failure. Twenty-five Jews were killed, and the rest were driven off.

The Arab suburb of Sheikh Jarrah, with its control over the road to Mount Scopus, was occupied on April 28 by troops of the Palmach's Harel Brigade, commanded by Yitzhak Rabin. The British demanded that these troops withdraw by six that evening or face attack. 'I proposed rejecting the ultimatum and not giving way,' Rabin later recalled. As the deadline expired, British tanks and artillery advanced towards the Jewish-held positions. Rabin, his only artillery being a single British army bazooka, ordered an immediate retreat to Mount Scopus.

*

The now almost entirely ineffectual British presence in Jerusalem had only two weeks to run. In anticipation of the imminent British withdrawal the battle for Jerusalem's suburbs intensified. A Truce Commission had been set up by the United Nations, to come into effect on April 23, consisting of the Consuls General of the United States, France and Belgium. Its work was virtually confined to the rooms of the French Consulate. The consulate itself was often hit by Arabs shooting from the Jaffa Gate into New Jerusalem. 'How could three consuls stand between Jew and Arab at this climacteric moment in their history?' the future Israeli diplomat Walter Eytan asked.

On the night of April 30, Jewish forces attacked the St Simeon Monastery, at the edge of Arab Katamon. The Arabs, including Arab soldiers from Iraq and some from Syria, were using the monastery as an arms supply dump and liaison centre, and as a base for attacks on Jewish suburbs around it. 'I saw some of the men go into action,' a Jewish journalist, Julian Meltzer, reported for the *New York Times*. 'They were all in their late teens and early twenties, and full of good humour and fighting spirit. There were girls among the fighters too, in battle-dress tunics and slacks, and carrying light carbines. They are always among the Palmach's best sharpshooters.' Outside the Hagannah command post, Meltzer added, 'children were playing in the street, unperturbed by the battle going on not 2,000 yards away; making use of the parking ground for the armoured vehicles that had left for the scene of the fighting.'

The monastery was taken. In the final struggle, ten Iraqi soldiers and seven Hagannah soldiers were killed. Then, as the fighting for Katamon itself intensified, the remaining Arab residents fled. Their homes had become a battlefield. By early afternoon on May 1 the whole Katamon suburb was in Jewish hands. Upper Bakaa was also taken, its Arab residents joining the refugees from Katamon on the Jerusalem-Bethlehem and Jerusalem-Ramallah roads. As the refugees set out on their long and traumatic journey, Arab artillery opened fire from Nebi Samwil on several Jewish suburbs. Eight Jews were killed, among them ten-year-old Yardena Shoshani, nine-year-old Esther Ben Shimon and eight-year-old Benjamin Yehezkel.

*

The Arab-Jewish conflict was intense throughout Palestine, as British concerns focused almost entirely on withdrawal. On May 3 the *Palestine Post* published the casualty figures for the whole of Palestine for the preceding five months: 3,569 Arabs had been killed, 1,256 Jews and 152 Britons, an average of a thousand deaths a month, or more than thirty deaths every day. On May 4 the British Red Cross began to remove the bodies of the Arab soldiers killed in the fighting for Katamon almost a week earlier. That day British soldiers looted the abandoned premises of the Dutch Consulate-General in Katamon, although the Netherlands flag was still flying on the building. After Dutch protests most of the looted property was returned. On May 5 six buses arrived from Egypt to evacuate 160 Egyptian nationals under the protection of the Red Cross flag.

In an attempt to secure a truce within the Old City, as requested by the United Nations General Assembly, two senior members of the Jewish Agency Executive, Golda Meyerson and Eliezer Kaplan, went to see the High Commissioner, General Cunningham, on May 6. He told them that the Arabs were prepared to ensure the safety of the Jews of the Jewish Quarter, and access by 'pious Jews' to the Wailing Wall. When they asked if Jews generally would be allowed free entry into the Jewish Quarter, and access to the Wall, Cunningham replied that 'the Arabs would not consent to such a condition'. To Kaplan's request that Jewish patrols participate in guarding the route from the Jaffa Gate to the Wall the Arabs sent back no answer.

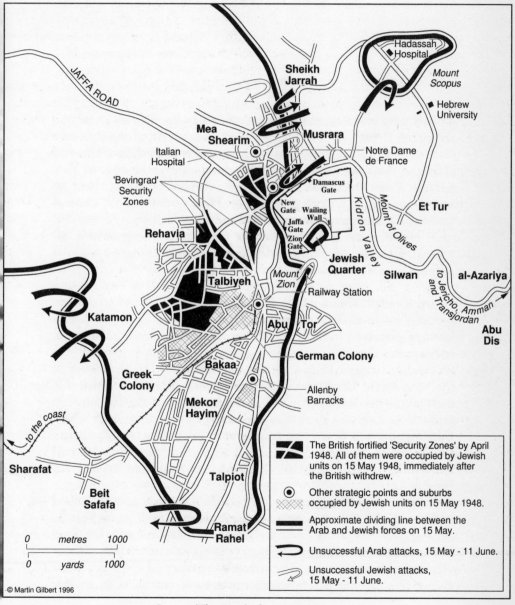

The Battle for Jerusalem

CHAPTER FOURTEEN

Two Weeks of War,
14–29 May 1948

At half past seven on the morning of Friday 14 May 1948 all the remaining British officials of the Chief Secretariat of the Palestine Government, and of British Army Headquarters, left their rooms and offices in the King David Hotel and drove out of the city. As they left, the Union Jack was lowered from the hotel parapet. Half an hour later, at eight o'clock precisely, the High Commissioner, General Sir Alan Cunningham, emerged from the covered portico of Government House wearing the field service uniform and insignia of a full general in the British army, and walked forward to inspect a guard of honour of fifty soldiers.

Earlier that year, in a foreword to a book by the city planner Henry Kendall, Cunningham had written: 'The City of Jerusalem, precious as an emblem of several faiths, a site of spiritual beauty lovingly preserved over the ages by many men's hands, has been in our care as a sacred trust for thirty years.' For Britain that sacred trust was ending. Cunningham entered his bullet-proof Daimler, drove to the King David Hotel and inspected a guard of honour which was itself about to leave, then drove north to the Kalandia landing-ground. At Kalandia there was another brief ceremony, after which Cunningham was flown in a small plane, piloted by the Air Officer Commanding, Palestine, to Haifa. There, at midnight, the formal moment of the ending of the Mandate, he embarked by ship for Britain.

At eight o'clock that morning, Pablo de Azcazarte and his United Nations Truce Commissioners reached Jerusalem from a visit to Amman. As they drove from the Damascus Gate towards the King David Hotel, 'we realised', he later wrote, 'that something strange was happening in the city. The streets were deserted and a profound silence reigned. But before we had time to comment on it, we discovered the reason for this extraordinary sensation: the city was occupied by British troops – machine-gun posts at each corner, troops stationed in the streets, and strict control of all non-military traffic. When I arrived at our offices I found the explanation for all this display of military force. The High Commissioner and the Chief Secretary had left Jerusalem that morning, after a brief ceremony in front of the King David Hotel, when the High Commissioner reviewed the troops drawn up there before going on to Kalandia airport, where an airplane was waiting to take him to Haifa.'

Pablo de Azcazarte was momentarily put out; he had expected to have an interview with General Cunningham that very morning. 'I must confess', he wrote, 'that it made a painful impression on me to see the High Commissioner and the Chief Secretary leave Jerusalem in this almost clandestine manner twenty hours before the official expiry of the mandate. This was bad enough, but it was not the worst. Though the British had never been willing to give us any indication of the date when the troops would evacuate Jerusalem, I had formed the idea (founded, as it turned out, more on wishful thinking than on sound reason) that it would be towards the end of the period envisaged for the total evacuation of Palestine by the British, which did not expire until the first of September. In my ingenuous optimism I had always counted on the British trying to hold off as long as possible (especially in Jerusalem) the chaos which must inevitably follow their departure, since the United Nations had been unable to establish a regime which, if nothing else, would have maintained a minimum of order and security; but it seemed that nothing was farther from their intentions than this reasonable and laudable project.'

De Azcazarte added: 'The troops we had seen drawn up in the streets were not there as a safety measure; they were, purely and simply, drawn up ready to march and, in fact, one detachment after another moved off until, at about two o'clock in the afternoon, not a single British soldier remained in Jerusalem. The time had come for the plunge into the unknown.'

As Cunningham's plane took off from Kalandia, the Union Jack was taken down from the flagpole on Government House. Within ten minutes of the flag's coming down a column of soldiers from the Hagannah advanced up the Jaffa Road and entered the three evacuated British security zones in the centre of the city. A few hours later they had secured the main buildings in the city centre, including the General Post Office, the main telephone exchange, the Generali Building, and the Russian Compound, in which was located the

Palestine Health Department. Arab troops had moved forward from the north-west corner of the city wall to the roads around the Barclays Bank Building, but were forced back by the Hagannah, which then entered the building. From its roof could be seen the full expanse of the city wall from the north-west corner to the Jaffa Gate.

At the Generali Building, overlooking several hundred yards of the Jaffa Road, the last British officer, leaving as the Hagannah entered, turned smartly towards the building, saluted, and walked briskly away. That morning the last British troops left Jerusalem, 250 vehicles in all: cars, lorries, armoured cars, Bren gun carriers and tanks. 'As the column lumbered partly along King George V Avenue in the heart of Jewish Jerusalem,' an eye-witness, Zeev Sharef, later wrote, 'multitudes stood and watched silently, thinking: "Well, they are going, really going, and what next?" '

What happened next was a dramatic moment in the Zionist story. It took place in Tel Aviv at 4.40 that afternoon, when David Ben-Gurion, the Chairman of the Jewish Agency, read out a Declaration of Independence and announced the establishment of a Jewish State, to come into being at midnight. It would be called 'Israel'. Six miles west of Jerusalem, at Kibbutz Maaleh Hahamisha, Jewish soldiers who had been fighting to keep the road to Jerusalem open, and were having a rare moment of rest, listened on their radio as Ben-Gurion proclaimed independence. 'Hey men, turn it off. I'm dying for some sleep. We can hear the fine words tomorrow,' one of them pleaded.

'Someone got up and turned the knob, leaving a leaden silence in the room,' recalled the men's commander, Yitzhak Rabin. 'I was mute, stifling my own mixture of emotions.'

By nightfall, before the new State had formally come into existence, five independent Arab States – Lebanon, Syria, Iraq, Transjordan and Egypt – gave orders to their armies to cross the borders of Mandate Palestine in force. Arab irregular troops had already surrounded the Jews in the Etzion Bloc of settlements ten miles south of Jerusalem: Revadim, Massuat Yitzhak, Ein Tzurim and Kfar Etzion. On the day before the declaration of statehood, all but Ein Tzurim had been overrun. Gloom and anger filled Jewish Jerusalem, when it was learned that a hundred of the defenders had been killed, fifteen of them machine-gunned by their captors after they had surrendered. Ein Tzurim fell on May 14, the day of independence.

Eight miles north of Jerusalem the inhabitants of the isolated Jewish suburb of Atarot, just next to the Kalandia airstrip from which Cunningham had been flown that morning, were under continual Arab attack, and had to be evacuated during the evening. They left on foot, southward to Neve Yaakov, a suburb only five miles from the city. At midnight news reached Jerusalem that the Arabs had set Atarot ablaze. That night a circular was distributed throughout Jewish Jerusalem, proclaiming that all men between the ages of eighteen and forty-five were 'at the disposal of the security forces'.

*

At nightfall on May 14 the forces of the Arab Legion, commanded by a British officer, Major-General John Bagot Glubb – 'Glubb Pasha' – and with thirty regular British officers among its senior commanders, reached the Jordan Valley from Amman and bivouacked on the Transjordanian side of the Jordan river. Shortly before midnight, its commander-in-chief, King Abdullah of Transjordan, stood on the Allenby Bridge, symbolically fired his revolver, and shouted to the troops around him: 'Forward!'

Crossing the Allenby Bridge, the Arab Legionnaires made their way up from the Rift Valley through the narrow defiles of the Judaean Desert to Jerusalem. They were the best-trained and the best-disciplined of all the Arab forces to enter Palestine as the British withdrew. 'The people expected us in two or three days to take Tel Aviv,' Glubb later wrote. He himself was pessimistic. 'I knew the extent of Jewish preparations. I knew that the Arabs had no plan and that there was no co-operation between them.'

Abdullah wanted Glubb to capture Jerusalem. When Glubb intimated that he hoped the United Nations would call a cease-fire and negotiate a truce with the two sides where they were, Abdullah wrote to him, as a spur and an order: 'My dear Glubb Pasha, The importance of Jerusalem in the eyes of the Arabs and the Muslims and the Arab Christians is well known. Any disaster suffered by the people of the city at the hands of the Jews – whether they were killed or driven from their homes – would have the most far-reaching results for us. The situation does not yet give cause for despair. I accordingly order that everything we hold today must be preserved – the Old City and the road to Jericho. This can be done either by using the reserves which are now in the vicinity of Ramallah or by sending there a force from the general reserves. I ask you to execute this order as quickly as possible, my dear.'

Glubb deferred to the King's wishes and devised an operational plan, to 'break into Jerusalem' from the north, take control of Sheikh Jarrah, and establish contact with the Old City. 'As soon as I reached home,' he recalled, 'I went to my room and wrote out the signal myself. "I have decided to intervene in force in Jerusalem." ' Glubb then gave the orders for the Arab Legion to attack Sheikh Jarrah in four days' time.

*

On 15 May 1948, the first day of Jewish statehood, the legal status of Jerusalem was altered for the first time in nearly thirty years, by facts on the ground. With the ending of the British Mandate, there was no external power, no nation or group of nations, or even the United Nations, in a position to replace the Mandatory authority in the city. Although Jewish Jerusalem was not, according to the United Nations, a part of the newly created State of Israel, the only forces available to defend it were Jewish forces. This had been increasingly true since the Partition vote six months earlier.

The fighting in Jerusalem was continuous on May 15. In the morning Arab irregular troops known as the Arab Liberation Army, commanded by Fawzi al-Kaoukji, who had spent some of the war years with the Mufti in Berlin, attacked the Jewish suburb of Neve Yaakov. The refugees from the more distant Atarot had found sanctuary there the previous evening. At midday the Hagannah defenders of Neve Yaakov telegraphed to their headquarters in the city: 'The settlement is subject to heavy gunfire. Send "birds" immediately, otherwise the place will be levelled to the ground.' But no aircraft – the 'birds' – could be spared, and that night, having buried four Hagannah men killed during the attack, the inhabitants of Neve Yaakov abandoned their homes and walked the five miles to the Hadassah Hospital on Mount Scopus.

Both Atarot and Neve Yaakov had been evacuated twice before, during the 1929 and 1936 riots. In both cases their inhabitants had returned within a few months and rebuilt their damaged homes. This time they were to be exiled for nearly twenty years. The American photographic journalist John Phillips, who had crossed the river Jordan two days earlier with the Arab Legion, reached Atarot shortly after its capture. 'By the time I got there,' he later recalled, 'only smouldering ruins remained. Airmail letters from the States and sheet music from Mozart's *Magic Flute* were scattered around. Most of the Holstein cows left behind had been slaughtered by the Liberation Army to prevent the Arabs from fighting over them.'

By nightfall on May 15, Jewish forces had overrun the Mea Shearim Police Station and Sheikh Jarrah, where, the *Palestine Post* reported, 'the Jewish flag was flown from the Mufti's house'. Four predominantly Arab suburbs – the Greek Colony, the German Colony, Bakaa and Talbiyeh – were also overrun that day. From them the Hagannah tried to link up with the isolated southern Jewish suburbs, and by the early morning of May 16 they were poised to reach the garden suburb of Talpiot. They were confronted on the way, however, by 300 Iraqi troops entrenched in the Allenby Barracks. That evening the barracks were captured, together with considerable stocks of arms and ammunition, including a British anti-tank gun.

By nightfall on May 16 the Hagannah had overrun both the railway station and Abu Tor, the one remaining Arab-held suburb just south of the city. The whole of the New City south of the walls was in Jewish hands. Just outside the north-west corner of the Old City, a continuous battle was being fought for control of the Notre Dame Monastery, through which the Arabs inside the walls hoped to penetrate into the centre of Jewish Jerusalem. But the monastery building was held by the Jews.

Other Arab attacks were also made that day, including a sustained one against Sheikh Jarrah, but the Hagannah held their positions there. Several Hagannah attempts to take over Musrara were repulsed, but the Mea Shearim Police Station, which the Arabs overran that day, was recaptured by the Hagannah in the evening. Thirty-seven Stern Gang members, who advanced towards the Jaffa Gate from the Barclays Bank Building, were pinned down by Arab gunfire. They were later rescued from a cellar by the Hagannah and brought back to the area under Jewish control.

*

As well as being a battleground, Jerusalem was still besieged. On May 17 a small convoy of a dozen trucks reached the city from the coast: it was a military convoy, with urgent army supplies, and brought with it no food for the civilians. That same day the Hagannah commander in Jerusalem, David Shaltiel, asked the officer commanding the Harel Brigade of the Palmach – the commando arm of the Hagannah – to come to Jerusalem. The officer, Yitzhak Rabin, was angered to find how few fighting men were at the Hagannah's disposal for the planned breakthrough into the Jewish Quarter. 'My rage was beyond restraint,' he later recalled. ' "Where are all the troops?" I railed at Shaltiel. "Are the eighty exhausted Palmachniks I lent you the only force that the Jewish people can muster for the liberation of its capital?" I was promised that reinforcements would be sent in after the breakthrough.'

The defenders of the Jewish Quarter, Rabin recalled, 'were sending out desperate appeals for assistance'. He was convinced that the attempt to break in through the Jaffa and Zion Gates was mistaken. 'Don't go charging head first right into a wall,' he told Shaltiel. 'I'll place the whole of the Harel Brigade under your command, but there must be a different plan.' The strategy Rabin proposed was, he later wrote, 'broader in conception. It called for closing in on the Old City from areas under our control in order to isolate it from the Arab forces before attempting to break in. But Shaltiel rejected my proposal and was adamant about implementing his own. I was furious with him and told him that his plan was idiotic and doomed to fail. But Jerusalem was much too dear to me to refuse even an attempt. We would carry out the diversionary attack as he requested.'

The attempt to break through the Jaffa Gate and advance to the relief of the besieged Jewish Quarter was launched on May 17. An Israeli flag was made, its design a blue Star of David on a white background, ready to raise above David's Tower. But the attack was repulsed: the saboteurs who were to have blown open the gate were killed before they could detonate their explosive charges. Within hours, Arab shells were falling again on western Jerusalem. 'The enemy surrounds us – is on our doorstep!' Pauline Rose wrote in her diary on May 18. 'Terrible battles are in progress. All sections of the Jewish city are being shelled. Heavy explosions continually rend the air, leaving behind a trail of destruction, death, pain, and shattered nerves . . . Jerusalem is a desolate city: no food, no water supply, no lighting, no news broadcasts . . . Jerusalem is like a city under sentence of death, bearing within it the certainty of life.'

That day, as the shelling of Jerusalem and the siege of the Jewish Quarter continued, a regiment of Glubb Pasha's Arab Legion occupied Latrun, a strategic hill on the road from the coast to the city. The regimental commander, Lieutenant-Colonel Habis Majali, fortified the British-built Tegart Fort there. It had been built in 1936 to deter Arab insurgents. Before the Israelis realised the full danger, Majali had obtained reinforcements, including Bren guns and heavy mortars. His position seemed, and proved, impregnable.

*

The diversionary attack on the Jaffa Gate having failed, in the early hours of May 19 a unit of Rabin's Palmach brigade, some sixty strong, made a second attempt to get through to the Jewish Quarter through the Zion Gate. The attack was led by twenty-three-year-old Major Uzi Narkiss. Advancing from the south, from the captured Arab suburb of Abu Tor, Narkiss's Palmach force overran Mount Zion and broke through the Zion Gate, making contact with the defenders of the quarter. The force brought with it weapons and ammunition, chlorine for the water cisterns, and supplies of blood plasma. It also evacuated the wounded. With the Palmach came eighty Hagannah men to join the 120 who had been in the quarter when the siege began.

The physical link established on May 19 could not, however, be maintained for long. A new factor was about to enter the battle for Jerusalem. That day, the British-trained soldiers of the Arab Legion, led by Glubb Pasha, and with many British officers at its head, entered the city from the north to spearhead the attack on the Jewish Quarter. At dawn the Arab Legionnaires drove the Jewish defenders from Sheikh Jarrah, and at midday they secured both the heights of French Hill, which controlled the northern approaches to the city, and the British Police Training Depot above Sheikh Jarrah, from which they were able to shell the Hadassah Hospital and the Mount Scopus enclave.

At six in the evening the Palmach force, whose task had been to reach the Jewish Quarter and supply it, but not to hold the link, was withdrawn. One of the sixty Palmach soldiers had been killed. There was later to be considerable controversy in Israel as to why some sort of link had not been maintained, at least by a small force of Hagannah men who had been left behind. The distance from the Zion Gate to the Jewish Quarter was less than 150 yards.

During May 19 there had again been heavy shelling throughout Jewish Jerusalem. Harry Levin wrote in his diary: 'The victory at Zion Gate warmed the hearts of the city this morning, but this fiendish onslaught has already driven it from people's minds. I have no idea of the number of casualties, but it must be large. Heard of three killed in one family; of a woman killed but her children unscathed while running for shelter. In King George V Avenue I saw a stretcher being carried towards an ambulance, a coarse grey blanket covering the body. Returning from the Jewish Agency's Press confer- ence at midday I twice took shelter in sandbagged doorways. Other people were there too, all tense and many frightened, but no panic. When the shelling moved away they slipped out in ones and twos, keeping close to house-walls for protection. I don't think there is a person not fully awakened now to the enormous danger of the whole city. All vague, thoughtless confidence has been blown to bits.'

*

Despite being driven out of the Old City, Jewish forces continued to hold Mount Zion, from which in the days following their incursion of May 19 they repelled a series of Arab Legion attacks. But Jewish units were never able to link up with the Jews in the Old City again. Meanwhile, considerable Arab artillery fire was being directed on the Jewish Quarter, whose situation was precarious, and where the defenders were outnumbered by twenty to one.

On the morning of May 21, just north of the city walls, the Arab Legion's tanks – more than a dozen of them – were in action for the first time. 'The Legion opened up with a terrific artillery barrage,' Harry Levin wrote in his diary. 'Thirty dead and I don't know how many injured in under two hours. Then the armoured cars and tanks advanced. Late this afternoon the news flashed through: the tanks had turned tail; three of them knocked out, two more disabled. I think many of us realised then that we were holding our breath.'

That same day, to the south, Kibbutz Ramat Rahel was the scene of a fierce artillery bombardment, with Egyptian forces leading the attack. Some of the settlers, elderly men unaccustomed to being under fire, suffered shell shock. On the following day the kibbutz was overrun. But it was recaptured a day later when, as the Israeli historian Netanel Lorch has written, Hagannah forces 'surprised the Arabs still busy looting and hunting chickens in the settlement courtyard'.

*

On May 21 the small Israeli air force was in action, bombing the Arab Legion base in the Arab village of Shuafat, just to the north of the city. A few days later the Arab artillery post on Nebi Samwil was bombed. But one of the most important, and most recent Jewish gains, the much-fought-over strategic crossroads of Sheikh Jarrah, was again recaptured by the Arab Legion on May 28. This ensured that Mount Scopus, with its Hebrew University and Hadassah Hospital under spasmodic artillery fire, could not be linked up to Jewish-controlled areas.

From Sheikh Jarrah, Arab Legion artillery fire, under the supervision of British officers, was directed on the northern suburbs of

Jewish Jerusalem, and considerable damage was done. The Egyptian army was firing artillery shells from its base at Mar Elias Monastery, on the outskirts of Bethlehem, into Jerusalem's southern suburbs, pounding Ramat Rahel and Talpiot, and reaching as far as the old Jewish quarter of Yemin Moshe, opposite the Jaffa Gate. The Hagannah had no artillery, and could not respond.

*

Entirely cut off, except by radio contact, from the rest of Jewish Jerusalem, the defenders of the Jewish Quarter of the Old City fought for nine days. On May 20 they were down to their last hundred grenades. Throughout the siege, medical services were maintained by a Hadassah medical unit led by Dr Avraham Laufer, an Austrian Jew who had studied at the University of Vienna, and served as a doctor in the Austro-Hungarian army in the First World War. The top floors of the Jewish Quarter hospital having been evacuated because of shelling, patients were treated in the basement, and in the adjoining synagogue. There was so little room for the large number of wounded that in some cases two patients had to share a single mattress.

Dr Laufer later wrote: 'I saw several men who were in and out of the casualty clinic two or three times in the same day and still went back each time to fight. I have to admit that men who would have been hospitalised under normal battle conditions were sent back to the front after being bandaged. We did this because we were so short of men and because while they were receiving treatment their places were being taken in the posts by children.

'There were men back at the loopholes whose fingers had been amputated a few days previously, or whose wounds were inflamed and suppurating, or who had one eye bandaged up.

'There was one case I shall never forget. A handsome boy about twenty years old was brought in. A piece of shrapnel had penetrated his eye.

' "How long will the operation take?" he asked.

' "About fifteen to twenty minutes," I answered.

' "Too long," he said. "The situation at our post is desperate right now. Just put a few drops of something in to kill the pain and bandage it. I'll be back as soon as we have driven them off."

'An hour later they brought him back. His handsome face was blown away by a shell. There was no need to trouble any further about his eye. He was dead.'

*

On the morning of May 22 the American Consul, Thomas C. Wasson, one of the three members of the United Nations Truce Commission in Jerusalem, telegraphed to Washington about Arab reactions to the recent decision by President Truman to recognise the State of Israel. The feeling was, Wasson reported, 'that United States has betrayed Arab States'. The Arab opinion reaching him was 'extremely bitter' against the United States. As for the Jewish reaction, he wrote: 'In Jerusalem Jews are faced with immediate and grim task of warfare and have not been able to give much thought to anything but business at hand.' Having sent his report Wasson went to a meeting of the Truce Commission at the French Consulate. Then, while returning to the American Consulate a short walk away, he was shot by an Arab sniper, and died later of his wounds.

That same day the United Nations Security Council issued a call for a cease-fire throughout Palestine, including Jerusalem. Israel accepted this on the following day, informing the United Nations that an order had been issued to all fronts to cease fire at the stipulated hour 'provided that the other side acts likewise'. But King Abdullah did not agree to halt his offensive. 'My soldiers did not enter Palestine to stop the war to no purpose,' was his response. The King, whose Arab Legion was poised to overrun the Jewish Quarter, instructed his government in Amman to make no reply to the Security Council. The other Arab States asked for a delay, in order, they said, to consult among each other. The delay was granted.

The Foreign Minister of the Provisional Government of Israel, Moshe Shertok, protested. 'While the delay was granted on the plea of a need of consultation,' he said, 'the shelling of Jerusalem from outside by foreign Arab armies is proceeding with unabated fury, and ancient Jewish synagogues in the Walled City are being destroyed one after the other as a result of Arab artillery fire.' That day an Arab-language broadcast from Ramallah described in lurid detail the first stage of the long-drawn-out destruction of the Hurva Synagogue in the Jewish Quarter.

On the afternoon of May 23 a further attempt was made by the Arab Legion to capture the Notre Dame Monastery, just outside the New Gate. The monastery served the Hagannah as an important fortified point protecting the central part of Jewish Jerusalem, which was only a few hundred yards away. It had been occupied by the Hagannah since May 14, when the British withdrew.

The Legion's armoured vehicles were able to advance unchallenged along the street outside the monastery. There were no anti-tank obstacles to impede them. Netanel Lorch, in his official history of the war, described the sequel: 'When the first armoured car was right under the windows of the monastery, heading for Jaffa Road, a Molotov cocktail, produced by Jerusalem's sappers with whatever they had at hand, was hurled at it from one of the upper storey windows by Jacques, a boy who was reputed to have fought with the Maquis in France though hardly sixteen years old.

'The second Molotov cocktail hit the armoured car and set it on fire. The burning vehicle proved an effective anti-tank obstacle. The vehicles following were forced to turn around and retreat. One vehicle, which had moved close to the first, presumably to evacuate its wounded, was also hit and damaged. The anti-tank obstacle had thus been strengthened. Meanwhile most of the defenders had descended to the ground floor of the monastery. They arrived in the nick of time: the assaulting infantry was stopped fifteen yards from the main building.'

Glubb Pasha later described the failure of the attack against Notre Dame as the worst defeat inflicted on the Legion throughout the war. At five o'clock that afternoon he called off the attack on Jewish Jerusalem. More than half the Arab Legion forces involved in the attack had been killed or wounded. Glubb did not want further casualties on that scale. He also had only two weeks' reserves of ammunition.

But the course of the battle was not yet determined. On May 23, as Glubb's forces fell back from Notre Dame, other Arab Legionnaires were in action sixteen miles west of the city, against the Israeli troops seeking to dislodge them from Latrun, overlooking the road from Tel Aviv to Jerusalem. More than 600 Israelis were killed. Many of them were survivors of the concentration camps, recently released from their long internment in Cyprus behind British barbed wire, and who, because of the emergency, had been sent into battle at Latrun with no training. The Arab Legion's superior artillery and firepower devastated the attackers, whose Sten and Bren guns, abandoned on the battlefield, were an important boost to the Legion's reserves.

*

On May 24, Egyptian forces overran Ramat Rahel, which the Hagannah had recaptured from them only three days earlier. 'An Arab flag flies over Ramat Rahel' was the terse radio message conveyed to Hagannah headquarters.

That evening Ramat Rahel was recaptured by the Hagannah. The kibbutz had changed hands three times in as many days. Even today the trenches of the defenders are clearly visible. From them, across southern Jerusalem, one can see, as the Egyptians saw during their brief occupation, the walls of the Old City.

From Ramat Rahel the Hagannah made a raid on Mar Elias, the monastery from whose grounds the Egyptians had launched their attacks on the kibbutz. The monastery was found abandoned, except for a single nun who had stayed on throughout the battle.

Outside Jerusalem, Glubb Pasha continued his efforts to dominate the road to the coast. Following the capture of Latrun, troops of the Arab Legion had taken one of the highest points in the Jerusalem corridor, Radar Hill, from which its artillery could fire on many stretches of the Jerusalem road, from the entrance to the city to Bab al-Wad.

*

Inside the Jewish Quarter of the Old City the situation was so desperate that on May 25 some of the inhabitants went to the Hagannah command and demanded that they open talks with the Arabs with a view to surrender. That day a radio message sent from the Hagannah unit inside the quarter reported that there were no grenades left, and that demoralisation was also spreading among the soldiers.

Arab morale in the attack on the Jewish Quarter had been boosted by the arrival of Arab Legion soldiers, who took up positions along-side men of the Muslim Brotherhood, a predominantly Egyptian-based fundamentalist group fiercely opposed to any Jewish State. Glubb was exhilarated to see his 400 men in such a setting. 'There was something strangely moving to me', he later wrote, 'in seeing my own soldiers on those historic walls, their rifles thrust through medieval loopholes, shaped long ago to the measurement of crossbows.'

A Jewish pilot, flying in a small plane, managed to drop guns and ammunition to the Jewish Quarter on May 26. But so much of the quarter had been overrun that these crucial supplies fell into Arab hands. That morning another radio message reported that the defenders had only 170 machine-gun bullets left. Attempts were made to use rifle bullets in the machine-guns, but these jammed the guns. Some of the fighting men said they would not go on duty the next morning unless help arrived from outside. But the Hagannah had no means of breaking through the Zion Gate as it had done seven days earlier. Plans were being made, but the forces were not yet ready.

During May 27 the Arab forces raised their flag on the roof of the Hurva, the main synagogue in the Jewish Quarter. The synagogue was then set on fire. First built in 1705, destroyed in 1720, rebuilt between 1856 and 1864, the Hurva's eighty-foot-high dome had been a prominent city landmark for almost a century. With the seizure of the Hurva, a third of the quarter was in Arab hands. That day the three senior Hagannah officers and the principal rabbis of the quarter met to decide what to do. The rabbis wanted to open negotiations with the Arabs. During the meeting a message arrived from Hagannah headquarters in western Jerusalem promising that an extricating action would be launched within two days.

This promise of a renewed Hagannah attack through the Zion Gate gave momentary hope to the defenders in their discussions with the rabbis. Their situation had indeed become almost hopeless. In the hospital the few remaining bottles of blood plasma that had been smuggled in eight days earlier were ruined when the power supply failed. The last of the anaesthetics had been used. Operations had to take place without anaesthetic, and by candlelight. The number of wounded – well over 100 – was increasing with the explosion of every shell. Among the most gravely wounded was an English girl, twenty-two-year-old Esther Cailingold, who had volunteered to go with the Hagannah into the Old City. She was not to survive. 'We had a difficult fight,' she wrote in a letter to her parents that was found under her pillow when she died. 'I have tasted hell, but it has been worthwhile because I am convinced the end will see a Jewish State and all our longings. I have lived my life fully, and very sweet it has been to be in our land.'

On May 28 a radio message from the defenders in the Old City reached Hagannah headquarters: 'There is no possibility from a military point of view of holding out here.' From outside, the Hagannah urged the defenders to hold out for another day, when a breakthrough would be attempted. The defenders, however, did not feel able to hold on even for twenty-four hours. At 9.15 that morning, with permission from the Hagannah officers inside the quarter, two rabbis went out towards the Arab post at the Zion Gate, carrying a white sheet tied between two poles, the white flag of truce, to seek a cease-fire. Among the Israeli soldiers on Mount Zion at that moment was the Palmach commander, Yitzhak Rabin. 'I witnessed a shattering scene,' he later wrote. 'A delegation was emerging from the Jewish Quarter bearing white flags. I was horrified to learn that it consisted of rabbis and other residents on their way to hear the Legion's terms for their capitulation.'

After a tense day of negotiations, at 4.36 that afternoon the commander of the Arab Legion in the Old City, Major Abdullah al-Tel, accepted the cease-fire. His two conditions were that the Jewish Quarter be occupied by Arab Legion troops, and that all Jewish 'fighters' be taken to Amman as prisoners-of-war. When al-Tel saw that the defenders had only a pitiful collection of weapons, he exclaimed: 'If I'd known this was your situation, I swear I would have conquered you with sticks.' Finding that there were only thirty-five Jewish soldiers left unwounded, he became even more angry.

In the last week of fighting in the Jewish Quarter sixty-two Jews had been killed and two hundred wounded. John Phillips, the *Life* photographer who entered the captured quarter with the victors, found among the Hagannah troops an Englishman who had earlier deserted from the British army and had joined the Jews.

*

For the first time ever there was to be no Jewish presence in the Jewish Quarter, and no means of Jewish access to the Wailing Wall. Before leaving for captivity in Transjordan, the Jewish soldiers had first to assemble so that an Arab doctor could decide which of them were badly enough wounded to be set free. Under the terms of the truce, all the able-bodied men between fifteen and sixty were to go to Amman. While the examination of the prisoners was proceeding, a mob of local Arabs threatened to lynch them. It was officers of the Arab Legion, some Arab and some British, who then gave the order to open fire on the mob, in order to protect the Jews. An Arab bystander who tried to shoot a Jew who was being led into captivity was himself shot dead by an Arab Legion soldier.

That evening a total of 1,300 refugees prepared to leave the Jewish Quarter for western Jerusalem. 'I was struck by their expressions, which had changed from a numb, empty look to one of grief,' Phillips later wrote. 'Yet no one wept. Tears were a luxury these people did not have time for. One hour was all they had to gather up the possessions of a lifetime.' Among those watching the refugees as they moved out of the Jewish Quarter under Arab guard was Pablo de Azcazarte, the head of the United Nations Truce Commission.

'Misery always wears the same face,' he told Phillips, who was standing next to him. 'I am a Spanish republican. It was just like this at Malaga during the civil war.'

A two-hour cease-fire was negotiated between the Arab Legion and the Israeli army, and the Jewish Quarter evacuees were sent through the Zion Gate. As they left they could see columns of smoke rising from the quarter behind them. The Hadassah welfare station had been set on fire, and, despite Abdullah al-Tel's curfew, the looting and burning of Jewish property was in full swing. Into the new city were sent 1,300 old men, women and children, and the wounded men. To a prisoner-of-war camp in Amman were sent 340 fighters, including fifty-four men who were listed as 'lightly wounded'.

On the morning of May 29 Pablo de Azcazarte visited the hospital in the Jewish Quarter. He was surprised to find that all the wounded had been transferred during the night to the Armenian Patriarchate, 'because some fires in the Jewish Quarter had spread so as to threaten the hospital and render its evacuation necessary. And here is the interesting part; it was those same soldiers of the Legion who had remained to guard and protect the hospital and who, according to the assistant director, were not going to leave a single wounded man alive on the following morning, who removed them to the Armenian Patriarchate and saved them from the fire. I confess that this was a great source of satisfaction to me, especially when Dr Laufer, the director of the hospital, beckoned me to one side and said more or less as follows: "You will remember my fear and mistrust that it was decided last night to leave the hospital under the protection of the Arab Legion. Well, now I want to tell you that the Legion has behaved as well as the best disciplined force of any European army, and I may say that I have served as a doctor first in the Austrian Army and afterwards in the British. Thanks to the soldiers of the Arab Legion and their magnificent behaviour, we have been able to save our wounded from the fire that was threatening the hospital." '

On May 29 John Phillips took one last look at the shell-battered streets of the Jewish Quarter. 'Down Beit El a proud Moslem led the way,' he later wrote, 'followed by his barefoot wife carrying three wooden containers of Sephardic scrolls from a nearby synagogue, and his daughter balancing a carton of matzohs on her head. Along Batei Mahse Street, which looks out on the Mount of Olives and the Russian church, Arab civilians were gathering up what little was left to plunder – nondescript pieces of shelves, window frames, boxes. Near Shaar Hashamayim a more fortunate Arab had found an entire door he was carting off.'

The refugees from the Old City were distressed at what many of them saw as the failure of the Hagannah to come to their rescue. Bernard Joseph later wrote: 'It is hard to forget a twelve-year-old girl who threw her ration of bread at the volunteer distributing the first meal, screaming, "Why didn't you send us arms before, instead of giving us bread now?" '

*

On May 29, the day after the fall of the Jewish Quarter, the United Nations Security Council passed a second resolution calling for a cease-fire, to be followed by a four weeks' truce throughout Palestine. On the following day the British Government, which had sponsored this resolution, ordered all British officers fighting with the Arab Legion to leave their commands and withdraw entirely from the battle. Concern had been expressed in the British Parliament at the participation of British officers in the onslaught on the Jewish Quarter. Winston Churchill had expressed his anxiety in a private message to the Labour Prime Minister, Clement Attlee.

'The withdrawal of the British officers was a shattering blow,' Glubb Pasha later wrote. 'They included all operational staff officers, both the brigade commanders, and the commanding officers of three of the four infantry regiments, and all the trained artillery officers. The artillery having only been raised three months before, none of the Jordanian officers were yet really competent to direct the fire of the guns.' These British regular officers, Glubb added, 'were therefore the keystone to the whole edifice in 1948'.

That keystone had been removed. With some distress Glubb wrote: 'Although the Arabs were favourably placed at the end of the first month of fighting, we knew that they had in reality shot their bolt. If on May 15th they had rapidly brought their full forces to bear, and had then advanced energetically, they might have succeeded in overrunning the Jewish State. But they were far from doing this. Most of them completely underestimated the task, despatched quite inadequate forces, and came to a halt as soon as they met resolute opposition.'

*

As well as the 1,300 refugees who had arrived in Jewish Jerusalem from the Old City there were several hundred more from the Etzion Bloc. These refugees, whose homes and possessions had been seized by the Arabs, were housed in Arab homes in Katamon and Bakaa. All the Arab residents of what was now West Jerusalem had fled during the fighting. On June 2 these former Arab residential areas were handed over by the Israeli military authorities to the Jerusalem Emergency Committee. The first step on their road to becoming an integral part of Jewish Jerusalem had begun.

*

Among the Arab forces that were fighting in and around Jerusalem there was no unity. The Egyptian military leaders, whose troops were at the southern entrance to the city, held in contempt the Jordanians, who were to the north and east. The Syrian Prime Minister, Jamil Mardam, who had promised his Arab colleagues an infantry division to fight on the battlements of Jerusalem, was fearful of King Abdullah's ambition, as he saw it, to restore Hashemite rule to Damascus, where Abdullah's brother had ruled briefly after the First World War, before being dislodged by the French. The senior British diplomat accredited to the Hashemite Kingdom of Transjordan, Sir Alec Kirkbride, who was present at many of the inter-Arab meetings in 1948, reported after one of them: 'Jerusalem was dismissed as saved, and the talk then turned to more pleasant matters such as the final offensive which was to sweep the Jews into the sea, and how the Jewish property would be divided among the Arab governments that had sent armies.'

*

As the siege of Jerusalem continued, seven public restaurants were opened in the Jewish sector, where meals were sold at minimum prices. Starting on June 1, some 5,000 three-course meals were provided each day. Each meal included 200 grams of bread.

The water situation was relieved for a while by the use of the water found in houses from which the Arabs had fled, most of which had cisterns. Water from the Romema reservoir was brought to the citizens by truck, often under shell-fire and sniping. The ration was at first two gallons of water per person, of which drinking water was four pints. By the beginning of June, the water ration had to be cut to six quarts per person per day. Bernard Joseph commented: 'One favourite device was to remove the stopper from the kitchen sink and place a bucket underneath the vent. The water thus trapped was used to wash floors and then to flush toilets.'

With incredible difficulty, a road was being built by gangs of Jews brought from Jewish Jerusalem. The aim of this new road was to bypass the Arab-held section of the Jerusalem road at Latrun. Known as the 'Burma Road', this Jewish lifeline was hacked and bulldozed out of the steep hillsides. At first there was a three-mile gap between the two main sections of the road. This could only be traversed on foot. Hundreds of men, mostly aged fifty years or over, carried forty-five-pound sacks of flour over this three-mile stretch, often making the journey twice a night. By the early days of June, trucks could drive, with difficulty, along the whole length of the new road, and about 100 tons of supplies were reaching the city every twenty-four hours. Over the steepest parts of the route the trucks had to be pulled by tractors.

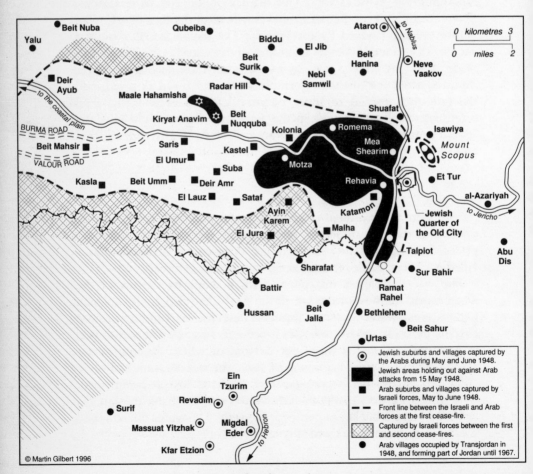

Jerusalem besieged 1948

CHAPTER FIFTEEN

Truce, Violence, Armistice and Renewal, June 1948 to December 1949

On 11 June 1948 the cease-fire called for by the Security Council nearly two weeks earlier was finally signed. The Arabs realised that there was no way they could penetrate, with any chance of meaningful success, into the Jewish-controlled area of the country. In Jerusalem all fighting and shelling ceased. That day the Central Bureau of Medical Statistics reported that 316 Jews had been killed in the city in the previous five weeks: 199 of them were civilians, 52 were soldiers not in action, and 65 were soldiers killed in action. More than 10,000 shells had fallen on the city. Two thousand homes had been seriously damaged. In the Old City, twenty-two of the twenty-seven synagogues had been reduced to rubble after the Jewish Quarter had been captured. At the same time, homes had been looted and vandalised, and most of the holy books had been destroyed.

With the coming of the truce, the road to Tel Aviv could be travelled for the first time in more than six months without the fear of sniping and attack. On the night of June 12 the Israeli diplomat Walter Eytan was among those who made the journey to the coast. He later wrote: 'Part of the route lay along the new "Burma Road", roughed out of the secret hills a few nights before. One stretch of it could still not take a loaded jeep; for half a mile we walked. All Israel seemed to be on the move that night – hundreds of volunteers carrying supplies to Jerusalem on their backs; silhouetted black against the stars; silent soldiers heading east and west like a straggle of ants, guided seemingly by instinct; political leaders on their way down to join the Government at Tel Aviv, others going up to see how Jerusalem had fared in the siege. Old friends met unexpectedly in the rocky night, stopped just long enough to exchange a few words.'

Bernard Joseph has left a picture of life in Jerusalem during the cease-fire. 'Young couples could be seen walking arm in arm. Just to go out in the bright sunshine of the high summer days was to gain a sense of freedom and release. People could be seen examining damage caused to their houses with a view to repairing them. A limited number of scavengers were on duty collecting broken glass in the streets. Schools resumed their studies. Movies were reopened. Cigarettes and talk were exchanged by our defence men and legionnaires near the city walls. The cafés were now open at night, but were still shrouded in darkness or semi-darkness. All they could offer their customers was a cup of coffee, sometimes a stale cake or pastry. One café was always noisy and full of heated discussion: the one commandeered by convoy drivers who were still in the city. Convoys had resumed under strict UN supervision, but there was as yet no transportation for passengers. Newspapers still did not come from Tel Aviv.'

On 12 June 1948 Count Folke Bernadotte, the United Nations Mediator, arrived in Jerusalem. Bernadotte was a Swedish diplomat who, at the end of the Second World War, had been involved in negotiations to save Jews from the concentration camps. Bernadotte's first intervention in Jerusalem was distressing to the Jews. 'I explained my views to them,' he later wrote. 'The supply system should be so organised that neither of the two parties would be in a more advantageous military position at the end of the truce than they had been before: food stocks should therefore not be increased.' It took long and difficult negotiations before Bernadotte agreed that the citizens of Jewish Jerusalem, who had been forced to such low rations during the siege only as a result of hostile action, could be allowed a near-normal ration during the cease-fire.

Under Bernadotte's eye the Arab Legion transferred military supplies from Jericho to Jerusalem. At Mar Elias, overlooking Ramat Rahel, the Egyptians established fortified positions in an area demarcated as No-Man's Land. Within Jerusalem, many new Arab fortified positions were built. There was sniping from several Arab suburbs into Jewish ones. From London *The Times* reported that the United Nations observers in Jerusalem, 'in an endeavour to maintain some semblance of control, reimpose a general cease-fire order and then have to declare special "no fire" periods in order to approach the front-line areas to arrange for further truce periods. The people of Jerusalem cynically ask which will finish first: the so-called truce, or the vocabulary of the truce-makers.'

*

On 28 June 1948 Bernadotte produced his own plan for Jerusalem: it would become part of an Arab State, with King Abdullah of Transjordan as sovereign. There would be 'municipal autonomy' in Jerusalem for the Jews, as well as 'special arrangements' for protecting the Holy Places. Israel's Provisional Government, meeting in Tel Aviv, rejected the plan, or any change from the United Nations resolution of November 1947, with its separate international regime for the city.

During the truce, both sides tended their wounded and consolidated their positions. The 'Burma Road', by-passing the Arab-held section of the coastal road at Latrun and enabling much-needed food and supplies to reach Jerusalem, was being completed. 'There are secret whispers of a new road being built,' Pauline Rose wrote in her diary on July 3. 'Nobody speaks about it. But a fresh hope filters through the fears of threatened danger.' Three days later the rumours were proved to have been true. 'Today there is great excitement in Zion Square', she reported. 'Several lorries have arrived with food-stuffs! Everybody is asking "How did they get through?" "Is it the new road?" We dared to believe the rumours. A convoy had come through. It means life.'

When on July 7 the truce period was about to expire, the Security Council asked each side if they would extend it for ten days. The Jews accepted this, the Arab States rejected it, and on July 9 fighting was renewed throughout Palestine. The Jewish armed forces were now a single entity: the Irgun terrorist group having been brought into the Hagannah to form a single entity, the Israel Defence Forces, Zahal (its Hebrew acronym), also known as the IDF. The Stern Gang remained in isolation.

*

The renewed fighting lasted for ten days. On July 10 an Egyptian Spitfire dropped a number of bombs on the Jewish sector of the city. Three children were killed. The Arab Legion made two attempts to break into the New City, one from Suleiman Street towards Notre Dame and the other from the Zion Gate towards Mount Zion. 'The assailants were repelled by the heavy fire our defenders opened on them,' Yona Cohen wrote in his diary, 'and turned back in confusion.'

From the first days of the fighting, the Jewish forces sought to secure the corridor from Jerusalem to the coast, which had proved so precarious a lifeline during the siege. Their efforts were successful. Not only was the corridor widened and secured, but the railway line to the coast was taken in its entirety. All thirty-five Arab villages in the corridor were overrun, and 50,000 Arabs from these villages fled across the fighting lines to the areas under Transjordanian control.

To the south-west of Jerusalem, just above the railway, the Arab hill village of Malha, from which the Arab Legion was bombarding the Jewish sector, was attacked by the Israel Defence Forces on July 13. The *New York Times* described the village as an 'important supply base and assembly centre' for the Arab forces. Egyptian troops were among those defending it. The attackers consisted of a company of former Irgun troops and two platoons from the Gadna, the youth battalions of the Palmach, working side by side. By July 16 the village was in Israeli hands. An Arab counter-attack that same day, in which fifteen of the Irgun men were killed, was driven off. Two days later the Arab village of Ayin Karem was overrun, thus ending, in the words of the Israeli commander of the Jerusalem area, 'a threatened Egyptian invasion' of the city.

*

The hopes of the Hagannah to regain the Jewish Quarter, and to capture Sheikh Jarrah, opening a way up to the Hadassah Hospital and the Hebrew University, were both frustrated. The main attempt to reach the Jewish Quarter was made on July 16, the day before a second truce, negotiated by Bernadotte, was to come into effect. Despite the use of a substantial charge of explosives set in the wall near the massively defended Zion Gate, it proved impossible to make a large enough breach to enter the Old City. A successful breakthrough into the more distant New Gate failed to make sufficient progress inside the wall to reach the Jewish Quarter. Essential reinforcements which the Jewish Quarter defenders had expected, and were dependent upon to maintain the defences, never arrived.

Of the final attempt to recapture the Jewish Quarter, Bernard Joseph has written: 'One of the accidents which had delayed the commencement of the action and so conditioned the subsequent withdrawal was that an Arab shell scored a lucky hit on an ammunition vehicle which was in one of the rear bases of the Etzel detachment. Thousands of bullets were destroyed and two men were killed. The other incident was at the New Gate. There the Arabs had built a road block of wood and shavings. This was ignited by a shell, and it took twenty minutes before the blaze could be extinguished and our men move forward. These were irrevocable, precious moments and it is on such flickers of fortune's eyelash that one can say the fate of the Old City was determined.'

The Old City was entirely in Arab hands, but several Arab attempts to capture Jewish-held Musrara outside the Damascus Gate were unsuccessful. The former Arab areas in western Jerusalem remained firmly in Jewish hands. 'While rummaging among the vandalised Arab houses in the neighbourhood,' Zipporah Borowsky wrote to her parents on July 16, 'I found some books. One, in particular, caught my eye, *Short Stories of Thomas Hardy*.' Forgetting the war for a few moments, she began to read. Her reading was interrupted by the arrival of a young man 'dripping with blood. I attended to his wound quickly and efficiently, marvelling at my calmness and warmth.'

Zipporah Borowsky had come to Jerusalem as a student less than a year earlier. Since the Ben Yehuda Street bomb, when she had found herself attending to the wounded, she had become an army nurse, attached to a unit based in Talpiot. 'The Sergeant-Major just came in to tell me we are on full alert,' she told her parents in her letter of July 16. 'This is the final hour before the enforced truce, accepted by everyone, goes into effect. Every last drop of energy will be used by us and the Arabs to push forward as far as possible. Already the bombardment is deafening.'

'God, last night was awful,' Zipporah Borowsky wrote to her parents on July 17, 'but not as awful for us as for those up front. The shells fell close. The house shook, the air was charged with explosives, one following the other relentlessly. No one knew a moment of peace until 5.30 a.m., when suddenly – synchronised silence.' Six Jews had been killed by shell-fire during the night. Then, after ten days of renewed fighting, the second truce came into effect in Jerusalem that morning.

*

There were two more days of spasmodic shell-fire from the Arab sector on to the Jewish side. No one was killed, but the Hadassah Hospital reported on July 19 that 'the vicious bombardment of the early afternoon resulted in some gruesome casualties'. An Arab attack on Musrara was driven off that day, when Arab troops, under a barrage of rifle and mortar fire, twice broke into the Mandelbaum House at the edge of Musrara but were driven off. From the safety of exile in Damascus, the former Mufti of Jerusalem, Haj Amin al-Husseini, denounced the truce as 'acquiescence in partition'. On July

23 two Israeli soldiers were killed by Arab firing from Abu Tor, and the King David Hotel was slightly damaged by shell-fire from the Arab village of Silwan.

On August 2 the Israeli Government proclaimed the areas of Jerusalem under Israeli control to be Israeli-occupied territory, and appointed Bernard Joseph as Military Governor. There was no longer any question of Jewish acquiescence in a United Nations *corpus separatum* or any other scheme for internationalisation. On August 5 the Israeli Government explicitly rejected the internationalisation proposals. Five days later, members of the Stern Gang gathered outside the Belgian Consulate in Talbiye as Count Bernadotte met with Bernard Joseph, and several leading Israeli political figures, to discuss the Jerusalem issue. The Stern Gang placards read: 'Stockholm is Yours; Jerusalem is Ours!' and 'Your Work is in Vain; we are Here!'

At the following day's meeting of his Cabinet, Ben-Gurion warned his colleagues that the Stern Gang might try to kidnap Bernadotte, not merely demonstrate against him. There was discussion about using force against the Stern Gang, but any decision to use force was set aside to enable talks to take place between the Government and the Stern Gang, with a view to dissuading them from any violent course.

*

Jerusalem's most troubled months were not yet over. On August 12 three Jewish soldiers were killed when Arab Legion shells fell on Mount Zion. The dead men were Moshe Eliash, Alfred Rabinowitz and Pinhas Solevetchik. That same day Arab Legion forces blew up the Latrun water pumping-station. Jewish Jerusalem was again entirely dependent for its water on the supplies stored in the cisterns of hundreds of private houses. In the city itself, violence was ever-present. On August 15 two Israeli and two Arab soldiers were killed during a second unsuccessful Arab attack on the Mandelbaum House, from which the Hagannah were protecting Musrara.

Breaches of the cease-fire continued throughout August 16, with Egyptian forces bombarding Israeli positions at Malha, and Arab snipers firing from Beit Iksa on to the Jerusalem-Tel Aviv road. Also that day the American Consul-General, James G. McDonald, was accompanied by Zeev Herzog, a Jewish liaison officer with the United Nations, to the only crossing-point between the Jewish and Arab sectors, near the Mandelbaum House to the north of the Old City. 'As Herzog stepped out of the United States car,' Bernard Joseph later wrote, 'he was shot by Arab snipers. McDonald drove off, leaving Herzog dead in the street.'

On August 19 Count Bernadotte telegraphed to the United Nations Secretary-General: 'Not only has firing practically never ceased in Jerusalem but the situation is getting out of hand.' Arab Legion efforts to infiltrate the No-Man's-Land areas, and the shelling of Jewish residential areas, continued throughout the autumn, and led to several deaths. On August 30 a Jewish worker was shot dead by sniper fire from the Old City walls while crossing a street on the Israeli side of the city.

*

Ben-Gurion's Cabinet failed in its efforts to persuade the Stern Gang to renounce violence. On September 7 Ben-Gurion ordered a military raid on the Stern Gang training camp. Bitterly, the Stern Gang denounced Ben-Gurion for his failure to continue the military struggle against the Arabs, and castigated Bernadotte, who had just returned to the region after a three-week absence, for wanting Jerusalem to be under Arab rule. A Stern Gang poster demanded that Bernadotte be banished from the country altogether.

Bernadotte's hopes for an Arab-ruled Jerusalem were unrealistic. The dividing line between Arab-held and Israeli-held Jerusalem ran right through the city, from north to south. Western Jerusalem was under the control of Israel and eastern Jerusalem under the control of Transjordan. This put an end to any practical solution for a single city under Arab rule, whatever safeguards might be proposed for the Jews. In a surprise development, King Abdullah, who recognised that the Jews would never accept Arab rule over the whole city, indicated on September 15 his willingness to divide the city with Israel. On the following day Bernadotte, who was then at the coast, submitted a final report in which, while giving up his earlier idea of putting the whole city under Arab rule, recommended, along the lines of the United Nations resolution of the previous November, that there should be an international regime for the city, which should be demilitarised.

On September 17, the day after submitting this report, Bernadotte made his fifth visit to Jerusalem. That afternoon he was driven from the former British Government House, where he had decided to establish his winter headquarters, to Rehavia, for tea at the home of Bernard Joseph, the Jewish Military Governor. On the way there, Bernadotte's car was ambushed by members of the Stern Gang (Lehi).

Shots were fired, and Bernadotte was killed. Also killed was a French army officer, Colonel André Pierre Serot, who was travelling with him. As a member of the French Resistance, Serot had saved many Jewish lives during the Second World War.

The idea of the murder 'was conceived in Jerusalem by Lehi members operating more or less independently,' one of the Stern Gang leaders later wrote in his memoirs. He was the Polish-born Yitzhak Yzernitzky (later, as Yitzhak Shamir, Prime Minister of Israel), a member of the Stern Gang's three-man Central Committee. 'Our opinion was asked', he wrote, 'and we offered no opposition.' But one of those involved later disclosed that the assassination had been decided on at a meeting eight days earlier by the Stern Gang's Central Committee, at which Shamir was present. The fatal shots were fired by Yehoshua Cohen, who had recently been released from a British prison.

Immediately after the killings, the Military Governor of Jewish Jerusalem, Bernard Joseph, consulted with the city's military commander, Lieutenant Colonel Moshe Dayan. 'We agreed', Joseph wrote on the following day, 'that the only practicable way of dealing with the situation was by a large-scale military operation to round up the whole Stern Gang.' From Tel Aviv, Ben-Gurion issued an order which began: 'One, arrest all Stern Gang members. Two, find and surround all Stern bases and confiscate all arms. Three, kill any who resist.'

Despite a curfew, a prolonged search, and 184 arrests in Jerusalem alone, the murderer of Bernadotte was never found. Leaflets were later left at the foreign consulates to say that the mediator had been murdered because he was 'a British agent carrying out British orders'. The Stern Gang claimed that they had been incensed by Bernadotte's plan that all Jerusalem should be under Arab rule. They had no idea that the mediator had given up that plan, and that, only a day before his murder, he had advocated the city's internationalisation.

*

On September 18, two days after Bernadotte's murder, a thirteen-year-old Jewish schoolboy, Yonathan Abramsky, was shot dead by an Arab sniper in the north of Jerusalem. Five days later a car in an Israeli convoy under United Nations protection was blocked on its way to the city. The United Nations observer in charge of the convoy, Colonel Henri du Marcel, told the passengers of the car to shelter in the roadside ditch, and went over to talk to the Arab soldiers. As he did so the soldiers opened fire on the passengers in the ditch. Marcel pleaded with them to stop firing – in vain. The Arabs went up to the ditch and fired into it at point-blank range.

All four of those in the ditch were killed: Gavriel Eliasburg of the fledgling Israeli Air Forces; John Locke Lewis of Philadelphia, an American railway expert whom the Government of Israel had invited to advise it on railway development; Mrs Simcha van Vriesland, the widow of the former Treasurer of the Zionist Executive; and Balfour Cohen, the son of one of Jerusalem's leading Sephardi families, who had been named after Lord Balfour, in honour of the Balfour Declaration. Cohen had accompanied the convoys, unarmed, as the United Nations observers had insisted. The road was not reopened for another three weeks.

In the United Nations, pressure for the internationalisation of Jerusalem continued. A leading Israeli politician, Rabbi Meir Berlin, wanted to accept it, arguing that the city would otherwise be divided into two parts, one Jewish and one Arab, and that 'all the remnants of our glory from ancient times' would be in Arab hands. At a Cabinet meeting on September 26 the Prime Minister of the new State, David Ben-Gurion, having already alerted the forces needed for the attack, proposed the renewal of military efforts to capture the whole city. His proposal was defeated by a majority of seven to four. On his copy of the Cabinet decision, Ben-Gurion noted, many years later: 'The proposal to renew the battle for the city is not yet for publication, because I do not want to shame those members of the Provisional Government who were opposed to it.' The Israeli Cabinet's decision that day was that 'if partition be essential, our delegation to the United Nations will agree'.

*

On October 10 the intensity of the Egyptian shelling on the southern suburbs was such that United Nations observers believed that a full-scale Egyptian assault on the city was imminent. On October 13 the observers reported that the Arabs had fired with automatic weapons 'for several hours, from areas under UN supervision, and without any provocation by Jewish Forces'. On October 16, Arab Legion forces at the Arab-held Zion Gate attacked the Jewish positions on Mount Zion, but were driven off after fierce fighting.

At a concert held in the Edison Film Theatre on October 16, Leonard Bernstein, who had come specially from the United States, conducted the newly-created Israel Philharmonic Orchestra. He did so amid the persistent background noise of rifle and machine-gun fire from the direction of the Old City. The climax of the evening was Beethoven's Fifth Symphony. 'Towards the end of the first movement,' an eye-witness, Tom Tugend, later recalled, 'machine-gun fire burst out in the Old City, held by Jordanian forces. The gunfire continued unabated throughout the performance. Lenny and the orchestra never missed a beat.' On October 31 the United Nations observers noted: 'Last night the cannons thundered again in most parts of the city. There were 108 instances of Arab firing at Jewish positions in the city during the last week.'

On November 2, the anniversary of the Balfour Declaration of 1917, the blackout in West Jerusalem was cancelled for the night. 'The city blazed with lights,' Bernard Joseph has written, 'and its citizens crowded the streets and cafés to taste the future they had fought for.' But on the following day there was more spasmodic shelling, and on November 5 Ben-Gurion reported to his Cabinet: 'Jerusalem has as yet hardly enjoyed one night of quiet.'

*

On November 28 the newly promoted Lieutenant-Colonel Abdullah al-Tel, representing all the Arab forces around Jerusalem, and Lieutenant-Colonel Moshe Dayan, the new commander of the Israeli forces in the Jerusalem area, met under United Nations auspices at Government House to discuss a return to an effective cease-fire. It was their second meeting in three days. Even as they were meeting, sniper fire broke out in the north of the city, and a Jewish Jerusalemite, Shlomo Mansur, was killed.

After more than four hours' discussion, Dayan and al-Tel reached agreement for 'a complete and sincere cease-fire in the Jerusalem area'. There was to be no movement by either side in the No-Man's-Land areas, and a positive effort to 'ameliorate' conditions generally within Jerusalem. When news of the agreement was announced, bonfires were lit in the Oid City and Arab Legion soldiers danced around them in joy.

Following the agreement large numbers of Arab refugees began to return to the Old City. It was also agreed that Jewish convoys could go up to the Mount Scopus enclave twice a month. But all attempts by the Jews to obtain the right to pray at the Wailing Wall, or to continue to use or even visit the Jewish Cemetery on the Mount of Olives, were rejected. On the day of the cease-fire agreement, Chaim Weizmann, who had been invited to accept the Presidency of the State of Israel, journeyed to Jerusalem for the first time since the fighting had begun more than a year earlier. 'Do not worry because part of Jerusalem is not now within the State,' he told the enthusiastic crowds that gathered to greet him. 'All will come to pass in peace.'

On December 12, less than two weeks after the signing of the final cease-fire, the new road running parallel to the 'Burma Road', but less precarious, was opened by Ben-Gurion as a secure by-pass for travel to Jerusalem from the coast. Known as the 'Valour Road', it was fifteen miles long, and had been built in eight weeks. It was possible at last for the journey to Jerusalem to be made without danger of sniping; all the Arab villages overlooking it had earlier been blown up by the Hagannah.

*

Despite Bernadotte's murder, the United Nations continued its efforts to find a way to implement his report on the internationalisation and demilitarisation of the city. On 11 December 1948 the General Assembly established a Palestine Conciliation Commission, made up of representatives from the United States, France and Turkey. One of its tasks, set out by the General Assembly, was to prepare proposals for the permanent international regime for Jerusalem, with 'maximum local autonomy consistent with the special international status of the Jerusalem area'.

Confronted by United Nations talk of internationalisation, and with it the demilitarisation of the city, both the Israelis and the Jordanians took steps to assert the permanence and primacy of their respective presences in East and West Jerusalem. At the end of December King Abdullah appointed his own nominee, Sheikh Husam a-Din Jarallah as Mufti of Jerusalem, thereby depriving the exiled Haj Amin al-Husseini of the post which, even in exile, he had used as a powerful lever for Palestinian-Arab nationalism.

On 2 February 1949 the Israeli Government in Tel Aviv announced that West Jerusalem was no longer 'occupied territory' but an integral part of Israel under civilian administration. Twelve days later, on February 14, the Israeli Parliament, the Knesset, which was to hold its regular meetings in Tel Aviv, held its first session specially in Jerusalem, in the Jewish Agency Building on King George V Avenue, when Dr Weizmann was formally elected President of Israel. 'The main streets, which have known pain and suffering, want and siege, took on a festive appearance,' Yona Cohen wrote in his diary of the festivities that day. 'A gate of honour was set up at Romema, bearing the inscription: "We have a strong city" (Isaiah). The President cut a ribbon that was stretched across the street and the Mayor, Daniel Auster, handed the President the key to the city and a scroll. In the square in front of the Jewish Agency buildings, the President reviewed a military guard of honour. To the sound of a shofar (ram's horn), the President entered the temporary assembly hall of the Knesset in the Jewish Agency building and swore an oath of loyalty to the State of Israel. Rabbi Abraham Haim Zwebner of the Mizrahi stood up and pronounced the benediction: "Blessed art Thou . . . who hast given of Thy glory to flesh and blood." '

At the end of Weizmann's speech of thanks, the seventy-eight-year-old Isidore Shalit, the sole surviving member of the 204 delegates who in 1897 had participated in Basle at the first Zionist Congress, of which Theodor Herzl had been President, went over to Weizmann and said: 'It has been a long, long way.'

Western Jerusalem was now under Israeli civilian administration, signalling its integration into the rest of Israel. The Jordanians also decided to pre-empt any United Nations decision for the internationalisation of the city by taking unilateral action. On March 17 King Abdullah established a Jordanian civil administration in the areas of Jerusalem under his military control. Since the end of the fighting, Abdullah had been the effective ruler of East Jerusalem. Palestinian-Arab hopes for a provisional Arab government for Palestine, to be established under the presidency of Haj Amin once the British had gone, were dashed.

*

On 3 April 1949 an armistice agreement was signed by Israel and Jordan. Under the agreement, Jerusalem was divided from north to south, along the November 1948 cease-fire line – the Green Line, as it would be called. Two demilitarised zones and several No-Man's-Lands, were created, to ensure that the points of contact between the two sides were kept as far apart as possible.

One Jewish-held area, the Hadassah Hospital and Hebrew University on Mount Scopus, was still entirely cut off from the Jewish part of the city. According to the armistice agreement, Jordan was committed to ensuring 'the normal functioning of the cultural and humanitarian institutions on Mount Scopus, and free access thereto', but in the months and years to come the government in Amman refused to discuss the practical implementation of this clause. Mount Scopus became an isolated enclave to which only minimal Israeli

16. In 1936, Arab schoolgirls march in Jerusalem with their headmistress, Hind al-Husseini, to protest against continuing Jewish immigration, and against British plans for the partition of Palestine into a Jewish and an Arab State. *(Hanna Safieh photographic archive)*

17. In 1939, Jews march in protest against the Palestine White Paper of that year, which curtailed Jewish immigration and land purchase. *(Keren Hayesod photographic archive)*

18. The destroyed wing of the King David Hotel, soon after it was blown up by Jewish terrorists in July 1946, when more than ninety people were killed. *(Imperial War Museum)*

19. The edge of the British Army's fortified zone in the centre of Jerusalem, known to the Jews as 'Bevingrad', from which Jewish and Arab cars and pedestrians were excluded. *(Jerusalem Post Picture Collection: photographer Hauser)*

20. Ben Yehuda Street, five minutes walk from 'Bevingrad', shortly after a bomb, placed there by British Army deserters in February 1948, killed more than fifty Jews. *(Jewish Agency Archives)*

21. British soldiers leave Jerusalem, May 1948. *(Keren Hayesod photographic archive)*

22. Arab legion shells strike the Jewish Quarter of the Old City, May 1948. To the left of the plume of smoke are the domes of the two main synagogues in the quarter, the Hurva ('Ruin') and the Tiferet Israel ('Hope of Israel'). Both were damaged in the fighting and destroyed immediately after it. *(Hanna Safieh photographic archive)*

23. The dome of the Hurva synagogue in the Jewish Quarter, badly damaged by Jordanian shellfire, and subsequently demolished. *(Hanna Safieh photographic archive)*

24. France Square in West Jerusalem. Residents of the Kings Hotel take tea on the balcony. Behind the hotel is the white dome of West Jerusalem's main synagogue. *(State of Israel Government Press Office)*

25. The 1950s: Jewish immigrant housing on the outskirts of Jerusalem. *(Keren Hayesod photographic archive)*

26. The Six-Day War of June 1967. An Israeli fighter plane bombards a Jordanian military position next to the Augusta Victoria Hospice on Mount Scopus. *(Jerusalem Post Picture Collection: Bemahane)*

27. Three Israeli generals, Uzi Narkiss (commander of the Central Command), Moshe Dayan (Minister of Defence) and Yitzhak Rabin (Chief of Staff) enter the Old City through St Stephen's – or Lions' – Gate on their way to the Temple Mount, June 1967. *(Jerusalem Post Picture Collection)*

28. Israeli soldiers reach the Wailing Wall. *(Photographer David Rubinger)*

29. One of the concrete walls dividing East and West Jerusalem being demolished, June 1967. *(Jerusalem Post Picture Collection: Photo Ross)*

30. Teddy Kollek, Mayor of Jerusalem from 1965 to 1993. This photograph shows him speaking at a memorial ceremony in 1974 for soldiers who had lost their lives during the battle for Jerusalem in 1967. *(Jerusalem Municipality Photographic Collection)*

31. The Arab war memorial at the north-east corner of the city wall, commemorating the Arab war dead of June 1967. Adnad Imhamad, aged 14, remembers his elder brother, killed in action. *(Jerusalem Post Picture Collection: photographer M. Goldberg)*

32.Israeli Prime Minister Menachem Begin and Egyptian President Anwar Sadat at a press conference in the Jerusalem Theatre in November 1977. On the far right, behind Sadat, is Colonel Menahem Milson, Sadat's Israeli Aide–de-Camp for the duration of his visit. Four years later Sadat was assassinated in Cairo by Muslim extremists. *(State of Israel Government Press Office)*

33. Memorial candles in front of the coffin of the Israeli Prime Minister Yitzhak Rabin, as he lay in state in front of the Knesset, November 1995. He had been murdered by a Jewish extremist. *(Photographer Isaac Harari)*

34. King Hussein of Jordan pays his respects at Yitzhak Rabin's grave immediately after the funeral at the military cemetery on Mount Herzl, Jerusalem, November 1995. *(Photographer Efraim Kilshtok)*

access was allowed, by means of a twice-monthly convoy. When the Jordanians, who controlled the supply of water and electricity to Mount Scopus, cut off supplies, it became impossible for either the hospital or the university to function.

*

Among the articles of the armistice agreement was one, Article VIII, under which Jordan guaranteed Israeli Jews free access to the Wailing Wall. In fact, during the nineteen years of Jordanian rule in East Jerusalem, no Israelis were allowed to visit this site which was most holy to them: the place where Jews had mourned the destruction of their Temple since Roman times.

The Israeli negotiators also failed in their attempts to secure right of access for Israeli Jews to the Jewish Cemetery on the Mount of Olives, the Kidron Valley tombs or the Tomb of Simon the Just. In the years following the armistice, many of the tombstones on the Mount of Olives were used as building materials. The Tomb of Simon the Just was used as a stable for horses.

*

On May 17, only six weeks after the armistice agreement, the Hebrew University-Hadassah Medical School was founded. The dedication ceremony, which should have taken place on Mount Scopus, took place instead in the open area of the Russian Compound, the centre, two years earlier, of Britain's fortified security zones in the middle of the New City, known to the Jews as 'Bevingrad' after the British Foreign Secretary, Ernest Bevin. Then no Jews were allowed into the area without special permits, few of which were granted. Now an audience of 2,000 attended, including the Prime Minister, David Ben-Gurion, and James McDonald, the former United States Consul-General, who had become the first United States Ambassador to Israel. 'There was also an "unofficial" audience,' the physician Dr Kleeberg recalled, 'consisting of riflemen of the Arab Legion, patrolling the top of the nearby wall of Suleiman the Magnificent, encircling the Old City. They were within stone's throw – let alone rifle range – of all the notables of Israel, assembled there for the occasion. But nothing untoward happened.'

*

A year after Count Bernadotte's murder, the United Nations Palestine Conciliation Commission produced its plan for Jerusalem. The city would be removed from the jurisdiction of both Israel and Jordan, to become a separate entity under United Nations control. The city would be divided into two zones, one Jewish and one Arab. There would be considerable local autonomy for both zones: the Jewish zone linked with Israel and the Arab zone linked with Jordan. A United Nations Commissioner would be charged with the protection of the Holy Places.

The administration of Jerusalem would be managed by a General Council, which would be composed of an equal number of Jewish and Arab members. The Council would deal with all matters that went beyond the specific needs of either zone.

The new plan was much discussed. The Vatican, conscious of its responsibilities for so many of the Christian holy sites in the city, supported it. So too did the Arab States, except Jordan. Abdullah wanted the eastern zone, which included the Old City and almost all the Holy Places, to remain under Jordanian control, as it had been for more than a year.

As the debate on the internationalisation versus the partition of Jerusalem continued, a British Christian thinker, James Parkes, pointed out what he regarded as the moral weakness in asking the Jews to 'make the sacrifice of their feelings and surrender Jerusalem', in response to the concern of 'millions of Christians' to the Holy Places. 'Had the millions of Christians, the Churches, and the governments which use this argument made a serious, even if unsuccessful, attempt to prevent the battle for Jerusalem,' he wrote in June 1949, 'or to relieve the Jewish civilians, women and children, who were on the point of starvation, they would at least have a moral right to put it forward. As it is, they have not.'

In November 1949 the Government of Israel, in an attempt to seek a meaningful compromise with the United Nations' call for internationalisation of the whole of Jerusalem, put forward a plan for the internationalisation of the Old City, some six and a half per cent of Jerusalem's municipal area. The Israeli plan would have made possible the return of Jews to the Jewish Quarter, albeit under United Nations control. It would also have opened many of the Holy Places for access to all. The United Nations rejected this proposal.

There were some at the centre of Israeli policy-making who did not reject out of hand the internationalisation of the whole city, Old and New, East and West. 'As a matter of fact, in terms of the cold logic of power politics,' wrote the United States Ambassador, James

McDonald three years later, 'Jerusalem was a liability to Israel. Situated on the borders of the country, connected with its coastal hinterland by a narrow corridor, it was exposed to attack and expensive to defend. If Israel were willing to give up Jerusalem, it could get substantial territory elsewhere in exchange. Moreover, the internationalisation of the city might prove to be of economic advantage to Israel. It would provide a trans-shipment point for re-establishing commerce between Israel and some of its neighbours; such commerce would be of immense value to Israel.'

Indeed, McDonald continued, 'there were some important Israeli leaders who considered the strategic vulnerability of Jerusalem and the economic advantages of its internationalisation more important than its historical and religious appeal. These "realists" would, had they dared, have favoured a compromise or at any rate a less unyielding attitude than that adopted by Ben-Gurion and his Cabinet. But none of them spoke out, because Israeli public opinion was simply adamant against any form of internationalisation of the New City, which was almost entirely Jewish and contained few Holy Places of any religion. Israel would not relinquish one hundred thousand of its Jewish citizens; moreover, Jerusalem had a special significance, a religious and national attachment of overwhelming proportions.'

The few Israeli politicians who might have considered Jerusalem 'a liability to Israel' in the strictest practical and strategic terms were far outnumbered by those who, reflecting the national mood, regarded Jerusalem as an integral, and central, part of any Jewish State. Amid all the talks and plans, the facts on the ground also made it clear that the internationalisation of the city would not take place. Israel, whose Government had been functioning from Tel Aviv since the declaration of statehood in May 1948, decided in December to end all ambiguity and speculation by moving the main organs of the administration to Jerusalem. On 5 December 1949, the Israeli Cabinet, meeting as usual in Tel Aviv, issued a public declaration that Jerusalem was the capital of Israel. Ben-Gurion went to Jerusalem to discuss the implications of this decision with Bernard Joseph, who later recorded the Prime Minister's discussion of the dangers 'of formally moving our entire capital to a city which the world still did not recognise as ours'.

Bernard Joseph was in confident mood, telling Ben-Gurion: 'From years of experience in this city, especially after the last thirty months, I think nothing is going to happen. There will be a lot of talk. But only what we do right here will count. It may be unpleasant for a while, but that's the only price we'll pay. The few people who dislike us anyway will dislike us a little more. The good people, who are usually in the majority, will admire us a little more for our courage. What we have done is good and just and will be recognised as such by all men of goodwill.'

The future of Jerusalem was again discussed by the Israeli Cabinet in Tel Aviv on December 10, when Ben-Gurion proposed transferring the capital to Jerusalem 'without delay'. Some of his ministers hesitated, not wanting to provoke world hostility. But Ben-Gurion was convinced that the move could be made without ill effect. When asked some years later why he had thought it would not be seriously opposed by the outside world, he replied: 'First of all, I knew we had an ally – Transjordan. If *they* were permitted to hold on to Jerusalem, why weren't *we*? Transjordan would permit no one to get them out of Jerusalem; consequently no one would dare to move us.'

Transjordan itself had been transformed, with the annexation of the West Bank, into the Hashemite Kingdom of Jordan. But Abdullah's occupation of the West Bank of the river Jordan, and the high ground of Judaea and Samaria, including Nablus and Hebron, was not recognised by the United Nations; only by Britain and Pakistan. The name 'Jordan' became, however, within a short time, the accepted name of the enlarged State.

*

On December 26 the Israeli Parliament, which had hitherto met in Tel Aviv for all but its opening session, moved permanently to Jerusalem. On 23 January 1950, determined to ensure the status of those parts of the city that were under Israel's control, the parliamentarians proclaimed Jerusalem 'once again' the Jewish capital. They added that 'Jerusalem was, and had always been, the capital of Israel', a reference to the Jewish kingdoms of two and three thousand years earlier.

The Israeli decision to make Jerusalem a capital city followed long periods when it had been ruled from other cities, often far distant. British rule had been, in effect, from London. Ottoman Turkish rule had been from Constantinople. Before that, Ommayad rule had been from Damascus. The only rulers who had made Jerusalem their capital since the defeat of the Bar Kochba revolt by the Romans in AD135 had been the crusaders, in the twelfth century.

One by one the Israel Government ministries moved to Jerusalem. The first to do so was the Ministry of Supply and Rationing, headed by the former Military Governor of Jerusalem, Bernard Joseph. For security reasons the Ministry of Defence remained in Tel Aviv, as for the next four years did the Foreign Ministry, to avoid, as Walter Eytan has written, putting 'forty miles of mountain road' between itself and the foreign diplomats who were almost all stationed in Tel Aviv, and whose governments did not recognise Jerusalem as part of Israel.

Tens of thousands of Arabs had fled from western Jerusalem. In the Mandate era their suburbs had been an integral and prosperous part of the city. They had been in the forefront of Jerusalem's social, intellectual and commercial life. After 1948 they were refugees. Some made their new homes in East Jerusalem. But as one of their number, Albert Hourani, who left Jerusalem to live in Britain, later wrote, 'a large part of the Arab bourgeoisie of Jerusalem, as of Haifa and Jaffa, settled in cities outside Palestine, and it was their capital and energy which were the main cause of the rapid growth of Amman'.

After 1950 an estimated 57,000 Jerusalem Arabs were refugees, part of the world-wide Palestinian diaspora. Among those who fled with his family from Jerusalem during the fighting was the four-year-old Sirhan Sirhan, who, eighteen years later, was to assassinate Senator Robert Kennedy in California, accusing him of bias towards Israel.

*

The war receded, but its legacy of bitterness and division was to plague the Jews and the Arabs of Jerusalem for many decades. Contact was immediately lost between the two halves of what, throughout the first half of the century, had been a single city.

In 1950 a tiny gesture of cooperation took place, born out of the absurdity of war. On Mount Scopus, the Jews of Jerusalem had, before the fighting, established a small zoo. During the fighting most of the 300 animals were killed by shell-fire or died after escaping from their cages and roaming through the inhospitable terrain. When the fighting ended the zoo was in the hands of the Jordanian army, which gave its consent in 1950 for the twenty surviving animals to be 'evacuated' to Jewish Jerusalem. There they formed the nucleus of a small Biblical Zoological Garden in Romema, where birds, reptiles, insects and wild beasts mentioned in the Old Testament were identified by an inscription giving the chapter and verse references to their mention in the Bible.

CHAPTER SIXTEEN

A Tale of Two Cities,
1950–1967

With West Jerusalem declared the capital of Israel, the Jordanians were in a dilemma. For them, their capital city was Amman, as it had been since 1921, first under a British Mandate and since 1945 as an independent State. East Jerusalem, however holy or important, was not the centre of their political or administrative life. But it was, from a national point of view, the centre of a rival nationalism, that of the Palestinian Arabs, who, while well represented numerically and even socially in Amman, were as proud of being Palestinians as the Jordanians were of being Hashemites.

In early 1950 negotiations of the most secret kind were begun between Israel and Jordan. Ben-Gurion had it in mind to hand over to Jordan some formerly Arab-inhabited areas of West Jerusalem that lay along the Israel-Jordan divide, as well as the Jerusalem-Bethlehem road, which, being in Israeli territory, necessitated a long and tortuous, and in places precipitous, eastward detour for the Arabs going from either Jericho or Ramallah to Bethlehem and Hebron. In return, Ben-Gurion wanted the Jordanians to restore Israeli sovereignty over the Jewish Quarter of the Old City and the Wailing Wall, as well as to guarantee secure access to the hospital and university on Mount Scopus (this had been guaranteed by the armistice agreement) and to the Jewish Cemetery on the Mount of Olives. In secret talks, these ideas were discussed between a group of Jordanians led by King Abdullah and Israelis led by Moshe Dayan. Although conducted in a spirit of goodwill and compromise, the talks came to nothing.

There was another point of difference between the Israeli and Jordanian view of Jerusalem – one that was deeper than the conflicting claims of two sovereign states. The Jordanian presence in the city dated back only to the Jordanian conquest of East Jerusalem in 1948, but Jews had been a majority in the city for more than a century, and pre-State Israelis had been an integral part of the city's life and administration throughout the British period.

On 24 April 1950 the Jordanian Parliament, meeting in Amman, ratified the Jordanian annexation of East Jerusalem and the occupied Palestinian lands on the West Bank of the river Jordan, including Nablus, Ramallah, Bethlehem and Hebron. At this same meeting, the Jordanian Parliament declared that Amman was the capital of the enlarged Jordanian State. This gave the Palestinian Arabs a sense of exclusion. For them, Jerusalem was to continue to be ruled from outside, and by outsiders, even though many of their leaders were to hold important positions in the Jordanian civil administration of the city, and even in the Jordanian Cabinet and Senate.

Many Jerusalem Arabs felt aggrieved at what they regarded as Jordanian neglect of their city. Their request for the establishment of an Arab University in East Jerusalem was rejected; the university was set up, instead, in Amman. The Jordanian decision to transfer government offices from East Jerusalem to Amman, just over forty miles away, provoked protests. In a letter to the Jordanian government, Anwar Nusseibeh, who was a member of the Jordanian Parliament for the Jerusalem region, complained that the constant discrimination was weakening Arab Jerusalem, in contrast to the continual developments on the Israeli side. But the growth of Amman was phenomenal, from a population of 22,000 in 1948 to a quarter of a million in 1961: this in itself greatly increased its importance as an Arab city. Many Jerusalem Muslims, businessmen and former Mandatory officials, were attracted to the new metropolis across the Jordan river.

Palestinian Arabs never gave up their desire for some form of independence from Jordan. In August 1950 one of their most outspoken sons, Arif al-Arif, was appointed Mayor of East Jerusalem. A distinguished former Mandate official, he had earlier been one of the chief agitators, with Haj Amin al-Husseini, against British rule and Jewish immigration; in 1920 the British had sentenced him to death for his part in the anti-Jewish riots that year. 'The city is wrestling with the ruins of destruction, writhing on the embers of poverty and destruction,' Arif al-Arif complained to King Abdullah shortly after his appointment as Mayor, 'and therefore requests you to abstain from damage to its standing, and to the livelihood of its citizens, by government departments being moved away to Amman.' This protest was to no avail. The departments were moved to Amman, where Jerusalem Arabs had to go if they sought favour or redress at ministerial level.

Palestinian bitterness against Jordanian rule created the tensions that led to violent extremism. On 20 July 1951 King Abdullah arrived in Jerusalem for prayers at the al-Aksa Mosque. He had come to speak the eulogy for Riad Bey a-Solh, Prime Minister of Lebanon, who had been assassinated in Amman four days earlier. It was said in the bazaars of East Jerusalem that a-Solh had been in Amman to discuss with Abdullah a peace treaty with Israel: for that 'crime' both men had been denounced. There was tight security around the King as he reached the mosque. 'Why do you imprison me between these close lines of soldiers?' he asked the guard commander. 'Let them fall back.' The commander protested that such security was necessary. 'This is God's house,' the King replied. 'Everyone is safe here.'

Hardly had Abdullah spoken these words than a shot rang out, and he fell down dead. He had been shot by a Palestinian gunman. As he fell, his grandson Hussein watched horrified at his side. Abdullah's assassin, Mustafa Shukri Ashu, was shot dead on the spot. Fearful of rioting by Palestinians in Jerusalem and on the West Bank, Glubb Pasha put the Arab Legion on full alert. In East Jerusalem the Legion meted out swift retribution to those who challenged it. On July 20 more than thirty Palestinian Arabs were shot dead, and hundreds were arrested. Four plotters were also arrested and hanged.

The fomentor of trouble, to whom the assassin and those who applauded his action had looked for inspiration in the holy struggle against the Israeli 'infidel', and who had fuelled their anger against those Arabs who tried to make peace with Israel, was the former Mufti of Jerusalem, Haj Amin al-Husseini. Thirty years since the British had supported his election as Mufti, fourteen years since he had fled from Jerusalem as a wanted man, Haj Amin was an exile in Egypt. Abdullah had refused him access to East Jerusalem and had him replaced as Mufti.

Abdullah's successors, first his son King Tallal and after him his grandson King Hussein, would not allow the former Mufti to return. Violence returned to the streets of East Jerusalem, however, after the Jordanian elections of October 1956, when those deputies who wanted closer links with Syria and Egypt were in conflict with King Hussein. Jerusalem was one of the centres of anti-Hussein riots. The Jordanian army was called in and opened fire to disperse the rioters, and several men, women and children were killed.

*

After Abdullah's murder there was no change in the Jordanian neglect of Jerusalem. When Arif al-Arif tried to extend the municipal borders to the south and east, in order to increase the area and population of East Jerusalem, he was dismissed by King Tallal. From January 1957 a new Mayor, Ruhi al-Khatib, fought hard for the elevation of the status of Jerusalem. He was successful, in that, on 1 September 1959, the Jordanians changed the status of the city from that of 'baladiya', a municipality, to that of 'amama', something given in trust, and thus equal to the Jordanian capital, Amman. Over the course of the next eight years of his tenure as Mayor, al-Khatib was often dissatisfied, however, with the reality of the change, feeling that it was not as effective as it ought to have been in making East Jerusalem a focal point and flourishing centre.

When Jordanian parliamentary elections were held in 1962, one of the Jerusalem Arab candidates bewailed the loss of Jerusalem's primacy. 'See the palaces which are being built in Amman,' he said, 'those palaces should have been built here in Jerusalem, but were removed from here, so that Jerusalem would remain not a city, but a kind of village.' To such complaints, the extension of the former British landing-ground to the north of the city into a municipal airport, making use of the lands of the destroyed Jewish agricultural farm at Atarot, was no compensation: the airport was only for light aircraft, or military ones.

*

Jewish Jerusalem recovered only slowly from the terrible events of 1947–8. It had to absorb Jewish refugees from the Old City, and Jewish immigrants from both Europe and the Arab world. Among those who came to live in the city were survivors of the Holocaust, with their own deep traumas. Ruined areas such as Ramat Rahel had to be rebuilt. Old institutions had to be housed in new buildings. A place had to be found for the Knesset, for the Supreme Court, and for various government ministries which had moved from Tel Aviv. The Hebrew University, as one of its luminaries, Norman Bentwich, has written, 'celebrated its Silver Jubilee in 1950 as a Displaced Person, in its temporary quarters in the Jewish city'. Its new quarters were in the Franciscan Terra Sancta College, surmounted then as today by a statue of the Virgin Mary. It was to be another decade before its new campus, on Givat Ram, was ready. A new Hadassah Hospital was being built to the west of the city.

Deserted Arab quarters such as Talbiyeh, Katamon and Bakaa, and abandoned Arab villages such as Ayin Karem and Malha, were becoming Jewish suburbs. To provide the increased amount of water needed, a twenty-four-inch pipe was laid from Eshtaol near the coastal plain to a reservoir in West Jerusalem. There were also several deep wells in the Jerusalem area that were dug for use when water consumption was particularly high.

Among the American-Jewish visitors to Jerusalem in 1950 was Benjamin Ferencz, a former Nazi war crimes investigator. He later recalled, in a letter to the author, how, among the Jews of the city, 'everyone seemed so full of hope and enthusiasm and incredulous expectations that a new era was dawning for them. And the children were all so beautiful and the source of so much pride to all and not merely to the parents. Everyone reminded me of my youthful days at a summer camp when everyone was filled with joy and anticipation of happy times to come. The Jews I knew back home were all lawyers, doctors or businessmen, and here I saw workers in the streets, cleaning and digging ditches, and Jews from Yemen and other far away places that had no connection to Brooklyn or the Bronx.'

A splendid Palace of the Nation, known more prosaically as the Convention Hall, was being built at the entrance to West Jerusalem. In 1951, even before the building was completed, it was decided to use it for the twenty-third Zionist Congress – the first Congress to be held in Jerusalem since the start of the Zionist movement in 1897. The journalist Elias Epstein recalled the state of the building as the delegates assembled from all over the Jewish world. 'It was a workmanlike, even artistic accomplishment,' he wrote, 'but it bore all the signs and scars of the upbuilding in progress, the flux of a dynamic movement in travail. The institutional exhibits, the traditional post office, the sentries bearing tribute to the heroes of our struggle, modified but could not eradicate the primitive nature of the externals of this significant gathering.'

Thirty years later, when the new Hebrew University buildings were being constructed on Mount Scopus, the governors of that renewed institution were to hold their annual meetings among the scaffolding and bare concrete pillars of another dusty building-site, to mark their similar confidence in an unfinished enterprise.

*

On 26 July 1951 David Ben-Gurion visited Jerusalem as part of his successful campaign for re-election as Prime Minister. At the entrance to the city he visited the abandoned Arab village of Lifta, where he saw many of the evacuees from the Jewish Quarter of the Old City. At the Jerusalem Shoe Corporation he was introduced to immigrants from thirty different countries who were cutting, sewing and gluing shoes. Beyond the former Allenby Barracks, in Talpiot, he visited some of the hundreds of immigrant houses, the maabarot, where Jews who had come from Arab lands were living.

Mary Clawson, an American from California whose economist husband had been asked by the Israeli Government to advise on agricultural economics, reached Jerusalem two years later, on 18 June 1953. Her letters to her family and friends in the United States described the Jewish side of the city as it struck a non-Jewish visitor who, on leaving the United States 'didn't even know the city was split between Israel and Jordan'. On the afternoon she arrived, she wrote in her first letter home, 'we took several walks. Almost everyone looked poor; I did not see a single woman wearing hose, and the men wore no neckties; I must say I think the lack of hose and neckties were both excellent ideas. There seemed to be an astounding number of good bookstores around.'

Five years after the battle for Jerusalem, rationing was still in force. 'We have no ration cards yet,' Mary Clawson wrote on June 21, 'so no coffee, eggs, meat, margarine, sugar, soap, etc. The neighbours have been unbelievably helpful and friendly and given or loaned us precious rationed things to eke out our meals, though I have been eating a huge amount of plentiful bread. I have never met so many people I like in so brief a time.' One of her Jewish neighbours tried to explain the local generosity. 'The Jews have been guests in every land until Israel was established. Everyone gets tired of being a guest, and now they are hosts, they want very much to be gracious hosts.'

Within a month, the first impression of the poverty of Jerusalem had worn off. On July 10 Mary Clawson was able to write to her sister: 'Now it looks quite prosperous and flourishing to me. The better residential districts are lovely with gardens and trees; the downtown shopping centre is a mixture of old and new – Arab-looking men riding donkeys down the street; bearded men with long earlocks and large felt hats, driving horses and wagons filled with kerosene; women shoppers with string bags like mine; bicycles, motorcycles, cars, horses moving helter-skelter through town; beggars squatting on corners offering to give you every blessing you can think of if you will give them a few piasters. And there are wonderful and beautiful corners. The School of Arts and Crafts and the Museum has an informal, easygoing courtyard I shall never forget. There are olive, fig, eucalyptus, pepper trees. Students work out of doors. The

Museum has marvellous exhibits inside. All this is half a block from my automatic laundry.'

Mary Clawson was living in one of the original pre-war Jewish garden suburbs, Bet Hakerem. The Israelis in her apartment building were mostly what are known in Jerusalem as 'Anglo-Saxons': Jews from English-speaking countries. 'They are professional people with good educations,' she told her sister. 'Most of them come from families with some money, and most of them have children, many young children. They come from England, Scotland, Canada, Australia, and one from the United States. One couple were originally from Belgium and then lived in the United States for about eight years. Three of the families are from Israel, though they speak English. Many of the neighbours have spent one to five years as members of kibbutzim.' The only stores in Bet Hakerem, she wrote, were 'small, darkish, fly-ridden'. The buses were 'shabby but not bad'.

The Jewish Sabbath was a time of particular serenity. 'The quiet that falls over Jerusalem on Friday evening', Mary Clawson wrote to her mother, 'is the peace of the Lord that passeth all understanding; it is like snow falling gently and quietly; it is the meaning of serenity. Buses stop running; all stores close; no money passes hands, at least legally or openly; few private cars can be seen on the highway, though some godless taxis run between Jerusalem and Tel Aviv; even the children quiet down considerably. Saturday morning you see men and boys returning from synagogues; women rarely go. The non-religious sleep late; around 10.30 or 11 in the morning, fathers take their young for a walk. Late Saturday afternoon all Jerusalem, as far as we can judge, goes for a Sabbath stroll, dressed in their Sabbath best. It is truly a day of peace and quiet for almost everyone, with the possible exception of parents of young children.'

On a visit to Ramat Rahel, Mary Clawson found that the kibbutz was 'almost completely rebuilt, except for a few walls or parts of walls, which are riddled with bullets and saved so that newcomers will be reminded of the brave men who fought there, and who died there too'.

Since 1948 Ramat Rahel had been on the border with Jordan. Jerusalemites went there to look out over Bethlehem. 'There was Bethlehem so near and so far away that it was frustrating,' Mary Clawson wrote. 'We could see an Arab herding sheep, just down below, a truck going sedately along the highway, and a car zooming past it; we could even hear the car honking at intervals. I think what really annoyed us, though, was the group of men who had come to Ramat Rahel and who were looking into Jordan at the same time we were; they were apparently diplomats and were talking in French about what it is like on the other side. It is really difficult for anyone who has not experienced it to understand what a sensation it is to be so close to a place and yet as far away as around the world; farther really, because with enough money and time anyone could get around the world, but you cannot get to Jordan if you are a Jew in Israel.'

Most frustrating of all for Jerusalemites was the border running through the centre of the city. There was only one international crossing-point, near the Mandelbaum House, and known as the Mandelbaum Gate, but this was closed to Israelis, who were not allowed to enter East Jerusalem or the Old City. On one of her very first excursions, Mary Clawson made her acquaintance with this barrier. 'We drove round the city yesterday,' she wrote to her mother on July 4, 'right up to the Arab frontier marked by barbed wire, stones piled up and a large sign in English, Hebrew and Arabic: FRONTIER. STOP. NO PHOTOGRAPHS PERMITTED.

'This morning we drove around, this time further west past groves of olive trees. Frontier police are very much on the alert at every point. We stopped on a dirt road under an olive tree to look around and in a short time a husky young man with a rifle and binoculars came up to see what we were doing.'

*

The diplomatic battle for the status of Jerusalem was continuous. On 12 July 1953 the Foreign Ministry of Israel transferred its offices from Tel Aviv to Jerusalem. Six governments protested – those of the United States, Britain, France, Italy, Turkey and Australia – each of which expressed adherence to the United Nations' desire that the city should have some form of international status. They all refused to accept that western Jerusalem was Israel's capital. Ironically, both Britain and the United States had voted against the most recent United Nations resolution on internationalisation. For many months diplomats boycotted ceremonies in Jerusalem. When, four years later, Cuba moved her legation to Jerusalem, she was persuaded by the United States to move it back to Tel Aviv within a few days.

Almost all foreign embassies remained in and around Tel Aviv. The only exceptions were those of The Netherlands, Greece, Guatemala and Uruguay. When any other ambassadors needed to consult with Israeli officials, they made their way to Jerusalem and held talks in the new Foreign Ministry there, before returning to the coast.

Whereas Israel prefaced its communiqués 'From Jerusalem', most foreign Governments, and most newspapers, issued their communiques 'From Tel Aviv'. While the first President of the State of Israel, Dr Weizmann, lived at Rehovot, in the coastal plain, ambassadors presented their credentials to him there. Following Weizmann's death in November 1952 he was succeeded as President by Yitzhak Ben-Zvi, a Jerusalemite, who transferred the President's office to Jerusalem. At first, foreign governments refused to let their ambassadors present their credentials there. A year after Ben-Zvi had become President, the Italian Ambassador, to avoid going to Jerusalem, insisted on presenting his credentials at Tiberias, on the Sea of Galilee, where Ben-Zvi was taking a short holiday. That was the last occasion of such a subterfuge; after that the Israeli Government made it clear that ambassadors would not be accepted if they did not present their credentials in Jerusalem. The next ambassador to arrive was from Switzerland. Despite considerable diplomatic pressure from the Arab States, the Swiss Government finally instructed him to make the journey to the divided, disputed capital.

*

On 27 July 1953, only two weeks after the Israeli Foreign Ministry moved to Jerusalem, King Hussein of Jordan declared that East Jerusalem was 'the alternative capital of the Hashemite Kingdom'. It would form an 'integral and inseparable part' of Jordan. This was a strong clarion call, but despite it, and to the distress of many Arab Jerusalemites, the Jordanian Government continued to discourage the economic growth of East Jerusalem, and to block the establishment of a university there.

*

It was not only Jews who suffered from lack of access to their Holy Places in East Jerusalem under Jordanian rule. The division of the city proved a blow to another aspect of worship that had hitherto been taken for granted. Under the Jordanians, the Christian and Muslim shrines in East Jerusalem were open to all Christians and Muslims worldwide, except for those who were resident in Israel. Thus tens of thousands of Israeli Arabs found themselves prevented by Jordan from praying at the al-Aksa Mosque, or from setting foot on the Haram.

At the end of December 1953 Mary Clawson and her husband

received a permit to pass through the Mandelbaum Gate to East Jerusalem. The eve of the visit had been quite worrying: 'The American Consulate has a sign posted to be read by those who are allowed to cross: "In crossing the lines from the Jewish-held section of Jerusalem to the Arab-held, you are advised to be closed-mouthed and as non-committal as possible about what you've been doing in Israel. Also carry with you as few souvenirs of obvious Israeli origin as convenient. The Arab authorities do not appreciate any evidence of pro-Israel sympathy on your part. Remember the Arabs and Israelis are still technically at war."

'We were in suspense until we got through the Arab check station, as you can be turned back, if after having completed all the preliminaries, your name, probably through a clerical error, does not appear on the list against which the Arabs check your passport, or in our case, your form. We could not use our passports as they have Israeli visas in them, so instead filled out a special form, signed by the American Vice-Consul. An English girl just ahead of us in the line got turned back; the last we saw of her she was striding off in a rage for the nearest phone to call the British Consul. Mandelbaum Gate is not a gate at all, merely a small house, once belonging to an unfortunate Mr Mandelbaum. We got approved by both sides without any trouble, and I was so delighted I beamed all over as we left the Arab station and headed for the Old City walls. To spend months looking at the walls and not be able to get inside is frustrating.

'We hired a car and a guide, practically a necessity to get around either at Christmas or Easter because of the mobs, and we saw just about everything we wanted to. It is an experience to go through Mandelbaum Gate; you go back at least 2,000 years in time. The Old City is picturesque as Algiers is, or as people say Cairo is, but it is also a disgrace when you think what lies on the other side of the Old City. Many children are barefooted and in rags, men bowed in two under huge loads, people begging everywhere. And there is also the Eastern servility in hopes of getting a little money. In Israel any shoeshine man, or garbage collector, or what have you, figures he is every bit as good as you, if not a little better, and lets you know it too, very much like the western United States, and I love it and laugh. But in the Old City, people bow to the ground in politeness, which I assume is far too often false.'

Mary Clawson's account continued: 'After we got around the closed-in corner known as Mandelbaum Gate, there were the walls of Jerusalem and there was Damascus Gate. Just outside this gate, buses from all over Jordan and neighbouring countries stop to let out their passengers. It is evidently always a busy centre: taxis were honking like mad; donkeys went by loaded high, some of them braying; there were policemen with spiked helmets; dozens of men wearing keffiyas, red and white, black and white, all white; black-veiled women, dressed all in black; little barefooted children begging from the tourists; and even a couple of disdainful camels picking their way through the traffic.

'Once we got inside the walls, I kept thinking, "Our feet are standing within thy gates, O Jerusalem." But though I was rejoicing at being within the gates, I also rejoiced that we lived outside them in Israel. Within the walls there are only three or four "main" streets north and south and an equal number east and west, and these are from ten to twenty feet wide, some just wide enough to let a car go by, if pedestrians and animals hug the walls. There are no sidewalks as such. Other streets are too narrow, too steep or have too many steps for auto traffic. A large part of the way these main streets are lined with shops; the shoppers were standing in the street as they shopped, although there are some fairly large shops too. I was impressed with the number of shops making shoes; usually one or two cobblers hammering and stitching in a dark little cubbyhole. I was even more impressed with the beautiful looking fruit and vege-tables (such apples as they have in Jordan! – none in the New City of Jerusalem, at least this time of year) and with the delicious pastry shops.'

While she was in East Jerusalem, Mary Clawson also visited the Wailing Wall, to which no Israeli Jew had been allowed access since 1948. The area was now entirely inhabited by Muslim Arabs. The few inhabitants of the former Jewish Quarter were also Arabs, mostly refugees from the Israeli side of the line. 'The Wall itself is interesting,' she wrote, 'long and high and made of huge stones, of at least two very different dates, with vines growing around many of the stones. It is undamaged but deserted except for a lone postcard peddler who tried to charge ridiculous prices and, as a result, got no business. He followed us for several blocks, wailing all the time. After we left the Wall, three or four barefooted, ragged, cold little girls also followed us begging. We wanted to give them money but did not, as it would have resulted in more right after them. We felt mean because the poor little things undoubtedly needed the money but to start giving money to children or adult beggars in such a city is like trying to sweep back the ocean.

'I was eager to see what the old Jewish quarter looked like, so I asked the guide whether he would be willing to take us around.

I cannot say he was enthusiastic about the idea, but he did not object. We walked through fairly extensive areas near the south wall where all the buildings have been destroyed, and many other areas where they have been damaged, but refugees were living in them. Washing was strewn around in odd places. In what had been the old Jewish market or bazaar street, a couple of the ancient synagogues are in ruins.

'In order to try to give you a bit of the feeling I had all day, I should keep repeating that all this is a few minutes' drive, or in some cases walk, from the New City where we have been living for six months. A couple of times our guide would say something about such and such "in Jerusalem" and I would start. I did not feel a bit as if I were in the Jerusalem I knew; I felt at least 2,000 miles away and 2,000 years back.'

*

Spanning the years 1953–4, Jewish Jerusalemites celebrated the three-thousandth anniversary of the founding of the Kingdom of David in Jerusalem. A climax of the celebrations was the first performance of an opera, *David*, composed for the occasion by Darius Milhaud, with libretto by Armand Lunel. In New York the celebrations in Madison Square Garden included singing by Frank Sinatra. In Jerusalem the Third Millennium celebrations were held, like many other international gatherings in the city, at the newly built Convention Hall, a theatrical, musical and cultural centre from which one could see on the eastern horizon the Mountains of Moab, to the north the Tomb of Samuel, and to the west Mount Herzl, to which Theodor Herzl's body had been brought from Vienna in 1949, and reinterred.

Among the events held at the Convention Hall during 1953 were a Festival of Hebrew Song, attended by 800 choristers gathered from all over the world, and an International Scientific Symposium, 'The Conquest of the Desert'. This symposium examined the most recent developments in soil maintenance, irrigation and reafforestation, and set out the practical means of rescuing desert, recultivating hitherto barren soil, and replanting forests. Almost every country in the world took part in the symposium, but not a single Muslim or Arab State agreed to send a delegation.

*

By January 1954 Mary Clawson had been in Jerusalem for seven months. In her letters home she gave many glimpses of life in the Jewish city. In a letter to friends on January 30 she described the generally low salaries of professional people in Israel – less than $2,000 a year for an occupation which in the United States would command at least $13,000 at that time. 'Do you have the remotest idea', she wrote, 'what such a low salary means? There is no money for a car; the food budget needs constant watching and scrimping, and no dining out; there is not enough money for clothes; the amount of insurance which can be carried as protection for a man's family is hardly excessive; there is money for very few gifts; few, if any face creams and hand lotions; no smoking or drinking and not much money for charity. There is no money in such a budget for household furniture and repairs; no item for upkeep of a garden, if you like to garden; much less is there any money left for the hobbies many Americans, especially at this job level, consider in the category of essentials.

'Most people have no money for a telephone. A phone is a real luxury in Jerusalem; we do not have one so I am in an excellent position to judge the additional work and planning required in a phoneless home. Phones are scarce in Israel, so to keep down the demand there is a neat system which requires a non-refundable payment of a fair amount of money to have one installed – two hundred pounds in Jerusalem. It works fine; furthermore, if you do scrape together the money for a phone, your monthly bill is relatively high.'

Because it was so unusual at that time, Mary Clawson added: 'It is not a wonder, therefore, that such a large proportion of Jerusalem middle-class women with children work outside their homes.' She also wrote in this letter of what she called a 'sweet Israeli, or at least Jerusalem' custom, 'the payment of salaries at late and irregular periods'. As she explained: 'Most of our neighbours have no idea when they will be paid; they are sure the salary will be late, but how late becomes a burning question. It could be a week or it could be, and often is, two or three months late. As a result, much of Jerusalem lives on credit. You owe the grocer, the butcher, the clothing store, the carpenter, and you go right on owing them for months and months. The carpenter who made us a clothes rack, for instance, did not give us a bill for it until seven months later, and another carpenter, who did a small job in the flat, finally came around four months after he had finished to ask for a few pounds. He so hated to ask for the money honestly due him.'

*

In March 1954 Mary Clawson visited the largest Jewish immigrant camp in Jerusalem. It was located in Talpiot, on part of the site that, thirty years earlier, had been designated as part of the Jewish garden suburb then under construction. Lack of money had prevented its completion then. The large empty space proved ideal for the immigrant camp, as several hundred thousand Jewish immigrants from Arab lands, among them Jews from Iraq, Kurdistan, Yemen and Morocco, arrived in Israel. Many had come from the utmost poverty and squalor. In addition, following the establishment of the State of Israel in 1948, they had been subjected in their Arab lands to various forms of discrimination and persecution, including pogroms in which dozens had been killed.

The settlement of so many Jews from Muslim countries, with their very different traditions, their background of poverty and their deep suspicion of the Arabs among whom they had lived for generations, proved a difficult economic and social burden for Israel. On March 27 Mary Clawson wrote to a friend: 'Monday I visited the large maabara (transient camp for immigrants) in Jerusalem where Dr Fanny Rabinowitz looks after the health of all those who are completely without means of support. She is responsible for about 2,500 people, mainly natives of other Near Eastern countries. There are about 7,500 or 8,000 people in the Talpiot maabara. A maabara is supposed to be a temporary place, but this one has people who have been there years and Fanny's patients are the ones who haven't much hope of getting out in the near future. I spent two hours in her dispensary and another hour touring the maabara. We went to see one patient, so I saw her hut without appearing to intrude.

'This maabara is a bit like a highly inferior Farm Security Administration camp of the 1930s; perhaps it is more accurate to say it is like a large gathering of Dust Bowl farm workers who haven't had any work to speak of for some time. There is one water tap for about twenty families, no toilets, just holes in the ground with walls around them for a certain number of huts and the smell emanating from them is nauseating.

'Most families have one hut about fifteen square metres in size, though if they have a large number of children they may get two huts. The huts, made of corrugated iron or with walls of old bits of canvas in wooden frames with corrugated iron roofs, are hot in summer and freezing in winter. Fanny's patients in particular suffer as they have no money for kerosene to heat the hut or to dry clothes. The mud in winter is also a nasty problem, especially when you remember everyone, children and the ill, must go out in pouring rain for toilet facilities. From the smell of urine everywhere in the maabara not everyone goes always to the prescribed holes.

'This maabara has its own stores and kiosks for those who have work and money to buy food, essential household equipment or even second hand clothes.'

Fanny Rabinowitz took Mary Clawson into her clinic. 'I will say, for the patients Fanny saw,' she wrote, 'they are not squashed. I would give a good deal to know how they acted in Iraq, Persia, Algiers, or Morocco or wherever they came from originally. I have a feeling that they think they are at last in their own land, among their own people, and can and will demand what they consider their rights. I do not have to deal with it every day, so I enjoyed seeing the supposedly downtrodden of this earth acting in this fashion. Heaven knows, they are not suppressed or in terror of their lives.

'Some of the patients were picturesque, certainly to a Westerner. There was an old bearded man, wearing a black turban, wide red band around his middle, holding a staff, who sat cross-legged on the waiting room floor. He was there to ask for a food ticket so he could sell it. He declared he was dying, but although he was ill from undernourishment, according to Fanny he was far from dying. He comes almost every week to ask for extra food tickets and to announce in energetic terms that he is dying.'

Dr Rabinowitz also visited immigrants in their homes. 'The patient we went to see after office hours', Mary Clawson wrote in her letter of March 27, 'is a woman of thirty who used to be one of the most ambitious of the social cases. She has ten children; they live in a hut, filled with beds of course. The husband just laughs if you suggest he work, and they all live almost entirely on bread and weak tea. Three months ago this woman went insane, screamed, yelled, sang all the time, declared various people were about to murder her. Fanny has been doing her best to get her into a hospital for the insane but Israel does not have enough mental homes. In the last three months there were five new insane people in Talpiot maabara alone.'

Mary Clawson discussed her visit to the immigration centre with her husband, Marion. It had been a harrowing experience, and Fanny Rabinowitz was not one to minimise the problems. 'Fanny waxes indignant about conditions in Talpiot maabara,' Mary Clawson wrote, 'but Marion says one must take the long view and look at Israeli statistics. Even with the recent immigration wave, which doubled the Jewish population, people in Israel live as long as in the United States and the infant death rate is lower. Admittedly conditions are dreadful where Fanny works, but also she works in one of the worse maabarot in Israel, where people have less hope than anywhere else.

'One reason I am so devoted to Israel and Israelis is because there are so many people like Fanny here: people who get upset about conditions which they consider inadequate, whether it is a maabara, the way the city of Jerusalem is managed, the school system, inequalities of various kinds, or something else. This country is filled with such people and as a result Israel has accomplished miracles in the past six years and is apt to go on accomplishing miracles.

'Let Fanny splutter and rage – I bet she manages to improve conditions by her wrath. In other Middle Eastern countries, no one gets excited about poverty or alleged mismanagement or dirt; it is the will of Allah. The Jews blow their tops, and I laugh and admire and respect them for it.'

*

Violence flared up in Jerusalem in the summer of 1954. On July 3 Mary Clawson wrote to friends in the United States: 'Who is it who advises people to live dangerously? We are following his advice these days all right. I suppose the Washington papers have reported that there has been shooting back and forth between the New and Old Cities of Jerusalem this past week.' On June 30 the Arabs had begun 'shooting over to this side and after waiting a brief time to investigate to be sure the shooting was not just a trigger-happy Legionnaire, the Jewish side returned the fire. Marion's building was hit too; the shooting was heavy enough and close enough so that he moved his desk into the centre of his office, well away from the windows. A pedestrian was shot almost directly in front of his building; no buses ran to his office. He loaded an order of groceries from Haifa into our car, but in order to do it, he had to find a parking place which was safe from gunfire. Friends of ours in Rehavia, which is a fair distance from the border, were kept awake all Wednesday night, and many parts of Jerusalem near the border were evacuated.'

On the Thursday, Mary Clawson tried to drive into the centre, to the YMCA, but was turned back twice. 'But I was stubborn so just wound around until we got there. It was not bright, probably, but I was not going to be intimidated by Arab shooting.' A friend of hers who returned from Tel Aviv that day with her husband reported that they had had 'a bad time' on June 30, their last night in Jerusalem. 'Their flat here was right on the border; their windows were broken with shots; they sat up all night leaning against a wall.' Mary Clawson added: 'I would give a lot to know what the Arabs think this kind of thing will do; it will not frighten the Jews; they do not frighten that way.'

Several people were killed and many injured, some seriously, in that particular shooting incident.

*

The future and status of Jerusalem remained an issue on the international agenda throughout the 1950s. The United States and Britain both continued to oppose the legal status of Jewish Jerusalem as Israeli, and of Arab Jerusalem as Jordanian. Lingering and tenacious support for the concept of internationalisation prevented any member State of the United Nations from accepting East or West Jerusalem as respectively Jordanian or Israeli. At a lunch at Buckingham Palace on 18 February 1955, Winston Churchill told a British diplomat, Evelyn Shuckburgh, whose father had been instrumental in drafting the clauses of the British Palestine Mandate thirty-three years earlier: 'You ought to let the Jews have Jerusalem; it was they who made it famous.'

*

Archaeology flourished in Jerusalem in each decade, for as the city grew the ancient buildings that lay beneath it were inevitably stumbled upon. In 1956, while the foundations of a house were being dug in Rehavia, a 2,000-year-old tomb was discovered, with rock-cut passages, chambers with burial niches, and wall decorations including a war-galley attacking a merchant ship. Hence the name given to it: the Tomb of Jason.

At Kibbutz Ramat Rahel, archaeological work had begun in 1954 on a site which proved rich in antiquities, dating back to the time of the kings of Judah 2,700 years earlier and including Roman and Byzantine structures. The hill on which the kibbutz was built was at the very southern border of the city. The Green Line, with its barbed wire and its military patrols, ran along its southern edge. From the border fence, the church steeples of Bethlehem could be seen clearly.

On 23 September 1956, during a gathering of the Israeli Archaeological Society's Congress at the Ramat Rahel excavations, a Jordanian soldier on the hillside facing the kibbutz opened fire with a Bren gun on more than 100 archaeologists and students: four of the archaeologists were killed. One of them, Jacob Pinkerfeld, had emigrated to Palestine from Poland in 1920, and had served as an architect in the Department of Public Works under the Mandate. At the time of his death he was Custodian of Public Monuments in the Israeli Government Department of Antiquities. His daughter was married to Golda Meir's son. A few hours before he was killed he had been giving a lecture on Jerusalem's synagogues in the Convention Hall. Eight years earlier, during the siege of Jerusalem, his nephew Uri Reich had been among the thirty-five Hagannah volunteers killed while on the mission to relieve Kfar Etzion.

Another of those killed at Ramat Rahel, Dr Rudolph Rudberg, who had come to Palestine from Germany in 1938, was President of the Israel Dental Association. Also killed was Baruch Shochetmann, a distinguished bibliographer who had joined the Hebrew University on his arrival from Russia in 1926 and was one of the editors of the quarterly journal of the Jewish National and University Library. 'For him', wrote the *Jerusalem Post* in his obituary, 'the past was not past, but ever present. Often he used to approach one of his close friends – he had no enemies, and could not have had – with a warm smile. "What happened twenty years ago today?" he would ask. Perhaps the answer was only that there had been a heat wave. He knew much that others had forgotten and in particular liked to recall the various memorable occasions of the Hebrew University.'

In a statement to the United Nations, the Jordanian Government said that the firing at Ramat Rahel had been the work of a single soldier, who had been 'taken by a madness'. But some of those under fire had seen two machine-guns firing, one manned by three soldiers and the other by five. A day after the Ramat Rahel attack, a Jordanian army patrol crossed the Israeli border at the village of Aminadav, just to the west of the city, opening fire on a group of women olive-pickers, and shooting dead Zohara Umri, a Jewish immigrant from the Yemen.

*

In 1957, as the result of the passage of a Knesset resolution four years earlier, a memorial centre was opened to commemorate the 6 million Jews murdered in the Second World War. It was also intended to celebrate the heroism of the wartime ghetto fighters, and to honour several thousand non-Jews 'who risked their lives in order to save victims of the Nazis'. The centre was established next to the Military Cemetery on Mount Herzl, and was given the name Yad Vashem: 'a place and a name'. The words were taken from God's promise in the

Book of Isaiah: 'Even unto them will I give in mine house and within my walls a place and a name ... I will give them an everlasting name, that shall not be cut off.'

Each year Yad Vashem grew in size and extended its activities, publishing books and journals, holding seminars and conferences, and collecting documents and personal testimonies. Almost every week a small ceremony is held in honour of a non-Jew who saved the life of a Jew in the war years. At this ceremony a tree is planted in a special avenue known as the Avenue of the Righteous Gentiles.

*

As Israel approached the tenth anniversary of statehood, West Jerusalem was, in the words of the British-born Israeli writer Naomi Shepherd, who went to live there in 1957, 'literally a dead end, the furthest accessible point of a territorial corridor leading up through the Judaean Hills from the coastal plain. The frontier which bisected the city was the frontier between Israel and the entire Arab world, between Israel and Asia. The coastline of Israel was the end of the Mediterranean, and Jerusalem gave me the feeling of running up against a wall, of being at the end of the world. One could go no further.'

As she came to know West Jerusalem, Naomi Shepherd began to 'decode' the presence of the different national groups in the city. 'The solid German bourgeoisie of Rehavia,' she wrote, 'behind neatly trimmed hedges, tended private libraries and window-boxes, while sonatas trickled out of well-aired rooms; old ladies with veils counted the grocer's change in German. In the former Arab areas, huge and dignified houses were broken up with partitions and extra stairways to accommodate immigrant families from North Africa and Eastern Europe. The ultra-religious quarters were designed like Polish or Hungarian ghettos ... with galleried courtyards and fur-hatted men – all that was missing was the marauding cavalry. There were no open boulevards and pavement cafés as in Tel Aviv, a real seaside town.'

It was to be another decade before West Jerusalem ceased to be a frontier town; three decades before its pedestrian malls and street cafés were to turn it into a bustling, if not a seaside, town. 'A sleepy border town,' the Israeli journalist Abraham Rabinovich recalled thirty years later, 'virtually cut off from the mainstream of life on the coastal plain, to which it was linked by a tenuous territorial corridor. Knesset committees preferred meeting in Tel Aviv rather than making the tedious hour and a half trip up the Judaean Hills, and their chairmen had periodically to be reminded that Jerusalem was still the nation's capital.'

The tenth anniversary celebrations of Israel's statehood in May 1958 saw great activity in Jerusalem. The Government of Israel decided to hold its main military parade in Jerusalem. The parade ended in the new university stadium on Givat Ram.

*

In 1960 Adolf Eichmann, the Nazi official who, from his office in Berlin, had coordinated plans for the murder of 6 million Jews, was captured by Israeli agents in the Argentine and brought to Jerusalem for trial. The impact of the daily testimony of witnesses brought home to Jerusalemites just how total had been the destruction of Jewish lives, and of Jewish life, throughout Europe during the Second World War. 'In a hall furnished with the trappings and panoply of a court of law,' recalled the chief prosecutor, Gideon Hausner, 'the whole sombre panorama of German Nazi oppression was to be revealed over the coming months in all its fiendishness.'

Eichmann's trial, and the sight of Eichmann himself in the dock, riveted the attention of the world on that courtroom for many months. Hannah Arendt, reporting the trial for the *New Yorker*, wrote of 'the man in the glass booth built for his protection: medium-sized, slender, middle-aged, with receding hair, ill-fitting teeth, and near-sighted eyes, who throughout the trial keeps craning his scraggy neck towards the bench'. When the trial ended in 1962, Eichmann was found guilty and executed.

Two years later, in 1964, world attention again focused on Jerusalem when Pope Paul VI visited the Holy Land. Like all travellers, he could cross from one side to the other of this populous city only by going through the Mandelbaum Gate. In doing so, he passed from one jurisdiction to another, as he made his way from Mount Zion in Israel to the Mount of Olives in Jordan. For the Christians of Jerusalem his visit was thrilling. But for Muslims and Jews, and even for Christian Arabs, who formed by far the largest Christian group in the city, he brought no palliative to the problem of a divided city; indeed, it seemed that the city would stay divided for as long as the Arab-Israeli conflict, itself apparently unending, remained unresolved.

*

The Jordanian presence in East Jerusalem helped to ameliorate the centuries-old conflict between the various Christian groups in the city. In 1961 King Hussein had succeeded in promoting an agreement between the divided Christians. He facilitated the restoration of the Church of the Holy Sepulchre, the holiest Christian site in Jerusalem, which had been allowed to fall into a sorry state of disrepair. But there were worldwide protests from Christian religious leaders when the Jordanian Government, in an about-turn, forbade the Christian churches to acquire any more property within the Old City.

Bloodshed flared in East Jerusalem on 23 April 1963, when Palestinian-Arab demonstrations against King Hussein, and in favour of a Jordanian-Arab republic on both sides of the river Jordan, were suppressed by the Jordanian army. Eleven of the demonstrators were killed and more than 100 injured.

Despite the elevation of Jerusalem to the status of a capital city, the Mayor of East Jerusalem, Ruhi al-Khatib, and his councillors were dissatisfied with what they regarded as a lack of real Jordanian commitment to the development of the city. For its part, the Jordanian Government was not pleased by the activities of the Municipal Council. Arif al-Arif was still a member of the council, and a focal point of Palestinian-Arab nationalism. He helped to prepare, and Ruhi al-Khatib personally greeted, the much publicised opening session of the Palestinian National Council. Meeting in East Jerusalem in May and June 1964, the council led to the foundation of the Palestinian Liberation Organisation (PLO), which was to find itself in open warfare with Jordan six years later.

Two Municipal Council meetings in East Jerusalem in October 1965 protested at 'discrimination against Jerusalem' by Amman. King Hussein had decided to increase considerably, and demonstrably, the Jordanian presence and activity in Jerusalem. In itself, this helped the city, but it was still seen by many Jerusalem Arabs as an outside initiative, not a local one by their own people. Under the King's patronage, the road from Jerusalem to Jericho (and Amman) was widened, in the course of which, to the distress of the Jews of West Jerusalem, a section of the ancient Jewish Cemetery was destroyed.

At the King's command, a hotel, the Intercontinental, was built on the top of the Mount of Olives, with a remarkable view across the Kidron Valley to the Haram, and over West Jerusalem. The black Dome of the Rock was transformed by the King, as it had been by Haj Amin al-Husseini forty years earlier, into a golden dome, this time by the use of anodised aluminium. A royal palace was under construction on a hill to the north of the city, Tel al-Ful, from the summit of which it was possible, on a clear winter day, to see both the Mediterranean and the Dead Sea.

Many Christian Arabs, unhappy at the growing preponderance of Islam in Arab Jerusalem, left the city in the 1960s for the Christian suburbs of Beirut, or for the West. In 1948 there had been more than 20,000 Christian Arabs in East Jerusalem; within two decades that number had fallen to just over 10,000. The Muslim population had risen, but only slowly, from 50,000 in 1961 to 56,000 six years later. Under Jordanian rule, East Jerusalem was still only a town, rather than a city.

The East Jerusalem municipality did have its own independent successes under Ruhi al-Khatib. The most important was the extension of the municipal boundaries northward, as far as Kalandia Airport, adjacent to the former Jewish suburb of Atarot, which had been destroyed in 1948. A master plan for East Jerusalem was also drawn up by a British town planner of the Mandate era, Henry Kendall, and was under active discussion.

*

Transformations were also taking place on the Jewish side of Jerusalem's divide. On 7 May 1965 the Israel Museum was opened, on a hill from which the Jordanian army post above Beit Jalla was clearly visible. The museum soon became a focal point of West Jerusalem's cultural life: a museum representing the whole spectrum of the Jewish experience from archaeology to architecture, from ancient artefacts to modern painting and sculpture. It was a museum that would bring to Jerusalem the finest works of artists of every religion and nationality: for its opening the British Rothschild family, under the inspiration of James de Rothschild's wife, Dorothy, gave five superb paintings: two by Van Gogh, one by Cézanne and two by Gauguin.

The second transformation in West Jerusalem that year was the election on 12 November 1965 of a new Mayor, Teddy Kollek. On arriving at his municipal office, less than 150 yards from the Jordanian sector of the city, Kollek discovered the architects' drawings, models and detailed plans for a new Municipality Building which was about to be built well away from the divided city's border, in the centre of West Jerusalem. 'I decided to drop the project, write off the investment, and stay where we were,' he later wrote. 'My principal reason was that to abandon the old City Hall would in a way mean accepting the division as permanent. But by staying put on the frontier, we were giving expression to our faith in the eventual unification of Jerusalem.'

Kollek had another reason for not moving City Hall. 'Since 1950,' he wrote, 'many of the new immigrants – largely from Arab countries but also from Europe, particularly Roumania – had been settled in neighbourhoods on the border. I felt it was immoral to leave these thousands of newcomers in such a vulnerable spot while the City Fathers moved themselves safely and expensively out of the danger zone. Besides, the cost of a new City Hall would have run into the millions, and that money could better be spent on many more urgent needs.'

Even before he formally took up his post, Kollek had obtained, during a visit to New York, the money needed to build a small garden and playground. Parks and gardens were to be a major theme of his many years in office – especially playgrounds for children. One of Kollek's friends was sceptical of this aspect of his vision. 'Why should you break your back over Jerusalem?' he asked. 'It's been dirty for two thousand years; you can't change it in a day.' The fifty-four-year-old Kollek, who had been born in a small Hungarian village in the Austro-Hungarian Empire, was not a man to give up. He wanted West Jerusalem to look and act like a capital city, not like a frontier town and dead-end. 'This half-city', he later wrote, 'was the only place in Israel, except for the border kibbutzim, where you constantly sensed an atmosphere of war and the enemy close by.'

Early in Kollek's mayoralty there was an example of the harshness of the division of the city. A Baptist minister, Dr Lindsey, who lived in West Jerusalem but also had parishioners on the Jordanian side, decided to seek medical care on the Israeli side for a young Jordanian boy. 'Dr Lindsey knew the Jordanians wouldn't let him out through the Mandelbaum Gate,' Kollek later wrote, 'so he tried to cross No-Man's Land at night and had a foot blown off.'

The divided city was a blemish and a danger. As Kollek recalled: 'Half the time you drove down a road or a side street, you ran into a sign reading: "STOP! DANGER! FRONTIER AHEAD!".' Kollek added: 'There was hardly a month in which somebody was not killed or wounded on the frontier, or at least struck by a stone thrown from the wall. When we complained to the Jordanians, they said, apologetically, "A soldier went mad." The city was divided by walls fifteen to twenty feet high wherever a through street had previously existed and by stretches of No-Man's Land, barbed wire fences, and mines. In a description which recalled Mary Clawson's experience twelve years earlier, Kollek added: 'There was only one crossing point, the "Mandelbaum Gate", though it wasn't actually a gate at all. The crossing was near a house that had once belonged to a Mr Mandelbaum, and the name stuck to the open roadway with a barrier across it. In the beginning of 1964, right before the Pope's visit, we put a roof over part of the crossing so that even in the rainy weather the departing Pope could step out of his car and bid goodbye to the people accompanying him. It finally gave the crossing an appearance that justified the word "gate".'

Clergy and diplomats were allowed to go through the gate and return, as were United Nations personnel. Tourists who were neither Israelis nor Jordanians could also cross, as Mary Clawson had done. 'After years of pressure from the Western countries,' Kollek wrote, 'Israeli Christians were finally allowed to visit their holy places on Christmas and Easter and then cross back. We had to present short-lists of these pilgrims, and the Jordanians cut the number down even further. The permits to cross were for only thirty-six to forty-eight hours. On the first Christmas after I became mayor, I accompanied the Israeli district commissioner to the spot between the two police stations at the Mandelbaum Gate. Without our knowing it, a press photographer snapped a picture of us together with the Jordanian governor, Anwar al-Khatib. The photograph appeared in the *New York Times* and apparently created quite some difficulties for the governor, because he was meeting not only with his official counterpart but with the Mayor of Jewish Jerusalem.'

*

From his first moments as Mayor, Teddy Kollek strove to bring culture, in all its guises, to West Jerusalem. Early in 1966 he persuaded Marlene Dietrich to give a concert in the city. The concert hall was filled, he later recalled, with the 'older generation' of German-speaking Jerusalemites delighted to hear songs 'from the days when they, and she, were young'.

Kollek was determined to continue to build up the Israel Museum into something special, and internationally known. One of those who expressed an interest in helping was the German newspaper magnate Axel Springer. 'I liked Springer immediately,' Kollek later wrote. 'We went up to the roof of City Hall, and I pointed out the dividing wall twenty yards away and the nearest Jordanian gun position about a hundred yards away. I also expressed my belief in the eventual unification of Jerusalem and explained why I had decided to keep the Municipality in the centre of the entire city. I did not know then that Springer, for similar motives, had decided to construct his own office building next to the Berlin Wall. Perhaps it was this comparison that moved him to offer a gift to Jerusalem. Since I was deeply involved with our fledgling museum, I suggested that he endow it with a library for art and archaeology. He asked to have time to consider my suggestion. That night he phoned me from Tel Aviv and asked me to meet him. By the next day, we had settled on a gift of about $1 million for a library and auditorium wing of the museum. There were no strings attached. Springer did not donate the money to immortalise his name. He did it because he cared about Jerusalem, cared about art and about books, and thought it was a fitting idea.'

On 10 July 1966, while the museum was still a building-site, the new Israeli Parliament building, the Knesset, was inaugurated on a nearby hill. It was a gift from a leading British philanthropist, James de Rothschild, who as an officer in 1918 had been active in recruiting Jews to serve in Allenby's army, and who, with his wife, Dorothy, was one of the main benefactors of Jewish Jerusalem. That same year another of Jerusalem's British benefactors, Miriam Sacher, who had lived in the city in the 1920s with her husband Harry Sacher, donated a vast, empty swath of land between the Knesset and the city, to be turned into a wooded park and gardens for the children of the poorer Jewish neighbourhoods nearby.

On the day of the inauguration of the Knesset, King Hussein declared East Jerusalem to be the 'spiritual capital' of Jordan. Jewish attachment to the city was also expressed that year by the Galician-born writer S. J. Agnon, who had lived in Jerusalem throughout the Mandate period, and whose house had been vandalised in the riots of 1929. On receiving the Nobel Prize for Literature in Oslo, Agnon declared: 'Through a historical catastrophe – the destruction of Jerusalem by the emperor of Rome – I was born in one of the cities of the diaspora. But I have always deemed myself a child of Jerusalem, one who is in reality a native of Jerusalem.'

*

On 15 May 1967, Israel's nineteenth Independence Day, the celebrations in West Jerusalem were intended to make the city the focal point of the national celebrations. Fireworks, a football match, an International Youth Bible Quiz and a military parade were among the highlights. 'Staid Jerusalem has been given an injection of colour by the Army preparations,' wrote the *Jerusalem Post* on May 14. 'The main streets, usually "rolled up" at about 10 p.m., were alive with people for more than an hour past midnight, as the motorised columns of tomorrow's parade held a dry run, headlights blazing on jeeps and trucks.' On the day of the parade, Jordanian Legionnaires with field-glasses studied the parade from the various vantage points on the Old City walls. The *Jerusalem Post* praised the military parade 'for the subtle reassurance it brought that Jerusalem is not really to be discriminated against, as some people had begun to fear – and others across the border, to hope'.

For the national song festival with which the Independence Day celebrations ended, a song competition had been commissioned by Teddy Kollek. He wanted at least one song to be about Jerusalem. It was written by Naomi Shemer, who spent, she later recalled, 'a whole day soaking up atmosphere in Jerusalem', but in the competition itself her song did not reach the top three. It was called 'Jerusalem of Gold', and a storm of applause greeted it when it was sung at the competition. When the winners were announced it was not their songs but 'Jerusalem of Gold' that the audience called for. When Kollek urged Naomi Shemer to sing it again, the audience joined in the lilting refrain. The words, which spoke of Jewish longings for the Old City, caught the imagination of all those who heard them. One line told of the impossible: 'To reach a wall where men stand weeping.' Within four weeks, that impossibility was to become reality for the Jews of West Jerusalem, after nineteen years of dreaming.

CHAPTER SEVENTEEN

The Six-Day War,
June 1967

On 16 May 1967, one day after the festive parade in West Jerusalem celebrating Israel's Independence Day, the Government of Egypt declared itself on a war footing. At the same time, from the Syrian capital of Damascus, the Syrian Government expressed its determination to support its Egyptian ally. For two weeks the world watched, expecting Israel to be attacked and overrun. In a successful and provocative move to block Israel's direct access to the Red Sea and the Indian Ocean, Egyptian forces closed the narrow Strait of Tiran, at the exit to the Gulf of Akaba. On June 3 King Hussein went up to East Jerusalem to inspect his troops. That same day an Israeli colonel, Mordechai Gur, was in West Jerusalem, making contingency plans for a raid by his Parachute Brigade to rescue the exposed and isolated Jewish garrison on Mount Scopus.

During June 4 there were several incidents in the city. Just before midday there were three bursts of machine-gun fire from a Jordanian army post facing Ramat Rahel. At 12.40 there were several further bursts in the Musrara border area. Five minutes later a *Jerusalem Post* reporter, driving through the Mahane Yehuda market, heard the 'sharp rattle' of machine-gun fire. 'And old lady to whom I had given a lift asked shyly, "Should one go home?" She was re-assured since no-one else in the crowded market area seemed to take any notice of the noise.'

On the night of June 4 the Voice of Palestine radio, broadcasting from Cairo, called on the Jordanians to prevent the Mount Scopus convoy from making its regular journey on the Wednesday morning, June 7. The Jordanians should 'turn Mandelbaum Gate into a second Tiran', the radio exhorted. This item of news appeared in the *Jerusalem Post* on Monday June 5 in the stop-press 'After Midnight' column. At 8.30 that same morning an Israeli lookout post near the

Jerusalem border with Jordan reported that the Arab workers who had been building King Hussein's palace on the hill of Tel al-Ful had stopped work and were leaving the area. Half an hour later, at nine o'clock, both Israel and Jordan radio announced that fighting had broken out between Israel and Egypt: Israeli war-planes had struck at the Egyptian air force at its bases deep inside Egypt, destroying many aircraft on the ground.

The Israeli Government, knowing that a Syrian attack on Israel was imminent, decided to seek Jordanian neutrality. The United Nations chief observer in Jerusalem, a senior Norwegian officer, General Odd Bull, was summoned from the United Nations headquarters to the Israeli Foreign Ministry in West Jerusalem, where he was asked to pass on an urgent message from the Israeli Prime Minister, Levi Eshkol, to King Hussein.

The Israeli message read: 'We are engaged in a defensive battle in the Egyptian sector, and we will initiate no action in the Jordanian sector unless Jordan attacks us. If Jordan attacks Israel, we will assault her with all our forces.' As well as approaching Jordan through General Odd Bull, the Israeli Government also asked the American Ambassador, Walworth Barbour, to transmit the Israeli offer from Washington to Amman. Israel's position was clear: if Jordan stayed out of the war, Jordanian rule in the West Bank and Jerusalem would not be challenged. East Jerusalem would remain in Jordanian hands. For King Hussein, however, the temptations of joining a victorious Arab coalition were too great. It seemed impossible that Israel could stand against the combined power of Egypt and Syria, or that a defeated Israel would not present to its Arab victors a vast array of gains and benefits. The very fact that Israel had made an offer of neutrality, and to maintain the status quo, seemed a desperate act sprung from a position of weakness and fear.

From Egypt came a powerful appeal from President Nasser to King Hussein. In a telephone call, the Egyptian leader told the King that Jordan's participation would divert Israeli forces from the Sinai front, and would enable the Egyptians to advance into the heart of Israel, as they had done in 1948. It seemed folly not to participate in the destruction of the enemy. If nothing else, it might be possible to make inroads into West Jerusalem; perhaps, if all Israel was besieged, to overrun the whole of the Jewish capital.

Nasser's telephone call was intercepted by Israeli intelligence, and the actual recording of the two men speaking was broadcast to the world within hours.

At 9.30 that morning, June 5, half an hour after General Odd Bull's drive to the Israeli Foreign Ministry, King Hussein broadcast from Amman: 'The hour of revenge has come.' Teddy Kollek gave West Jerusalem's answer: 'We shall not be conquered.' It was not clear, however, if the Jordanians had any plans to attack, let alone conquer, West Jerusalem.

Then, half an hour after King Hussein's broadcast, Radio Amman declared: 'Israel's end is in your hands. Strike at her everywhere, until victory!' No shots had been fired, and none were heard for another fifteen minutes, when small-arms fire began, followed by machine-gun fire and the explosion of Jordanian mortar and artillery shells in West Jerusalem. Shells burst in the streets, on houses, shops and gardens. But no attempt was made by the Jordanians to cross the border.

At 10.30 a.m. an announcement over Radio Amman boasted the capture of Jebel Mukabber, a hill in the neutral zone which overlooked Jerusalem from the south, and the site of the United Nations headquarters (the former British Government House). As no attack had been made on this hill, or on the building, the announcement was interpreted in Israel as bluster and fantasy.

Three-quarters of an hour later, at 11.15 a.m., Jordanian troops opened fire with light mortars on various Israeli border outposts. Then, fifteen minutes after this somewhat desultory bombardment, Jordanian twenty-five-pounder field-guns fired at Jewish positions at Kibbutz Ramat Rahel at the southern extremity of the city – the same kibbutz that had been overrun three times by the Egyptian army in 1948 but had survived within the borders of Jewish Jerusalem. A few moments later a volley of mixed Jordanian mortar and artillery fire struck the Mount Scopus enclave.

At first the Israeli commander of Central Command, General Uzi Narkiss, thought that the Jordanian shelling of Israeli military positions must be mere bravado, to put up a show for Egypt. It seemed impossible that the Jordanians would really attack, risking the loss of East Jerusalem, and much more beside, by aggressive action on the ground. At about 11.30 a.m., however, a unit of 150 Jordanian troops, commanded by Major Badi Awad, crossed the demarcation line between Jordan and the southern neutral zone, and took up positions in the wood around the United Nations headquarters.

When the Jordanian unit then tried to set up an artillery piece in one of the second-floor windows, the United Nations staff, who numbered about 100, intervened to try to prevent them. They were pushed aside. The United Nations commander, General Odd Bull, argued with Major Awad, but did so in vain. From this new position, Jordanian artillery opened fire on the Israeli battalion stationed in the Allenby Barracks. Several Israeli soldiers were wounded and the battalion withdrew.

No Jordanian troops had yet crossed the 1949 cease-fire line, the Green Line, into Israel. Perhaps they had no plans to do so. 'If they occupied the UN headquarters in the old Government House,' the *Jerusalem Post* wrote on the following day, 'it may have been as a result of Nasser's urgent appeal that they occupy some small corner of Israel territory for the sake of Arab prestige.' But then, in their first ground attack on Israel proper, Jordanian troops advanced through the neutral zone west of the United Nations headquarters to attack the Jewish Experimental Farm in Talpiot, at the edge of the zone. 'They were stopped cold,' one of the Six-Day War's historians, Eric Hammel, has written, 'when the farm director's wife and an elderly auxiliary policeman fired an ancient Czech light machine gun at them.'

As the Jordanian troops moved back into the wood to prepare a second assault, two Israeli companies reached the hill and occupied the farm in force. Two more companies made their way along the crest to Ramat Rahel, reaching it before the Jordanians could attack.

*

At 3.30 that afternoon Israeli forces began their counter-attack on the United Nations headquarters. After an eleven-minute battle, in which one Israeli and five Jordanian soldiers were killed, Major Awad evacuated the summit of the hill. For a while he was given artillery support for a renewed attack, but by 3.45 p.m. the Jordanians switched their artillery fire to West Jerusalem, using the prominent façade of the King David Hotel as their central aiming-point to straddle the whole Jewish built-up area. This left the Israeli troops at the United Nations headquarters free to attack Major Awad's force and drive them off the hill altogether. Fifteen Jordanians and one Israeli soldier were killed in this renewed assault.

Israeli troops then advanced on the two main fortified Jordanian positions further south: the 'Sausage' position along the ridge and the 'Bell' position facing Ramat Rahel. In the battle for the 'Sausage' thirty Jordanian soldiers were killed and one Israeli was wounded. In the battle for the 'Bell' twenty Jordanians and five Israelis were killed. By early evening both positions were under Israeli control, and the whole of southern Jerusalem east of the Green Line was in Israeli hands.

Elsewhere during the afternoon of June 5, Israeli aircraft flew a series of bombing sorties over the Judaean Desert, where a Jordanian armoured brigade was struggling up the winding road from Jericho with orders to reach Jerusalem that day. Further bombing sorties were ordered east of the river Jordan, on an Iraqi infantry brigade that was trying to reach, and cross, the river.

*

The Jordanian shelling of West Jerusalem during the late morning and throughout the afternoon of June 5 gave the Jordanians no military advantage. Throughout the day, Teddy Kollek visited the areas under bombardment. When he was on his way to the Jewish Experimental Farm in Talpiot a bullet went through his car. No one was hurt. A shell also exploded at the Israel Museum, blowing down a door. It seemed that its true target was the nearby Knesset building. That morning, as a precautionary measure, Kollek had given the order for the precious Dead Sea Scrolls, the jewel in the museum's crown, to be lowered into their shelters below the building.

Arthur Veysey, the correspondent of the *Chicago Tribune*, was with Kollek as he left to drive through the city. He reported to his paper on a visit to a border suburb where children were playing behind sandbags, watched by their parents: 'Some adults talked excitedly, but the Mayor calmed them. Suddenly there were three loud crumps, and grey-white clouds rose among houses on the crest of the hill. The people vanished in a whiff.' Kollek got back into his car and sped up the hill 'smack through the still rising clouds. He wanted to see how much damage such mortars could do. It was gratefully small, only craters, six inches deep, two or three feet wide, in the street.'

The Mayor drove on to the railway station. As he reached it, a mortar shell burst on the other side of the tracks. 'The Mayor paused to look,' Veysey reported. A few minutes later, in Rehavia, 'a row of tanks clattered by. People hearing them coming ran out and cheered them on, and the tankmen, standing upright through open hatches, waved back. "They are ruining our streets," the Mayor said jokingly, critically looking at the chopped-up asphalt.' The next stop was the Rehavia High School. 'School was breaking up and teenagers strolled along the tree-shaded streets laughing and joking, pausing to examine every branch knocked down by a shell.'

As West Jerusalem submitted to a barrage of shell fire, Israeli troops in the Jerusalem corridor were driving the Arab defenders from the heights of Radar Hill, and from the villages of Biddu and Beit Iksa, overlooking the approaches to Jerusalem.

*

During ten hours of shelling, ten West Jerusalemites were killed and 100 injured. That evening more than a hundred foreign and local journalists crowded into the Knesset to try to find out about the course of the battle. 'Shortly after eight o'clock,' the *Jerusalem Post* reported, 'a bomb fell right by the building' – it was in fact a shell – 'shattering windows in the canteen. All present were shepherded into the shelter, where eminent personalities such as . . . Mr Ben-Gurion and Mrs Golda Meir sat with senior officials, clerks, cleaning workers and a British TV technician clutching his tapes – all in high spirits and good humour.'

That night most of the citizens of West Jerusalem took to their shelters. While they slept, or tried to sleep, in Stygian gloom beneath their apartment buildings, Israeli troops occupied the heights of Nebi Samwil, to the north of the city, and advancing eastward along almost the exact line taken by Allenby's troops fifty years earlier, reached the Jerusalem-Ramallah road and the heights of Tel al-Ful. Israeli command of the air enabled a substantial Jordanian counter-attack by a superior force of tanks to be beaten off. With the Israeli capture of Tel al-Ful, the Jordanians in Jerusalem could get no reinforcements from the north.

*

On June 6 General Narkiss had decided to make a direct assault on the Jordanian positions between the Green Line and Mount Scopus. The attack was commanded by Colonel Gur. Throughout the day the fighting was heavy and the losses on both sides considerable. At Ammunition Hill, the main fortified Jordanian outpost in the northern sector of Jerusalem, there was fierce Jordanian resistance. Before the position was overrun by the Israelis, sixty-seven Jordanian Legionnaires and twenty-six Israeli soldiers were killed. In the hand-to-hand fighting there, the initiative and courage of a Jordanian infantry officer, Captain Suliman Salayta, was acknowledged by both sides.

There was further intense fighting that morning against the fortified Police School in Sheikh Jarrah, on the Ramallah Road, where forty Israeli soldiers and more than 100 Arab Legionnaires were killed before the building was overrun by the Israelis. Then the American Colony Hotel was taken and, after fierce fighting, the Ambassador Hotel, where Jordanian snipers continued to seek out victims from every floor. Advancing from the north of the city other Israeli units attacked the Jordanians on French Hill – named after a British colonel who had been billeted there in 1918 – from where the Israelis hoped to move straight on, along the ridge to Mount Scopus. But, as they began to move forward, they were attacked in error by their own fighter and tank forces, and were forced to withdraw.

By midday the Israeli army had taken most of East Jerusalem outside the city walls. Learning that the road to Mount Scopus, the scene of so much sniping and killing in 1948, was no longer in Jordanian hands, and that the Jordanian forces besieging the Mount Scopus garrison had melted away, General Narkiss drove with the Israeli Minister of Defence, Moshe Dayan, to the top of the enclave, where they overlooked the embattled city. The moment was marked by a lunch, cooked for them by the garrison cook. 'What a fantastic view,' was Dayan's comment. At 12.30, while Dayan and Narkiss were on Mount Scopus, Israeli intelligence intercepted a telegram from King Hussein to President Nasser. 'The situation rapidly worsens,' the King reported. 'In Jerusalem it is hopeless.'

Among the Arab suburbs captured by Israeli forces that day were the Arab section of Abu Tor, the village of Silwan, and Sheikh Jarrah, from which so many Arab attacks had been launched on Jewish cars and buses in 1948. Also captured was French Hill, the high ground just to the north of the city which the Arab Legion had taken on its march into Jerusalem nineteen years earlier.

During the battle for French Hill, shells fell on the Jerusalem Biblical Zoo, which lay in the line of fire of the combatants. Twenty animals were killed, as well as seventy parakeets whose cage took a direct hit. At the height of the shelling, the three orang-utans cried so bitterly that the zoo staff transferred them to the greater safety of a closed room. When the shelling was over, one of the orang-utans was reported by the zoo Director to look 'ten years older'.

*

On the morning of June 6, the Shaare Tzedek Hospital in the Jaffa Road had received two direct hits from Jordanian shells. One of the shells rolled into a storage space overlooking the corridor of the maternity ward, where twelve mothers and babies were sleeping. Fortunately it neither rolled further nor exploded. By the evening Shaare Tzedek had taken in seventy-five civilian casualties of the day's shelling. Five of them died of their wounds. Bikur Holim Hospital took in nine civilian casualties, two of whom died. 'Bikur Holim was rather proud of having a Jordanian major upstairs,' Malka Rabinowitz reported for the *Jerusalem Post*. 'The captured officer, wounded in the hands and legs, had the usual chart at the foot of his bed.' His name was Major Abdul Azziz Yassin.

At the Hadassah Hospital below Ein Karem, rebuilt there after the closing of Mount Scopus, wounded Israeli and Arab soldiers were in the same wards. 'I saw one stretcher-case,' the Israeli journalist Philip Gillon reported, 'with shocking wounds – the soldier had lost one eye, and the other was badly damaged. He seemed to be just as stoical as any of the others, but he was a captured Arab Legionnaire.' The doctor told Gillion: 'The only words he knows in Hebrew, which he said over and over when he came in, were: "We are brothers, we are brothers." '

*

In the hills just above the coastal plain, the monastery, pumping-station, and Mandate police fort at Latrun, where the Arabs had cut Jerusalem off from the coast in 1948, were captured from the Jordanians on June 6. That day, eighty miles to the south, Israeli troops advanced into the Sinai desert. During the afternoon Teddy Kollek crossed through the Mandelbaum Gate to visit East Jerusalem. Several minutes after he went through the crossing-point a soldier was fatally wounded by sniper fire there.

Kollek went first to Mount Scopus, where he visited the Hadassah Hospital and Hebrew University buildings, deserted except for a small garrison since 1948. Then he went down to the Ambassador Hotel in Sheikh Jarrah. At the hotel he gave a press conference. When a journalist asked him if he expected very soon to become Mayor of a greatly expanded city, he replied: 'I was elected Mayor of the area for which I am responsible today. But my Council is considering the problem of giving aid to the other part of Jerusalem as soon as hostilities cease – we can expect grave difficulties with regard to water supply, garbage collection, and possible outbreaks of disease.'

Did Kollek not want Israel to include ancient Jerusalem in the Jewish city, another journalist asked him. 'Every Jew has dreamed of this for 2,000 years,' he replied. 'But we are aware that it cannot be done in a hurry.'

Asked about the future of access to Mount Scopus, Kollek replied: 'I am not the proper person to deal with such a question. If we had been planning this war for months, I might have given the matter more consideration, but only last Saturday we were worrying about whether they would let the convoy through to Mount Scopus today.'

Turning to the question of the battle for the Old City, the Mayor was asked if he did not regard Israel's declared policy of 'self restraint' as 'a great handicap to our soldiers'. He replied: 'Certainly. There are many holy sites in a very small area. This obviously poses a very real problem for our soldiers.' The Arabs, he pointed out, had not accepted such 'shackles'. In their earliest bombardments on June 5 they had hit the Church of the Dormition, the Hadassah Hospital, the Knesset and the Israel Museum.

Kollek's press conference was conducted 'with considerable good humour,' the *Jerusalem Post* reported, 'although he had to endure some rather fierce competition from machine-guns, guns and bombs, which were exploding at various points in Arab and Jewish Jerusalem. When a particularly effective Israeli bomb set the Arab Legion's fortified position near the Mar Elias Monastery violently ablaze, the conference broke up at great speed, to enable foreign correspondents to file their stories.'

The Mayor returned to West Jerusalem. An Israeli soldier, recognising him, remarked, 'We've made your city bigger,' to which he replied: 'A bigger headache, you mean.' That evening, the *Jerusalem Post* reported, Israeli troops driving back through the Mandelbaum Gate into the Jewish suburb of Mea Shearim 'were greeted by large crowds of excited residents from the neighbourhood, clapping and cheering them on. The men were dog-tired; they just smiled.'

*

On the evening of June 6 an Israeli attempt to seize the Mount of Olives failed, when the tank column took the wrong road and, instead of climbing the Mount, was trapped in the Kidron Valley. But the Jordanian commander of the Jerusalem region, Brigadier Ata Ali Hazzaa, realising that it was only a matter of time before the

Old City was surrounded, had decided not to endanger the lives of his soldiers unnecessarily. At five that afternoon he had ordered the Jordanian military units that were gathering to the east of the city, just below the Mount of Olives, to pull back towards Jericho.

Towards dusk, Major-General Mohammed Ahmed Salim, the Jordanian commander of all the forces on the West Bank, ordered the evacuation of all Jordanian military units in the Jerusalem area. They were to take the road down to Jericho, the only road out of East Jerusalem that was still open to them. As darkness fell, only the Jordanian troops inside the Old City, about 600 men in all, remained at their war stations.

That night the citizens of West Jerusalem again took to their shelters. Although the Old City and the Mount of Olives were still in Jordanian hands, there was a sense among all Jewish Jerusalemites that the city was about to be reunited. On the morning of June 7 the *Jerusalem Post* editorial declared: 'The battle for Jerusalem has been won. Its brave, heroic, and weary citizens are unlikely to have to spend a third night in their hot, cramped shelters.' The two days of battle had been 'a brief taste of the drawn-out trial of 1948, when the city remained on starvation rations and almost without water for many weeks. But there is a difference. In 1948 there was a deep fear that Jewish Jerusalem might fall – as the Jewish Quarter of the Old City had fallen after long and heroic resistance, when its ammunition gave out. There was no such fear this time, and the aimless shelling was doubly resented as mere obedience to Nasser's order for a diversionary move that would cause Israeli forces to be withdrawn from the Sinai front for the defence of their capital.'

No such diversion had been necessary. King Hussein's actions had been of no value to the Egyptian army. The Jordanians, wrote the *Jerusalem Post*, were Nasser's 'unwilling supporters, who have been dragged into a battle that is not of their own choosing'. There was no evidence that Hussein had any intention of attacking Israel in force 'or of making any move in Jerusalem'. What he had done was 'likely to cost him his position in Jerusalem, if not his crown or his life'. The King remained on his throne, but East Jerusalem, which his grandfather had acquired by conquest in 1948, was to be Jordan's no more.

Even with the Old City still under Jordanian control, it was assumed by all Israeli commentators that the battle on June 7 would see it fall. The *Jerusalem Post* was already looking to the future. 'In a hard and costly fight', it declared on the morning of June 7, 'the City has been surrounded, and it is not expected to resist very long in this condition. The Jews of Israel will once more practise the ancient custom of visiting the Western Wall of the ancient Temple for prayer and remembrance. Israel cannot permit itself to be locked out of the Old City again, or to rely on the uncertain services of the United Nations for its right of access. The division of the city has been a painful and expensive anomaly for twenty years. Now it looks as though some entirely new solution to this problem will have to be found.'

The editorial did not say what that solution might be. The plans and developments of municipal and civic administration would have to wait until the aftermath of battle. Unknown that morning to the newspapers, or to the Jewish Jerusalemites, Brigadier Hazzaa had decided, some two hours after midnight, that the Old City could not be defended, any more than the Mount of Olives, and that all those troops who wanted to do so should leave. The Israelis had deliberately avoided advancing to the Dung Gate to enable just such an exodus to take place. More than 450 Jordanian soldiers availed themselves of this escape route. Then, at three in the morning of June 7, Brigadier Hazzaa, his intelligence officer, his driver, and the second most senior officer under his command, also left, setting off on foot across the Kidron Valley to the Jericho Road.

At five o'clock that morning, as Brigadier Hazzaa and his men were making their way eastward, leaving the Old City poorly defended, the Israeli Cabinet, meeting in emergency session in Tel Aviv, was discussing whether to attack the Old City at all. General Dayan opposed any such attack, fearing a terrible loss of life in what he thought would be intense hand-to-hand fighting. Other ministers feared that, once Israeli troops entered the Haram, an Islamic Holy War might break out throughout the region. But the balance of opinion, strongly supported by the ministers representing the religious parties, was to try to capture the Old City, and with it the deserted Jewish Quarter, overrun by the Jordanians in 1948.

The Cabinet's decision was sent to General Narkiss. His military Order of the Day was phrased in confident tones. 'Today Jerusalem is to be liberated,' it declared. 'In the centre and in the north, the city of our ancestors is in our hands. Our army is still poised. Men of the Regional Command, be resolute. Do not waver.'

At seven that morning, the Israeli Deputy Chief of Staff, General Chaim Bar-Lev, arrived in the city by air from Tel Aviv to oversee the attack. He was particularly concerned that no Holy Places, Muslim, Christian or Jewish, should be damaged in the fighting. As Bar-Lev was on his way to Colonel Gur's headquarters, which had been set up in the Rockefeller Museum just outside the north-east corner of the city wall, Gur himself was supervising a sudden and effective assault on the remaining Jordanian fortified positions at the Augusta Victoria Hospice and on the Mount of Olives.

Before the heights were captured, Jordanian mortar shells, falling on Gur's headquarters, killed several Israeli paratroopers who were unable to get to the fortified rooms in time. Among the dead was a young Italian Jew, Natan Schechter, who had arrived in Israel from Italy only three days earlier and was serving as a medical orderly. Several Jordanian Legionnaires who were being held prisoner in the headquarters were also killed by the bombardment.

*

The assault on the Mount of Olives was launched at 8.30 on the morning of June 7. As the assault began, Israeli air force planes dive-bombed the Jordanian military positions around the Augusta Victoria. Several bombs hit the building itself – the first bombs to fall on it since 1917. When the infantrymen advanced up the hill, they were buoyed up by the news that King Hussein had just instructed his soldiers in the Jerusalem area to give up their positions and leave the city. The attack on the ridge was a gamble. Had there been 'any kind of force in the Augusta Victoria,' General Narkiss later wrote, 'we should have been cut down like toy soldiers. Every man was exposed, a sure target, virtually like figures on a target range.'

As the crest of the Mount of Olives was stormed, Giora Ashkenazi, a company commander, was hit by an isolated volley of shots. 'This was the only casualty of the Battle of Augusta Victoria,' the paratrooper Eli Landau wrote, 'and it cast a shadow on the joy of the victorious soldiers as they climbed the ridge.'

The ridge having been conquered, Colonel Gur hurried to the Intercontinental Hotel at the southern end of the Mount of Olives. From there he looked down over the whole of the Temple Mount. After a few moments' contemplation, looking at a scene no Israeli had been allowed to contemplate for nineteen years, he gave the orders for an assault to be launched through St Stephen's Gate, the only entrance to the city on the eastern side of the city wall. Then he spoke through his radio link to his commanders. 'We are going up to the Old City, to the Temple Mount, to the Wailing Wall,' he said. 'For thousands of years the Jewish people has prayed for this moment. Israel is awaiting our victory. Good luck!'

In advance of the assault, Gur ordered an air strike on the Jordanian defenders who remained along the eastern and northern sections of the Old City wall, and on the north-eastern suburb inside the wall. 'A terrific artillery barrage was laid down,' he recalled a week later. 'This quarter could have interfered with our plans. All our tanks and recoilless guns opened fire as well, plastering the wall itself, from St Stephen's Gate northwards. Not a single shot was fired at any of the Holy Places. The City Wall quaked. The stones on the embrasures seemed to dance. When I saw the tanks approaching the wall I jumped into a half-track and ordered the tanks to speed up more. We intensified our artillery barrage.' During the firing a shell pierced the roof of the crusader church of St Anne. But the church, a Christian Holy Place, and one of the few complete crusader buildings in Jerusalem, was otherwise intact.

*

It was 9.45 in the morning. The tank in which Colonel Gur was riding approached St Stephen's Gate, known also as the Lions' Gate because of the two ornamental stone lions carved on it by Suleiman the Magnificent in 1538. 'I told Ben Tsur, my driver, to step on it,' Gur recalled. 'Ben Tsur stepped on it. He put all his ninety kilos on the accelerator. We passed the tanks spearheading the way, and firing away with all their might. There was a burning bus in front of us, and behind it was the Lions' Gate. There should have been men with hand grenades on top of that gate.'

The Lions' Gate was unmanned. The bazookas and store of shells carefully positioned above it had been abandoned. 'Ben Tsur continued to step on it,' Gur recalled. 'We crashed through the gate, climbing over the stones that had toppled from the wall. There was a man standing there. We swerved past him, through the second gate blocked by a motor cycle. We wondered whether it was mined and rode it down. And then we arrived in front of the Dome of the Rock.'

Gur had entered the Haram through the Absat Gate, the very gate through which, according to Muslim tradition, the tribes of Israel used to enter in ancient times on their way to pray at the Temple. There was no opposition, only a Jordanian army field kitchen, its cauldrons still boiling, but its pots and pans abandoned. All firing had stopped. As more troops followed swiftly behind Gur and his driver, they saw the Kadi of Jerusalem and the Jordanian Governor approach them. The two Muslim dignitaries brought a message that there was 'a unanimous decision to cease all opposition'. Gur, for his part, pledged that he would 'try to mop up the town without firing a single shot'. As the negotiators spoke they could hear firing on the city walls, the final brief skirmishes as Israeli soldiers mounted the walls at their three most sensitive points: above the Damascus Gate, facing Mount Zion, and facing the Yemin Moshe quarter.

At that moment General Narkiss was on his way by jeep to the Lions' Gate. As he approached the gate he contacted Colonel Gur by radio 'to find out where he was'. Gur answered: 'The Temple Mount is ours!' Narkiss could not believe him, and said so. 'I repeat,' said Gur. 'The Temple Mount is ours. I'm standing near the Mosque of Omar right now. The Wailing Wall is a minute away.'

*

It was midday as the first Israeli troops hurried down from the Temple Mount towards the Wailing Wall, to which Israeli Jews had been denied access since 1948. The final obstacle, the Moghrabi Gate, was opened by a wizened old Arab who, speaking Hebrew, appeared as if from nowhere and produced the key. From this gate, steps led straight down to the Wall. At that moment a paratrooper was shot and killed by a sniper's bullet from the direction of the Wall. His comrades fired back, and the sniper was killed. Then a small group of Jordanian soldiers was seen in a truck at the base of the stairway, towing an anti-tank gun. The Jordanians opened fire with their rifles. When the Israelis returned fire the Jordanians sheltered under their truck. It was hit by Israeli fire and exploded. All the Jordanians were killed.

A few moments later the first Israeli troops reached the Wall and began to pray. They were quickly joined by dozens more. Even as sporadic sniping and fighting continued in other parts of the Old City, the Wall became a magnet. It was a moment which, thirty years later, still excites vivid emotions in Israel whenever it is recalled. 'Tough Israeli troops covered with dust wept like small children at the sight,' reported Robert Musel, a foreign correspondent who had reached the Wall with them. When General Narkiss arrived he was deeply moved as 'the restrained weeping became sobs, full-throated, an uncontrolled emotional outburst'.

Israeli troops made their way across the Old City to the Jaffa Gate. Others hurried to the Jewish Quarter. Everywhere white sheets were hanging out of windows. The battle for Jerusalem was over. It had been short but intense. During less than three days of fighting, 180

Israeli soldiers and 14 Israeli civilians, and 350 Jordanian soldiers and 249 Jordanian civilians, had been killed.

That night, paratrooper Eli Landau recalled, as the soldiers crowded near the massive stones of the Wailing Wall, 'a medical officer, Captain Uri, was called to one of the houses in town. A Moslem woman was about to give birth. The doctor was led through the narrow streets to a small alcove lit by a street lamp. The woman was contorted in pain. He delivered her – a sub-machine gun slung over his shoulder, a steel helmet on his head. When he returned to the Wall, a soldier offered him some coffee in a tin can. While sipping the hot liquid, the paratroopers talked to each other, saying that "perhaps this birth signalled a new better day".'

*

The excitement in Israel, and particularly in Jerusalem, that the whole city was under Israeli control was intense. The Jewish Quarter of the Old City, lost in 1948 and reduced to rubble, was once more in Israeli hands: about a third of its buildings had been demolished by the Jordanians in 1948, and soldiers wept to see the extent of that destruction, which included the Hurva Synagogue, where the Chief Rabbis used to be inaugurated, and where the flags of the Jewish battalions of the First World War had been kept.

As to the Wailing Wall, so many struggles for access to it had been fought, first in Turkish times and then under the Mandate. Streams of Israeli soldiers were reaching the Wall throughout the afternoon of June 7, 'some to pray, others just to stare', the *Jerusalem Post* reported. 'Many put petitions for the health of their dear ones in the spaces between the giant stones that Solomon had emplaced for the Glory of God.' Those particular stones had been put in place by Herod, a thousand years after Solomon, but that was a minor quibble at such a time of high emotion.

That afternoon many Israeli leaders also made their way to the Wailing Wall. One of the first to do so was the senior chaplain to the Israeli forces, Rabbi Shlomo Goren. He came, the *Jerusalem Post* reported, 'at an eager run'. He was carrying a Scroll of the Law, and recited the prayer thanking God for allowing him to live to see that moment. Goren stayed at the Wall for several hours, reciting psalms of praise for the victory and prayers for the souls of those who had been killed in securing it. As Goren's prayers were relayed over Israeli army radio, they were picked up by a unit of soldiers that had just entered the Etzion Bloc, from which the Jews had been driven out in 1948. The Jordanian army camp there had been abandoned.

Shortly after Rabbi Goren reached the Wall, the Defence Minister, Moshe Dayan, arrived, together with Generals Narkiss and Rabin. 'I felt truly shaken and stood there murmuring a prayer for peace,' Rabin later recalled. 'Motta Gur's paratroopers were struggling to reach the Wall and touch it. We stood among a tangle of battle-weary men who were unable to believe their eyes or restrain their emotions. Their eyes were moist with tears, their speech incoherent. The overwhelming desire was to cling to the Wall, to hold on to that great moment as long as possible.'

'We have united Jerusalem, the divided capital of Israel,' Dayan declared. 'We have returned to our holiest of holy places, never to part from it again. To our Arab neighbours we extend, also at this hour – and with added emphasis at this hour – our hand in peace. And to our Christian and Muslim fellow citizens, we solemnly prom-ise full religious freedom and rights. We did not come to Jerusalem for the sake of other peoples' holy places, and not to interfere with the adherents of other faiths, but in order to safeguard its entirety, and to live there together with others, in unity.'

Dayan, Rabin and Narkiss were followed at the Wall by many other leading figures. Among them were the former Foreign Minister (and later Prime Minister) Golda Meir, whom the soldiers hugged; David Shaltiel, the commander of the Hagannah forces in Jerusalem when the Wall was lost in 1948; and Bernard Joseph, the Military Governor during the siege, who had felt so keenly then that the loss of the Jewish Quarter could have been avoided. Also visiting the Wall that afternoon was the Prime Minister, Levi Eshkol, 'the first leader of a Jewish Government to visit the site of the Temple since its loss 1,897 years ago', commented the *Jerusalem Post*, which went on to report: 'The Prime Minister, robustly cheered by the tired but elated boys and men who had freed the Holy City, was accompanied by the two Chief Rabbis. It was approaching dusk and, because the city's tortuous alleyways still possibly concealed last-ditch snipers, the official party's escort tried to speed their return to the newer city. But all still lingered, perhaps not fully realising that they have plenty of time to go again, and again.'

*

As the Sephardi Chief Rabbi, Yitzhak Nissim, crossed the Temple Mount on his way to the Wall, a long file of Jordanian prisoners-of-war in front of the Dome of the Rock was parted to enable him to go by. Around the corner from the Wall, the singer Yaffa Yarkoni was leading a singsong. 'Again and again,' the *Jerusalem Post* reported, 'the boys went tirelessly through "Jerusalem of Gold", the song commissioned by the Mayor for the Independence Day Song Festival held twenty-three eons – or was it just days? – ago.'

An Israeli journalist, Lea Ben-Dor, was in West Jerusalem, at the entrance to the ultra-Orthodox section of Mea Shearim, on the afternoon of June 7. 'Bearded dignitaries crowded the pavements of "Sabbath Square",' she wrote, 'to cheer passing truck-loads of soldiers. This is the corner that has been the favourite point for protests against Sabbath drivers, who often cannot pass there for fear of stones being thrown at them. The old men looked embarrassed as they applauded the men who had given the Jewish people back the Western Wall for the first time, with Jews to guard it instead of British policemen. But they were shy of cheering the soldiers whom they have reviled so often for their lack of orthodoxy. The Yeshiva boys cheered wildly, relieved to be able to join wholeheartedly for once in a general celebration.'

The Israeli journalist Philip Gillon was among a group of newsmen who were taken up to Mount Scopus that day. They were driven through Sheikh Jarrah, part of which, he noted, 'had taken a hammering'. 'Suddenly, at the side of the road, we saw a very bald man, dead, his trunk twisted, his legs crumpled up under him. Then we came to Embassy Row in Sheikh Jarrah – the Turkish Consulate, the British Consulate, Shepherd's Hotel, the American Colony Hotel, the great Hotel Ambassador, and one magnificent stone mansion after another. This is as lovely a suburb as I have seen in many a day. A few Israeli soldiers wandered around. No civilians were visible, but on the houses fluttered white handkerchiefs.'

Driving on the road which led up from Sheikh Jarrah to Mount Scopus, Gillon noticed a Jordanian army bunker, completely demolished. 'But otherwise there were few signs of the savage fighting that had liberated Scopus only a few hours before. The monument to the Australian Imperial Forces of 1915–1918 seems to be completely untouched. Just beyond it, the Hebrew University Medical School, the Hadassah Hospital, and the University buildings are in poor condition, and will need considerable attention. From the University, we looked breathlessly across Jerusalem the golden – naturally, at that precise moment, the strains of Naomi Shemer's most appropriate of song hits reached to us from somebody's transistor, perhaps due to super-planning by the Army spokesman. And then we saw, intact, the amphitheatre, where Weizmann, Balfour and Allenby dedicated the University, and below it the valleys marching down to the Dead Sea.'

With the closing of the road to Mount Scopus in 1948, the number nine bus, which had so often run the gauntlet of stones and rifle fire, could run no more. Its number had not been allocated to another bus route, but had been discontinued. On June 7 the first bus to make that journey in 1967 carried a cardboard sign with '9' in its number slot. The route was immediately reinstated. It was still in operation nearly thirty years later, when a suicide bomber killed four passengers who were on their way to the university.

Those who went into the Jewish Quarter of the Old City during June 7 were shocked by the destruction that had been caused in 1948 and the devastation that remained. Amid the ruins of the great nineteenth-century Hurva Synagogue (its Hebrew name means 'ruin', it having been destroyed twice by the Muslims after it was first built in 1705) was found a broken stone fragment, dated 1857, on which were inscribed the words 'This is the gate of the Lord which the righteous shall enter.' The fragment, from the synagogue façade rebuilt in the nineteenth century, had been part of a lintel smashed during the bombardment of 1948.

It was to the Wailing Wall that the largest numbers made their way. 'Isolated Jordanians were still firing from rooftops,' a Holocaust survivor who had just flown in from America later recalled, 'but thousands of Jews rushed to the Old City. No force could deter them. Rabbis and merchants, Talmudic students and farmers, officers and schoolchildren, artists and scholars – all left whatever they were doing and converged on the Wall, and when they reached it, kissed the stones and shouted ancient prayers and requests. On this day everybody was running. I did too. Never did I run so fast, or say "Amen" with such fervour as when I heard the parachutists reciting the minha prayer.' That survivor was Elie Wiesel.

*

Plans had to be made to repair the damage of the war, and to cope with a city that now had an Arab sector and an Old City. There was accommodation to be arranged for 1,200 families who had been evacuated from their shell-damaged homes in the former border areas. There were barriers to be taken down at the borders, and barbed wire to be cleared, as well as mines. A notice in the newspapers on June 7, addressed to 'Citizens of Jerusalem!' by the municipality, warned: 'The border with the Old City is mined. The Jordanian snipers are still active, and two people have been killed by snipers in the Old City. The military command has strictly prohibited approaching the border, or entering the Old City until further notice.' Despite the warning, three children were killed by mines on the following day.

*

Every Israeli newspaper was ecstatic that Jerusalem was one city again. *Hayom* declared on June 8: 'Millions of Jews for many generations have been dreaming of this great day.' The ultra-Orthodox *Shearim* wrote: 'With God's help we have liberated Jerusalem from alien captivity, and hoisted on her walls the flag of free and liberated Israel – after she had fallen to Edom 1,900 years ago, and 19 years ago to Ishmael.' 'Jerusalem is no more divided, but united under the flag of Israel,' declared *Haaretz*. 'All of Jerusalem is ours. Rejoice and be merry, people of Zion.'

Whatever might be the political future of East Jerusalem, responsibility for its sanitation, water, lighting and rubbish collection was suddenly on the shoulders of Teddy Kollek and his West Jerusalem Council. There was no one else willing to take on that costly burden. On June 8 a 'United Jerusalem' fund was established by the municipality. In making it public, Teddy Kollek said he hoped that the coalition of parties that made up his council 'would prove up to uniting the two cities'. Kollek visited the East Jerusalem City Hall, to speak to the Jordanian Mayor, Ruhi al-Khatib, himself a Hebronite. 'Seven or eight of his councillors were there,' Kollek later wrote, 'and we discussed means of co-operation. They were greatly troubled and in a state of shock. When we arrived we found our city flag flying outside their building.'

*

On June 8, as the final battles of the Six-Day War were being fought in the Sinai and on the Golan Heights, there was a notice in all the Israeli newspapers, placed there by the Tel Aviv municipality, urging every householder to fly the Israeli flag 'in honour of undivided Jerusalem'. Among those who reached the Wailing Wall that day was Doris Lankin, an Israeli journalist who had last been there in 1947. In those days, she wrote, 'to my unaccustomed Western eyes the streets looked grim and unsanitary and the atmosphere was one of a grimy Eastern bazaar. It has not changed very much. But the rubble of war and the bodies of dead Arabs along the roadside were new. The rows upon rows of bearded, unkempt but laughing young soldiers was new. And the Western Wall was also new. It was a singing, shining wall. Even the old Jew who prostrated himself at the foot of the wall and kissed it hysterically with the tears streaming down his beard, rose up and sang, in a voice growing ever stronger, the Psalm of David. The song was taken up by the young, talit-enwrapped soldiers reciting the morning prayers at the Wall for the first time in nineteen years. It was taken up by the hard-boiled, cynical journalists, by the ubiquitous sightseers and it rang out in the confined space of the slum-area surrounding the Wall. But the slums went unnoticed. All eyes were turned to the Wall, to the singing, shining Wall.'

At that moment the Israeli President, Zalman Shazar, arrived, and began to recite his own prayers. 'As the assembled throng repeated the words of the prayer in unison,' Doris Lankin noted, 'sporadic shooting in the neighbourhood broke out. The President continued his prayers and the crowd answered in unison. As the Presidential party took their leave, four blindfolded Arab snipers were led out of the room behind the Wall in which they had been hiding. The last resistance was being broken. The last resisters were being mopped up. The Old City, and the old, singing Wall were ours, forever.'

*

During June 8 the 'grand old man' of Israeli politics, David Ben-Gurion, who had been Prime Minister until four years earlier, went to the Wailing Wall. At his side, visiting the Old City for the first time, was Shimon Peres, later to be twice Prime Minister of Israel. 'It was the end of an era for Israel,' Peres later wrote, 'the start of a new and very different period in the life of the nation.' At that moment an episode took place which typified this new period. The narrow passageway in front of the Wall had been called by the Arabs 'Al-Burak Road', in honour of the horse on which Mohammed had ascended to Heaven from the rock on the Haram above: the name was engraved in Arabic and English on a ceramic tile, with the words 'Wailing Wall Road' in brackets. There was no Hebrew name on the tile.

Ben-Gurion looked at the tile with distaste. 'This is not right,' he said. 'It should come down. Does anyone have a hammer?' A soldier hurried forward, climbed up to the tile, and began to hack at it with his bayonet. 'No, no,' Ben-Gurion called out, 'you may damage the stone. Hasn't anybody got a hammer?' Producing a small axe, another soldier worked with great care to erase the name from the tile, but not to harm the ancient stone to which it was affixed. The crowd cheered. 'This is the greatest moment of my life since I came to Israel,' Ben-Gurion declared.

The mood of exhilaration spanned the hopes of both communities. 'Anyone who visited Israel in the summer of 1967,' Golda Meir later wrote, 'will testify to the extraordinary euphoria that gripped the Jews and appeared also to affect the Arabs. It was, in short, as though a death sentence had been lifted – which was, after all, literally true. If I have to choose one particular aspect of that immediate post-war period as an illustration of the general atmosphere, I would certainly point to the tearing down of the concrete barricades and barbed wire fences that had separated the two halves of the city of Jerusalem ever since 1948. More than anything else, those hideous barricades had signified the abnormality of our life, and when they were bulldozed away and Jerusalem overnight became one city, it was like a sign and symbol of a new era. As someone who came to Jerusalem then for the very first time said to me: "There is light from within the city," and I understood exactly what he meant. "Very soon," I told my grandchildren, "the soldiers will come home; there will be peace; we will be able to travel to Jordan and to Egypt and all will be well." '

Throughout Jewish Jerusalem there was an enormous sense of relief and desire to celebrate. On June 9 the flag of the Hebrew University was hoisted on the university buildings at Mount Scopus, shortly after which the Hadassah flag was raised above the Hadassah Hospital, re-establishing the links that had been so abruptly severed nineteen years earlier. In the Chemistry and Mathematics Institutes at the university, the instructions about lectures and seminars on the students' notice-boards were all dated 1947. That same day, while walking in the Old City, the Dutch-born pilot, inventor and writer Wim Van Leer founded, on the spur of the moment, a $1,000 prize, to be given each year for the best broadcast on an Israeli subject. He then said that he was going to announce the first award himself, and did so there and then, giving it to General Chaim Herzog, the Israeli Military Governor of the West Bank and Jerusalem, and later President of the State of Israel, for his morale-boosting radio broadcasts during the war.

On June 10, the last day of the Six-Day War, several thousand Jerusalemites crowded into the National Convention Centre at the entrance to the city to hear a concert conducted by the Indian conductor Zubin Mehta. 'I am sorry I am not one of you,' Mehta told the audience. 'I wish you a successful peace so that you may work in music. And I hope the only language you speak here in future will be the language of music.' Mehta was later to make a substantial contribution to music in Israel, as the conductor of the Israel Philharmonic Orchestra.

The star performers of that musical evening were the cellist Jacqueline du Pré and the pianist Daniel Barenboim. Three pieces of music were played: Saint-Saëns' Concerto for Cello and Orchestra, and Beethoven's Piano Concerto No. 5 and Fifth Symphony. Four days later Teddy Kollek was present at a special presentation in Jerusalem by the Haifa Municipal Theatre of *For Jerusalem with Love*. The advertisement for the performance stated: 'All proceeds will go for the reconstruction of Jerusalem.'

It was not only the damaged buildings of West Jerusalem that were to be repaired: the future of the destroyed Jewish Quarter of the Old City was likewise under daily discussion. On June 11 a delegation of former residents of the Jewish Quarter asked the municipality for permission to rebuild their old homes. The Deputy Mayor, Rabbi Shear Yashuv Cohen, told them that the municipality would 'do everything in its power to bring about a revival of Jewish life' in the Old City. That day Teddy Kollek arranged for 20,000 bottles of milk for infants to be taken in to the Muslim, Christian and Armenian Quarters of the Old City. And at the former Jordanian police station in Wadi al-Joz, just north of the city walls, the Israeli occupation authorities prepared to enlist for duty all former Jordanian policemen up to the rank of captain who answered an Israeli call for volunteers.

*

Israel was in a stronger position in Jerusalem than it had been at any time in the nineteen-year history of the State. One of the first changes made was in front of the Wailing Wall. For two days bulldozers were at work knocking down and clearing away the twenty-five Arab houses immediately to the west of the Wall in order to make a larger space for worshippers. The families living there who had not fled were given summary notice to leave.

'Yesterday afternoon,' the *Jerusalem Post* reported on June 12, 'a bulldozer was overturning the last of the houses. Protruding from the rubble were beds and bedding, other items of furniture and kitchen utensils, food and shoes, presumably abandoned by those who had fled the area during the fighting for the city. When the general public is admitted to the area sometime later this week they will find that the slum buildings which had cluttered the place for more than a century have been razed. There is now a large square before the Wall, which rises in its splendour before the visitor, the moment he turns right from the path leading in from the Dung Gate.'

Among those who came to see the demolition work at the Wall was the French Jewish philanthropist Baron Edmond de Rothschild. It was his grandfather, also Baron Edmond, who in 1887 had offered to purchase this same area in front of the Wall from the Muslim religious trust that owned it. Despite the approval of the Turkish Governor of the time, the project had fallen through.

By June 14 the space in front of the Wall had been cleared and levelled, and anyone who wished to visit the Wall could do so. It was the Jewish pilgrim festival of Shavuot (Pentecost, or the Feast of Weeks). To the surprise of many, an estimated 200,000 West Jerusalemites and Israelis from much further afield, some from the Upper Galilee, came to celebrate. For thirteen hours they made their way to the Wall, through six successive police barriers, set up to maintain an even flow. At 9.30 in the morning Teddy Kollek appeared. 'He was hugged and cheered,' reported the *Jerusalem Post*, 'as the first "Mayor of Greater Jerusalem".'

On the following day the *Jerusalem Post* described the implications of the scene. During the nineteen years when the Jordanian authorities refused to allow any Israeli to visit the Wall, the paper wrote, 'perhaps many Israelis, and even the citizens of Jerusalem, were only dimly aware of the fact that to be cut off from this ancient monument, from this physical link with the nation's past, gradually assumed the character of a new exile. It is not chance that an almost life-size photographic reproduction of a section of the Wall occupies a place of honour in the new Knesset. The nation's historic link with its origin and history in this country is preserved chiefly in its writings – the foremost in the Bible – in the nation's collective memory, and in archaeological finds. The Western Wall, and the living city of Jerusalem in which it stands, are the only visible, tangible survivors of a distant glory.

'For centuries the Wall has been a place of pilgrimage to Jews, the religious first of all, but the non-religious as well. In the years of the British Mandate, people not only went to pray there, but annual pilgrimages, without any organisation or appeal, mobilised practically every Jew whose feet would carry him there and back. The tradition was renewed yesterday with an enthusiasm and fervour and in such numbers as must have astonished even those who were aware that these great blocks of stone that are said to date back to the Temple, recipients of the fervent prayers of so many generations, have acquired a national symbolism quite unmatched in Jewish life, which has dealt so largely in abstractions.'

Two hundred thousand people 'undertook the hot and laborious pilgrimage up Mount Zion and down again, down a long road that finally brought them face to face with the Wall,' the *Jerusalem Post* wrote. 'Many more thousands may be expected in the coming days, and without doubt it will become the focus of every Jewish visitor's journey to Israel, and that of many Gentiles as well. Yesterday's pilgrims were the ordinary citizens, not the privileged who had already had a glimpse of the Wall since the capture of the Old City last week.' Many were soldiers with only a few hours' leave from their units.

Considerable efforts had been made by the municipality to transform what had been a neglected border area into a route that the multitude could take without difficulty. 'They found that their city had served them well,' wrote the *Jerusalem Post*, 'in choosing a wide road, building the missing sections, providing an exit in a different direction to maintain one-way traffic, supplying police to control the crowds and soldiers to protect them, water to drink on the way, and in clearing the open space in front of the Wall to accommodate many thousands, and all in a surprisingly short time. In due course, no doubt, the great square created will be paved, and more trees planted to join the ancient fig tree fortunately preserved in the middle, and benches to rest on.'

The newspaper's conclusion was emphatic. 'If there was anyone, here or elsewhere, who still had any shadow of doubt concerning the future of Jerusalem,' it wrote, 'yesterday's pilgrimage provided the answer: under no circumstances, whatever the pressures may be, will the citizens of Israel allow anyone to cut them off again from the Wall that stands at the centre of their city and is the essence and reason for its existence.'

*

On June 17 Moshe Dayan ordered the responsibility for the Haram, which had been under Israeli military control for a week, to be restored to Muslims. He also insisted that the Haram should be open to all Muslims from throughout Israel as well as from the West Bank. Six days later, the first Friday after Dayan's decree, five thousand Muslims prayed on the Haram, including a thousand Israeli Muslims who had been denied access during the nineteen years of Jordanian rule.

On June 28 several thousand Jews returned to the Hebrew University amphitheatre on Mount Scopus, the scene of the inauguration of the university in 1925, cut off from the rest of Jerusalem since 1948. Among those present at the ceremony were the Nobel Prize-winner S. J. Agnon and the President of the University, Eliahu Elath, who, as Eliahu Epstein, had been present at the opening ceremony in 1925. Nelson Glueck, the pre-war and wartime Director of the American School of Oriental Studies in Jerusalem, who was visiting the city from the United States, wrote in his diary that when General Rabin, the Chief of Staff of the victorious armies, took his place on the platform 'a great swell of emotion and applause swept through the packed audience'.

In his speech, accepting an honorary doctorate, Rabin spoke of peace and reconciliation. 'The price paid by the enemy also weighs upon our soldiers,' he said. 'Conditioned by its past, the Jewish people have never been able to feel the conqueror's pride or victor's exaltation.' Elie Wiesel, who was in Jerusalem that day (like Rabin, he was later a Nobel Prize-winner), noted the 'moving restraint' of Rabin's speech. In his book *A Beggar in Jerusalem*, written in those June days, Wiesel echoed Rabin's reflections on the sadness felt by the Israelis in the faces of the vanquished Arabs, 'especially the children who saw them as victors and therefore capable of doing them harm'. Wiesel later recalled: 'I saw such children in the Old City . . . They were afraid of us, of me. For the first time in my life, children were afraid of me.' And in his diary he wrote that June: 'The victors, in fact, would have preferred to forgo battle. Saddened, they returned to their homes without hate or pride, disconcerted and withdrawn.'

Following the honorary-degree ceremony on Mount Scopus, the Hebrew University Board of Governors decided to rebuild the original campus and to return to it, making it 'a revitalised centre of teaching and research'. It was to be a ten-year project, costly and ambitious, but a symbol of the determination of the Jews of Jerusalem to renew and strengthen their physical and spiritual contact with Mount Scopus. The Hadassah Hospital would likewise be restored.

*

Among the rumours circulating in East Jerusalem in the aftermath of the war of 1967 was one concerning the Jewish religious seminary

Torat Hayim, located since 1894 on the Via Dolorosa, which had been abandoned by its occupants after the riots of 1936, and left in the care of its Arab janitor. This janitor had died just before the war of 1948 but had given the keys of the building to his brother. With considerable courage, the brother, while subsequently renting out the lower rooms to Arab tenants, had reportedly managed to seal off and preserve the synagogue and library on the upper floor. On hearing the rumour, the Israeli Military Governor, Chaim Herzog, went to the building and found that the synagogue and its library of 3,000 books were indeed intact. The Arab janitor was asked: 'Weren't you afraid to watch over the synagogue when all the other synagogues in the old city were demolished?' To which the janitor replied: 'The holy place watched over me more than I watched over it.'

CHAPTER EIGHTEEN

Reunification: The First Two Years, 1967–1969

On 28 June 1967 the Israeli Government announced that the official reunification of Jerusalem would take place on the following morning. To the somewhat compact 8,750 acres of West Jerusalem would be added the more sprawling 18,750 acres of East Jerusalem. Some people feared that too swift an opening of the nineteen-year-old barriers would lead to tensions and violence, but the Minister of Defence, Moshe Dayan, was emphatic that there should be no hesitations and no delays.

'Dawn came and we did it,' Teddy Kollek later wrote. 'We removed all the fences, dismantled all the check posts, and started blowing up the dividing walls – first the two big walls near the Municipality that closed off Jaffa Road and Suleiman Street. And along with those walls came all those structures built up against the ancient city walls over the last century and buildings that had deteriorated into slums. Eventually it cost us a lot of money to compensate the owners for those torn-down buildings, but the results were well worth it: the beautiful Old City walls were visible again and a green belt could be laid out around them. We did almost too good a job. I remember the army engineers saying, "Here you need so-and-so many pounds of explosive, but to make sure add fifty percent", and the individual sappers added even more. The results were a few broken windows in a fairly wide circle, which we had to repair.'

Jerusalem was once again a physical unity, a single city. 'At first a few crossed the frontier lines, watchful and timid,' Kollek recalled. 'There were police and soldiers around, but they just looked on. Then, in the afternoon, there was a tremendous flow of people. It was contrary to all predictions – except Dayan's. Many Jews were scared. Some people said that families with teenage daughters would not go on living in Jerusalem for fear of the Arabs. Others made all sorts of dire predictions. None of these came true. In one radiant day, Dayan was proved right. The Arabs were astonished at what they saw and heard as they walked around and looked at houses they had lived in. They knocked on the door, were invited in for a cup of tea, and sat down to discuss with their Jewish hosts whether they would have their property returned or what compensation would satisfy them. Jews did the same in the Jewish Quarter. Both sides believed that all problems would be solved easily. I gave an interview for foreign television networks. As I stood with the Wall in the background, the United Nations was meeting to express loud disapproval. My only comment on that was: "If the UN delegates could see how this is working, they would talk differently. If they left us alone, this is how we would live together in Jerusalem." '

That was also an Arab perspective, 'Hundreds of former friendships were brought back to life,' Nabil Khoury wrote in the Beirut weekly *al-Hawadith*. 'On June 29, in Jaffa Road, the main street of Jerusalem, the Hebrew tongue disappeared. On that day, along the entire length of the street, only Palestinian Arabic, in all its different dialects, was heard.'

A Jewish Jerusalemite, Moshe Kohn, who also witnessed the transformation, wrote in the *Jerusalem Post*: 'Jerusalem of the thousand faces' – as a poet defined the city before barbed wire and cement firewalls obscured many of these faces from each other's view nineteen years ago – yesterday leapt to a vigorous new life. Tens of thousands of residents of each side of the city moved freely past the newly lifted barriers to rediscover those faces and plumb the mysteries created by the two decades of separation. Thick knots of vehicles – Israeli and Jordanian, with the word "Jordan" on many licence plates covered or painted over – and pedestrians moved at a turtle's pace past each other through the connecting arteries. The twisting cobble-stoned alleys of the Old City and the relatively broad main streets of the New City and some of its quarters were thickly packed with Jews and Arabs, Moslems, Christians of the different churches, laymen and clerics in all varieties of garb, complexion, eye-colour, physiognomy, and dialect that comprise Jerusalem-United. They gawked at each other and at one another's architecture – in the Old City, some wondering at a life in such patchwork habitation, while others, in the New City, amazed that the tall office buildings did not totter and collapse on their pillar-foundations. With increasing frequency through the day, and with decreasing diffidence, they greeted each other in various languages. They did commerce with each other in a volume that the city probably had never before in its history seen.'

The poet whom Moshe Kohn had quoted was Judah Stampfer, an ordained rabbi, whose poem *Jerusalem Has Many Faces* had appeared a few years earlier in a book of that same name.

*

In Tel Aviv, on the evening of June 29, David Ben-Gurion addressed a rally of his political supporters, the breakaway Rafi Party. The rebuilding of Jerusalem must be 'at the centre of the national effort', he told them. At least 100,000 Jews should be settled around the Old City, 'especially in the empty areas around Mount Scopus'. Not one Arab resident of Jerusalem would have to be moved, he said. But, making use of the 'unprecedented enthusiasm' created by the Israeli victory, tens of thousands of Jews should be encouraged to come from abroad and to build up Israel, 'especially Jerusalem'. He also urged the 'immediate resettlement' of Jews in the Jewish Quarter of the Old City.

The Jewish Cemetery on the Mount of Olives, which had not only been cut off from Jewish Jerusalem but also much vandalised in the years since 1948, was again to be the burial place of Jews from Jerusalem and all over the world. The first burial there after the 1967 war took place on 13 November 1967. It was of Celina Sassoon, whose family plot lay just below the Jerusalem-Jericho road; a road that, when widened by the Jordanians in 1966, had been driven through many tombs.

*

For many of the 199,000 Jews and 66,000 Arabs of Jerusalem, the prospect of cooperation led to hopes for a new and better era. Among the first measures Kollek took – one which the Arabs appreciated – was to give permission for a monument to be erected in the city for the Arab war dead. Some of Kollek's city councillors disapproved: 'Where, I was asked, was there a monument for the Germans in France or in England? I explained that the situation was not comparable. The Arabs were living in Jerusalem.'

There was also a dark side to reunification. The following summer bombs went off in several places in West Jerusalem, and several Jews were hurt. 'That same evening,' Kollek recalled of one such incident, 'some young Israelis went on a rampage, turned over an Arab car, and broke an Arab store window. The terrorists almost accomplished what they had set out to achieve: tension between the city's two communities. The next morning Arabs were afraid to come to work and Jews were reluctant to go shopping in Arab stores. That day, Minister of Police Eliahu Sasson and I spent the day walking around from shop to shop, and one café to another to demonstrate that there was nothing to fear. Our appearances helped to diminish the impact of the bombing and stress the theme of co-operation in our city. We also did everything possible to explain to the Jews that violent reaction was just what the terrorists were hoping for.'

*

Jerusalem had not been mentioned in the United Nations Security Council Resolution 242 of 22 November 1967, which sought to reverse the territorial results of the Six-Day War. But both the Israeli reunification of the city, and the building of new Jewish suburbs across the former cease-fire line, were condemned by the international community. Each Israeli action in the city was examined with critical scrutiny by the United Nations, where there was anger on 8 March 1968 when the Israeli military authorities, using a British Mandate regulation, blew up, in Wadi al-Joz, the two-storey house of Kamal Namari, the Jerusalem commander of the Arab bombers, who had been captured the previous month. The explosion was heard throughout the northern part of the city. Due to a mistake in the calculation of the amount of the explosives needed, twenty other dwellings were damaged, as well as a school and an archaeological institute.

Teddy Kollek let it be known that he was distressed at the decision to blow up the house. It was argued by many Jewish Jerusalemites that the military law in use on the occupied West Bank could not apply to Jerusalem, which according to Israel's own assertions was part of Israel. The army accepted this argument, apologised for the damage, sent girl soldiers to give out sweets to the children of Wadi al-Joz, allowed the municipality to clear up the rubble, and paid compensation to the owners of the damaged houses. For the next five years, no more houses were demolished. But the rancour created by the incident could not be easily assuaged.

On 21 May 1968 the Security Council, meeting in New York, passed Resolution 252, stating 'that all legislative and administrative measures and actions taken by Israel, including expropriation of land and properties thereon, which tend to change the legal status of Jerusalem, are invalid and cannot change that status'. The resolution was supported by the United States, Britain and the Soviet Union. It was to be followed by many more. But the Israeli position was not to be changed by critical resolutions. A total of 4,666 acres of Arab-owned land were expropriated beyond the armistice lines, for the building of five substantial new Jewish suburbs, to the north, east and south of the city.

Determined to restore the destroyed Jewish Quarter of the Old City, the Israeli Government set up a Company for the Reconstruction and Development of the Jewish Quarter. Plans were drawn up for residential, commercial and public buildings to enable 650 families to live in the quarter – the same number that had been dispossessed at the time of the Jordanian conquest in 1948. The ground area of the quarter was to be the same as before 1948: thirty acres. Almost every foundation that was dug there revealed some archaeological treasure. Strenuous efforts were made to preserve these, and to make them accessible, or visible. At one point the visitor today can look down a well-lit shaft to see walls dating from biblical times.

*

In October 1968, during the showing of a John Wayne film at the Zion Cinema, someone noticed that two black girls, Nubians from the 200–strong black community in the Muslim Quarter of the Old City, had left the cinema early, leaving a parcel behind. An usher took it out of the cinema, and a policeman ran with it to police headquarters, 200 yards away. It exploded a minute later. 'In the cinema,' Naomi Shepherd recalled, 'the explosions in the last reel had been so deafening that we hardly noticed the thud of the real explosion just down the road.' Fortunately no one was hurt.

In a gesture of defiance to the anonymous bombers, on the following evening the Israeli film star, Uri Zohar, came up to Jerusalem from Tel Aviv and, with other popular figures in the Israeli entertainment world, gave a midnight show at the cinema. 'We made a gala occasion of it,' Kollek recalled. 'In fact, so many thousands came that we had to move the show from the movie house to the square outside. Large crowds stayed until two in the morning as a communal gesture of defiance: we would not be frightened out of going to a movie!'

The two perpetrators of the Zion Cinema bomb were tracked down, and the man who had sent them on their errand was caught with them. He was Omar Audah Khalil, known as 'Dr Nur', who had organised a sabotage group of thirty members. His group was broken up, but others survived, and the Zion Cinema bomb was followed by another a year later, on November 22, in the Mahane Yehuda Jewish open-air market on the Jaffa Road. Twelve people were killed, all Jerusalemites, including two Arabs. Fifty-three people were injured. The bomb, placed in a car, had been parked outside a barber's shop. Among the dead were forty-year-old Yisrael Schnitzer, who had been having his hair cut, and twenty-five-year-old Rami Cohen, one of the barber's assistants. One of the Arabs killed was seventy-one-year-old Sabri Hassan Mustafa Zaanin, from Wadi al-Joz; the other Arab was a young boy.

The Jerusalem Arab newspaper *al-Kuds* condemned the killings. 'The explosion shook not only the foundation of the city,' its editorial insisted, 'but the conscience of every inhabitant of the town, Arab and Jew, who desires peace and hates the killing of innocent people.'

More explosions were to follow, however, over the following three years, and more deaths, stirring anti-Arab feeling among the Jews. The municipality did its best to curb this. But Arab extremists had decided to register their hatred of the occupying power. On one occasion a rocket was fired from the Judaean Desert into West Jerusalem. A home was damaged, but no one was hurt. In the streets of West Jerusalem, vigilance replaced carefree strolling. 'We got used to looking out for unattended parcels and unexpected letters,' Naomi Shepherd wrote, 'and to opening handbags for inspection at cinemas and theatres.'

*

In 1969 the Security Council met again to discuss the various Israeli measures in East Jerusalem, both in the Jewish Quarter and in the outer suburbs. The United States representative, Ambassador Charles W. Yost, spoke critically of what Israel had done in the city. 'The expropriation or confiscation of land,' he said, 'the construction of housing on such land, the demolition or confiscation of buildings, including those having historic or religious significance, and the application of Israeli law to occupied portions of the city are detrimental to our common interests in the city.'

The United States considered that the part of Jerusalem 'that came under the control of Israel in the June War, like other areas occupied by Israel, is occupied territory and hence subject to the provisions of international law governing the rights and obligations of an occupying power. Among the provisions of international law which bind Israel, as they would bind any occupier, are the provisions that the occupier has no right to make changes in laws or in administration other than those which are temporarily necessitated by his security interest, and that an occupier may not confiscate or destroy private property.'

The American Ambassador then explained that the 'pattern of behaviour' authorised under the Geneva Convention and international law was clear: 'the occupier must maintain the occupied area as intact and unaltered as possible, without interfering with the customary life of the area, and any changes must be necessitated by immediate needs of the occupation.' He went on to tell the Security Council: 'I regret to say that the actions of Israel in the occupied portion of Jerusalem present a different picture, one which gives rise to understandable concerns that the eventual disposition of East Jerusalem may be prejudiced and the rights and activities of the population are already being affected and altered.'

The American rebuke to Israel over East Jerusalem was a formidable one. 'My Government regrets and deplores this pattern of activity,' said Yost, 'and it has so informed the Government of Israel on numerous occasions since June 1967. We have consistently refused to recognise these measures as having anything but a provisional character and do not accept them as affecting the ultimate status of Jerusalem.'

The Ambassador concluded that a 'just and lasting' peace in the Middle East 'will not be found through terror bombings, which inevitably harm innocent civilians, any more than through unilateral attempts to alter the status of Jerusalem. It will be found only through the instruments and processes of negotiation, accommodation and agreement. It will come only through the exercise by the parties of the utmost restraint, not just along the cease-fire lines or in public statements, but also on the ground in Jerusalem itself.'

Israel did not accept the premise of Ambassador Yost's proposal, at the end of his Security Council speech, 'to request the parties to lay aside their recriminations, to desist from any action, in Jerusalem or elsewhere, that might be construed as prejudicing or prejudging a final, comprehensive settlement of a just and lasting peace.' If the words 'any action' meant, as they were intended to mean, the building of new Jewish suburbs beyond the Green Line, or the rebuilding of the destroyed Jewish Quarter of the Old City, these would go on. No resolution in New York, even when supported by the United States, could halt it.

Israel had no intention of halting the creation of Jewish suburbs beyond the Green Line, arguing that the Green Line was no more than the point at which the armies had ceased firing in 1949, that it had no demographic or urban significance, and that a city could not be condemned never to grow. Jews wished to live in Jerusalem, attracted by the work and the climate, and did not see why they could not expand the Jewish suburbs of the city on hillsides which were empty of all building. Almost every new Jewish suburb was being built on non-arable, stony wasteland. Some land was, however, expropriated from its Arab owners, and some Arab houses found themselves cut off from the Arab suburbs of which they had been a part by the new Jewish houses.

In the building of one of the new suburbs, East Talpiot, several acres of orchards and cultivated land belonging to the Arab village of Sur Bahir were expropriated. This created great anger, which was to intensify when, as East Talpiot continued to grow, yet more cultivated land was taken. Other than the houses that were knocked down in front of the Wailing Wall, however, few Arab houses were being expropriated – unlike in 1948, when the Arab residential areas of West Jerusalem had been taken over by Israel in their entirety and several thousand Arab houses had been given to Jews.

The Arab suburbs of East Jerusalem were also able to expand after 1967, and did expand considerably. The road running north from French Hill became a continuous belt of Arab houses, some of them of considerable size and prominence, as far north as the airport at Kalandia. At the same time, the municipality was committed to improving Arab urban services, most of which had been greatly neglected under Jordanian rule.

For the Arabs of Jerusalem, the sight of the new Israeli building was ominous. As the suburbs of Ramat Eshkol, French Hill, Gilo and East Talpiot were under construction, each being built beyond the Green Line, and each on high ground, they were clearly part of a deliberate plan to encircle the city with a ring of building, to surround it, and, by creating facts on the ground, to strengthen the case for Israeli sovereignty throughout Jerusalem. Although the Arab suburbs were also growing, the initiative lay with Israel. No month passed without Arab protests. On the 'Night of the Grenades', 18 August 1968, sixty-nine Israeli soldiers, women and children were injured when grenades were thrown at buses bringing celebrants to a recruiting swearing-in ceremony at the Wailing Wall.

Teddy Kollek called on the heads of the Arab community to denounce such acts of terror, but they refused to do so. The grenade attack was followed by strikes and shop closures, culminating in a general commercial strike that began on Balfour Day, November 2.

Many Arab shopkeepers stood in front of their shuttered stores, telling passers-by: 'We've been forced to join this strike, but please come back tomorrow.' After the first day's closure, however, the Israeli army confiscated fifteen shops in retaliation, and as a deterrent. But however strong might be the Arab desire to trade, hostility to the occupation of East Jerusalem could not be assuaged.

Teddy Kollek made every effort to draw Arabs into the work of his extended municipality. Some, like Sami Mustaklim, remained in their former positions: Mustaklim had been head of the East Jerusalem fire brigade. The former Town Clerk of East Jerusalem, Salah a-Din Jarallah, was appointed Assistant Town Clerk of the wider municipality. The former East Jerusalem City Engineer, Yousef Budeiry, became Deputy City Engineer, and Mohammed Zuatier was appointed Assistant Director of the crucial water-supply department.

Several hundred East Jerusalemites were employed in the different municipal departments. The streets of the Old City were paved, more than 1,000 street lamps were erected, new saplings were planted in municipal gardens, new waste-removal equipment was supplied, and water pipes were laid at such a rapid rate that an average of fifty Arab houses were connected to the municipal water system every week.

Like East Jerusalem, West Jerusalem was also reviving in the aftermath of the war. The former border areas were no longer at risk from sniper fire, or disfigured by coils of barbed wire and the adjacent ruins of 1948. Yemin Moshe, which had once been prosperous but had fallen on hard times as a border area, was transformed into a leafy residential area. Just below the Jaffa Gate, Jorat al-Anab, which before 1948 had been the home of poor Sephardic Jews and Muslim and Christian Arabs, was restored. Craftsmen arrived to take up residence in the new shops. In 1969 the Israeli silversmith and gemologist Gideon Flanter was one of the first. Slowly, as with so much in Jerusalem, the area, now known as Khutsot Ha-Yotser (Arts and Crafts Lane) began to flourish. Twenty-five years later the annual Arts and Crafts Fair was to be held here, a focal point of city life, resplendent with displays of every type of artist's work.

The most difficult work of restoration was the Jewish Quarter of the Old City. Visiting the quarter in 1968 a British traveller, Colin Thubron, wrote: 'I met a Jewish girl there, who had known the quarter as a child before 1948. She walked in confidence – a girl of barbarian beauty – speaking of streets where I saw only rubble, remembering houses, synagogues and friends. Here and there a Hebrew notice hung on a locked door, telling whose home it had been, and whose it would be again. "The people will come back," said the girl. "It will be built again as it was. It is part of our soul." '

Thubron also visited the venerable Palestinian nationalist leader Arif al-Arif, who had been the Mayor of the city in Jordanian times. 'Jerusalem was his passion,' Thubron wrote, 'his native city.' Al-Arif told him: 'In the 1948 war Jerusalem suffered more than any other place. Even in this last war four hundred were killed. It is a hard place. Bitter. There is little water and not much arable land. Yet people have to live. They cannot fill their stomachs with religion.' Thubron noted: 'He stabbed with his fingers, as if pinning down the truth as it flew by.' 'This is why Moslems here are sometimes austere,' al-Arif continued. 'They rarely drink and you don't hear much music. There is scarcely a prostitute in the place and a few women still wear the veil. I think we are more temperate too in our loves and hates. It is said we have *Helem* (patience), that we are not excitable. But we are desperately devoted. Scarcely anybody emigrates. Whereas in Bethlehem and Ramallah for instance . . . half Ramallah is in America!'

'Those who leave Jerusalem,' Thubron said, 'must feel they're leaving the centre of the world.' 'The *Sakhra*, yes – the rock beneath the Dome – this is the world's centre,' replied al-Arif. 'We say that *al-Yom* – the Last Day – will be inaugurated there; that Jerusalem will be a part of *al-Aher*, of paradise. It has been promised, and may God will it.' Al-Arif's fingers struck down at the table with force, as he declared: 'There's an irony for you! Jerusalem a paradise!'

*

May 1968 saw the twentieth anniversary of the founding of the State of Israel. Colin Thubron was in the city that day, observing the local customs. 'The streets of West Jerusalem,' he wrote, 'burst into gorges of light where the crowd's heads moved in congested thousands under tinselled discs suspended from the houses, or were swept into dancing to the lilt of accordions. The young spirit of the nation was pulsing through the streets in jeans and Victory hats, natural and exuberant as a new Rome with Hannibal retreated from the gates. Everyone held a plastic hammer which uttered a blink-blink as he hit his neighbour on the head. The strange music had a touch of the East. Fireworks left their smoke like cobwebs on the stars. I went back to East Jerusalem. Its battlements were lit, but behind the walls was a profound silence – the Arab city lost in sleepless gloom – only the lamps' gilding on the lanes, and cats tense and hissing in the dark.

Long afterwards, as dawn spread, I could still hear singing outside the walls, and the chatter of the hammers.'

*

Increased trade, growing prosperity, the continual efforts by the municipality under Teddy Kollek to improve the quality of life in East Jerusalem: all suffered frequent setbacks, sometimes by incidents which had nothing to do with Arab-Jewish conflict. One such incident, which had enormous repercussions, took place on 29 August 1969, when a deranged Australian tourist, the twenty-eight-year-old Denis Michael Rohan, a fundamentalist Christian, set fire to the al-Aksa Mosque. Rohan believed that this, the destruction of one of 'Satan's temples', was the first step in a sequence of events that would make him King of Jerusalem and enable 'sweet Jesus' to return and pray in the rebuilt Temple. Rohan started the fire by setting alight the superb twelfth-century cedar-wood pulpit, carved in Aleppo in 1187 and brought to Jerusalem by order of Saladin. The pulpit was destroyed, as was the mosque's dome and ceiling. When Jewish firemen struggled to put out the blaze, Arab women tried to pull the hose away from them, fearing that they were deliberately pouring petrol, not water, on the blaze.

*

'Logically,' wrote Teddy Kollek, 'the Arabs in Jerusalem knew we were in no way responsible. But deep in their hearts they wanted to believe we were. Ultimately they interpreted the al-Aksa incident as divine punishment because the Holy Places were under the control of infidels. The infidels in question happen to be Jews, but it would have been just the same if the British, the UN, or the Pope were ruling Jerusalem.'

Kollek was at a municipal meeting when news reached him that the mosque was ablaze. 'By the time I reached the site, the fire brigade was at work (though stories quickly circulated that the fire brigade was deliberately slow in arriving). The Arabs were trying to put out the blaze with buckets and sentiment, and the scene of the flames, with thousands of Moslems weeping, was heartbreaking. In the afternoon I returned to the mosque with Golda (who was then Prime Minister) and Dayan. Both of them promised help, but their offer was never officially accepted by the Arabs. Nevertheless, all the gifts that came in – marble from Italy and similar donations – were allowed into the country without customs levies and import licences. We also provided cement at a time when there was a severe shortage.'

The repairs to the mosque were expertly done. 'Even ancient crafts have been revived for the purpose,' Kollek wrote, 'particularly the cutting of gypsum windows at a special angle so that when the sun shines through the coloured Hebron glass at various hours, it creates different colour combinations that are of particular beauty. The old man who knew this special craft trained several younger people to work with him, and thus the art is being preserved. However, the occasion was also used to replace Crusader capitals at the mosque by modern copies of Moslem-style capitals, so that any indication of Christian influence would disappear.'

Although the fire had been the work of a madman, an Arab Commission of Investigation found cause to censure the Israelis. 'The occupation authorities, being as they are, cannot escape their security responsibilities. The guardians of the Muslim shrines have no security jurisdiction or function,' the three commissioners, Anwar Nusseibeh, Anwar al-Khatib and Baid Alla al-Adin, concluded. This situation was changed. Following the fire, the Israeli authorities appointed an armed police unit of Muslim, Christian and Jewish police to guard the Haram, commanded, since then, by a Muslim officer. Although at the time of the fire there were no signs of Israeli sovereignty, such as flags or notices, on the fifty-acre Haram, the Israeli Government stressed that none were to be erected in the future.

*

The hopes that Teddy Kollek had of bringing the Arabs of Jerusalem into the municipality as equals and active city administrators were not realised. The morale of the 500 Arab staff members of the municipality was undermined when some dozen Arab employees of the former Jordanian municipality were promised employment but received none. 'The hope, co-operation and enthusiasm vanished, to be replaced by a mood of despair and bitterness,' Gideon Weigert, a reporter on Arab affairs for the *Jerusalem Post*, wrote in 1973.

One reason for the deterioration in the Arab mood, Weigert noted, was a series of small but significant Israeli actions against Arab buildings: the demolishing of houses rented by Arabs in the Jewish Quarter, the Israeli army's seizure of a Muslim religious school to make room for a rabbinical court, the take-over of a Muslim court building to ensure security measures for visitors to the Wailing Wall, and the refusal of the Israeli authorities to consider any restoration of Arab property in West Jerusalem to its pre-1948 owners. East Jerusalemites could visit their former homes, and ask to be shown round them, but there was no mechanism whereby they could seek to return to them.

No Arab stood as a candidate in the October 1969 municipal elections, although a special Israeli law had been passed to enable Arabs to do so. After the elections, in which many Arabs cast their votes for Israeli parties, and especially for Teddy Kollek, a dozen East Jerusalemites were asked if they would serve on municipal committees affiliated to the city council. A number agreed to do so, on condition that their names were kept secret. When their names were leaked to the press, all of them withdrew. They were frightened of reprisals from among their own people.

*

The Arab-Israeli dispute in Jerusalem had its amusing moments. Teddy Kollek later recalled an episode that took place shortly after the 1967 war. A well-known British Lord was visiting Jerusalem with his wife, and Kollek invited them to dinner with several other guests. He later recalled how the Lord's wife, 'who had spent the morning touring Jerusalem and Bethlehem, sat through most of the meal extolling the accomplishments of the Israelis to her dinner partner, whose name she apparently hadn't caught. "How were you able to fight against such odds? How have you managed to build up the city as you have done?" Towards the end of the meal her dinner partner mentioned something about London, prompting her query: "What did you do in London?" Anwar Nusseibeh's reply was simple: "I was Jordanian Ambassador to the Court of St James." '

Fifteen years after reunification, Anwar Nusseibeh expressed to me, in conversation at his East Jerusalem home, his sadness at so much Israeli building in and around the city after 1967. This sadness, he explained, was in part the political dislike of a Palestinian Arab for Israel's efforts to bring more Jewish residents and activities to the city and to extend the Jewish suburbs far across the Green Line, in a half-circle around the Arab sections. It was also in part nostalgia for the days when, under the Mandate, Jerusalem was more modest in size. Teddy Kollek also had nostalgic memories of the much smaller, provincial-style city of Mandate times, but for him there was an element of real and even urgent benefit to all Jerusalem's citizens in what he sought to do: to make Jerusalem a more modern, and, at the same time, a more attractive city.

Kollek's aim was to improve the city for Jews and Arabs alike, and also for the tourists and foreign visitors who, after 1967, began to arrive in ever-increasing numbers. 'Once,' Kollek recalled, 'when I was touring the city with an American columnist, he asked me whether I didn't find all this furious activity a little futile. "At worst", I said, "we are like ants building the most beautiful ant heap that was ever created, and we hope it will continue to exist undisturbed. But who knows? Maybe a man with a stick will come along, poke it into our masterpiece, and part of it will be destroyed. If so, here we are, like ants. And we will build it again and again, as well and as beautifully as we know how." '

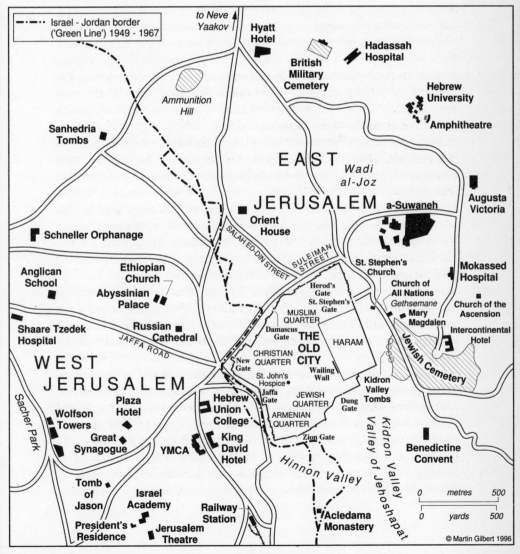

Central Jerusalem

CHAPTER NINETEEN

The Search for Harmony,
1970–1980

The new decade opened in Jerusalem with violence. In the Old City the crowds were busy sightseeing and shopping on the morning of 1 January 1970 when a grenade was thrown at a passing Israeli military jeep in an Arab market near the Church of the Holy Sepulchre. The grenade missed the jeep and exploded in the street. Five Arabs were injured. One of them, Ahmed Mohammed al-Afi, from Silwan, died shortly afterwards of his wounds.

Such incidents always led, briefly, to the closing of shops and the dispersion of tourists in the streets near the attack. But within a few hours the hustle and bustle of the bazaar would return. The mood and demeanour of the Old City remained that of a vibrant market-place, drawing in the visitor by its commercial clamour and babble of tongues. Among the languages heard in the homes and court-yards of the Old City in the 1970s were, most frequently, Arabic, English, Hebrew and French; not infrequently Yiddish, Armenian and German; and in certain streets, from time to time, Turkish, Spanish, Aramaic, Greek, Italian, Coptic, Amharic and Romany. Russian, the language of many recent Jewish newcomers, was also in evidence. In all, twenty-five different 'native tongues' were recorded among the inhabitants of the Old City in the last decade of the twentieth century.

Every guidebook tries to capture the variety of life in Jerusalem. Nitza Rosovsky did so several years after reunification, in her descrip-tion of the square just inside the Jaffa Gate, where she noted 'graceful Arab women in embroidered dresses carrying large baskets on their heads; Hassidic Jews in eighteenth-century Polish garb, sidelocks dangling beneath their *streimels*, the fur hats of the ghetto; bare-headed Franciscan friars in sandals and brown cassocks; elderly Arabs on their way to the coffee house wearing the traditional *tarboosh* or *kaffiyeh*; a few remaining monks from Ethiopia, silent shadows gliding by, cut off from their homeland; Border Patrolmen in green berets, carrying guns, reminders of conflict yet unresolved. And of course the tourists, in groups, in pairs, by themselves.'

Among those who visited Jerusalem in the new decade was the British writer David Pryce-Jones. 'United again,' he wrote, 'Jerusalem becomes its mixed provincial-cosmopolitan self, as it was in the Mandate. Unity – Annexation.' Among those whom Pryce-Jones visited in East Jerusalem was the former Jordanian Governor of the city, Anwar al-Khatib, of whom he wrote: 'He wishes that the Israelis were severe and tyrannical so that the population would rise against them. Arab labourers should not be constructing Israel. The bridges should be closed, the issue should be forced, never mind the misery.'

Walking around East Jerusalem, Pryce-Jones reflected: 'The Rivoli Hotel, the Ritz, the Paradise, Palmyra, the Cleopatra, the names on and around Saladin Street have the touch of absent glamour . . . But at the end of Saladin Street is the Jordanian army building into which the Israeli military government has moved. One or two Israelis are sometimes sitting and joking on its steps. A scruffy rope and a slouching soldier in a helmet bar entry. On the top flies the blue and white flag and it can be glimpsed from the office windows above the pines and low-pitched Jerusalem roofs; it is always in the background and flaps to every passing wind.'

*

Each visitor to Jerusalem treasures his or her own first memories of the city. Mine date from the summer of 1971. The city was still basking in the unusual situation of unification. My host on my first night was the Viennese-born Israeli writer Amos Elon, one of the pioneers in the moves for Arab-Jewish reconciliation at that time. As a gesture of the new-found spirit of compromise and harmony, he and his wife, Beth, had taken up residence east of the city's Green Line, in a flat attached to the newly built church of St Stephen. This had been constructed in the last year of Jordanian rule just below the Lions' Gate, amid the palms and vines of the Kidron Valley. From the Elons' windows one could look up to the Golden Gate, and down the Kidron Valley to the magnificent south-east corner of the Temple Mount. The Garden of Gethsemane was adjacent to their garden.

Amos and Beth Elon would go shopping in the stores of Arab East

Jerusalem. They would dine in Arab restaurants, and have animated discussions with Arab friends. This seemed the dawn of a new age, a period of reconciliation, the potential of which appeared limitless. But the expectations of those days were soon to be disappointed. The Arabs of East Jerusalem, though many had been discontented under Jordanian rule, were even less eager to embrace the Israeli presence. 'I weep to think of what we imagined then,' Beth Elon commented twenty-five years later. As Mayor of West and East Jerusalem, Teddy Kollek – like Amos Elon, a Viennese-educated Jew of culture and charm – did his utmost to draw the Arabs into his plans and his improvements. But the divide was always there. The breaking-down of the physical barriers in 1967 had not removed it.

The sharp increase in building activity in consequence of the reunification of the city expressed itself most visually in changes in the skyline of West Jerusalem. High-rise buildings were beginning by 1971 to intrude on what had been a silhouette of low-lying buildings moulded to the shape of the ground in a hilly landscape. The Plaza Hotel, against the construction of which public protest had been in vain, blocked out the skyline of the Mount of Olives from part of King George V Avenue. The Wolfson Towers dominated the hitherto pastoral scene of the Sacher Park and the Monastery of the Cross. 'The process which is now beginning to alter Jerusalem's basic form and character', wrote the American architect and town planner Arthur Kutcher in 1973, 'is similar to a process which has been occurring in many other cities throughout the world.' That was indeed true, but there were those for whom the appearance of a growing number of tall blocks of buildings, offices, apartment houses and hotels, thrusting themselves into the West Jerusalem sky, was cause for sadness. In 1973, looking over the western city from the Mount of Olives (itself somewhat disfigured by the hotel built there in the last year of Jordanian rule), Kutcher identified twenty-six high-rise projects.

In 1972 Kutcher had been among those who, with the active support of two British-born architects, David Fields and Mike Turner, both on the staff of the City of Jerusalem Planning Department, led the campaign to stop several high-rise buildings being constructed in West Jerusalem. The main focus of their efforts was a group of eight high-rise residential towers planned for the Omaria Park, just below Talbiyeh, one of which had already been built. On 7 January 1972 the *Jerusalem Post* reported a meeting of indignant citizens who started collecting signatures for 'action committees' against the Omaria project. Kutcher later recalled: 'Public action had begun. It was concerted and passionate. Thousands of cards and letters were sent to officials. A demonstration was held with school children planting trees on the site of the proposed towers. A press and television campaign was undertaken. In the face of this vigorous action, the official plans simply withered away. The scheme for the additional towers was dropped and the area is for the present at least to remain open.'

The public coalition which had achieved this 'remarkable success', Kutcher wrote, 'was an improbable mixture of left-wing students and right-wing extremists, new immigrants and veteran residents, religious fanatics and atheists, solid citizens and eccentric artists. Ultimately the coalition came to include Jews and Arabs. It was in fact a cross-section of the city's population mosaic, and was motivated by the one force which unites all of Jerusalem's divergent communities: a clear and powerful awareness of her special quality.' Kollek had also been unhappy at the way in which commercial interests, the search for high rents, and the pressures of building space, had led to the upward thrust of so many new buildings.

The public's Omaria protest had been successful. It was followed by two more: one against a twenty-two-storey annexe to the King David Hotel, the other against a twenty-three-storey Hyatt Hotel on the lower slopes of Mount Scopus. As a result of these public protests both the King David and Hyatt high-rises were abandoned, the owner of the King David telling the *Jerusalem Post* on 1 September 1972: 'I wouldn't rest quietly in my grave if people said I ruined Jerusalem.' In the two decades since then the municipality made strenuous efforts to prevent further high structures. Some, nevertheless, were built, including an ugly bank building at the bottom of Ben Yehuda Street that dwarfs part of the precinct area beneath it and can be seen, one Jerusalemite declared, 'from London'.

The high-rise issue, together with the increase in building activity, and the opportunity offered by reunification to create a unified city plan, stimulated the debate over town planning for Jerusalem. This debate was an intense one, on the need to balance the historical, traditional and spiritual interests of the city with the demands of a modern urban scene in which, as in every city in the world, the motor car was becoming the personal means of transport of more and more citizens. Before 1967 a master plan had been devised for West Jerusalem by three Israeli planners, the brothers Arieh and Zion Hashimshony, and Joseph Schweid. When the city was reunited they extended their plan to include East Jerusalem. It was published in 1968. A dominant feature was the road system, accepting the supremacy of the motor car and the need for fast roads, by-passes, intersections and all the paraphernalia of a modern European or American city.

It was clearly possible to bulldoze the ground to make way for a grandiose scheme, should one be approved. Among several old buildings demolished and cleared away for modern development after 1967 were the Alliance Israelite Universelle vocational school on the Jaffa Road, built in 1882, and the Talitha Kumi Monastery on King George V Avenue (I remember wandering through the empty rooms of this lovely building just before it was levelled to the ground). Unattractive multi-storey commercial buildings now stand on both sites.

After long discussions, in 1972 the Hashimshony-Schweid plan was submitted by Teddy Kollek to a specially constituted Jerusalem Committee, consisting of leading town planners, architects and scholars from all over the world – though not from the Arab world, whose town planners declined to participate. These experts, asked to consider the place of Jerusalem in the world as well as on paper, threw the plan out in its entirety. Teddy Kollek then decided to invite an international figure to head the city's Planning Department and to prepare a new plan from scratch. A distinguished British town planner, Nathaniel Lichfield, himself a Jew, was made Chief City Planner in mid-1972. He and his staff sought to reconcile the special needs of Jerusalem with the demands of accelerating modernity. Under the new form of planning, Lichfield later explained, 'the spirit and structure of Jerusalem would dominate everything'.

At a meeting of the Jerusalem Committee on 20 June 1973, Lichfield, after noting that there were as many as forty 'big projects' under consideration in the central area of the city, declared: 'Jerusalem is a big building camp at the moment.' The Jerusalem public, he added, had become 'terribly aware of what is going on in this city. They are very concerned. They want it to be a fine city.' Eagerly, he presented his approach to the new plan, and his emerging proposals, planning systems and philosophy. He was warmly received and supported. But the decision to accept his ideas was never made, and no master plan was adopted. The baton then passed to Joseph Schweid, who had been Lichfield's deputy. But again the search for a master plan came to naught: Jerusalem is still (in 1996) without one, and remains subject to the whims of changing and political desires.

'Jerusalem planning was a scene of many fatalities,' Lichfield reflected twenty years later. 'I was but one of a series of figures who came and went.' A leading Jerusalem architect, the Danish-born

Ulrich Plevsner, some of whose planning schemes are among the most impressive in Israel, was appointed City Architect. 'He lasted six months,' noted Lichfield, 'but was ignored.' Also ignored was one of Lichfield's own staff, the Czech-born Berthy Hofnung, who had earlier worked in Britain on the problem of traffic in towns under the British expert Professor Sir Colin Buchanan. Hofnung wanted to constrain the number of vehicles on any given road in Jerusalem to its environmental capacity, by not funnelling too many cars through the centre of the city, and not building ring roads and by-pass roads through what were still essentially rural areas on the periphery. His aim was to design the road aspects of the master plan accordingly. He prepared a scheme, but it got no further than the Lichfield ideas of which it was a part.

Most cities in the world can continue their town-planning discussions, and all their social and cultural debates, in relatively uninterrupted leisure, if there is no war. But, for the fourth time in three decades, war returned to Israel in 1973, disrupting the calm and normality of life in Jerusalem. On 6 October 1973 the State of Israel was attacked simultaneously by the armies of Egypt and Syria, when Egyptian forces crossed the Suez Canal, and Syrian forces broke into the Golan Heights. The date chosen for this attack was Yom Kippur, the Day of Atonement – the most solemn date in the Jewish calendar. In West Jerusalem, as throughout the country, the news that Israel had been attacked became known while many people were in synagogue, at prayer and fasting. Call-up notices were brought to people while they were praying. A few minutes after 2 o'clock, as people hurried home, the air-raid siren sounded. Half an hour later, Israel Radio broke its traditional Yom Kippur silence, to announce that the siren had not been a false alarm, and that when it went again, everyone should go to the air-raid shelters in their basements. Nothing was said on the radio of any attack. The transmission continued with music, including Beethoven's 'Moonlight' Sonata. Then, an hour and a half later, an announcer came on to say that Egypt and Syria had attacked, and that partial mobilisation had been instituted. For the rest of the afternoon the radio broadcast coded mobilisation instructions. Throughout the city, men and women changed into their uniforms and hurried off to report to their military units.

That night, with the moon illuminating Jerusalem like a floodlight, many citizens feared a Jordanian attack across the river Jordan. A blackout was in force. Only the lights of the Arab suburbs twinkled in the clear, still night. Cars drove with masked headlights.

*

The bright moon seemed an invitation to the Jordanians to try to regain the lost land between the city and the Jordan, and perhaps to reach the city itself. No such attack came. But for twenty-four hours the city, virtually undefended as the battles raged far to the south and north, was in a highly nervous state.

Within a few days there was mourning in many Jerusalem households, as news came in of heavy casualties, and of many deaths, in the Sinai and on the Golan Heights. One of the most harrowing tasks in the city, at a time when all official vehicles had been commandeered for military purposes, and most postmen had been mobilised, was to drive schoolchildren volunteers, with telegrams announcing the deaths of soldiers in action, to the homes of bereaved parents. I was one of those drivers.

*

After three weeks of fighting, the war of October 1973 came to an end. Israel had beaten off the attacks but at a heavy cost in life and morale. Following the war, a series of discussions initiated by the Arab States at the United Nations repeatedly condemned Israeli actions in Jerusalem. These condemnations were regularly supported by the world's three most populous nations – the Soviet Union, China and India – as well as by almost all the Third World, some diplomats of which, as I later learned from personal experience, could not even locate Israel on the map. One area of condemnation concerned the archaeological excavations which Israel had initiated inside the Old City. Quite overlooked was the fact that, before 1967, considerable archaeological work had been done in East Jerusalem by the distinguished British archaeologist Kathleen Kenyon, who had uncovered some of the oldest of the Jewish walls in David's City, just south of the Temple Mount, and had also excavated inside the Old City, at the Muristan and the Armenian Gardens. Her impressive work had never been condemned.

On 7 November 1974 the United Nations Educational, Scientific and Cultural Organisation – UNESCO – condemned the Government of Israel for what it described as 'altering the cultural and historical character' of Jerusalem by its excavations at Muslim and Christian sites. These Israeli excavations had already been the subject of a UNESCO inquiry, but the result of that inquiry, conducted by a Belgian professor, Raymond Lemaire, was ignored. According to

Lemaire: 'The excavations are being carried out by a perfectly well-qualified team of experts of various kinds, who are extremely attentive to all aspects and to all the periods of which remains have been found on the site.' In answer to Muslim criticisms, Lemaire wrote: 'The same care is expended on the preservation of remains of the Ommayad palaces as on those of the Herodian period.'

During the excavations just inside the wall of the Jewish Quarter of the Old City, the Israeli archaeologist Benjamin Mazar had uncovered not only a large Herodian house, dating back to the time of the Second Temple two thousand years earlier, but also several previously unrecorded Muslim buildings from the very first period of Muslim rule in Jerusalem, from AD637. These historic Muslim remains were preserved as carefully as the Herodian ones, as were the Christian churches, and an impressive crusader street, uncovered at the same time.

*

Israeli rule continued to rankle among the city's Arabs, for whom East Jerusalem remained a city under occupation. Despite the efforts of Teddy Kollek to improve and extend municipal services, extremism never died, and when it re-emerged it did so with terrible consequences. On 4 July 1975 a refrigerator was left outside a shop in Zion Square. When it exploded, forty-five minutes later, fourteen people were killed in the blast and more than seventy people were wounded.

Among the dead in Zion Square were a Jewish couple visiting Jerusalem from Eilat, Meir and Rosa Zimmerman, and their nine-year-old daughter Ahava. A thirty-four-year-old social worker, Mira Berger, was also killed. She worked at the Hadassah Hospital, and was specially trained in preparing relatives of terminal patients to cope with death. Another of those killed was Naziha Mohammed Hamed, a twenty-five-year-old Arab girl from Wadi al-Joz, who was in West Jerusalem with her sister and her aunt to buy a bridal dress for her wedding the following week. Her sister, Arib Hamed Abu Khadija, had come from Jordan for the wedding. Both she and the girl's aunt, Fatima Moussa Hamed, were also killed.

Through a spokesman in Cairo, the Palestinian Liberation Organisation claimed responsibility for the bomb. Its self-styled Jerusalem Committee, headed by Mustafa Liftawi and Mahmoud Aloul, had masterminded this attack. In the nearby suburb of Musrara, a group of Jews tried to attack Arab passers-by, but were dispersed by the police, using water hoses. Visiting the scene in Zion Square, Teddy Kollek asked the citizens of Jerusalem 'to show patience towards the Arab residents of the city'. Two days after the bomb the *Jerusalem Post* commented: 'Jerusalem has suffered much through the decades and shown astonishing resilience. It was no different with Friday's death machine.'

Among those most sympathetic to Arab needs in Jerusalem was Meron Benvenisti, the Deputy Mayor, who had been appointed by Kollek 'administrator of the eastern sector' of the city after the 1967 war. Benvenisti worked with great energy to create fair and decent conditions for the Arab population, and was often criticised by right-wing members of the municipality for his sympathetic attitudes. 'There is no place which arouses such deep, fanatical feelings as does Jerusalem. The city's atmosphere nurtures an exclusive possessiveness,' he wrote in May 1976, in the introduction to his account of his stewardship. 'There is no other place where one feels the tragedy of two nations fighting for their homeland more than in Jerusalem. This is the only place in the world today where Jews and Arabs live side by side, and where the struggle is a real, everyday occurrence and not an abstraction. He who decides to judge between the two sides must remember that only in fairy tales is one side all good and the other all bad.'

Benvenisti added. 'I belong to a nation fighting for its soul, and its soul is Jerusalem. I identify with my nation's longing for Jerusalem. I, too, experienced the transcendental experience of our return to the holiest of our places. At the same time, I am a son of this city and know the meaning of a son's love for it. I cannot, and will not, forget the love, which is as strong as my own, of the Arab residents of Jerusalem for this city. In the light of this tragic conflict, which has racked Jerusalem during the past generation, an observer longs for catharsis, for an end to the damaging myths spread by both sides, and for the transformation of the love that both sides have for this city into a uniting, rather than a dividing, force. Right now, this is only wishful thinking, but perhaps past experiences will help to bring about its realisation.'

Benvenisti dedicated his book 'to all Jerusalemites who pray for the mending of this torn city.'

*

In the nature of the historical narrative, it is the tearing and the suffering and the killing that constantly intrude on the description of the city's life, scarring each decade, and each year, with some ugly scene that darkens the page and tarnishes the memory. But the nature of life in Jerusalem can also be utterly pleasing. It is a city in which musicians and writers, poets and painters, seek, and sometimes find inspiration. In the old Montefiore Houses, built in the 1860s for poor Jews who wished to live outside the insanitary clutter of the Old City, and restored after 1967, the Jerusalem Foundation provides visitors with a haven of peace. Among those who came there, watching each night the golden glow of the setting sun on the Ottoman walls, and busy with paints or pens, were the painter R. J. Kitaj and his wife, Sandra Fisher, who painted a magnificent canvas, *Kitaj in Jerusalem*. Erich Segal, author of *Love Story*, wrote his novel *Acts of Faith* while staying there. Herman Wouk did the research for his two volumes on the history of Israel, *The Hope* and *The Glory*. Saul Bellow wrote a reflective volume, *To Jerusalem and Back*.

Creativity is prized. Yet even amid creativity there is a sense of danger. 'The city is a modern city with modern utilities,' Saul Bellow wrote after his visit in 1975, at the time of the Zion Square bomb. 'You shop in supermarkets, you say good morning to friends on the telephone, you hear symphony orchestras on the radio. But suddenly the music stops and a terrorist bomb is reported. A new explosion outside a coffee shop on the Jaffa Road: six young people killed and thirty-eight more wounded. Pained, you put down your civilised drink. Uneasy, you go out to your civilised dinner. Bombs are exploding everywhere. Dynamite has been thrown in London; the difference is that when a bomb goes off in a West End restaurant the fundamental right of England to exist is not in dispute. Here you sit at dinner with a charming host in a dining room like any other. You know that your hostess has lost a son; that her sister lost children in the 1973 war; that in this Jerusalem street, coolly sweet with night flowers and dark green under the lamps, many other families have lost children. And on the Jaffa Road, because of another bomb, six adolescents – two on a break from night school – stopping at a coffee shop to eat buns, have just died.'

*

Below the Montefiore Houses lies the Hinnom Valley, otherwise known as Gehenna, where in pre-biblical times the believers in Moloch would sacrifice their children. Inside the rock caverns, the tombs of antiquity, Saul Bellow peered. 'Now truck fenders are rusting there,' he wrote, 'the twentieth century adding its crumbling metal to the great Jerusalem dust mixture.' Like almost all visitors, Bellow also went to the Via Dolorosa. He was accompanied by an Israeli friend. Ten years earlier no Israeli would have been allowed to accompany him. After 1967, however, the Israeli Government, unlike its Jordanian predecessor, allowed unrestricted access to the Holy Places to people of all faiths, from all lands, and refrained from interference in Christian and Muslim places of worship. Nevertheless, one of the main and repeated condemnations of Israel at the United Nations during the twenty years after reunification concerned the Holy Places.

On 10 November 1976 the United Nations Security Council issued a Consensus Statement, supported by the United States, the Soviet Union and Britain, which warned Israel 'that any act or profanation of the Holy Places, religious buildings and sites, or any encouragement of, or connivance at, any such act, may seriously endanger international peace and security'. Ironically, the first Israeli interference with worship in Jerusalem was made against the Jews, whom the Israeli authorities prevented from praying on the Haram, in deference to Muslim sensitivities. When a group of young Jews tried, in defiance of regulations, to pray on the Haram in 1976, arguing that it was the Temple Mount sacred to Jews, they were arrested by the Arab police there and brought to trial.

The magistrate found in favour of the young men and asserted that Jews had 'an inherent right' to pray in what is also the holiest of Jewish sites. Despite a statement by the Israeli Minister of Police, negating the magistrate's ruling by forbidding Jewish prayer on the Mount, there were serious Arab demonstrations throughout the Old City. Then the Israel High Court, to which the magistrate's original ruling had been submitted, overruled the magistrate's decision. Since then, Jews seeking to pray on the Mount are turned back, or removed, by the police.

*

On 19 November 1977 both East and West Jerusalem were electrified by the arrival in Israel of the Egyptian President, Anwar Sadat. His was a totally unexpected mission to make peace with Israel – the first breach in the thirty-year-long, much-publicised determination of the Arab States to destroy Israel altogether. His only previous visit to Jerusalem had been in 1955, when, as Secretary-General of the Muslim Congress, an organisation vehemently opposed to the Israeli presence in the city, he had spent several days in Jordanian East Jerusalem.

The first day of Sadat's 1977 visit fell on the Muslim Id al-Adha, the Feast of the Sacrifice. As there were ferocious protests throughout the Arab world at Sadat's visit, in particular from the Palestine Liberation Organisation, the Israeli authorities decided that Muslim worshippers would not be allowed to attend prayers at al-Aksa that day, for fear of violence. Sadat, who had expressed a keen desire to pray in the mosque, would have to pray alone.

Protocol required President Sadat to be accompanied by an Israeli aide-de-camp. The man chosen was Colonel Menahem Milson, a Hebrew University professor who had become head of the Military Government on the West Bank and was fluent in Arabic. 'I saw myself as the representative', Milson later wrote, 'of Israel's students of Arabic and Islamic culture who for decades had immersed themselves in the literature and history of Israel's Arab neighbours, hoping that their knowledge would somehow help build bridges of peace and understanding.' Milson persuaded the authorities to allow 2,000 Arabs known to be in favour of Sadat's initiative to enter the Haram and to pray in the mosque with the Egyptian leader.

During his three days in Jerusalem, Sadat stayed at the King David Hotel. Before setting off for the al-Aksa mosque on the morning of November 20, he performed a private prayer in his room. At the Haram he was met by several Palestinian Muslim dignitaries, among them the Chief Kadi, Sheikh Hilmi al-Muhtasib; the former Jordanian District Governor, Anwar al-Khatib; and the chief custodian of the Haram mosques, Mustafa al-Ansari.

Milson later recalled: 'The worshippers welcomed Sadat with shouts of "Long live the hero of peace" and "We'd give our lives for you, Sadat." I could see Sadat's face light up and congratulated myself on having arranged for Muslim worshippers to be present. A small boy of about ten managed to sneak in uninvited and he ran along Sadat's procession jeering: "Some hero! Some President!" He was quickly chased out. If Sadat heard him, he gave no sign. I prayed he did not.'

From the Haram, Sadat went to the Church of the Holy Sepulchre. There, rival Ethiopian and Egyptian Coptic priests, who have been in dispute for many generations over their respective jurisdictions inside the church, put their grievances before their distinguished visitor. The Egyptian Copts naturally hoped for a preferential judgement. 'Sadat's face as he listened to them showed only impatience,' Milson recalled, 'and little interest in the centuries-old dispute.'

Later that day Sadat went to the Knesset, laid a wreath at the monument to the Israeli war dead, and addressed the Knesset, where he received five ovations. He then held a joint press conference with the Israeli Prime Minister, Menachem Begin, in West Jerusalem's spacious Jerusalem Theatre, and visited Yad Vashem, the Holocaust memorial in the west of the city. There he signed the visitors' book with the words 'May God guide our steps towards peace. Let us end all suffering for mankind.' In a series of talks in the King David Hotel between Sadat and Begin, a political settlement was outlined, the first between Israel and any of its four Arab neighbours.

*

Violence in Jerusalem did not cease with Sadat's visit, even though a peace treaty was subsequently signed between Israel and Egypt, and the armies facing each other in the Sinai were withdrawn. On 29 June 1978 an Arab terrorist bomb in the Mahane Yehuda market in West Jerusalem killed two people and injured thirty-seven. The bomb had been hidden in a box of fruit and placed under a fruit stall. The two people killed were a worker in the market, the twenty-four-year-old Shimon Haim ('Life'), and an eighty-year-old shopper, Zvi Hirsch Goldberg. The Palestine News Agency in Beirut announced that the bomb had been placed there by a member of the Palestine Liberation Organisation. Visiting the market shortly after the explosion, Teddy Kollek declared: 'The world must know that nothing will deter us from working for a unified Jerusalem, neither terrorist bombs nor the refusal of nations to recognise unification.'

The German Foreign Minister, Hans-Dietrich Genscher, who was visiting Jerusalem at the time of the explosion, was one of the first to go to City Hall and extend his condolences to the Mayor.

*

A physical transformation had taken place in Jerusalem in the decade since the Six-Day War. It was a transformation which began slowly, but it was visible to all the city's inhabitants by 1979. That year Yael Guiladi wrote in her book *One Jerusalem*: 'From an enclave which for many led only to Heaven; a town whose western half was blocked from north, south and east, cutting it off from its natural hinterland; a site that was militarily insecure; a city whose life was lived as a small, peripheral appendage of a country which, in Israel's case, helped support its existence artificially, and in Jordan's, left it to stagnate; a place that went to bed early and from which one "escaped" to Tel Aviv or to Amman – Jerusalem has acquired the air of a thriving metropolis with all its attendant advantages. Needless to say, every section of the population has benefited from this prodigious development of Israel's capital. From all over the world tourists flock to it, some for the pleasure of contemplating its beauty now that the scars of its division have been healed, its monuments restored, its parks replanted and its past revealed, others for religious reasons now that complete freedom of worship is guaranteed them. But in fact most of them come for a combination of both, for in Jerusalem the secular and the religious remain inseparable.'

*

Population growth demanded much new building, both Jewish and Arab, even if there was no master plan to control or direct it. The Muslim Arab population, which was slightly above 60,000 in 1967, reached 92,000 in 1979, with several Arab suburbs, notably the northern suburb of Shuafat, growing considerably. The Christian Arab population, which under Jordanian rule had declined to less than 11,000, rose again to just over 12,000. The Jewish population, for which several substantial new suburbs had been built beyond the Green Line, grew most rapidly of all, from just under 200,000 to more than a quarter of a million.

Although there was no master plan for the expanding city, there was still one dominant political guideline for all Israeli building beyond the Green Line: that the new Jewish suburbs would be constructed in such a way as to create as unbroken a circle as possible of Jewish buildings. The blocks of flats constructed at French Hill, to the north of the city, in East Talpiot to the east and in Gilo to the south were tall, packed closely together, dominating the hilltops on which they stood. In each case, smaller Arab villages lay on the slopes opposite them across shallow valleys.

In June 1979 the then City Engineer, Amnon Niv, wrote with candour: 'Ours is a pluralistic city of Jews, Arabs and Christians, of the well-do-do and the indigent, of secular and orthodox. It is difficult to find unanimity or general agreement among them all as to various problems of planning and implementation. There are many personal philosophies and conflicts of interest, making it difficult to satisfy all equally.'

Individual architects worked to create harmonious, low-lying buildings, including the Hebrew Union College, not far from the

Jaffa Gate, and, in a later decade, the Supreme Court. Most ambitious of all, a compact and substantial neighbourhood was being created in the Jewish Quarter of the Old City, from the rubble of the houses and synagogues destroyed in 1948, revitalising an area which had been desolate for nineteen years.

The rebuilding of the Jewish Quarter took more than a decade. As it progressed, further incredible archaeological discoveries were made, including a Hasmonean wall dating from 135BC, and the basement of a house burnt by the Romans in AD70, complete with a spear and the skeletal arm of a young woman who was apparently unable to escape when the house went up in flames. Also discovered, by workmen preparing the foundations of one of the houses to be rebuilt, was a Byzantine church from the time of the Emperor Justinian.

The most spectacular architectural find came during the construction of a new commercial centre in the Old City in 1976. Archaeologists led by Professor Nachman Avigad unearthed part of a monumental arcaded street of shops and columns. This was the sixth-century Cardo, as depicted in the Byzantine mosaic map in the Jordanian town of Madaba. Following the peace treaty between Israel and Jordan signed in 1994, Jewish Jerusalemites can visit, in the course of a single morning if they wish, both the street itself and the mosaic on which it is depicted; for the mosaic is in a church only thirty miles to the east, across the river Jordan.

CHAPTER TWENTY

From Annexation to Intifada, 1980–1989

In 1980 the Arabs of Jerusalem constituted 27 per cent of the total population, the Jews 73 per cent. This balance was changing further in favour of the Jews, as the expansion of Jewish suburbs across the former Green Line continued. In March 1980 the Israeli Government, which since 1977 had been led by the Likud leader Menachem Begin, expropriated more than 500 acres of Arab-owned land just to the east of the Ramallah road, on the edge of the Judaean Desert. The few Arab houses there were to be left undisturbed, but the unbuilt-on land was to be used, Begin explained, to build a substantial Jewish suburb on the eastern slope. This would link the existing Jewish suburb of Neve Yaakov, which had itself been built beyond the Green Line after 1967, with the equally new Jewish suburb on French Hill.

The new houses would create a belt of Jewish urban habitation to the east of the Arab suburb of Shuafat. Teddy Kollek opposed the plan, saying that it could only 'unduly exacerbate tensions between Jews and Arabs'. His protest was in vain. A decade later, a large Jewish suburb, Pisgat Zeev, was in place on the ridge, and still expanding.

The Israeli Government did not intend to stop at new building. On 22 July 1980, in a move which created instant international protest, the Knesset voted by ninety-nine votes to fifty-one to annex East Jerusalem. 'Jerusalem, complete and undivided, is the capital of Israel,' the Jerusalem Bill began. One of its clauses read: 'State institutions shall grant special economic, financial and other priorities to the development of Jerusalem.'

Within ten days the bill had been turned into law. A critical leading article in the *New York Times* was headed 'Capital Folly in Jerusalem'. The article itself called the law 'gratuitous and provocative', and commented: 'A final peace may one day provide for a symbolic sharing of sovereignties in Jerusalem, and define rights of access to the holy shrines of three religions. But that is for the end of the peace process, when passions have been cooled by the vision of a new future. To play upon these passions now is reckless.' In a letter to the London *Daily Telegraph*, Abba Eban, a former Israeli Foreign Minister, and one of the fifty-one parliamentarians who had withheld their support for the bill, pointed out in favour of the unity of the city under Israel that 'the modern international system is a system of States, and Jerusalem has to be governed by someone. No historic imagination should be affronted by the idea that the responsibility has come to repose upon the people that gave Jerusalem its original fame and its universal resonance.'

The formal Israeli annexation of East Jerusalem under the Jerusalem Bill took place while talks were in progress between Egypt and Israel about future Palestinian autonomy on the West Bank. The reiterated annexation was a clear sign by the Israeli Government that it did not regard the future of Jerusalem as part of the negotiating process. Between the occupation of East Jerusalem in 1967 and its formal annexation in 1980, Israeli building east of the Green Line had been on a vast scale. Within thirteen years, 12 per cent of the total population of the city were Jews living in the new neighbourhoods across the Green Line. There were five of these: French Hill, Ramot and Neve Yaakov to the north, East Talpiot to the east, and Gilo to the south – what the Jerusalem town planner David Kroyanker called the 'external neighbourhoods'. These provided an outer bastion of Jewish settlement, with the most southerly houses in Gilo looking across only a few fields to the Arab town of Beit Jalla, and East Talpiot divided only by a road from Jebel Mukabber and by a narrow valley from Sur Bahir.

In reaction to Israel's formal annexation of East Jerusalem, Prince Fahd of Saudi Arabia declared that it had to be reversed, even if it meant a jihad, or Holy War, to do so. Western nations, including the United States and Britain, made it clear that they did not recognise the annexation. Thirteen nations, twelve of them Latin American, and The Netherlands, each of which had moved their embassies to Jerusalem after 1967, removed them to Tel Aviv. The United Nations Security Council voted fourteen to nil on a resolution denying Israel's rights to change the status of Jerusalem and calling on Israel to end its 'prolonged occupation of Arab territories, including Jerusalem'. The American and British Consuls in East Jerusalem continued to serve as the conduit for local Arab grievances.

As well as annexing Jerusalem, Menachem Begin announced in

July 1980 that he was moving the Prime Minister's office to East Jerusalem. The veteran Israeli diplomat Walter Eytan wrote to the *Jerusalem Post*: 'If Jerusalem is Israel's single, undivided and indivisible capital, under all-encompassing Israeli sovereignty, it surely makes no difference where, within its city limits, the Prime Minister's office is located. The only things that should count are the adequacy of its premises and the Prime Minister's convenience. At present his office lies within easy distance of the Knesset and the main Government departments. What sense is there in moving it three or four kilometres away, with one-way streets and downtown traffic the way they are? The proposed transfer suggests uncertainty, a hidden fear that we may yet lose East Jerusalem, and a belief that the chances of this loss would be reduced if the Prime Minister worked there. There is no sound ground for believing any such thing.'

In the event, the Prime Minister's office was not moved. But the anger caused by that proposal, as earlier by the annexation, was a pointer to the continuing sensitivities of Jerusalem. Any ill-considered move on either side of the Arab-Jewish divide could intensify and exacerbate those sensitivities. Jewish Jerusalem was itself divided, and sometimes violently so, with 20 per cent of the Jewish population being ultra-Orthodox Jews who were prepared to demonstrate, to build roadblocks, and to throw stones to prevent the majority of secular and less Orthodox Jews from driving through Orthodox neighbourhoods on the Sabbath. Repeated ultra-Orthodox protests made travel between the centre of the city and some of the outlying suburbs a dangerous thing to undertake on a Friday night or a Saturday. The ultra-Orthodox also used their political influence to prevent a football stadium being built to the north of the city, arguing that those going to the stadium, and those playing the game, would violate the Sabbath. Their protests were taken up again, but ultimately failed, when the stadium project was moved to the south of the city, where the ultra-Orthodox presence was minimal.

Bitterness between the majority of secular and non-Orthodox Jews in Jerusalem and the ultra-Orthodox minority created an unpleasant situation in the city in the 1980s. The apprehension of many secular Jews was heightened when a growing number of ultra-Orthodox families bought houses in previously non-Orthodox areas. Only the influx of tens of thousands of mostly secular Russian Jews, once the Soviet Union opened its gates from 1987, began to alter the Jewish demographic balance in Jerusalem, and to lessen fears among the secular of an eventual Orthodox majority.

A murder in London, Paris or New York is seldom headline news. A murder in Jerusalem can unsettle the mood of millions: Muslims, Christians and Jews. In April 1982 the American-born Alan Harry Goodman, a deranged Jewish follower of the extremist Rabbi Kahane, and a recent recruit of the Israeli army, entered the Haram and opened fire with an automatic rifle. Haj Salah Yamani, an unarmed Muslim guard at the Dome of the Rock, was killed.

On being arrested, Goodman declared that his purpose was to liberate the Temple Mount from the Muslims and to become 'King of the Jews'. This was not unlike the claim of the Australian tourist Denis Rohan, who, in setting fire to the nearby al-Aksa Mosque in 1969, had declared that he had wanted to become 'King of Jerusalem'.

Muslims all over the world were outraged by Goodman's act. Inside Jerusalem, tensions grew. On the Mount of Olives, Jewish tombstones were smashed. At the village of Battir, Muslim youths stoned the Haifa-Jerusalem train. But strenuous efforts were made by the municipality to reduce the tension. 'I don't despair particularly,' Teddy Kollek commented a week later. 'It just makes life much more difficult.' The municipality would push ahead with what Kollek called the 'physical revitalisation' of the Muslim Quarter of the Old City and the outlying Arab areas of East Jerusalem.

'We are presently devoting great energies to planning Jerusalem's Arab neighbourhoods,' Kollek wrote in March 1985. 'Orderly planning will make organised, speedy development possible for the first time, after many decades of spontaneous, unsupervised building and an absence of even minimal infrastructure and public service systems. These efforts will reduce much of the housing distress of a population which has doubled since 1967 to about 130,000. We harbour the hope that this process will also alleviate the fears of a minority that the authorities could affect its land privileges. We entertain no illusions that this will defuse the existing political contradictions; these, with patience and tolerance, may be solved in another generation or two. At the same time, we believe our objective will signify a step of sorts towards narrowing the gaps, allowing for more amenable conditions for co-existence. We pursue our goals expecting neither sympathy nor gratitude from a population which cannot alienate itself from its national emotions.'

The national emotions of a few extremist Palestinian Arabs were still turning to violence. In December 1983 five Israelis were killed and forty-three injured when a bomb exploded on a bus in West Jerusalem. Among those killed were sixteen-year-old Esther Pollack and her eleven-year-old sister Nurit. Another eleven-year-old girl, Eti Adi, was also killed. Responsibility for the attack was claimed by the Palestine Liberation Organisation, whose Cyprus-based news agency reported that 'forty Israeli soldiers' had been either killed or wounded; but in Jerusalem itself the killings were condemned by five leading Palestinian Arabs, including Anwar Nusseibeh, then chairman of the East Jerusalem Electric Company, and Hanna Siniora, editor of the Jerusalem Arabic daily newspaper *al-Fajr*.

Two months later, in February 1984, twenty-one Israelis were injured in an Arab grenade attack outside a clothing shop on the Jaffa Road. In October 1986 one Israeli was killed and seventy were injured when three grenades were thrown at families and soldiers leaving the Dung Gate after a military graduation ceremony at the Wailing Wall. The dead man, Dov Porat, had come from his home on the coast to watch the swearing-in of his son. A twelve-year-old Arab was also injured in the blast; his uncle, an Arab shopkeeper, was seen covered in blood as he helped carry the wounded Israelis to the ambulances. The attackers, who were later arrested, belonged to Islamic Jihad ('Muslim Holy War'), a fundamentalist Muslim group that had its origins in Gaza and the West Bank.

Exactly a month after the Dung Gate grenade attack, a young religious Jew, Eliahu Amedi, was attacked by three Arabs in the Old City. While one of the Arabs pinned back his arms he was stabbed to death by the other two. The killers were caught. It emerged that they had come from the town of Jenin that afternoon and had picked their victim at random. He was the first young Jew whom they had managed to find alone.

By chance Amedi belonged to a Jewish nationalist right-wing group, the Penitent Sons, whose seminary was located, deliberately and provocatively, in the Muslim Quarter of the Old City. Amedi's funeral procession to the Mount of Olives turned, as it reached the Damascus Gate, into a series of frenzied attacks by the mourners on Arab shops and cars. 'At one stage,' recalled the Jerusalem writer Naomi Shepherd, 'the bearers of the corpse, carried in a winding sheet according to Jewish custom, on a stretcher, set the stretcher down and took part in the riot; as they passed the Basilica of the Agony at Gethsemane, they tried to break into the grounds. The police escort was forced to fire into the air as a warning.' On the following day a young Arab student at the Hebrew University was forced off a bus in north Jerusalem by an Israeli soldier, and so badly beaten up that he needed hospital treatment.

For almost a week, Jews stoning Arab cars replaced Arabs stoning Jewish cars in the streets of Jerusalem. In place of the cry 'Death to the Jews!' was heard 'Death to the Arabs!' Israeli riot police dispersed gangs of Jewish youths as earlier they had dispersed Arab youths. Teddy Kollek, while condemning the murder of Amedi, said that he was even more shocked by the rioting. 'Death to Teddy!' was the crude response of the Jewish rioters. As the rioting continued, and the Penitent Sons gutted an Arab cobbler's shop in an attempt to make him move out, young Arabs turned again to violence.

Summoning the leading Arab merchants and communal leaders, Kollek warned them about their passivity while Arab youths terrorised the city. 'In your schools, in your cafes, pass on the message!' he urged them. But he also recognised the Arab sense of grievance. 'I don't say it's an ideal situation,' he told them, and he added, with the blunt honesty that was his hallmark: 'I wouldn't want to be an Arab in Jerusalem.'

*

Despite the outbreak of violence, the 1980s saw much building in Jerusalem. Architects were in creative mood. In 1987 Moshe Safdie, the man responsible a decade earlier for the Habitat Exposition in Montreal, designed a children's memorial at the Holocaust museum, Yad Vashem, in which, by the light of a few candles reflected by many mirrors, an intensely moving image and mood are created, by which every visitor is affected, and some are overwhelmed. The memorial was financed by an American Jew, Abraham Spiegel, who had lost his two-year-old son at Auschwitz. It was opened on 28 June 1987. 'It was a brilliantly sunny day,' Safdie later recalled, 'and hundreds of guests listened to the speeches. And then, as the ribbon was cut, they descended down the ramp into the darkness. Mrs Spiegel had not seen the memorial under construction. I guided her into the place of infinite candles. I cried as she cried.'

Another feature of Jerusalem in the 1980s was the effort made on behalf of those Jews in the Soviet Union who wanted to leave, but were refused permission to do so. Among the many marches and demonstrations which were held under the banner 'Let My People Go' was a march to the Wailing Wall in support of Anatoly Shcharansky, who had been imprisoned on a trumped-up charge of spying for the United States. Shcharansky's wife Avital, who had been allowed to leave Moscow for Israel, was at the forefront of the march. As part of the Soviet Jewry campaign, schoolchildren would gather in the Knesset Rose Garden, or outside the Jerusalem Theatre, holding photographs of the twenty or more Jewish prisoners, each one incarcerated because of his or her desire to live in Israel.

In 1986 Shcharansky was released. On the night of his arrival in Israel, 11 February 1986, he was taken to Jerusalem, and on reaching the plaza in front of the Wailing Wall was carried through an excited crowd to the Wall itself. There, clasping the very Book of Psalms which he had always refused to give up while in prison, he gave thanks for his deliverance. It was a solemn moment seen by millions of television viewers throughout the Western world. Then, as he left with his wife to go to their apartment in Jerusalem, the city in which she had waited for him for more than eleven years, the vast crowd sang the Jewish and Israeli anthem 'Hatikvah' ('Hope'). It was the anthem that had been sung by Shcharansky's friends outside a Moscow courthouse in July 1978 when they learned that he had received a thirteen-year sentence.

One of the events in which Shcharansky participated after his arrival in Jerusalem was the opening of a small park in East Talpiot as a gesture of support for another long-term prisoner, Josef Begun. He, too, was released in due course, and went to live in Jerusalem.

*

In June 1987, on the eve of the twentieth anniversary of the incorporation of East Jerusalem into Israel, Hanna Siniora, the Palestinian-Arab editor of *al-Fajr*, stated that his decision to run for municipal office that summer 'does not mean we relinquish sovereignty over East Jerusalem. I believe Jerusalem should be an undivided city with dual sovereignty, the capital of both a Palestinian State and of Israel.' For most Israelis, these views were anathema, and yet the search for a compromise was uppermost in the minds of all those who felt that Arab aspirations in the city had somehow to be satisfied.

Not compromise, however, but confrontation had come in January 1987 to the border between the Jewish suburb of East Talpiot and the Arab village of Sur Bahir. In the determination of the Jewish National Fund to build a park for the residents of East Talpiot, sixty village-owned olive trees were uprooted and several thousand pine saplings were planted in their place. This was the culmination of a series of land expropriations by East Talpiot, starting when 500 acres of Sur Bahir had been expropriated for the building of the new

Jewish suburb in 1970, and a further 75 acres taken for a park. The expropriation of the olive trees led to an unprecedented protest, when Jews and Arabs combined to seek an end to the taking away of precious land. In a clear criticism of the hard-line policy of the new Likud Government headed by Yitzhak Shamir, which had come to power in October 1986, Teddy Kollek told the press: 'Neighbours are working together, standing together in what seems to be a matter of justice. I hope that we will succeed.'

For three months the dispute continued, but the protests were successful. It was agreed that no more Arab trees would be uprooted, and that the villagers could continue to tend those trees still standing on the land that had been taken for the park. No Jewish National Fund forest would be planted there. It was a small victory for joint Arab-Jewish cooperation. 'This land has been cultivated by the Arabs for generations,' Kollek told the Israeli journalist Louis Rapoport. 'We have to find a compromise in the city, to live together in tolerance, understanding and mutual respect, and this is a classic example of how that can be done.'

Brave words, and true, but within five months such hopes as the East Talpiot-Sur Bahir compromise might have raised were soon dashed. On 9 December 1987 a Palestinian uprising, known as the Intifada, broke out. In Arabic, the word *intifada* means 'a shaking-off'. The violent challenge to Israel's occupation started in Gaza, the day after four Arabs had been killed by an Israeli driver in a road accident. Within a few days, violence, at first dominated by the hurling of stones and rocks and slabs of concrete at Israeli troops and cars, spread to the West Bank and East Jerusalem. As the confrontations became more violent, blocking roads and endangering the lives of Israeli soldiers on patrol, the Israeli army retaliated with raids, beatings, arrests, detention without trial, and collective punishment. When stone- and rock-throwing by youths from the Arab village of Jebel Mukabber against East Talpiot reached a pitch of intensity, the whole village had its electricity cut off.

One weapon used by the leaders of the Intifada was to close all Arab shops. There were many days when East Jerusalem was shuttered and deserted. The Israeli military authorities ordered shops to be opened at certain times. Shopkeepers defied these orders and had their shutters prised open by the soldiers: this happened for the first time on 18 January 1988, but the shopkeepers still refused to trade. Some shopkeepers were arrested. Others refused to pay their fines. At a press conference held at the National Palace Hotel in East Jerusalem, Arab merchants from Ramallah and al-Bireh pledged to continue their strikes until all Palestinian 'national demands' were met.

The battle for the shops was an ugly one. There were occasions when Israeli soldiers, after forcing open the shutters, would run amok inside the shop, ruining foodstuffs and other produce. The Israeli military authorities made every effort to punish such excesses, but the ferocity of the verbal and physical attacks on Israeli patrols was often an unbearable provocation for soldiers who were seldom much older than their tormentors. On February 16, as Arab anger intensified, a general strike was called which brought East Jerusalem's trade to a halt. As a gesture of solidarity with the shop-owners, Arab bus and taxi companies also refused to operate. These protests hurt most of all those who participated in them. Walking in East Jerusalem became a nerve-racking and even dangerous thing for anyone who might be thought of as a Jew. Nor did the desperate cry 'I am not Jewish!', by a visiting journalist or tourist, always serve as a protection.

Violent Arab protests spread from the Arab to the Jewish section of the city. The burning of Jewish-owned cars became a nightly hazard, with dozens of cars being destroyed each night. The stabbing of Jewish Jerusalemites as they shopped in markets, stood at bus stops, and even played in their school playgrounds, became increasingly common. East Talpiot was one of the worst-affected areas. 'Youths from Sur Bahir', Louis Rapoport wrote in his account of the first year of the uprising, 'started stoning the houses of their Jewish neighbours. At the home of Judy Segal and her family, who emigrated to Israel from the United States after the Yom Kippur War, the shutters were closed and the Segals stayed away from the windows. "We kept hearing the glass breaking," she told a reporter after fifty Arab youths pelted the house with hundreds of stones. Even after the border police came, the kids kept coming back, taunting the police to chase them. Four of Segal's neighbours on Meir Naqqar Street, just across from Jebel Mukabber, also came under attack.'

The Segals were left-wing supporters of the Israeli peace movement, Peace Now. 'But it's easier to be leftist when people aren't throwing stones at you,' Judy Segal told Rapoport. 'I have no hatred for the Arabs. I would be willing to give back territory for peace. But in the meantime it has to be made clear to them that this cannot continue.'

Israeli police later entered Sur Bahir in force, breaking into homes, smashing furniture, and roughing people up. The police spokesman, Rafi Levy, declared: 'Those who take part in disturbances have to take into account the fact that the police will respond. The adults of Sur Bahir should control their young people, and then no one's property will be damaged.' After the police raid, Hillel Bardin, one of the East Talpiot residents who had worked particularly hard to find common ground with his Arab neighbours, was in despair, telling Louis Rapoport: 'I am opposed to violence, and I wish there was a non-violent path which could give the people of Sur Bahir what they want.'

Teddy Kollek, 'always on the scene of any disturbance with his instinct for conciliation,' wrote Rapoport, 'stood amid the shards of glass and the wafting smoke, looking desolate, bitter and exhausted.' Looking into the Israel Television camera, Kollek swept his arm across the vista of East Talpiot, and said: 'Coexistence is dead.' Later, after he had recovered his composure, he denied that he had said the words that the whole nation heard. What he meant, he said, was 'almost dead'. There was a very narrow line between the two, and the longer the Intifada lasted, the narrower that line became.

*

In 1988 the Palestinian Liberation Organisation, meeting in exile in Algiers, proclaimed the establishment of a Palestinian State 'in the name of Allah, with its capital Holy Jerusalem'. The Israeli writer Amos Elon, a resident of West Jerusalem, commented: 'The declaration was dismissed by the Israeli government as a worthless piece of paper that would soon be forgotten. There was an unexpected irony in the fact that Jews, who owed their present prominence in Jerusalem to their extraordinary memory of their own past, were now counting on the Arabs to forget theirs.' Elon noted that Palestinians today 'make every effort to remember Jerusalem – as the Jews have, for generations – in their customs, their songs, their prayers', and that stylised views of the city 'hang on the walls of countless homes all over the Near East'.

The magnetic attraction of Jerusalem not only to its inhabitants, but to Jews, Christians and Muslims throughout the world, led Amos Elon to reflect, in 1989: 'In our time, men have stepped on the moon seeking new Jerusalems in foreign galaxies, but so far the old Jerusalem has not been replaced. She retains an extraordinary hold over the imagination, generating for three hostile faiths, in perfectly interchangeable phrases, the fear as well as the hope of Apocalypse.' The Intifada had introduced an imbalance, however, between Jews and Arabs. 'After twenty years of occupation,' the Israeli journalist

Eric Silver wrote in the London *Jewish Chronicle* on 2 June 1989, 'Jerusalem is still a divided city – divided for the Jews, if not for the Arabs, an irony of occupation.' Arabs still worked and shopped in West Jerusalem, and shopped in even larger numbers than before, as a result of the continual shop closures and strikes in East Jerusalem. But few Jews took the eastward path any more. 'Israelis no longer shop in Salah ed-din Street outside the walls,' Silver wrote. 'They no longer walk in the Arab quarters of the Old City, or take their cars to be resprayed in Wadi Joz. Drivers no longer take the short cut past the American Colony to French Hill and Mount Scopus. The Dolphin fish restaurant, a popular symbol of Jewish-Arab co-ownership opposite the Rockefeller Museum, has closed.'

Reflecting on the Arab reaction, that 'the Jews are afraid', Eric Silver commented: 'The Jews say it is not so much fear as prudence. Why risk a knife in the back, a rock through the windscreen? Who needs it?' On 22 June 1989, three weeks after Silver wrote those words, a Hebrew University scholar and member of the Israel Academy of Sciences and Humanities, Professor Menachem Stern, was stabbed to death by two teenage Arabs. The killing took place in West Jerusalem. Professor Stern, who had come to Jerusalem from Poland as a teenager fifty years earlier, was walking from his home through the valley of the Monastery of the Cross to the National Library on the Givat Ram campus. His most important published work was a three-volume anthology of the writings of Greek and Latin authors on Jews and Judaism. His two attackers later told the police that they had killed Stern as an 'initiation rite', in order to qualify for membership of Yassir Arafat's 'Fatah' ('Conquest') movement. They had not known who Stern was, nor had they cared.

The site of Stern's killing was a popular park. The murderer could not have chosen 'a better arena for his despicable crime to elicit revulsion and terror among Jerusalemites,' Menachem Shalev wrote in the *Jerusalem Post*. The pleasant valley, in which several Israeli youth movements held their weekly meetings, had been turned 'into an ugly place which, henceforth, will fill parents' hearts with foreboding'.

Innumerable Israeli police and army raids into East Jerusalem sought out the perpetrators of these Intifada attacks. There was increased nervousness in the streets of West Jerusalem after each incident. Suspicion mounted on each side of the divide, with hatred often breaking to the surface. The Israeli police and army resorted to tear-gas and rubber bullets, and to live ammunition. At night, an incident would often be followed by the release from helicopters of intensely bright magnesium flares, to illuminate an area through which police and soldiers would search for some fugitive who had just killed or maimed.

An American journalist, Thomas Friedman, had been reporting from Jerusalem for the *New York Times* since 1984. Before that he had been reporting from Beirut in Lebanon. A week before leaving Jerusalem for a new assignment he decided to take his wife, Ann, and their two daughters, Natalie and Orly, for a family lunch at the Intercontinental Hotel, overlooking the Temple Mount. 'Ann drove and the two girls sat in the back seat,' he recalled a few months later. 'As our little Daihatsu chugged slowly up Mount Scopus, a teenage Palestinian suddenly stepped out from behind a wall, stood in front of us, took careful aim, and threw a stone at Ann's face. It shattered the windshield into a spiderweb, but fortunately did not penetrate the glass. Orly saw the whole thing and began screaming hysterically from the back seat. Ann was paralysed with fear. "Keep driving," I shouted at her, as the Palestinian youth loped away into the adjacent Arab village of a-Suwaneh.

'None of us was hurt from the small shards of glass that dusted the interior of the car, just shaken. The only lasting scar from the incident seems to have been inflicted on Orly's psyche. She still asks about the "man with the stone", and I am afraid that as she grows older this incident will remain one of her earliest childhood memories. The Palestinian wasn't aiming at us specifically. He had simply seen the Israeli licence plates on the car and that was enough for him to throw a stone and to inflict pain, no matter who was inside.

'How ironic, I thought afterward. I had seen marching armies and many nations pass through Beirut and ultramodern fighter jets flash above its skies. I had seen the battleship *New Jersey* fire shells as big as Chevrolets, and I had seen my own apartment house in Beirut reduced to dust by a pound of the most sophisticated high explosives known to man. I had seen massacres and car bombings and heard snipers until they had almost become routine. I had dodged them all for ten years, only to get hit by a stone.'

*

During 1989, five Israelis were killed in the streets of Jerusalem by Intifada activists. In July there was a particularly destructive attack five miles west of the city which intensified the feelings of anger and bitterness by which so many Jewish Jerusalemites were being affected. On July 6, three miles west of Motza, just below Telshe Stone, an

Arab passenger on the regular 405 bus from Tel Aviv to Jerusalem seized the wheel from the driver. Crying out 'Radwan, Radwan' – the name of a friend who had been injured in the Intifada – he forced the bus off the road and into a ravine. Tumbling to the bottom of the ravine, the bus burst into flames. Sixteen people were killed. Many of them were burned while still trapped in their seats as a strong wind fanned the flames. Among the dead were Etti and Yitzchak Naim, a married couple on their first holiday alone in twenty-two years. They had intended making the journey in a friend's car, but it had broken down.

The youngest person killed was the fourteen-year-old Kinneret Cohen. She was returning from a shopping expedition in Tel Aviv. Among those injured was Eliezra Cassuto, the fifty-three-year-old granddaughter of Eliezer Ben Yehuda, the founder of modern Hebrew. The Palestine Liberation Organisation's news agency, Wafa, called the attack 'a heroic act of a new type'. But among those helping to succour the survivors were many Israeli Arabs from the nearby village of Abu Ghosh, among them Issa Jabber, an architect, and Abdul Rahman, a Jerusalem waiter, who told the *Jerusalem Post*: 'If anyone saw what it looked like in that wadi, he would feel the same pain I did. Whoever carried out that attack was not a normal human being.'

That evening, at a concert in Jerusalem, the conductor Zubin Mehta asked the audience to stand in silence for two minutes before the concert started, and to refrain from applause during the performance. That night, when I passed the spot on my way from the airport, the smell of burning was still acrid in the warm night air. A large area of the hillside had been charred by the windswept flames.

The twenty-five-year-old Arab who had forced the bus into the ravine, Abed al-Mufti Gneim, was from the Nusseirat refugee camp in Gaza. His wife, a Negev Bedouin, was expecting their first baby. One of his brothers had been arrested in the first months of the Intifada. Gneim survived the downward plunge of the bus and the fire, and was imprisoned for life. He belonged to no Arab faction, and had acted alone. In the following three days, twenty-four Jews were arrested by the Jerusalem police for throwing stones at Arab cars and trying to attack Arabs in the streets. In retaliation, petrol bombs were thrown at Jewish buses, but no one was hurt. A Jew who threw a stone at an Arab truck was sentenced to eight months in prison. At six o'clock on the evening of July 13 all public transport in West Jerusalem stopped for one minute, in memory of the victims of the bus attack. Private drivers also stopped in tribute.

*

As the 1980s came to an end, Jerusalem remained in a state of nervous tension. Daily life went on, with all its joys and ordinariness, its pattern of meals and work, of school and playground, of family and friendship, of holidays and prayer; but it was often over-shadowed by items of news that caused anguish, sadness and pain.

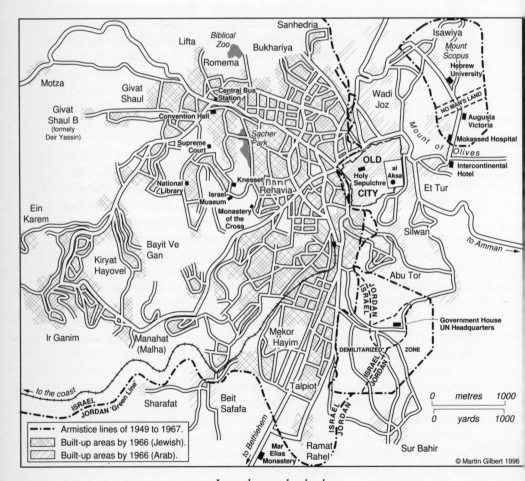

Jerusalem and suburbs

CHAPTER TWENTY-ONE

Towards the Twenty-First Century: Struggle, Uncertainty and Hope

The 1990s were to see as dramatic and positive changes in Jerusalem as any decade in the twentieth century. The new decade began without much apparent hope. The Intifada had entered its third year, bringing almost every week some tensions to Jerusalem – tensions which intruded uneasily into the steady, pleasing patterns of daily life. When, on 11 April 1990, Jewish settlers moved into a building in the Old City which they had leased from its Armenian leaseholder, there were immediate anti-Israeli demonstrations in the streets of Arab Jerusalem.

The building involved was the St John's Hospice, owned by the Greek Orthodox Church. The settlers belonged to a group that was determined to expand the Jewish presence in the Christian and Muslim Quarters of the Old City. The Greek Orthodox Church denied that the Armenian had the right to transfer his lease, and denounced the 'occupation' of its property. When the settlers placed a Star of David on the building, the Arabs tore it down. On April 27, in further protest at the Jewish leasehold, all Christian shrines throughout the city were closed to visitors. There were renewed street demonstrations in East Jerusalem when it was revealed that the Israeli Housing Minister, David Levy, had secretly provided almost $2 million, through a Panamanian holding company, to help the settlers buy the lease.

Sometimes the moment of danger could fade away, as when Kay Thomson, a visitor from England, drove along the road to the northern Jewish suburb of Neve Yaakov. 'We drive through Arab suburbs,' she wrote in her diary on 18 May 1990. 'Three very young boys have strung a wire across the road, and have stones ready to throw, but remove themselves at our approach.' That same day, a fire bomb was thrown by an Arab, and a woman's car was overturned near Sheikh Jarrah, on the road leading up to the Hebrew University, the scene of so many such incidents in 1948.

There was some incident almost every day. On May 19 Kay Thomson recorded in her diary: 'We go to Rimon café bar on Luncz Street, just off the main street, and drink Coca-Cola. A police van appears in the adjacent main street with a loud speaker, and people are warned to move out of the area. It clears people away towards me. The people and police look worried. Soldiers help in clearing people away and then a police officer starts to clear people from café bar tables in our street. We sit, I pay for our drinks, realising that we will be told to move at any moment. We move back. A man appears in a flak jacket, helmet and mask, at the corner of the main street, and takes something away. We are allowed to return to the café. An Arab family in white clothing appears. All is back to normal.'

But not quite normal. On Yassir Arafat's orders, the Jerusalem Arabs were closing their shops on three or four days each week, except for bread shops, which were allowed to stay open. In mid-August two Jewish teenagers, eighteen-year-old Ronen Karami and seventeen-year-old Lior Tubul, were stabbed to death near Ramot. Angry Jewish youths threw stones at Arab vehicles passing near the Shmuel Hanavi neighbourhood, and on the Hebron Road. Then, in an incident reminiscent of the Wailing Wall riots of 1928 and 1929, violence returned to the Old City. A tiny extremist Jewish group, the Temple Mount Faithful, had been refused permission by the Israeli authorities to lay the cornerstone of the Third Temple. They petitioned the Israeli High Court, but their petition was thrown out. On October 8, however, when there were several thousand Muslim worshippers on the Haram, calls over the loudspeaker system warned that the site was in danger, and there were strident cries over the loudspeakers of *'Allahu Akbar'* ('God is Greatest'), *'Jihad'* ('Holy War'), and *Idbah al-Yahud'* ('Death to the Jews').

About 2,000 Arab youths began to gather large stones and building blocks from the various buildings being renovated on the Haram. They then advanced against the small Israeli police station on the Haram, hurling their stones and forcing the dozen policemen to flee through the Moghrabi Gate. The crowd then gathered at the western edge of the Haram and began to hurl stones and rocks down on to the Jewish worshippers at the base of the Wailing Wall. It was the Jewish festival of Succot (Tabernacles), and several thousand worshippers were gathered there. As the stones began to fall, nine worshippers were injured.

The Israeli police managed to force their way back on to the

Haram, when they too were attacked by stones, rocks and iron bars, and nineteen policemen were hurt. They began to fire tear-gas and to shoot rubber bullets against the rioters. Several of their tear-gas canisters were thrown back at them. When these methods failed to disperse the rioters, live ammunition was fired, first in the air, and then directly at them. Eighteen Arabs were killed. When the rioters retreated into the al-Aksa Mosque, the order was given to cease fire.

Following the cry for the Arab deaths to be avenged, and a false rumour that the Israelis had fired into the mosque, three Jews were stabbed to death in the Old City, and an Israeli taxi-driver, Rafi Avrahamov-Doron, was shot through the head. When another Arab crowd was dispersed by tear-gas on the Temple Mount on October 9, one of those overcome by the fumes and taken to hospital was the eighty-year-old Mufti of Jerusalem, Saad a-Din al-Alami. At the same time, the Deputy Mufti, Muhammad al-Jamal, was arrested for incitement to riot. Twelve days later, on the morning of October 21, an eighteen-year-old Jewish girl soldier, Iris Azoulai, was brutally stabbed to death in the West Jerusalem neighbourhood of Bakaa, while walking on the street. Her assailant, Omar Abu Sirhan, repeatedly struck her in the chest with a forty-centimetre-long bayonet.

A few minutes later Sirhan came upon a Jewish nurseryman, Eli Altaratz, who was delivering a potted plant in the neighbourhood, knocked him to the ground, and lunged at him with the bayonet. 'What do you want from me?' Altaratz cried out, 'I am a Jew!' Sirhan continued stabbing, shouting loudly: '*Allahu Akbar!*', 'God is Greatest!'

An off-duty policeman, Shalom Chelouche, who had a gun, tried to stop Sirhan by firing first in the air and then at his legs. This had no effect, but Chelouche would not shoot to kill. 'No, I'm afraid of hurting him,' he told the bystanders. He then seized Sirhan and pushed him to the ground, attempting to disarm him. Sirhan, still calling out '*Allahu Akbar!*', stabbed Chelouche to death. Chelouche's wife was pregnant with their first child.

That evening Teddy Kollek called for more Russian-Jewish immigrants to be settled in Jerusalem. 'The Arabs,' he said, 'should not delude themselves that they can weaken us by acts of terror.'

Three hours after the triple murder, the journalist Louis Rapoport, who had known Iris Azoulai and her family well, saw a group of Jews hurling stones near the murder scene at the house of a leading Jewish supporter of reconciliation with the Arabs. Rapoport tried to stop the stone-throwing. He was set upon by the Jews and savagely beaten. His life was saved by two passing policemen.

*

Not only internal Arab terror, but the external threat from Iraq caused many days of fear in Jerusalem. From the moment of the Iraqi seizure of Kuwait in August 1990 the danger of a gas attack on Israel was ever-present. The speed of the Scud missiles which Iraq had threatened to use against Israel was such that there would be no time to go into the air-raid shelters which were in the basement of almost every building in the city. Indeed, the nature of the gas might be such that even the most substantial shelters, because of their air ventilation systems, would not have been gas-proof. Every family was therefore asked to prepare a special sealed room, in which all sources of outside air would be cut off by masking-tape.

All Jerusalemites, including the Arabs, were given gas masks. Each one bore a label stating that it was not to be used except in case of emergency. The labels were printed in Hebrew, English, Arabic and, in view of the large numbers of recent Russian-Jewish immigrants to the capital, in Russian.

In the early hours of 18 January 1991, within twenty-four hours of the outbreak of the Gulf War, the first Scud missiles landed near Tel Aviv. Jerusalemites spent the period of alert in sealed rooms, awaiting the explosions that never came. The main target area, and most of the damage, was in and around Tel Aviv. In the course of one alert in the capital, during a concert by Isaac Stern in the Jerusalem Theatre, most of the audience put on their gas masks but remained in their seats. Stern and the orchestra, having begun to leave the stage as the alert sounded, returned at once and continued playing.

The Intifada did not end with the Gulf War. There were some on the Arab side of the Jerusalem divide who had gone to their rooftops and cheered when Scud missiles fell on Tel Aviv. For those who lived in West Jerusalem each such episode, and each moment of violence, were moments of despair, compounded of sadness and anger. On 28 February 1991 a twenty-five-year-old Jewish religious student, Elhanan Atali, was found in an abandoned storeroom in the Muslim Quarter of the Old City. His throat had been slit and he had been stabbed in the back. On March 10 that year four Jewish women were stabbed to death in the western suburb of Kiryat Hayovel. One of them, Bella Levitsky, aged sixty-one, was a recent immigrant from the Soviet city of Baku, on the Caspian Sea.

*

In May 1991 a new wave of immigrants came to Jerusalem: more than 1,000 Ethiopian Jews, part of the airlift of 14,000 Jews that month from Addis Ababa. They joined the Russian immigrants in the absorption centres at Gilo and in East Talpiot, and took their first steps towards becoming an integral part of the city's life.

On the last day of 1991 an Arab woman from Bethlehem was preparing an explosive charge in a toilet in the Mahane Yehuda market, the main Jewish market of West Jerusalem, when the charge exploded, killing her. No one else was hurt.

*

Israel's annexation of East Jerusalem had worried those Israeli thinkers, politicians and journalists who felt that the Palestinian Arabs would never accept such complete Israeli control over their homes, lives and livelihoods. On 19 December 1991 Professor Avishai Margalit of the Hebrew University put forward, in the *New York Review of Books*, a plan that sought a way towards a Jerusalem settlement acceptable to both sides. He suggested a form of joint sovereignty, whereby Jerusalem would be the capital of both Israel and a future Palestinian State, with the daily operation of the city's needs to be maintained by a joint municipal council. To get round the problems of joint sovereignty, Professor Margalit proposed 'granting Jerusalem a special status, so that it would have its own laws, which would be agreed upon by the parliaments of the two States, and would be part of the laws of each one of them'. In this way, Jewish and Arab individuality and separateness would be upheld, and equality of status secured, but the city would remain a single city, without the need to return to the barbed wire, concrete walls and No-Man's Lands that had effectively made it two cities between 1948 and 1967.

A dozen variants on Professor Margalit's plan have since been put forward, each with the same goal. When Jerusalem becomes part of the agenda in talks between Israel and the Palestinians, a plan such as this may provide a basis for negotiation.

*

In March 1992 an accident brought the Jews and Arabs of Jerusalem to each other's side. When a wall collapsed in an Arab coffee-house in East Jerusalem, twenty-three of those inside the building were killed. Israeli troops from the Special Evacuation Unit, which had gone to Armenia after the earthquake in 1988, hurried to the scene and, alongside Arab volunteers, helped clear the rubble. Arab Red Crescent and Israeli Red Shield ambulance teams worked side by side. The injured were taken both to the nearby Arab Mokassed Hospital and to the Hadassah Hospital. Teddy Kollek and the Deputy Mufti, Sheikh Jamal a-Rifai, were both at the scene to bring comfort. It was the Jewish Sabbath, but an ambulance crew of religious Jews from the Ramot neighbourhood left their synagogue in order to help. 'Enmities seemed to disappear in the common effort,' commented the *Jerusalem Post*.

Yet there were a few moments which showed how fragile the amity could be, when a small group of Arab youths pelted the Israeli army rescuers with rocks, and a few Arab stretcher-bearers refused to let Jewish doctors take some of the badly injured to the Hadassah Hospital's special trauma unit. An Arab doctor persuaded the hot-heads to desist.

The intensity of the Intifada waned in the summer of 1992, when, starting in June, a new Israeli Government, led by Yitzhak Rabin, sought a political agreement with the Palestine Liberation Organisation. The uprising had already lasted more than four years. Since 1987, 697 Arabs had been killed throughout the West Bank and Gaza by the Israeli army. The dead included seventy-eight youngsters aged fourteen or under. A further 528 Arabs had been killed, on the West Bank, in Gaza and in East Jerusalem, by fellow Arabs, some accused of collaboration with Israel, others accused, by the fundamentalist Islamic Jihad movement, of theft, drug-dealing and prostitution. Many of the Arabs killed by Arabs were knifed, bludgeoned or hacked to death. Thirteen Israeli soldiers and twelve Israeli civilians had also been killed in knife attacks.

*

On 12 June 1992 Professor Edward Said, a Palestinian living in the United States, landed with his family at Israel's Ben-Gurion Airport. He had been born in Jerusalem's Talbiyeh suburb in November 1935. Towards the end of 1947, before the arrival of Israeli forces, he and his family had left the city. He had not seen West Jerusalem since then, and had returned only once to East Jerusalem, briefly in 1966, shortly before it too was occupied by Israel. A distinguished literary scholar in the United States, he had become an active and articulate advocate of the Palestinian cause.

Said's first visits on his 1992 journey were to East Jerusalem and the Old City. 'The Holy Sepulchre, that centre of centres, was exactly as I recalled it,' he wrote, 'an alien, run-down, unattractive place full of frumpy middle-aged tourists milling about in the decrepit and ill-lit area where Copts, Greeks, Armenians, and other Christian sects nurtured their unattractive ecclesiastical gardens in sometimes open combat with each other. I remembered being carried around it on my father's shoulders, wondering who those bearded foreigners were, and could this be the actual site of Christ's last hours?'

That afternoon Edward Said made his way into West Jerusalem, and to Talbiyeh, in search of his former home. 'I saw no Arabs, although the handsome old stone houses still bear their Arab identity. I remember the house itself quite clearly: two stories, a terraced entrance, a balcony at the front door, a spacious (and at the time) empty square, designated as a park, that lay before the room in which I was born, facing towards the King David and the YMCA.' For a while, after 1948, Martin Buber, the city's most distinguished Jewish thinker, had lived in the house.

The Arab inhabitants of the Mandate years had all gone. Said's Palestinian guide 'called out the names of the villas and their original Palestinian owners – Kitaneh, Sununu, Tannous, David, Haramy, Salameh families – a sad roll call of the vanished past'. And then 'there the house was, I suddenly knew, with its still impressive bulk commanding the sandy little square, now an elegant, even manicured park. My daughter later told me that, using her camera with manic excitement, I reeled off twenty-six photographs of the place which, irony of ironies, bore the name plate "International Christian Embassy" at the gate.' To have found his family house now lived in not by an Israeli family but by a Christian pro-Zionist group was, Said wrote, 'an abrupt blow for a child of Palestinian Christian parents. Anger and melancholy took me over, so that when an American woman came out of the house holding an armful of laundry and asked if she could help, all I could blurt out was an instinctive "No, thanks." More than anything else, it was the house I did not, could not, enter that symbolised the eerie finality of a history that looked at me from behind the shaded windows, across an immense gulf I found myself unable to cross.'

Almost half a century after the Arab suburbs of Bakaa, Talbiyeh and Katamon became part of West Jerusalem, several hundred of the often magnificently designed Arab houses remain unchanged, or have gained a floor or two. Those living in them are no longer occupiers, as Edward Said called them: they are the children or grandchildren of those who took them over in 1948. Some of the first Jewish inhabitants of the Arab neighbourhoods were Jewish refugees from

Arab lands who had been dispossessed in 1948 from their homes in Morocco, Iraq and elsewhere. These houses are now Jewish homes in entirely Jewish parts of the city. The same is true for the more outlying areas that were once lived in by Arabs, including the villages of Malha (now Manahat) and Ayin (now Ein) Karem to the south-west.

*

Returning to East Jerusalem, Edward Said had a series of encounters with the past. 'I took my family to St George's to visit the old "Bishop School", as it is known in Arabic,' Said wrote. 'There I showed my son Wadie his grandfather Wadie's name on the cricket and football First Eleven boards from 1906 till about 1911. In the assembly room where morning prayers used to be held, a seventy-year-old caretaker asked us shyly whether we'd like to see old school pictures. He brought up four – a class picture from 1942, the staff in 1927 etc – from the cellar (they're about to be thrown out, he said), one of which riveted my attention. A work of great formal beauty, it was signed "Kh. Raad", the name of Palestine's most famous photographer, Khalil Raad, a nervous but gifted man whom I remember would fussily arrange and rearrange us for group pictures during weddings and confirmations. There seated on the floor next to a young man carrying a football with "1906" written across it, was in fact my father as a boy of twelve or thirteen.'

During his visit to Jerusalem, Said visited Faisal al-Husseini, the acknowledged leader of the Palestinian Arabs in Jerusalem, and the son of Abd al-Khader al-Husseini who had been killed in the battle for Jerusalem in 1948. 'The night I saw him,' Said recalled, 'he showed me a piece of paper announcing an agreement between him, as representative of the "National Movement", also known as the Delegation, the PLO, Fatah, whatever, on the one hand, and Hamas, the Islamic movement in the Territories, on the other. All sweetness and light, the document presented a reasoned argument for peaceful cooperation and political savvy in dealing with the Occupation and the peace process. Then, Husseini said, "Look at this other paper," which was dated a week later than the other. It was a circular purporting to issue from Hamas, denouncing Husseini and the Delegation as collaborators, traitors, sellouts.'

Said had stumbled upon one of the tragedies of East Jerusalem: what he called the 'internecine Palestinian conflict'. Those Palestinians who wanted to strike at Israel by violent means were still, in the year of his visit, trying to create an atmosphere of tension, hatred and mutual misunderstanding between Jews and Arabs in Jerusalem, even as the peace process initiated by Yitzhak Shamir at Madrid in October 1991, and considerably accelerated by Yitzhak Rabin from the moment of his election in June 1992, went forward.

In July 1992 the American Secretary of State, James Baker, was in Jerusalem as part of a peace mission that also took him to Egypt, Jordan, Syria and Lebanon. Israelis and Palestinians were also talking peace at official meetings in cities all over the world: Washington, Ottawa, Brussels, Vienna, Tokyo and Moscow. But in November 1992, the month before the fifth anniversary of the Intifada, there were in Jerusalem alone 24 stabbings of what was called the 'non-fatal' variety, 3,000 stoning incidents, and 400 Israeli cars gutted by fire. In the middle of the month a sixty-two-year-old Arab shopkeeper was killed by a grenade thrown by a Jewish extremist in the Old City. Elsewhere in Israel, more than a dozen Israelis and Palestinians were killed in a series of bloody incidents and confrontations. In December, during a curfew in the village of Beit Sahur, just south of Jerusalem, Abdel Rahman Uzoum, a masked Arab youth wearing an Israeli army uniform, who ignored an order to halt, was shot dead by soldiers.

Abdel Rahman Uzoum was eighteen years old. His death was one of the last of the Intifada in Jerusalem. With the petering out of the Intifada in the early months of 1993 something, but not all, of the vibrant life of the bazaars returned. The Intifada had come to an end after more than five years. Meetings began to be held between Israelis and Palestinians about the future of Jerusalem. On 15 March 1993, at one such meeting, which took place in the Notre Dame Centre in Jerusalem, there was an indication of the problems that would beset future negotiations when an Arab historian, Nafez Nazzal, a Professor of Arab and Islamic Studies who was teaching at the Jerusalem Centre of Near Eastern Studies, told a group of Israeli and Palestinian intellectuals: 'Even if Jerusalem is excluded as an item for negotiation, the Palestinians of the city will themselves make sure that Jerusalem will erupt into communal warfare.' Professor Nazzal continued: 'After the October 8, 1990 clash on the al-Haram al-Sharif in which eighteen Palestinians were killed by Israeli troops, the Palestinians of Arab Jerusalem were proud that they had provided their city, and the city of the prophets, with so many martyrs.'

Although Israeli sensitivities about any possible change in the status of the city were strong, in May 1993 the Israeli Government agreed that Faisal al-Husseini, Jerusalem's leading Palestinian activist, could participate in the Palestinian delegation which was about to renew negotiations with Israel in Madrid. These negotiations were to prove the start of a series of agreements leading to the withdrawal of Israeli troops and administrators from the West Bank and Gaza, and the establishment there of a Palestinian self-governing Authority.

*

Spasmodic acts of terror after the ending of the Intifada continued to mar the return to Jerusalem's previous civic bustle and varied and vigorous social and cultural life. On 1 July 1993 a Jewish woman, Olga Khaikov, was killed when terrorists tried to seize a bus near French Hill. She was a new immigrant from Russia, with an eleven-year-old daughter. The terrorists then seized a car belonging to a Jewish Jerusalemite, Jeannette Kadosh-Dayan, a mother of four, and forced her to drive them through the city. At Gilo junction to the south of the city they tried to break through an army roadblock, but Jeannette Kadosh-Dayan managed to signal to the soldiers on duty that something was wrong. As the soldiers opened fire she was shot dead by her hijackers, and her body thrown out of the car. The terrorists were killed in the car. They were later identified as members of the military wing of Islamic Jihad, the avowed enemies of compromise between Israel and the Palestine Liberation Organisation. From the site of the roadblock could be seen the spires of the churches of Bethlehem.

Each terrorist incident was unnerving to those for whom Jerusalem had always been a city of constructive activity, a cultural and spiritual magnet. Among the most moving episodes that take place on a regular basis is the tree-planting ceremony at Yad Vashem, where those non-Jews who had saved the lives of Jews in the Second World War are honoured for their courageous acts. On 22 July 1993 an Israeli Supreme Court Justice, Aharon Barak, was present at Yad Vashem to watch seventy-six-year-old Ceslovas Rakevicius plant a tree. Rakevicius had saved Barak, his brother and his parents, and more than twenty other Jewish families, by smuggling them out of the Kovno Ghetto in 1944. The eight-year-old Aharon had been smuggled out in a potato sack. Tears flowed at Yad Vashem as he embraced his rescuer.

*

On 13 September 1993, in Washington, Israel and the Palestine Liberation Organisation signed a Declaration of Principles, which had been negotiated in great secrecy in Oslo, aimed at furthering Palestinian self-government throughout the West Bank and Gaza. In view of the difficulties of the Jerusalem issue, the negotiators agreed that the future of the city would not be included in the various self-government arrangements that were to be put into effect in the coming two years. Instead, Jerusalem would be one of several subjects, including Palestinian refugees and Israeli settlements, that would be dealt with later, during the negotiations on the 'permanent status' of the Palestinian areas – negotiations that would start in 1996. It was also agreed in the Declaration of Principles that 'Palestinians of Jerusalem who live there' would have the right to participate in the future elections for an interim Self-Governing Authority for the West Bank and Gaza.

On October 11, a month after this agreement was signed, the Israeli Foreign Minister, Shimon Peres, its signatory on the Israeli side, sent a letter to the Norwegian Foreign Minister, Johan Jørgen Holst, in which he confirmed that 'the Palestinian institutions of East Jerusalem and well-being of the Palestinians of East Jerusalem are of great importance and will be preserved'. All Palestinian institutions in East Jerusalem, Peres added, including all economic, social, educational and cultural institutions, as well as the Christian and Muslim Holy Places, 'are performing an essential task for the Palestinian population'. The Government of Israel 'will not hamper their activity; on the contrary, the fulfilment of this important mission is to be encouraged'.

This letter appeared to give authorisation to a development which greatly angered many Israelis: the establishment, in a former hotel in East Jerusalem, Orient House, of the headquarters of several Palestinian institutions. The Peres letter, which was kept secret for almost a year, until it was leaked, was in apparent contradiction to the Declaration of Principles, in which it was stated that the offices of the Palestinian Authority must be located 'only in Gaza and Jericho'. Peres later explained that what he had been referring to in his letter was not political or governmental bodies, but municipal institutions serving the Arab population of Jerusalem.

The Palestinian Authority had been set up as part of the Palestinian-Israeli agreements to be the vehicle whereby Palestinian self-governing institutions would operate throughout the West Bank and Gaza. Those institutions whose headquarters were established in East Jerusalem, rather than Jericho or Gaza, seemed to many Israelis, and indeed to many Palestinians, to reinforce the Palestinians' claim that East Jerusalem must be their capital – not, as Israel wished, at some point in the future, Ramallah or Bethlehem.

The activities at Orient House included meetings between the Palestinian officials working there and several visiting Foreign Ministers. This was deemed by Israel to be out of accord with the Declaration of Principles, and strenuous objections were lodged. But, despite repeated demands by Israel that at least some of the institutions leave Jerusalem altogether, they remained there. By September 1995 there were eleven Palestinian Authority institutions located in Orient House, operating with their own ministers, civil servants and clerks. These included the Palestinian Ministry of Religious Affairs, the Palestinian Broadcasting Council, the Palestinian Bureau of Statistics, the Health Council, the Economic Council for Development and Reconstruction, and the Palestinian Housing Council. This latter offered mortgages to the Arab residents of Jerusalem. Also at Orient House was the office of the Mufti.

*

During a visit to East Jerusalem in August 1994 the chief negotiator of the Palestine Liberation Organisation, Nabil Shaath, called for Jerusalem to be made the 'capital of Palestine'. With him at the press conference was Faisal al-Husseini, who told reporters that he 'envisioned Jerusalem remaining an undivided city, with the eastern half under Palestinian rule'. Al-Husseini wanted Jerusalem to 'remain an open city', with security matters maintained jointly by Israel and the Palestinian Authority. 'Why can't we see Jerusalem as a special place', he asked, 'as the capital of capitals?'

In 1994, as part of the Declaration of Principles signed by Israel and the Palestine Liberation Organisation, the political future of Jerusalem was under continuous, though tentative discussion between Israeli and Palestinian negotiators. Sometimes an external event could eclipse the importance of such talks by its dramatic impact. One such moment came on 3 August 1994, when East and West Jerusalemites looked up with amazement into the sky as a jet aircraft, bearing the crown and insignia of the Royal Jordanian Airlines, flew over the city and circled the Temple Mount. Many people turned on their radios in order to discover the reason for such an extraordinary event. They learned that the plane was being piloted by King Hussein of Jordan himself.

On entering Israeli airspace, the King had spoken by telephone to the Israeli Prime Minister, Yitzhak Rabin. It was the first time that Hussein had flown over Jerusalem. From above he could see the Dome of the Rock, which had been recently gilded, and the al-Aksa Mosque, where he had been at the side of his grandfather the Emir Abdullah when the Emir was assassinated in 1951. That evening the King's gesture in flying over the city was the talking-point in thousands of homes, where the royal flight was seen as a harbinger of better times and wiser counsels.

The future of the Christian Holy Places was also the subject of wide concern. Both the Vatican and the Russian Government wanted to impress upon the Government of Israel their special interest with regard to the city. The first-ever Papal Nuncio to Israel, Andrea Cordero Lanza di Montezemolo, in presenting his credentials in Jerusalem on August 16, said that the voice not only of the Roman Catholic Church but of all Christian denominations should be heard with regard to the city's Holy Places. Nine days later the head of the Middle East Department of the Russian Foreign Ministry, Victor Posuvaliuk, during a visit to Jerusalem, stated that Russia both deserved and demanded a say in the political status of the holy sites. 'Russia possesses the largest Christian Orthodox community in the world,' he pointed out.

*

Extremist Islamic terror continued in Jerusalem. On 9 October 1994, only two months after King Hussein's historic flight over the city, a nineteen-year-old Jewish girl, Maayan Levy, and a thirty-five-year-old Arab, Samir Mugrabi, were both killed, and fourteen people injured, when two Arab gunmen opened fire in the crowded Nahalat Shiva shopping and restaurant quarter, a few moments' walk from Zion Square. Mugrabi, a father of two children, had been a supporter of the peace process. The 'armed wing' of the fundamentalist Islamic group Hamas claimed responsibility for the attack.

That autumn Hamas kidnapped a nineteen-year-old Israeli soldier, Nachshon Wachsman. On October 13, while Wachsman was being held by his captors at a secret hide-out, 50,000 Jews gathered at the Wailing Wall to pray for his life. He was killed the next day, when the Hamas hide-out was discovered by Israeli troops and an attempt was made to rescue him. His father Yehuda was an advocate of improved Jewish-Arab relations, and a supporter of the peace process.

As well as seeking an agreement with the Palestine Liberation

Organisation, the Rabin Government had pursued with tenacity the path of a negotiated peace with Jordan. In the peace treaty signed by Jordan and Israel on 26 October 1994, ending forty-six years of hostility, the Government of Israel acknowledged Jordan's position with regard to the Muslim Holy Places in Jerusalem. The text read: 'Israel respects the present role of the Hashemite Kingdom of Jordan in Muslim Holy Places in Jerusalem. When negotiations on the permanent status will take place, Israel will give high priority to the Jordanian historic role in these shrines.' These two sentences were resented by many Palestinian Muslims.

On the death of the Mufti, the Jordanian Government announced the appointment of Sheikh Abd al-Khader Aabdin as his successor. A few days later Yassir Arafat announced the appointment of Sheikh Ikrima al-Sabri as Mufti. A number of Palestinians from the Palestinian Authority area in Jericho then came to Jerusalem and prevented Arabs from entering Aabdin's office at the al-Aksa Mosque. For a few weeks Aabdin stayed away; then he came to his office once or twice a week, but exercised no authority. For the vast majority of Palestinians in Jerusalem, and on the West Bank, Sheikh al-Sabri was the true Mufti, and their spiritual leader. The Jordanian influence had been successfully challenged.

*

In East Jerusalem a Palestinian cultural renaissance was taking place. On 14 November 1994 the al-Wasiti Art Centre was opened in Sheikh Jarrah after six years of planning. Its first exhibition of paintings was entitled 'From Exile to Jerusalem'. Among the Palestinian artists whose work was on show were Kamal Bullata from Washington, Samir Badran from Barcelona, Laila Shawa from London and Sami Salaamed from Paris. A special tribute was made to the Bethlehem-born Jabra Ibrahim Jabra, a resident of Baghdad, who had founded an art and music appreciation club in Jerusalem in 1944. The club had lasted for four years. 'Even though we have not had such a centre in Jerusalem since that time,' Tania Nasir, a supporter of the new centre, told the opening ceremony, 'culture has always been a part of the network in Jerusalem.'

Violence was now infrequent, but when it came it cast the city into turmoil. On December 25 thirteen Israeli soldiers and civilians were wounded when a suicide bomber tried to board their bus at the entrance to the city but was foiled when the bus driver managed to close the door. The bomber was killed. Hamas claimed responsibility for the attack. Eight months later, in August 1995, five Jews were killed when a suicide bomber blew himself up on a bus in the suburb of Ramat Eshkol. It was the seventh suicide bomb in Israel, where, within a year, more than eighty Israelis had been killed. Among the dead in the Jerusalem bomb was forty-five-year-old Joan Davenny, an American teacher who was on her way to the Hebrew University. Her parents, the Edelsteins, had lived in Jerusalem for nineteen years. The restaurant which they had owned at Jebel Mukkaber, just east of Government House, on the very border of an Arab neighbourhood and with a stunning view of the Dome of the Rock, had been burned down several times during the Intifada by Arab youths. These youths rejected this well-meaning attempt to create a bridge between the two communities.

A month after Joan Davenny's death, her father, Burt Edelstein, reflected: 'We have absolutely no feeling of animosity against Arabs. From the moment we heard the news, we never thought, "Ah, the Arabs did this." It never crossed our minds. We have some dear Arab friends who went to pieces when they heard that our daughter was one of the victims on that bus.'

The bomber, Sufiyan Jabareen, blew himself up with his six-kilo-gram explosive suitcase. He was twenty-six years old, an unemployed labourer. In clinical, callous language, the Nablus man who had sent Jabareen on his suicide mission, and had himself been captured by the Israelis, told his captors: 'Hamas does not waste senior members with proven military successes on suicide missions. Our suicide bombers are merely human fuses replacing a chemical or electrical device.'

For twenty-four hours Jerusalem was in a state of shock. Yet the emerging and widening accords between Israel and Yassir Arafat's recently-established Palestinian Authority seemed to offer some hope. The continuing killing was aimed at destroying agreement between Israel and the Palestinians. It was to try to prevent such a destruction that in the last week of August, following Sufiyan Jabareen's act of terror, the Palestinian police in Gaza arrested a Hamas activist whom they said was 'on his way to blow himself up at Jerusalem's Central Bus Station'.

*

Part of the debate in 1995 was whether the two sides of the Jerusalem divide could ever come together. Whenever a terrorist attack took place, optimism waned. Yet efforts at reconciliation continued to be made. By chance, on entering the Jerusalem hill resort of Arza in the summer of 1995, I found the Palestinian flag flying alongside the Israeli flag. A group of Jewish and Arab youth movements had come together for a few days of discussions, sleeping in separate buildings but sitting on the lawns and in the conference rooms in amicable if heated debate. An outside observer at the meetings, an American journalist, told me that he doubted whether there would be any agreement among the young people, except to disagree. But the effort was being made.

In the Young Women's Christian Association technical college in East Jerusalem, a special class was held on 25 May 1995 to encourage some fifty Palestinian-Arab girls, mostly Muslims between the ages of eighteen and twenty, to express their opinions freely in the political debates then centring around the forthcoming Palestinian elections. Many Jerusalem Arabs will have a vote in these elections, even though Israel has excluded Jerusalem from the Palestinian Authority's area of responsibility.

The aim of the meeting at the technical college was to encourage debate across a spectrum of Arab concerns, including freedom of speech, equality for women, and minority rights. The Executive Director of the Palestinian Centre for Peace and Democracy, Naseef Muallem, told the young women: 'You cannot say democracy is only elections, which are only once every four years. Democracy is a way of life in society. Democracy begins in the family.'

The process of creating a democratic system, while the rights of the Palestinian Arabs in Jerusalem are still curtailed, is a hard one. Among those who persevere in trying to enhance it is Marwan Burgan, the Director of the Washington-based International Foundation for Electoral Systems. He organised 153 seminars in Arab schools in three months, many of them in Jerusalem. He is aware of the strength of Islamic feeling in the city, and of the reluctance of many Muslims, not only fundamentalists, to regard democracy as something other than alien and hostile to Arab aspirations and ideology. 'You cannot really champion democracy from outside,' he warned. 'One of the great challenges is to define democracy in Islamic terms. We try to look for examples in the Koran. One can find elements of democracy there. But there is a school of thought which rejects democracy as a Western concept.'

The struggle for the peaceful future of Jerusalem is also a struggle for the disposition of the whole region among its divergent, and often conflicting, peoples. Men like Muallem and Burgan are not willing to despair. What the future may bring is inevitably obscure, but the forces of confrontation and those of conciliation are in almost daily, often visible, conflict. This was seen in the first months of 1995 when the pine-covered hillside between Jewish Ramot and Arab Shuafat was cleared to create a new Jewish neighbourhood, Reches Shuafat (Shuafat Ridge), with 2,100 housing units for ultra-Orthodox Jews. The most easterly houses of the new Jewish suburb were only a few yards from the built-up Arab area.

*

During 1995 many schemes were floated for the future of Jerusalem. One which represented a radical departure from the norm, but was nevertheless not beyond the realm of possibility, was put forward by the historian Bernard Wasserstein in a public lecture in London on 19 June 1995. 'Throughout the whole of its modern history,' he said, 'Jerusalem has been a divided city. It is still a divided city today. And I venture to predict that it will remain a divided city in the future.' Wasserstein proposed Palestinian-Arab control of a narrow strip of Arab-inhabited suburbs and areas from Ramallah in the north to Sheikh Jarrah, then 'broadening out' to include the Arab-populated districts of Wadi al-Joz, the Muslim Quarter of the Old City and possibly Silwan to the south – an area with about 30,000 Arab residents which 'although it lies within the municipal borders of Jerusalem, still retains much of the character of an Arab village'.

The Israelis would retain the rest of the Old City, and the post-1967 Jewish suburbs in the south, east and north. 'Under such a scheme,' Wasserstein wrote, 'nearly all Jews and a majority of Arabs in the Jerusalem area would live under their own sovereignty, and would control their own holy places. International guarantees would secure the interests in the holy places of Christians and Muslims in general. Each side would be free to declare Jerusalem its capital. And each side could plausibly maintain that the swap of territory did not affect its vital interests and was broadly equitable.'

Wasserstein concluded: 'Such a proposal is not quite as alien to Israeli or Palestinian thinking as one might imagine. Indeed, the Israeli Government has on occasion in the past considered a settlement that would involve Israeli sovereignty over the whole city, save for a sovereign Arab corridor to the Temple Mount which would be under Arab sovereignty.'

*

On 2 November 1993 Teddy Kollek had been defeated as Mayor of Jerusalem, after twenty-eight years of mayoral responsibility. His successful opponent was a member of the opposition Likud Party, Ehud Olmert, who was supported by the Orthodox Jewish political parties. There was a mood of frustration among Kollek's supporters that it was Olmert who would reap the benefits of Kollek's decision, while he was still Mayor, to celebrate, starting in September 1995, the three-thousandth anniversary of the city's foundation by King David.

The launching of the 'Jerusalem 3,000' campaign was fraught with difficulties, although it was only the older residents who remembered that the same anniversary had been celebrated in Jerusalem forty-three years earlier. Seventeen months of festivities were to commemorate the rule of King David who, 3,000 years earlier, had purchased the threshing field from a local Jebusite woman, as the ground on which his son Solomon was to build the first Temple of Jerusalem. At the opening ceremony, held on 4 September 1995, the Israeli Prime Minister, Yitzhak Rabin, declared: 'Undivided Jerusalem is the heart of the Jewish people and the capital of the State of Israel. Undivided Jerusalem is ours.'

Of the seventy foreign diplomats invited to the opening ceremony, only seventeen agreed to be present. Jewish Jerusalemites were particularly disappointed, and some were angry, that the United States Ambassador, Martin Indyk, the first Jew to hold that post, also stayed away from the celebrations. The new Mayor of Jerusalem, Ehud Olmert, went so far as to describe the issue of Jerusalem as 'an open wound in the relations between us and the United States'.

The main ceremony on the opening day took place amid the 3,000-year-old remains of the fortified Jerusalem of antiquity in the City of David. Just to the east, across a narrow valley, the Arabs of the village of Silwan held a silent protest during the ceremony. As the ceremony ended in the City of David, hundreds of balloons were released from Silwan in the Palestinian national colours: red, black, green and white.

Despite the balloons over Silwan, the slow, steady progress of Arab-Israeli reconciliation continued. On 21 September 1995 the head of the Palestinian Red Crescent Society, Dr Fathi Arafat, the younger brother of the Chairman of the Palestinian Authority, met his Israeli opposite number, Professor David Barzilai, head of the Magen David Adom (Red Shield), in the King David Hotel. They discussed the possibility of cooperation between their two societies in emergency medicine, and in the establishment of a blood bank. It was a constructive step forward.

This important development was the precursor of several other constructive initiatives across the fifty-year-old divide. But the depth of that divide, and in particular the clash of aspirations between Israel and the Palestinian Arabs over Jerusalem, was heightened on the following day, September 22, when the *Jerusalem Post* published an interview with Ehud Olmert. In the interview, Olmert set out his plan, as Mayor, 'to fill in the gap' between the northern suburb of Pisgat Zeev and the centre of the town, so that 'in all the area there will be one continuity of Jewish neighbourhoods, all the way from Pisgat Zeev across to French Hill down to the centre of the city'. As to the possibility of the current Arab population of 160,000 increasing by immigration, Olmert was emphatic: 'The only needs for the Arabs are their own natural growth, because we will not allow the immigration of Arabs from outside the city into the city. This is not the policy of the city. This is not the policy of Israel. We are not opening Jerusalem for Arab immigration from across the world. Jerusalem is part of the State of Israel. They do not want to be part of the State of Israel. What purpose do we have in bringing Arabs to aggravate the problems that we already have?' Olmert explained that his goal was to increase the Jewish population by at least half a million 'in the next twenty-five years'.

Despite Olmert's emphasis on the future and permanent Israeli nature of Jerusalem – an emphasis which most Israeli Jerusalemites supported – the question of the future status of East Jerusalem remains on the Israeli-Palestinian agenda, and on the wider Arab agenda. Speaking in Strasbourg, to the Parliamentary Assembly of the Council of Europe, on September 25, King Hussein of Jordan envisaged Jerusalem as the capital of both Israel and the Palestinians, and spoke of the Holy City as 'a platform for reconciliation'. Its history, he said, 'should never again be "liberation" for some and "loss" for others. Its rightful place in history is where the three faiths – Judaism, Christianity and Islam – converge, and where sovereignty is God's alone.'

King Hussein did not believe that the 'problem of Jerusalem' presented an insuperable difficulty. 'The Greater City of Jerusalem,' he said, 'can be the capital of both the State of Israel and Palestine. Jerusalem should be a shining symbol and the essence of peace for ever between Palestinians and Israelis, as well as all the followers of the three great monotheistic religions.'

On 10 October 1995, as part of Israel's agreement with the Palestine Liberation Organisation, two members of the PLO's former Jerusalem Committee, Mustafa Liftawi and Mahmoud Aloul, crossed into Israel from Jordan as a prelude to becoming Governors of Ramallah and Nablus respectively. Twenty years earlier they had been on Israel's list of most wanted men, having masterminded the Zion Square bomb in which fourteen people, including three Arabs, were killed. Some Jewish Jerusalemites were bewildered, others angered to read the *Jerusalem Post* headline 'Returned terrorist chieftains to govern Ramallah, Nablus.' That same day the Israeli military authorities on the West Bank handed over the civil administration of the first of 460 villages to the Palestinian Authority. The first village to be transferred that day was Salfit, near Nablus. As the Israeli trucks drove out of the village, the villagers raised a banner with the words 'Today Salfit, tomorrow Jerusalem'.

For almost all Israelis, this slogan was a challenge and a danger. 'There are not two Jerusalems,' the Israeli Prime Minister, Yitzhak Rabin, said in Washington on October 25. 'There is only one Jerusalem. For us, Jerusalem is not subject to compromise, and there is no peace without Jerusalem. Jerusalem, which was destroyed eight times, where for years we had no access to the remnants of our Temple, was ours, is ours, and will be ours – for ever.'

The conflicting views appeared unbridgeable. But the reality can often tend towards compromise. On October 27 Rabin himself, seeking a way to break the deadlock and the tension with regard to Jerusalem's Arab population, agreed that when the time came for the Palestinian elections, early in the new year, election posters could be placed anywhere in East Jerusalem, and that the voting in the city would be supervised by the Palestinian Central Election Commission. An important Israeli gesture had been made to the Arabs of East Jerusalem. But Rabin's efforts to seek accommodation with the Palestinian Arabs were denounced by the Opposition parties in the Knesset, and pilloried in the streets on wall posters in which he was denounced as a traitor. Near his official Jerusalem residence in Balfour Street, posters were put up showing him in Arab headdress. On October 28, during an opposition rally in Zion Square, a photographic montage was circulated showing him in Nazi uniform. A week later, on the evening of Saturday November 4, at the end of a peace rally in Tel Aviv, he was assassinated by a Jewish fanatic.

Rabin's murder sent a shudder of despair throughout Israel. In the streets of Jerusalem men and women wept openly. At Zion Square, the scene of the hostile rally a week earlier, a makeshift memorial was set up, with a photograph of Rabin, cut from a newspaper, pasted on to a lamp-post. Flowers were placed there, and memorial candles were lit by the roadside. Throughout the following day, and throughout the night of November 5, an estimated one million people, coming from all over Israel, and many from overseas, filed past Rabin's coffin as it lay in state in the forecourt of the Knesset. Some people collapsed in grief. Many cried. Others were unwilling to move on, unable to tear themselves away from the coffin, unable to say a last farewell. Thousands of bunches of flowers were brought, and hundreds of memorial candles were lit around the coffin. Young boys and girls sat on the ground in groups, singing quietly.

At midday on November 5, as the coffin was driven slowly through the streets from the Knesset to the Military Cemetery on Mount Herzl, hundreds of people lined the roadside in silence, standing impassive, shocked, saddened and grieving. As the funeral service began, sirens wailed loud and piercing in unbroken agony for two minutes that seemed an eternity. The mourners stood in silence. In the streets, tens of thousands of people who had been walking towards Mount Herzl stopped and stood to attention. Motorists stopped their vehicles and stood by their open doors in tribute and solemn contemplation. As the sirens' wail continued, many of those in the streets, and in their homes, bowed their heads and wept.

At the funeral ceremony, attended by 4,000 invited guests, representatives of eighty-six nations were present. These included more than forty Heads of State and Prime Ministers. King Hussein of Jordan and President Mubarak of Egypt were among those who delivered eulogies. Mubarak had never been in Jerusalem before, the city where his predecessor Anwar Sadat had been a surprising, and honoured, visitor in 1977. Nor had King Hussein ever been in the Jewish part of the city. Forty-four years earlier, however, he had been present in East Jerusalem, on the Haram, at the assassination of his grandfather King Abdullah.

In the whole history of Jerusalem in the twentieth century, no day was as sombre, as silent, as full of individual sorrow and collective contemplation, as the day of Rabin's funeral. 'How can you try to comfort an entire people?' his granddaughter, Noa Ben-Artzi Filosof, asked in her eulogy, 'or include in it your personal pain, when grandma does not stop crying, and we are mute, feeling the enormous void that is left only by your absence?'

In the week following Rabin's funeral, hundreds of thousands of

Jews came to his grave to pay their respects, to stand in silence with heads bowed, and to light memorial candles. Several thousand letters of farewell were placed by visitors at the graveside. On November 12, when the week of mourning came to an end, his family and close friends returned there for a short ceremony. 'A young cedar tree spread its shade over the grave,' wrote Batsheva Tsur in the *Jerusalem Post*. 'The smell of wax wafted into the chill of the air as hundreds of the memorial candles lit by pained citizens continued to flicker. Early in the morning, a group of soldiers had carefully rearranged them – tall candles in the centre, a candle holder in the shape of a white dove to the side – so the grave would be more accessible to the mourners. An olive tree sapling was moved close to the trees in the grove. The thousands of letters written by citizens were gathered into bags.' Family and friends said prayers, seeking solace in each other's company. Then Rabin's wife, Leah, led the mourners around the grave.

Batsheva Tsur's account continued: 'Generals saluted before the grave of the first son of Jerusalem to be buried in the section reserved for the Great of the Nation. Eitan Haber, Rabin's longtime bureau chief, lingered, then came back, unable to tear himself away. Softly sobbing secretaries placed red roses and white lilies on the flower-laden grave. Medics and soldiers on duty at the site began streaming past. Even the media, speaking in unusually hushed tones, went to pay their last respects.'

Rabin's last resting place had become a place of solemn pilgrimage. When the Russian Minister of Defence, Pavel Grachev, visited Jerusalem three weeks later, there were two special points on his itinerary: Yad Vashem and Rabin's grave.

On December 5 a large gathering of mourners, including more than two hundred Jewish leaders from abroad, representatives of twenty-five Diaspora communities, placed wreaths on Rabin's grave at the end of the traditional Jewish thirty days of mourning. That afternoon, in the Convention Hall at the entrance to the city, his life and work were commemorated before a large gathering of family, friends, colleagues, citizens, visitors from abroad and diplomats. His part in the battle for Jerusalem in 1948 was recalled, and his remark many years later about the heavy fighting that year to keep open the road to Jerusalem: 'I still remember the pain echoing. I still remember the silence of death.'

That Rabin had been born in Jerusalem, the only Israeli Prime Minister in forty-eight years of whom that could be said, was a source of pride to those who had gathered to remember him.

The future of Jerusalem remains the subject of discussion and disagreement. As King Hussein of Jordan had envisaged it in September
1995, the city could be the 'essence of peace'. It could equally be the
source of conflict. It had been in the past, and could be in the future,
the scene of riots or of reconciliation; the focus of celebration or of
protest; of religious devotion or religious hatred; of quiet contemplation or loud exhortation.

In the early months of 1996, two acts of terror in Jerusalem shocked
the whole of Israel. On Sunday February 25, twenty-six people were
killed in an explosion on a bus near the Central Bus Station. One of the
dead was the Palestinian-Arab suicide bomber. The others killed were
Israeli soldiers, students, workers, and seven recent immigrants from
Russia, including Boris Sharpolinsky, who had been in Israel for just
eight months. Two of those killed, Matthew Eisenfeld and his fiancée
Sara Duker, were American Jews studying in Jerusalem. Also killed
was a twenty-three-year-old Palestinian, Wael Kawasmeh. A week
later, on Sunday March 3, nineteen people were killed on a bus near the
Main Post Office. Among them, as well as the suicide bomber, were
Israeli soldiers and students, several workers from Roumania, and two
Palestinians. These killings cast a pall of fear over the process of
Arab–Jewish reconciliation, the vision close to the heart of Rabin's
successor, Shimon Peres.

The twentieth century has often been a bloody one for Jerusalem.
But it has also been a century of creativity and satisfaction, exuberant
life, determination, civic achievement, and perpetual hope. 'Jerusalem
has a thousand faces,' Yitzhak Rabin had told his listeners in Washington in October 1995, 'and each one of us has his own Jerusalem.'

Bibliography of works cited in the text

REPORTS AND OFFICIAL STATEMENTS
(in chronological order)

The Times History of the War, volume XV, Printing House Square, London, 1918.

A Brief Record of the Advance of the Egyptian Expeditionary Force, July 1917 to October 1918, His Majesty's Stationery Office, London, 1919.

The War Graves of the British Empire, The Register of the names of those who fell in the Great War and are buried in the Jerusalem Group of Cemeteries, Palestine, Imperial War Graves Commission, London, 1927.

Report of the Commission on the Palestine Disturbances of August 1929, Command Paper 3530 of 1930, His Majesty's Stationery Office, London, 1930.

The Hebrew University Jerusalem, 1929/30, Jerusalem, September 1930.

Report of the Executives of the Zionist Organisation and of the Jewish Agency for Palestine, Jerusalem, 1937.

Palestine Royal Commission Report, Command Paper 5479 of 1937, His Majesty's Stationery Office, London, 1937.

Palestine Partition Commission Report, Command Paper 5854 of 1938, His Majesty's Stationery Office, London, 1938.

Hadassah Medical Organisation, *Report for 1939*, Jerusalem, 1940.

Report of the Anglo-American Committee of Enquiry regarding the problems of European Jewry and Palestine, Command Paper 6808 of 1946, His Majesty's Stationery Office, London, 1946.

The Hebrew University, Jerusalem, Its History and Development, Third Edition (Revised), Jerusalem, 1948.

Progress Report of the United Nations Mediator on Palestine, Command Paper 7530 of 1948, His Majesty's Stationery Office, London, 1948.

Geographical Section, General Staff, *Jerusalem Town Plan, Compiled and drawn by the Survey of Palestine, 1945*, War Office, London, 1952.

United States Mission to the United Nations, *Press Release*, USUN-70 (69), 1 July 1969.

364

Bibliography

R. Lapidoth and M. Hirsch (editors), *The Jerusalem Question and Its Resolution: Selected Documents*, Martinus Nijhoff, Dordrecht, 1994.

Elihu Lauterpacht, *Jerusalem and the Holy Places*, Anglo-Israel Association, London, October 1968.

The Planning of Jerusalem, Association of Engineers and Architects in Israel, Tel Aviv, April 1974.

Ora Ahimeir (editor), *Jerusalem, Aspects of Law*, The Jerusalem Institute for Israel Studies, Jerusalem, 1983.

David Kroyanker, *Jerusalem, Planning Developments, 1982–1985, New Trends*, Jerusalem Committee and others, Jerusalem, March 1985.

Address by His Majesty King Hussein to the Parliamentary Assembly of the Council of Europe (speech), Strasbourg, 25 September 1995.

Menahem Milson, *Sadat's Visit, A Personal Memoir (November 19–21, 1977)*, Jerusalem, October 1995.

GUIDEBOOKS
(in chronological order of publication)

E. A. Reynolds-Ball, *Guide to Jerusalem*, London, 1901.

Rev. J. E. Hanauer and Dr E. G. Masterman (editors), *Cook's Handbook for Palestine and Syria*, Simpkin, Marshall, Hamilton, Kent, London, 1907.

Father Barnabas Meistermann, *New Guide to the Holy Land*, London, 1908.

Rev. J. E. Hanauer, *Walks About Jerusalem*, London Society for Promoting Christianity Amongst the Jews, London, 1910.

G. E. Franklin, *Palestine Depicted and Described*, London and New York, 1911.

A Guide Book to Southern Palestine, Based upon the well-known enemy publication Baedeker's Palestine and Syria and augmented by numerous editions, Palestine Pocket Guide-Books, volume 1, Cairo, 1918.

Fr. Vester, *A Guide-Book to Jerusalem and Environs*, American Colony Stores, Jerusalem, 1920.

Harry Charles Luke (editor), *The Traveller's Handbook for Palestine and Syria*, Simpkin, Marshall, London, new edition, 1924.

J. E. Hanauer, *Walks in and around Jerusalem*, London Society for Promoting Christianity Amongst the Jews, London, 1926.

Christopher Lumby (editor), *Cook's Handbook to Palestine and Syria and Iraq*, Simpkin Marshall, London, 6th edition, 1934.

Zev Vilnay, *The Guide to Israel*, Ahiever, Jerusalem, 1955 (16th edition, 1973).

Elian-J. Finbert, *Israel*, Librairie Hachette, Paris, 1956.

Father Eugene Hoade, *Guide to the Holy Land*, Franciscan Press, Jerusalem, 4th edition, 1962.

Sarah Kaminker, *Footloose in Jerusalem, eight guided walking tours*, Footloose Publishers, Jerusalem, July 1970 (7th edition, 1988).

Nitza Rosovsky, *Jerusalemwalks*, Holt, Rinehart and Winston, New York, 1982.

David Benvenisti, *Tours in Jerusalem*, Kiryat Sefer, Jerusalem, 1985.

Bibliography

Arlynn Nellhaus, *The Heart of Jerusalem*, John Muir, Santa Fe, 1988.

Kay Prag, *Jerusalem* (Blue Guide), A. & C. Black, London, 1989.

Martin Lev, *The Traveller's Key to Jerusalem, A Guide to the Secret Places of Jerusalem*, Harrap, London, 1990.

Alan Mirsky, *Point by Point in the Jewish Quarter*, Jerusalem, January 1993.

BOOKS

Zvi Abells and Asher Arbit, *The City of David Water Systems, Plus Brief Descriptions of Aqueducts, Storage Pools and the Present Day Supply of Water to Jerusalem*, privately printed, Jerusalem, 1995.

David Aberbach, *Bialik*, Peter Halban, London, 1988.

Fannie Fern Andrews, *The Holy Land Under the Mandate*, 2 volumes, Houghton Mifflin, Boston, 1931.

Hannah Arendt, *Eichmann in Jerusalem*, Viking Press, New York, 1963.

C. R. Ashbee, *A Palestine Notebook, 1918–1923*, William Heinemann, London, 1923.

C. R. Ashbee (editor), *Jerusalem, 1920–1922*, John Murray, London, 1924.

Pablo de Azcazarte, *Mission in Palestine, 1948–1952*, Middle East Institute, Washington DC, 1966.

Michael Bar-Zohar, *Ben-Gurion*, Weidenfeld and Nicolson, London, 1978.

Alex Bein (editor), *Arthur Ruppin: Memoirs, Diaries, Letters*, Weidenfeld and Nicolson, London, 1971.

Saul Bellow, *To Jerusalem and Back, A Personal Account*, Viking Press, New York, 1976.

Shimon Ben-Eliezer, *Destruction and Renewal, The Synagogues of the Jewish Quarter*, Rubin Mass, Jerusalem, 1975.

Margery Bentwich, *Thelma Yellin, Pioneer Musician*, Ruben Mass, Jerusalem, 1964.

Norman Bentwich (editor), *Hebrew University Garland, A Silver Jubilee Symposium*, Vallentine, Mitchell, London, 1951.

Norman Bentwich, *Judah L. Magnes, A Biography of the first Chancellor and first President of the Hebrew University of Jerusalem*, East and West Library, London, 1955.

Norman Bentwich, *My 77 Years, An Account of My Life and Times, 1883–1960*, Routledge and Kegan Paul, London, 1962.

Meron Benvenisti, *Jerusalem, The Torn City*, Isratypeset, Jerusalem, 1976.

Folke Bernadotte, *To Jerusalem*, Hodder and Stoughton, London, 1951.

Estelle Blyth, *When We Lived in Jerusalem*, John Murray, London, 1927.

H. Eugene Bovis, *The Jerusalem Question, 1917–1968*, Stanford, California, 1971.

Randolph S. Churchill and Winston S. Churchill, *The Six Day War*, Heinemann, London, 1967.

Mary Clawson, *Letters from Jerusalem*, Abelard-Schuman, London, 1957.

Bibliography

Israel Cohen, *Travels in Jewry*, Edward Goldston, London, 1952.

Saul B. Cohen, *Jerusalem, Bridging the Four Walls, A Geopolitical Perspective*, Herzl Press, New York, 1977.

Yona Cohen, *Jerusalem Under Siege, Pages from a 1948 Diary*, Ridgefield, Los Angeles, 1982.

Larry Collins and Dominique Lapierre, *O Jerusalem!*, Weidenfeld and Nicolson, London, 1972.

Ruby Cromer, *The Hospital of St John in Jerusalem*, London, 1961.

Richard Crossman, *Palestine Mission, A Personal Record*, Hamish Hamilton, London, 1947.

Hillel Danziger (editor), *Guardian of Jerusalem, The Life and Times of Rabbi Yosef Chaim Sonnenfeld*, Mesorah Publications, New York, 1983.

Joan Dash, *Summoned to Jerusalem, the Life of Henrietta Szold*, Harper and Row, New York, 1979.

Amos Elon, *Jerusalem, City of Mirrors*, Weidenfeld and Nicolson, London, 1990.

Elias M. Epstein, *Jerusalem Correspondent, 1919–1958*, Jerusalem Post Press, Jerusalem, 1964.

Walter Eytan, *The First Ten Years, A Diplomatic History of Israel*, Simon and Schuster, New York, 1958.

Captain Cyril Falls, *Military Operations, Egypt and Palestine*, 2 volumes, Macmillan, London, 1930.

Leslie Farmer, *We Saw the Holy City*, Epworth Press, London, 1944.

Isaiah Friedman, *The Question of Palestine, 1914–1918, British-Jewish-Arab Relations*, Routledge and Kegan Paul, London, 1973.

Isaiah Friedman, *Germany, Turkey, and Zionism, 1897–1918*, Clarendon Press, Oxford, 1977.

Thomas Friedman, *From Beirut to Jerusalem*, Collins, London, 1990.

P. Gillon (editor), *Recollections of a Medical Doctor in Jerusalem, From Professor Julius J. Kleeberg's Notebooks, 1930–1988*, Karger, Basel, 1992.

Nelson Gluek, *Dateline: Jerusalem, A Diary by Nelson Gluek*, Hebrew Union College Press, Cincinnati, 1968.

Miss A. Goodrich-Freer, *Inner Jerusalem*, London, 1904.

Robert H. Goodsall, *Palestine Memories, 1917–1918–1925*, Cross and Jackman, Canterbury, 1925.

Arthur A. Goren, *Dissenter in Zion, From the Writings of Judah L. Magnes*, Harvard University Press, Cambridge, Massachusetts, 1982.

Stephen Graham, *With the Russian Pilgrims to Jerusalem*, Thomas Nelson, London, 1914.

Philip Graves, *Palestine, The Land of Three Faiths*, Jonathan Cape, London, 1926.

Yael Guiladi, *One Jerusalem*, Keter, Jerusalem, 1979.

Eric Hammel, *Six Days in June, How Israel Won the 1967 Arab-Israeli War*, Charles Scribner's Sons, New York, 1992.

S. F. Hatton, *The Yarn of a Yeoman*, Hutchinson, London, no date.

Bibliography

Gideon Hausner, *Justice in Jerusalem*, Schocken Books, New York, 1968.

Joseph Heller, *The Stern Gang, Ideology, Politics and Terror, 1940–1949*, Frank Cass, London, 1995.

Theodor Herzl, *Altneuland, Old-New Land*, illustrated English-language edition, Haifa Publishing Company, Haifa, 1960 (first editions in German, Yiddish, Polish, Hebrew, Russian, French, Roumanian, Hungarian and Dutch, 1902–3).

I. W. J. Hopkins, *Jerusalem, A Study in Urban Geography*, Baker, Grand Rapids, Michigan, 1970.

Albert Hourani, *A History of the Arab Peoples*, Faber and Faber, London, 1991.

F. Robert Hunter, *The Palestinian Uprising, A War by Other Means*, I. B. Tauris, London, 1991.

Albert M. Hymanson (editor), *The British Consulate in Jerusalem in relation to the Jews of Palestine, 1838–1914*, Edward Goldston, London, 1941.

Dov Joseph, *The Faithful City, The Siege of Jerusalem, 1948*, Simon and Schuster, New York, 1960.

Mousa J. Kaleel, *When I was a Boy in Palestine*, George G. Harrap, London, April 1920.

Ruth Kark, *Jerusalem Neighborhoods, Planning and By-laws, 1855–1930*, Magnes Press, Jerusalem, 1991.

Menahem Kaufman, *America's Jerusalem Policy, 1947–1948*, Hebrew University of Jerusalem, Jerusalem, 1982.

Edward Keith-Roach, *Pasha of Jerusalem, Memoirs of a District Commissioner under the British Mandate*, Radcliffe Press, London, 1994.

Henry Kendall, *Jerusalem, The City Plan, Preservation and Development During the British Mandate, 1918–1948*, His Majesty's Stationery Office, London, 1948.

Walid Khalidi (editor), *All That Remains: The Palestinian Villages Occupied and Depopulated by Israel in 1948*, Institute for Palestine Studies, Washington DC, 1992.

Sir Alec Kirkbride, *A Crackle of Thorns*, John Murray, London, 1956.

Dr Joseph Klausner, *Menachem Ussishkin, His Life and Work*, Joint Zionist Publication Committee, London, no date.

Teddy Kollek and Moshe Pearlman, *Jerusalem Sacred City of Mankind: a history of forty centuries*, Steimatzky's Agency, Tel Aviv, 1968.

Teddy Kollek, *For Jerusalem*, Weidenfeld and Nicolson, London, 1978.

Teddy Kollek, *Jerusalem*, The Washington Institute for Near East Policy, Washington DC, 1990.

Joel L. Kraemer (editor), *Jerusalem, Problems and Prospects*, Praeger, New York, 1980.

David Kroyanker (editor), *Jerusalem, Planning and Development, 1978/79*, Jerusalem Institute for Israel Studies, June 1979.

David Kroyanker, *Jerusalem architecture*, Tauris Parke, London, 1994.

Arthur Kutcher, *The New Jerusalem, Planning and Politics*, Thames and Hudson, London, 1973.

Bibliography

Eli Landau, *Jerusalem the Eternal, The Paratroopers' Battle for the City of David*, Otpaz, Tel Aviv, 1968.

Harry Levin, *Jerusalem Embattled, A Diary of the City under Siege, March 25th, 1948 to July 18th, 1948*, Victor Gollancz, London, 1950.

Major H. O. Lock, *With the British Army in the Holy Land*, Robert Scott, London, 1919.

Lieutenant-Colonel Netanel Lorch, *The Edge of the Sword, Israel's War of Independence, 1947–1949*, G. P. Putnam's Sons, New York, 1961.

R. A. S. Macalister, *A Century of Excavation in Palestine*, London, 1925.

James G. McDonald, *My Mission in Israel, 1948–1951*, Simon and Schuster, New York, 1951.

Neville J. Mandel, *The Arabs and Zionism before World War I*, University of California Press, Berkeley and Los Angeles, 1976.

W. T. Massey, *How Jerusalem Was Won, Being the Record of Allenby's Campaign in Palestine*, Constable, London, 1919.

Basil Mathews, *The Freedom of Jerusalem*, London, 1918.

Golda Meir, *My Life*, Weidenfeld and Nicolson, London, 1975.

Abraham E. Millgram, *Jerusalem Curiosities*, Jewish Publication Society, Philadelphia, 1990.

Benny Morris, *The birth of the Palestinian refugee problem, 1947–1949*, Cambridge University Press, Cambridge, 1987.

H. V. Morton, *In The Steps of the Master*, Rich and Cowan, London, 1934.

General Uzi Narkiss, *The Liberation of Jerusalem, The Battle of 1967*, Vallentine, Mitchell, London, 1983.

Monsignor John M. Oesterreicher and Anne Sinai (editors), *Jerusalem*, John Day, New York, 1974.

James Parkes, *The Story of Jerusalem*, The Cresset Press, London, 1949.

Helen Palmer Parsons (editor), *Letters from Palestine: 1868–1912, Written by Rolla Floyd*, privately printed, Jerusalem, 1981.

Lieutenant-Colonel J. H. Patterson, *With the Judaeans in the Palestine Campaign*, Hutchinson, London, 1922.

Maurice Pearlman, *Mufti of Jerusalem, The Story of Haj Amin El Husseini*, Victor Gollancz, London, 1947.

Shimon Peres, *Battling for Peace, Memoirs*, Weidenfeld and Nicolson, London, 1995.

John Phillips, *A Will to Survive*, Dial Press, New York, 1977.

Y. Porath, *The Emergence of the Palestinian-Arab National Movement, 1918–1929*, Frank Cass, London, 1974.

Zipporah Porath, *Letters from Jerusalem, 1947–1948*, Association of Americans and Canadians in Israel, Jerusalem, 1978.

Terence Prittie, *Whose Jerusalem?*, Frederick Muller, London, 1981.

David Pryce-Jones, *The Face of Defeat, Palestinian Refugees and Guerrillas*, Weidenfeld and Nicolson, London, 1972.

Yitzhak Rabin, *The Rabin Memoirs*, Weidenfeld and Nicolson, London, 1979.

Bibliography

Abraham Rabinovich, *The Battle for Jerusalem, June 5–7, 1967*, Jewish Publication Society, Philadelphia, 1972.

Abraham Rabinovich, *Jerusalem on Earth, People, Passions, and Politics in the Holy City*, Collier Macmillan, London, 1988.

Louis Rapoport, *Confrontations*, Quinlan Press, Boston, 1988.

Malkah Raymist, *The Stiff-Necked City, A journalist's personal account of the Siege of Jerusalem, 1948*, Gefen, Jerusalem, 1989.

Anat Reisman-Levy (editor), *Jerusalem: Perspectives Towards a Political Settlement*, United States Institute of Peace, Washington DC, July 1993.

Pauline Rose, *The Siege of Jerusalem*, London, 1951.

Trevor Royle, *Glubb Pasha, The Life and Times of Sir John Glubb, Commander of the Arab Legion*, Little Brown and Company, London, 1992.

Harry Sacher (editor), *Zionism and the Jewish Future*, John Murray, London, 1916.

Moshe Safdie, *Jerusalem, The Future of the Past*, Houghton Mifflin, Boston, 1989.

Edward W. Said, *The Politics of Dispossession, The Struggle for Palestinian Self-Determination, 1969–1994*, Chatto & Windus, London, 1994.

Edwin Samuel, *A Lifetime in Jerusalem, The Memoirs of the Second Viscount Samuel*, Vallentine Mitchell, London, 1970.

Simon Schama, *Two Rothschilds and the Land of Israel*, Alfred A. Knopf, New York, 1978.

Abdullah Schleifer, *The Fall of Jerusalem*, New York, 1972.

Gershom Scholem, *From Berlin to Jerusalem, Memories of My Youth*, Schocken Books, New York, 1980.

Yitzhak Shamir, *Summing Up, an autobiography*, Weidenfeld and Nicolson, London, 1994.

Zeev Sharef, *Three Days*, W. H. Allen, London, 1962.

Arieh Sharon, *Planning Jerusalem, The Old City and its Environs*, Weidenfeld and Nicolson, London, 1973.

Naomi Shepherd, *The Mayor and the Citadel, Teddy Kollek and Jerusalem*, Weidenfeld and Nicolson, London, 1987.

Naomi Shepherd, *Alarms and Excursions, Thirty Years in Israel*, Collins, London, 1990.

Evelyn Shuckburgh, *Descent to Suez, Diaries, 1951–56*, Weidenfeld and Nicolson, London, 1986.

Bernard Spolsky and Robert L. Cooper, *The Languages of Jerusalem*, Clarendon Press, Oxford, 1991.

Ronald Storrs, *Orientations*, Nicholson and Watson, London, 1943.

Yehuda Taggar, *The Mufti of Jerusalem and Palestine Arab Politics, 1930–1937*, Garland, New York, 1986.

Eliezer Tauber, *The Arab Movements in World War I*, Frank Cass, London, 1993.

Colin Thubron, *Jerusalem*, William Heinemann, London, 1969.

Bibliography

Bertha Spafford Vester, *Our Jerusalem*, Doubleday, Garden City, New York, 1950.

Bernard Wasserstein, *Herbert Samuel, A Political Life*, Clarendon Press, Oxford, 1992.

Gideon Weigert, *Israel's Presence in East Jerusalem*, Jerusalem Post Press, Jerusalem, 1973.

Elie Wiesel, *All Rivers Run to the Sea, Memoirs*, Alfred A. Knopf, New York, 1995.

J. E. Wright, *Round About Jerusalem, Letters from the Holy Land*, Jarrolds, London, 1918.

RECENT ARTICLES
(in chronological order of publication)

Haim Shapiro, 'Vatican's nuncio says all Christians should have a role in Jerusalem's holy places', *Jerusalem Post*, 17 August 1994.

Alon Pinkas, 'Russia demands say on status of Jerusalem', *Jerusalem Post*, 26 August 1994.

Dalia Habash, 'Palestinian cultural centre inaugurated in Jerusalem', *Jerusalem Times*, 18 November 1994.

Ronny Reich, 'Archaeology in Israel 1995', *Ariel*, numbers 99–100, Jerusalem, 1995.

Rami Tal, 'The Israeli Press', *Ariel*, numbers 99–100, Jerusalem, 1995.

Moshe Dector, 'A Passion for Jerusalem', *Midstream*, New York, May 1995.

Jon Immanuel, 'Young Palestinians learn democracy', *Jerusalem Post*, 26 May 1995.

Herb Keinon, 'Jerusalem 3000: Bring out the calculators', *Jerusalem Post*, 26 May 1995.

Bernard Wasserstein, *The Question of Jerusalem* (a lecture given on 19 June 1995), Institute of Jewish Affairs, London, 1995.

Myles Crawford, 'Alienated women in a patriarchal society', *Jerusalem Times*, 21 July 1995.

Ahmad Bukhari, 'Jerusalem in History, An Arab, Islamic Perspective', *Jerusalem Times*, 1 September 1995.

Paul Goldberger, 'Passions Set in Stone', *New York Times Magazine*, 10 September 1995.

Netty C. Gross, 'Is Forgiveness Possible?', *Jerusalem Post Magazine*, 22 September 1995.

Tabitha Yelloz, 'The politics of housing', *Jerusalem Post*, 22 September 1995.

Greer Fay Cashman, 'Read the Signs', *Jerusalem Post*, 8 October 1995.

Batsheva Tsur, 'Family, friends bid farewell to Rabin,' *Jerusalem Post*, 13 November 1995.

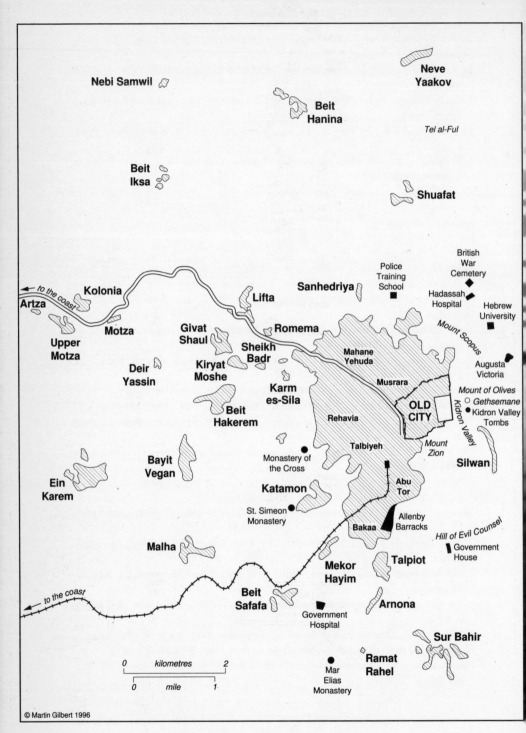

Neve
Yaakov

Nebi Samwil

Beit
Hanina

Tel al-Ful

Beit
Iksa

Shuafat

British
War
Cemetery

Police
Training
School

Sanhedriya

Hadassah
Hospital

Hebrew
University

to the coast

Kolonia

Lifta

Artza

Romema

Mount Scopus

Motza

Givat
Shaul

Sheikh
Badr

Mahane
Yehuda

Upper
Motza

Deir
Yassin

Kiryat
Moshe

Musrara

Augusta
Victoria

Karm
es-Sila

OLD
CITY

Mount of Olives

Gethsemane

Beit
Hakerem

Rehavia

Kidron Valley

Kidron Valley
Tombs

Ein
Karem

Bayit
Vegan

Monastery of
the Cross

Talbiyeh

Mount
Zion

Silwan

Katamon

Abu
Tor

St. Simeon
Monastery

Bakaa

Allenby
Barracks

Hill of Evil Counsel

Malha

Government
House

Mekor
Hayim

Talpiot

to the coast

Beit
Safafa

Arnona

Government
Hospital

Sur Bahir

0   kilometres   2

Mar
Elias
Monastery

Ramat
Rahel

0   mile   1

© Martin Gilbert 1996

Jerusalem and immediate environs 1917–1947

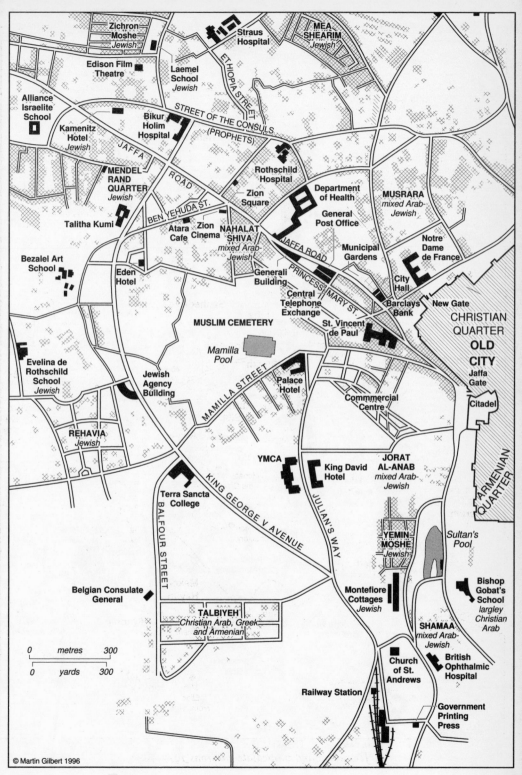

Western Jerusalem 1917–1947

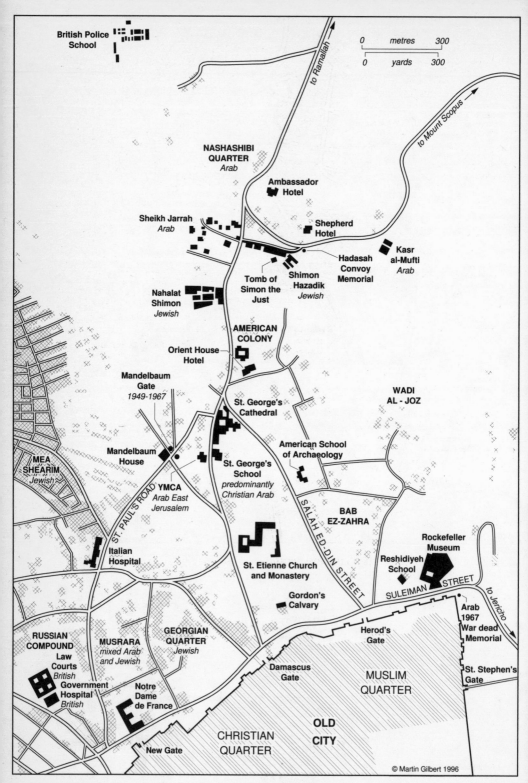

British Police
School

NASHASHIBI
QUARTER
Arab

Ambassador
Hotel

Shepherd
Hotel

Sheikh Jarrah
Arab

Kasr
al-Mufti
Arab

Hadasah
Convoy
Memorial

Tomb of
Simon the
Just

Shimon
Hazadik
Jewish

Nahalat
Shimon
Jewish

AMERICAN
COLONY

Orient House
Hotel

WADI
AL - JOZ

Mandelbaum
Gate
1949-1967

St. George's
Cathedral

American School
of Archaeology

MEA
SHEARIM
Jewish

Mandelbaum
House

St. George's
School
*predominantly
Christian Arab*

BAB
EZ-ZAHRA

Rockefeller
Museum

YMCA
*Arab East
Jerusalem*

Reshidiyeh
School

Italian
Hospital

St. Etienne Church
and Monastery

SULEIMAN STREET

to Jericho

Gordon's
Calvary

Arab
1967
War dead
Memorial

RUSSIAN
COMPOUND
Law
Courts
British
Government
Hospital
British

MUSRARA
*mixed Arab
and Jewish*

GEORGIAN
QUARTER
Jewish

Herod's
Gate

St. Stephen's
Gate

Notre
Dame
de France

Damascus
Gate

MUSLIM
QUARTER

OLD
CITY

New Gate

CHRISTIAN
QUARTER

© Martin Gilbert 1996

to Ramallah

to Mount Scopus

ST. PAUL'S ROAD

SALAH ED-DIN STREET

| 0 | metres | 300 |
| 0 | yards | 300 |

Eastern Jerusalem 1917–1947

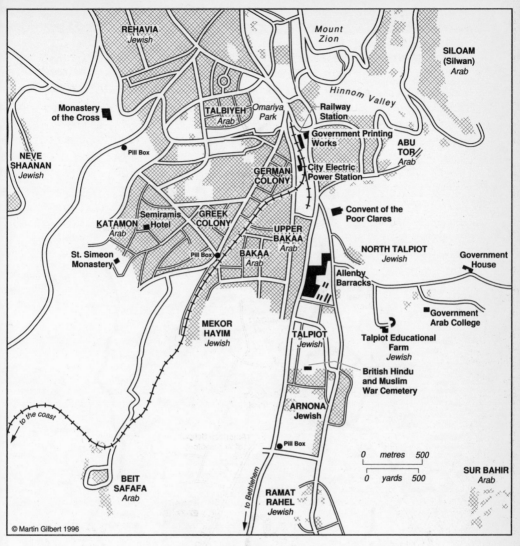

REHAVIA
Jewish

Mount
Zion

SILOAM
(Silwan)
Arab

Monastery
of the Cross

TALBIYEH
Arab

Omariya
Park

Hinnom Valley

Railway
Station

NEVE
SHAANAN
Jewish

• Pill Box

Government Printing
Works

ABU
TOR
Arab

GERMAN
COLONY

City Electric
Power Station

Semiramis
Hotel

GREEK
COLONY

KATAMON
Arab

UPPER
BAKAA
Arab

Convent of the
Poor Clares

St. Simeon
Monastery

• Pill Box

BAKAA
Arab

NORTH TALPIOT
Jewish

Government
House

Allenby
Barracks

MEKOR
HAYIM
Jewish

TALPIOT
Jewish

Talpiot Educational
Farm
Jewish

Government
Arab College

to the coast

British Hindu
and Muslim
War Cemetery

ARNONA
Jewish

BEIT
SAFAFA
Arab

• Pill Box

| 0 | metres | 500 |
| 0 | yards | 500 |

SUR BAHIR
Arab

RAMAT
RAHEL
Jewish

to Bethlehem

© Martin Gilbert 1996

Southern Jerusalem 1917–1947

375

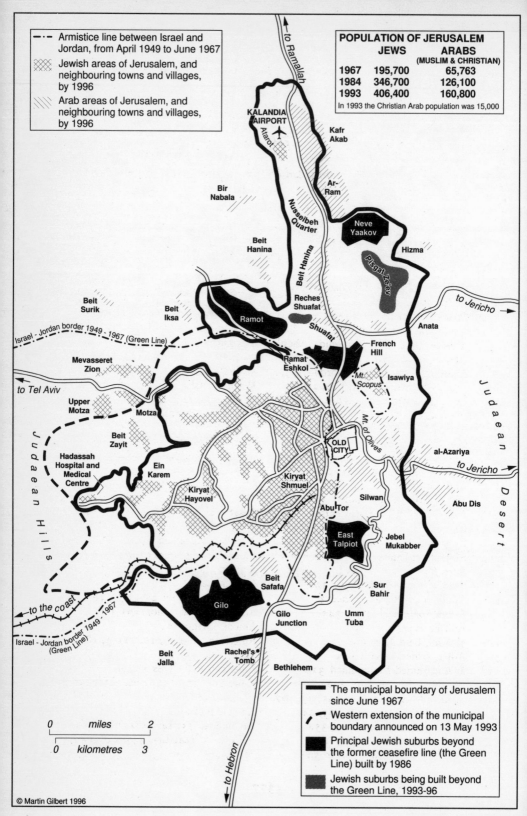

Legend:

- –·–· Armistice line between Israel and Jordan, from April 1949 to June 1967
- ⨯⨯⨯ Jewish areas of Jerusalem, and neighbouring towns and villages, by 1996
- ⫽⫽⫽ Arab areas of Jerusalem, and neighbouring towns and villages, by 1996

POPULATION OF JERUSALEM

	JEWS	ARABS (MUSLIM & CHRISTIAN)
1967	195,700	65,763
1984	346,700	126,100
1993	406,400	160,800

In 1993 the Christian Arab population was 15,000

to Ramallah

KALANDIA AIRPORT

Atarot

Kafr Akab

Ar-Ram

Bir Nabala

Nusseibeh Quarter

Beit Hanina

Beit Hanina

Neve Yaakov

Hizma

Pisgat Ze'ev

Beit Surik

Beit Iksa

Ramot

Reches Shuafat

Shuafat

to Jericho

Anata

Israel - Jordan border 1949 - 1967 (Green Line)

Ramat Eshkol

French Hill

Mt. Scopus

Isawiya

Judaean Desert

Mevasseret Zion

to Tel Aviv

Upper Motza

Motza

Mt. of Olives

Beit Zayit

OLD CITY

al-Azariya

to Jericho

Hadassah Hospital and Medical Centre

Ein Karem

Kiryat Shmuel

Kiryat Hayovel

Silwan

Abu Dis

Abu Tor

East Talpiot

Jebel Mukabber

Judaean Hills

to the coast

Israel - Jordan border 1949 - 1967 (Green Line)

Beit Safafa

Sur Bahir

Gilo

Gilo Junction

Umm Tuba

Beit Jalla

Rachel's Tomb

Bethlehem

to Hebron

0 — miles — 2

0 — kilometres — 3

© Martin Gilbert 1996

Legend (bottom right):

- —— The municipal boundary of Jerusalem since June 1967
- – – – Western extension of the municipal boundary announced on 13 May 1993
- ■ Principal Jewish suburbs beyond the former ceasefire line (the Green Line) built by 1986
- ▨ Jewish suburbs being built beyond the Green Line, 1993-96

Jerusalem since 1967

Index

compiled by the author

377

Index

Index

Index

Index

Index